COLONIALITY AND RACIAL (IN)JUSTICE IN THE UNIVERSITY

Counting for Nothing?

Edited by Sunera Thobani

Coloniality and Racial (In)Justice in the University examines the disruption and remaking of the university at a moment in history when white supremacist politics have erupted across North America, as have anti-racist and anti-colonial movements. Situating the university at the heart of these momentous developments, this collection debunks the popular claim that the university is well on its way to overcoming its histories of racial exclusion.

Written by faculty and students located at various levels within the institutional hierarchy, this book demonstrates how the shadows of settler colonialism and racial division are reiterated in "newer" neoliberal practices. Drawing on critical race and Indigenous theory, the chapters challenge Eurocentric knowledge, institutional whiteness, and structural discrimination that are the bedrock of the institution.

The authors also analyse their own experiences to show how Indigenous dispossession, racial violence, administrative prejudice, and imperialist militarization shape classroom interactions within the university.

SUNERA THOBANI is a professor in the Department of Asian Studies at the University of British Columbia.

Coloniality and Racial (In)Justice in the University

Counting for Nothing?

EDITED BY SUNERA THOBANI

UNIVERSITY OF TORONTO PRESS
Toronto Buffalo London

ISBN 978-1-4875-0533-2 (cloth)   ISBN 978-1-4875-3205-5 (EPUB)
ISBN 978-1-4875-2381-7 (paper)   ISBN 978-1-4875-3204-8 (PDF)

Library and Archives Canada Cataloguing in Publication

Title: Coloniality and racial (in)justice in the university : counting for nothing? /
    edited by Sunera Thobani.
Names: Thobani, Sunera, 1957–, editor.
Identifiers: Canadiana (print) 20210293152 | Canadiana (ebook) 20210293799 |
    ISBN 9781487523817 (softcover) | ISBN 9781487505332 (hardcover) |
    ISBN 9781487532055 (EPUB) | ISBN 9781487532048 (PDF)
Subjects: LCSH: Racism in higher education – North America. | LCSH:
    Discrimination in higher education – North America. | LCSH: Minority college
    students – North America. | LCSH: Minority college teachers – North America. |
    LCSH: Eurocentrism.
Classification: LCC LC212.43.N7 C65 2022 | DDC 378.1/9820971 – dc23

This book has been published with the help of a grant from the Federation for the
Humanities and Social Sciences, through the Awards to Scholarly Publications
Program, using funds provided by the Social Sciences and Humanities Research
Council of Canada.

University of Toronto Press acknowledges the financial assistance to its publishing
program of the Canada Council for the Arts and the Ontario Arts Council, an agency
of the Government of Ontario.

 Canada Council **Conseil des Arts**
for the Arts **du Canada**

ONTARIO ARTS COUNCIL
CONSEIL DES ARTS DE L'ONTARIO
an Ontario government agency
un organisme du gouvernement de l'Ontario

Funded by the   Financé par le
Government   gouvernement | Canada
of Canada   du Canada

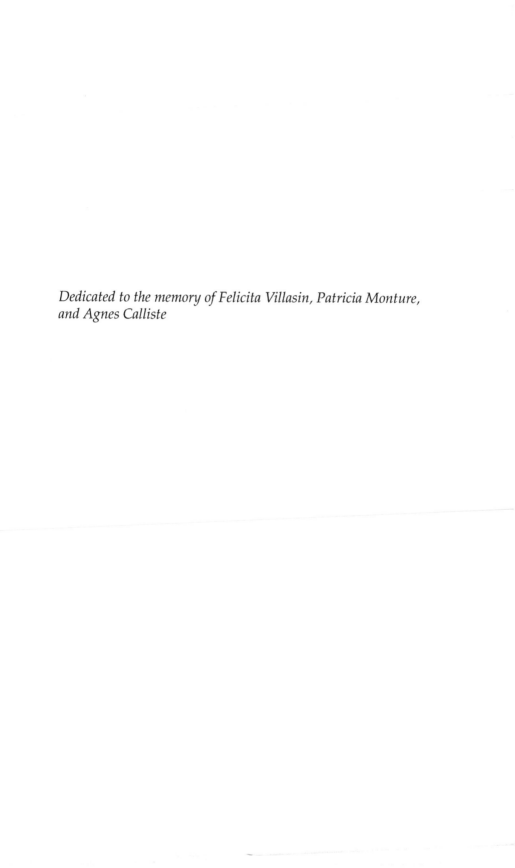

Dedicated to the memory of Felicita Villasin, Patricia Monture, and Agnes Calliste

When I dare to be powerful, to use my strength in the service of my vision, then it becomes less and less important whether I am afraid.

– Audre Lorde

Contents

Foreword

It was at the end of August 2020 when we both decided to launch Scholar Strike Canada, a two-day labour strike, with a series of teach-ins by academics, students, and staff across Canadian universities. We had both seen Twitter feeds and other social media posts and heard media reports of the scholar strikes planned across US universities to protest the police killings of George Floyd and other Blacks in the United States.

The political resurgence that was taking place globally led by Black, Indigenous, racialized, queer, trans, and two-spirited youth and students motivated us to create this labour action with teach-ins on anti-Black, anti-Indigenous racialized and settler colonial violence that encouraged faculty, students, and staff to pause their teaching, learning, and labour for two days. The teach-ins featured Black and Indigenous faculty and activists of colour such as Rinaldo Walcott, Bonita Lawrence, Eve Tuck, Andrea Davis, Courtney Skye, Chris Ramsaroop, and many others.

This labour action that we staged on 9 and 10 September 2020 provided faculty and students a space to engage the global racial and anti-colonial reckoning that had taken place in Canada during most of the spring and summer. Many of us participated in the uprisings organized by Black Lives Matter and other Black activists to protest police brutality and killings of Black, Indigenous, and racialized peoples here in Canada during the COVID-19 outbreak and lockdown.

The Scholar Strike Canada teach-ins allowed for bold conversations and critiques of the white supremacist neoliberal university and its subjugation of radical, Black, Indigenous, and decolonial knowledges and practices. Many academics, activists, and students had seen their university's statement on ending anti-Black racism and other forms of racism and recognized it as a statement of performance and not of change. Rinaldo Walcott (2018, 89) has referenced these practices as "institutional claims of performative non-performativity in service of the status quo."

The collection titled *Coloniality and Racial (In)Justice in the University*, edited by Sunera Thobani, could not have been timelier. Thobani's introduction provides a deliberate, incisive, and prescient critique of the university's investment in what she refers to as an "equity/diversity" regime that acts as a containment zone to radical, decolonial, and insurgents' knowledges and practices. This regime of power she speaks of is deployed to suppress any possibility of concrete action from the institution. She writes, "The ease with which the university set into gear its equity/diversity/inclusion machinery to counter the global wave of anti-racist protests galvanized by the Black Lives Matter movement in the United States, Canada, and elsewhere in the wake of the killing of George Floyd and countless other Black, Indigenous, and Brown people, as well as by the COVID-19–related explosion of anti-Asian violence, demonstrates just how indispensable this technology has become to institutional modes of power."

At the time we launched Scholar Strike Canada, we were not certain how this online platform would evolve. We were clear, however, that it had to be independent of any form of institutional control. The series of teach-ins that launched Scholar Strike Canada created spaces of conversations, imaginings, and strategies for scholars, students, and activists in a time of reckoning.

Scholar Strike Canada has since then organized and streamed several events this year. In April, the live-streamed Rally-On-Wheels action exposed the brutal corporatization and financialization of the university as was witnessed by the draconian cuts to programs, faculty, and staff at Laurentian University. In May, Scholar Strike Canada openly declared its support for the Canadian Association of University Teachers (CAUT) censure of the University of Toronto. The university administration, due to interference from a corporate donor, cancelled the hiring of a legal scholar whose research criticized Israel's human rights violations in the Occupied Palestinian Territories. Scholar Strike Canada organized and live-streamed a conversation on donor influence, racism, and academic freedom.

At the end of May, we organized and streamed a two-day series of panels by artists, activists, and scholars on anti-Asian racism in Canada and globally. It brought together a convergence of political Asian scholars, activists, and artists to speak to their long histories of struggles, activism, and intellectual work in the Canadian diaspora. The

Anti-Asian Racism Undone series revealed how the lived experiences and activism of migrant sex worker rights activists, like Mina Do and Elene Lam, have shaped theorization of these issues in the context of care, mutual aid, and abolition.

Scholar Strike Canada is a space committed to insurgent knowledges and practices that foster abolition, Indigenous self-determination, and decolonization. It is a space where scholars can boldly critique and refuse the destructive global racist, settler colonial, anti-Black, corporatized, capitalist, and carceral university unapologetically.

Scholar Strike Canada was borne out of the realization that the university is not the place of political, cultural, and ethical transformation. The university as it exists in the present is "the academy of misery" (Harney and Moten 2013, 10). Audra Simpson (2014) insists that we engage a politics of refusal in the university. Robin D.G. Kelley (2016) in his *Boston Review* article titled "Black Study, Black Struggle" cautioned faculty and students to not "seek love from an institution incapable of loving them." Instead, he insists that we connect our intellectual work to the long history of street activism.

We will continue to care for this online space in the hope for something new – not of the university or of the world as it currently exists but something "otherwise." Sunera Thobani's introduction insists that we remain attentive to the multiple ways that the university as an institution depoliticizes and deradicalizes through a process of containment. It is crucial, then, that Scholar Strike Canada remains this space of creative possibilities, imaginings, and strategies – "a space, not of reform, but newness making otherwise" (Brand 2021).

Beverly Bain and Min Sook Lee,
Scholar Strike Canada (SSC)

REFERENCES

Brand, Dionne. 2021. "A Short Entry on Time: Capitalism, Blackness, Time,
    and Writing." Jackman Humanities Institute Lecture, University of
    Toronto, 3 March 2021.
Harney, Stefano, and Fred Moten. 2013. *The Undercommons: Fugitive Planning
    and Black Study*. Brooklyn, NY: Minor Composition.
Kelley, Robin D.G. 2016. "Black Study, Black Struggle." *Boston Review*,
    7 March 2016. http://bostonreview.net/forum/robin-d-g-kelley-black
    -study-black-struggle.
Simpson, Audra. 2014. *Mohawk Interruptus: Political Life across the Borders of
    Settler States*. Durham, NC: Duke University Press.
Walcott, Rinaldo. 2018. "Against Social Justice and the Limits of Diversity:
    Or Black People and Freedom." In *Toward What Justice: Describing Diverse
    Dreams of Justice in Education*, edited by Eve Tuck and K. Wayne Yang,
    85–99. New York: Routledge.

COLONIALITY AND RACIAL (IN)JUSTICE IN THE UNIVERSITY

Counting for Nothing?

Introduction

Present Pasts: The Anxieties of Power

SUNERA THOBANI

It is not clear to me that we can confidently say there has been a recognition that the Canadian education system has been widely recognized as "unrealistic and paternalistic," or as racist and colonial. The experiences of Aboriginal women in institutions of higher education remain largely invisible. If the experiences remain personal and are told only anecdotally among ourselves (when we have the opportunity), then the hope that things will change is built on utter foolishness. Although I have indeed experienced the sharp edge of backlash, I speak to these issues because it is the only way to unmask and destabilize the power held over so many of us. And if I cannot hang on to the hope of transformative change, then I cannot continue to engage the university.

– Patricia Monture-Angus

A university is a curious accretion of historical conflicts that it has systematically forgotten. Each of its divisions reflects a history of ideological conflicts that is just as important as what is taught within the divisions yet is prevented from being foregrounded by the divisions themselves.

– Dominick LaCapra

Globalization takes place only in capital and data. Everything else is damage control. Information command has ruined knowing and reading.

– Gayatri Spivak

It was a beautiful West Coast morning, the crisp chill in the air melting into the warming rays of a sun determined to dissipate the clouds. First Nations Elders, members of the Musqueam, and the president of the University of British Columbia (UBC) had gathered on the Vancouver campus, along with deans, faculty, staff, students, and guests, invited to the dedication of the Musqueam Post being gifted to the institution (see UBC News 2016). The main campus for UBC, which ranks among

Canada's top tier research universities, is located on the unceded territory of the Musqueam: the post being commemorated that morning recounts the origin story of the Musqueam people.

Following the traditional welcome ceremony, a relative of Brent Sparrow Jr., the post's carver, took to the podium to honour the artist for the majestic work he had created. "Welcome to the Musqueam Take Back UBC Rally," the speaker began. A momentary hush fell on the gathering; dignitaries fidgeted in their seats. "Sorry, wrong speech," quipped the speaker as he pulled out another sheaf of paper. This time his comment was met with laughter that was a little too brittle.

The message was as pointed as it was on target. In that one instant, the speaker cut through the rhetoric of "reconciliation" recently embraced by UBC, like other Canadian universities, state institutions, and corporations, to expose the underlying colonial relationship that shapes their interactions with Indigenous peoples (see, for example, UBC n.d.-a). That morning, the double-headed serpent of the creation story of the Musqueam stood tall and proud on their traditional lands and at the very heart of the UBC campus. The post would henceforth remind all who walk by of the Musqueam's history and of their unmitigated claim, printed on the program for the dedication ceremony (6 April 2016): "We, the Musqueam people, have been here as long as there has been land to live upon; our lands and waters serving as a source of knowledge and memory, encoding our teachings." This message, too, is unmistakable: the very sense of *being* of the Musqueam is rooted in *this* land. The post attests not only to these Indigenous origins, pasts, and presents but also to possible futures. In other words, colonial conquest has yet to destroy Indigenous horizons.

The dedication of the Musqueam Post took place during UBC's centennial year, a landmark notable for an earlier incident also reflective of the institution's racial – and gender – politics. The UBC president who spoke at the ceremony that morning, Dr. Martha Piper, held the position on an interim basis. Having previously served as UBC president, she had hastily stepped in to tide things over upon the abrupt ouster of the first person of colour to hold that office, Dr. Arvind Gupta. The actual circumstances that led to Dr. Gupta's ejection from the presidency some thirteen months into his appointment remain shrouded in mystery, despite the incident becoming something of a national scandal. The fractious nature of the relations between this president and the UBC Board of Governors has been covered in the media (Brown 2016), as has the story of a member of the UBC faculty who reported being "intimidated" for suggesting that Dr. Gupta had lost a "masculinity contest." While media accounts pointed to conflicting visions for resource allocation, fiscal responsibility, and administrative positions between the board and the ousted president, many in the Asian-Canadian community read Dr. Gupta's sudden departure in the context of the controversy sparked by a leading Canadian magazine, *Maclean's*, which had published an article questioning whether UBC had become "too Asian" (Findlay and Köhler 2010). A faculty colleague close to the Gupta affair suggested to me as we chatted informally at an event that powerful networks within the university found it unacceptable to have "a brown man serving pakoras to brown people" in Norman Mackenzie House, the president's official residence.

Thus it was that Dr. Piper spoke for the university at the dedication ceremony. UBC's commitment to "strong relationships with Aboriginal people" was dutifully reasserted, as was its pride at being located on the site that was a place of learning for the Musqueam for centuries. Her inane comments – the likes of which can be found almost verbatim in such proclamations produced routinely by universities following the publication in 2015 of the Calls to Action by the Truth and Reconciliation Commission of Canada – skirted two essential questions: What kind of learning drives the university's objectives? What ends does this learning serve? These are the questions taken up in the chapters of this collection.

Coloniality and Racial (In)Justice in the University examines how the structuring racial-colonial logics and practices that shape the North American university are finding realignment in the crisis-managerial exigencies of the present juncture. The collection is informed by radical traditions within critical race studies and decolonization frameworks that are historically grounded in the praxis – that is, the intellectual thought *and struggle* – of abolitionist, Indigenous, and people of colour movements. Approaching the university as a prime site for the organization of racial injustice and settler colonial relations, the following chapters examine different aspects of the production, institutionalization, and dissemination of the forms of dehumanization that characterize the condition of coloniality more generally. The traditions drawn upon by the authors were forged in struggles to transform the socioeconomic, epistemological-political, and psycho-affective structures, ideologies, and discursive-institutional practices that have historically produced race, coloniality, gender, and sexuality in mutually constitutive ways. This collection hence furthers the study of how the university is productive of – as well as produced by – the racial-colonial and gender-sexual hierarchies that structure nation, state, and capital within local and global contexts. As each chapter interrogates the specific ways in which the institution is enmeshed in the perpetuation of the racial injustice and colonial violence that underwrites its very existence, it also documents and analyzes the forms of everyday resistance that are instantiated in response. Building this collective analysis and resistance is the driving impetus for the book.

In the Canadian context, this collection moves academic debates about the relation between race and coloniality, and the nature and workings of the university, beyond the "equity/diversity" and "anti-oppression" frameworks, analytics that are particularly dominant in current scholarship. By centring racial injustice and linking settler colonialism in North America to colonization as a global dynamic and ongoing structure, the collection breaks new ground. As will be discussed more fully below, the "equity/diversity" regime is here critiqued as a *containment zone* for the radical praxis and insurgent scholarship of women/queers of colour and Indigenous women within this institution. The work of these scholarly communities not only produces knowledge grounded in the historical consciousness of colonized and enslaved peoples; it also contests the power and authority of the university by revealing how this site is imbricated in their brutalization and subjugation. The ease with which the university set into gear its equity/diversity/inclusion machinery to counter the global wave of anti-racist protests galvanized by the Black Lives Matter movement in the United States, Canada, and elsewhere in the wake of the killing of George Floyd and countless other Black, Indigenous, and Brown people, as well as by the COVID-19–related explosion of anti-Asian violence, demonstrates just how indispensable this technology has become to institutional modes of power. Engaging and disciplining insurgent demands into equity and diversity portfolios to advance inclusion is now the entirely predictable form of officially sanctioned "social justice" on offer within the institution.

For its part, the "anti-oppression" framework is eschewed in this collection for its flattening and emptying out of the content and form of the "oppressions" to which it alludes. This approach ejects the specificities of race and coloniality, as well as the historically contextualized critiques of asymmetrical forms of exploitation and violence, by conceiving of all forms of oppression – class, race, gender, sexuality, disability, and so on – as analogous and interchangeable. It would not be going too far to argue that, in so doing, the "anti-oppression" framework renders anti-racist, anti-capitalist, and anti-colonial praxis misguided, if not entirely superfluous. Every chapter in this collection draws attention to the specificity of settler colonialism and to how sexuality, class, and gender are tied to processes of racialization and the condition of coloniality; each also attends to the intersection of race with nation, state, and neoliberalism. Taking up the concrete manifestation of these axes of power, the authors bring into focus their cross-cutting and constitutive – yet distinct – form and organization. Consequently, dehumanization, dispossession, extraction, genocide, appropriation, demonization, and retribution are the collection's main thematics, not exclusion, discrimination, and marginalization.

This collection is also distinguished by its attention to positionality and the hierarchical relations of power among and between Indigenous peoples; Black, Muslim, Asian, and other people of colour; and the "Canadians" and "Americans" whose belonging and sense of entitlement are beyond question in the university, as in the nation. Indeed, the university's functioning relies on the assertion of just this sense of belonging and entitlement – presently expressed as the power to include Others – as constitutive of its whiteness. Situating the university squarely within processes of nation and state formation, as well as within the reorganization of global capital and its attendant international order, this book draws attention to how racial injustice, while distinctly national in scope, is global in reach.

Crisis, Ruins, Reorders

To say that the university is in crisis is to state the obvious, although it should be noted that neither the institution's governing elites nor the states that fund it seem able or willing to acknowledge the extent of the predicament. Likewise, to say that this crisis is sparked by larger challenges to the colonial-racial matrix of power is also clearly undeniable. To make these statements together as a woman of colour is to be visited by the full wrath of the institution, for these truisms are met with outrage, or sometimes fervent protestations of good intent, by those empowered by the institution. Past experience has shown that such protestations soon turn to rage at who/what is then construed as the vengeful origin of the critique.

At the close of the twentieth century, Bill Readings (1996) argued that the university had entered an age of doom in which its future had become uncertain. The decline of the nation-state, in his view, made it increasingly obvious that the modern university (based on the German model) was no longer tethered to "national culture" and was instead being transformed into a "transnational bureaucratic corporation" (3). Readings's study, supported by the Quebec and Canadian academic funding bodies, defined this shift as part of the process of "Americanization" that was remaking the university in the image of the corporation, not only in the United States and Canada but also across Europe. Within academia, Readings also argued, the idea of "national culture" was itself being replaced by a vacuous notion of "excellence," empty of any particular meaning or content. This development was a death blow to a liberal education, such that the humanistic traditions that had shaped it were no longer viable and the institution had "outlived itself" (6). With this demise of the liberal university, the Subject who embodied its ideals was also fast disappearing: the "enlightened and liberal administrator" would henceforth be the "hero" of the transformed institution, not the scholar-professor-teacher, nor the student who was newly turned into a consumer. Readings's study of the university in which market criteria dominate led him to describe an institution in "ruins" – in terms of its mission (reason, nation, culture, and so forth), function (national integration, production of the citizen-subject, and other such objectives), and content (the humanities, liberal arts, among other disciplines).

Even as concern over the corporatization of the university became more pronounced in critical scholarship, the limitations of Readings's critique of the changing fortunes of the institution were pointed out by Dominick LaCapra (1998). The "university of culture" valorized by Readings, LaCapra pointed out, was a phantasm, given that the institution had actually been "born in ruins insofar as it was class-based, sexist and ethnocentric" (39). Moreover, LaCapra argued, "the contemporary university is based on a systemic, schizoid division between a market model and a model of corporate solidarity and collegial responsibility" (32). These contradictions could be seen in the new figuration of the ideal faculty member as the "entrepreneurial globetrotter" – a highly adept dealmaker and fundraiser, very marketable and always on the go – in contrast to the "local hero," who remains closely tied to the institution, faithful to its structure and the realization of its objectives. Periodic assaults on the institution by neoconservative think tanks and their affiliates, who lament the decline of undergraduate education, compound this divide. LaCapra also argued that the nation-state was hardly disappearing and that "crisis" was a more apt reading of the condition of the university. His point was that the neoliberal transformation of the institution was more complex and uneven than suggested in Readings's account. The acceleration of this transformation in the ensuing decades has only worsened the standing and condition of the institution.

Critical left scholarship in this vein continues to focus in Canada on the toll taken on the university by deregulation and privatization. Funding cuts, tuition hikes, and pressures to compete in a global marketplace are identified as increasing the institution's reliance upon, and ties to, the corporate sector, so that the latter's values, objectives, and practices now reign supreme in higher education (Davidson 2015; Brownlee 2014; Westheimer 2010; Giroux 2014; see also Harvey 2005). This critique also highlights how the acceleration of these pressures has been met with dissension within the ranks of the academy, particularly against unsustainable faculty workload, the push to "publish or perish," use of quantitative performance indicators, increasing commodification of education, and casualization of the professoriate (Westheimer 2010; Newstadt 2008). As noted by the president of the Canadian Association of University Teachers, for one example, these conditions demonstrate that "utilitarian managerialism [is] the dominant ethos of most Canadian university administrations today" (Compton 2016).

However, much of this scholarship, like the policies and priorities of representative professional bodies, does not centre race or coloniality among its issues of concern. Even when reference is made to these relations of power, as is presently the case with the heightened visibility of Indigenous resistance, Black Lives Matter, and other anti-racist movements, any significant reshaping of the Western analytic frame or reassessment of priorities that actively engage critiques of the structure of whiteness, which is constitutive of the institution, is yet to come.

Roderick Ferguson (2012) takes up this critique in his study of the contemporary university, *The Reorder of Things*, which centres the question of difference and the post-1960s emergence of the interdisciplines related to race, ethnicity, and gender. Ferguson foregrounds the constitutive relation of the university to state and economy as he interrogates these interdisciplines, and although his focus is on the US university, the parallels with the Canadian university are striking. Moreover, they reveal how closely interlinked are these North American institutions. Asking how modes of power "are exercised upon the daily lives of minoritized subjects and knowledges," Ferguson argues that these subjects are "caught in a new configuration of power" such that it is their "ruin" that is "prefigured by courtship, invitation, and acknowledgement" by the university (4). Ferguson's larger argument is that the revolutionary movements of the 1960s, including student movements, were fuelled by an "insurgent articulation of difference" to which state, capital, and university responded by institutionalizing modes of difference that could be managed to advance the latter's own interests (5). The radical struggles of the period led to the creation of new interdisciplinary fields, such as Black and African American studies, Asian-American and ethnic studies, as well as women's studies, which sought to transform the traditional university. In turn, the institution's technologies of power advanced to redirect these movements' insurgent and redistributive potentialities in service of capital and state. This move to containment is the "crisis" of the institution, Ferguson argues, as he eschews the idea that the university is derivative of, or subservient to, state and economy. Attending to these momentous shifts within the academy in order to "re-know state and capital as interlocutors with rather than determinants of American university life" (6), Ferguson demonstrates that the university "is not simply an entity that social-izes people into the ideologies of political economy" (9). Rather, the movements of the 1960s "point to an institution that socializes *state and capital* into emergent articulations of difference" (9; emphasis in original). Pointing to the mutually constitutive relation that binds the three, he explains that "power" – in the Foucauldian sense – "enlisted the academy and things academic as conduits for conveying unprec-edented forms of political economy to state and capital" (8). Key to the success of this enlistment of "the academy and things academic" was their transmutation of insurgent expressions of minority difference – fuelled by revolutionary and redistributive politics – into abstract and bureaucratic forms of minoritization (8). Where Readings (and much of the left critique that followed from his work) considers the decline of the university's status and power to result from the eclipse of national culture, Ferguson argues that "the American academy and things academic would become the place where enfeebled institutions might make sense of difference, its fortunes and its disruptions" (27). In other words, rather than the demise of national culture, the conflicts within the university point to how the institution reworked and rein-vigorated outmoded and contested notions of "national culture" into newer modalities to secure the power of state and capital, along with restabilizing the authority of the university.

The movements of the 1960s certainly exposed and challenged the ties between the state, the military, corporations, and the university, as Ferguson and other scholars have noted. These movements' contesta-tion of the racial-gender ideologies and Eurocentric epistemologies that shaped the liberal education also undoubtedly plunged the university into a crisis of legitimacy. But the difference in the challenges mounted by the various movements, like the difference in the modalities of their integration into the university, requires closer attention. While the uni-versity led "the ways in which power worked through the 'recogni-tion' of minoritized histories, cultures, and experiences" and shaped such "recognition" to "secure its status" (Ferguson 2012, 13), the pro-cesses of minoritization deployed by – and within – the academy fur-ther deepened the racial-gender-colonial divides within and between these newly "recognized" communities. Studies of the longer histories of the university, of state and nation formation, reveal how deep are the divides between these communities and how these divisions carried into the interdisciplines. These histories are ever present; they shape the anxieties of power today.

The long histories of North American universities demonstrate that the institution was founded by the missionary and settler projects engaged in the genocide of Indigenous peoples across the Americas. They also show how the institution became crucial to the modalities of power that incorporated these regimes of violence and dispossession, enslavement and commodification, and indentureship and migration across the colonial order by tying the Americas to Europe, Africa, and Asia. The early North American schools, colleges, and universities were established on Indigenous territories by church organizations and slave owners, colonial intellectuals and administrations, all enmeshed in Europe's colonizing ventures that tied the Atlantic to the Mediterranean as well as to the Pacific. The emergent racial hierarchies within this order – global in form, global also in the ambitions of elites – were shaped by Euro-American Christian *and* secular values, epistemological traditions, and sociopolitical institutions (Wilder 2008; Schuessler 2013; Hampton 2020).

It is in the context of this long historical view that the university has been defined as "the third pillar of a civilization based on bondage," the first two being the church and state (Wilder 2008). So, for example, Harvard, Yale, Columbia, Princeton, and Georgetown are among the elite institutions to have benefitted directly from Indigenous dispossession, the slave trade, and enslaved Black labour. In Canada, of the seventeen degree-granting institutions that had been established in the founding provinces at Confederation, four had "a non-denominational basis," while the remaining thirteen "were Church related and controlled" (Anisef, Axelrod, and Lennards 2015). Moreover, the precursor to the prestigious University of Toronto, King's College, was founded by Royal Charter, and McGill University by a slave owner. All are predicated on ongoing Indigenous dispossession, a process in which these institutions played, and continue to play, an active role (Grande and Anderson 2017). In the case of UBC, for example, "the university's arrival" on Musqueam lands is considered to mark "the final alienation of these lands from Musqueam use and control" (UBC n.d.-b).

Secularization was pushed onto the institution through the introduction of the liberal arts and sciences, and by financial pressure from provincial governments. In turn, "the growth of public higher education raised the issue of university protection against government interference," which led to the adoption of the bicameral system – faculty senate responsibility for academic policy, and citizen board of governors overseeing fiscal and other related matters (Anisef, Axelrod, and Lennards 2015). The state's reliance on the university for scientific research and training during the Second World War and the post-war flocking of veterans into universities in an extensive affirmative program expanded the public education system, the benefits of which were then available to the baby boom generation that soon followed (Anisef, Axelrod, and Lennards 2015). The North American university was thus not just born of, but remained integrally involved in, the organization and development of its respective nation-state and economy at successive junctures; the institution's subsequent liberalization during the 1970s added "equality of opportunity," that is, the incorporation of minority difference, into its mandate.

Ferguson's (2012) study of the university's reworking of insurgent articulations of minority difference into integrationist modalities of power is certainly indispensable to understand contemporary formations of state, capital, and academia across North America. The chapters of this book subtend *and* extend such an analysis by focusing on race *as well as* coloniality as the symbiotic thread that links university, state, nation, and economy. These chapters also attend to the intersectional and conflictual nature of the "difference" – that of race, gender, class, sexuality – contained within the umbrella term "minority difference." That is, the authors of this collection eschew the dominant tendency within the university to reduce such "difference" to the "difference that make no difference," to borrow the phrase from Stuart Hall.[1] They do this in several ways: first, by examining how the discourses and epistemologies presently privileged by the university articulate to its foundational logics, defined as colonial-racial; second, by keeping in focus the "land question" – which is also the sovereignty question – as one that is yet to be resolved; and third, by following how the institution's entrenched racial divides inform its contemporary governance practices. As illustrated in the earlier discussion about the dedication of the Musqueam Post, the ground upon which Canadian and American universities literally stand remains contested. Colonialism is "predicated on profitability," Joyce Green explains, and "profitability increases with the amount of land and resources stolen" (Green 2020, 247). Moreover, as noted by Michelle Daigle (2019), Indigenous nations "host Universities across Canada," and the "spectacular performances of recognition, remorse, and multicultural celebrations" that are now constantly on display on campuses are "constitutive to the larger terrain of affective governance" (6).

In the United States, "land grants" were historically used by states to develop "the new public universities that would research and educate American settlers in agriculture, science and mechanical arts" to service industry (paperson 2017; see also Ferguson 2012). In the process, the very meaning of these lands was transformed by the university, for "land as capital and not as campuses is an innovation of the land-grant university," la paperson explains; this development "incentivized land speculation" and fuelled the westward expansion of the US empire. Land has become "a motor in the financing of universities, enabling many of them to grow despite financial crises" in the present, argues la paperson. The capitalization of university lands is abundantly and everywhere visible in the real estate boom – occupation as "liberal education" transmogrified into high-end real estate.

Ferguson (2012) ties the land-grant institutions directly to the production of "excellence," for among their objectives was the upliftment, through access to education and training, of "poor and working class whites for the good of an industrializing agricultural economy" (84). The idea of excellence hence became encoded within a cross-class casting of whiteness in what would eventually be described as a meritocracy. Along with these institutions, African American institutions were funded in the South during the late nineteenth century so that the development of education, industry, and commerce became organized along bifurcated racializing lines. Ferguson argues that these institutions can be read as "an attempt to resolve the tension between racial hierarchy and democracy in ways that were consistent with the state's new project – segregation" (86). Excellence, rather than being an empty signifier, thus came to function as an exalted characteristic of whiteness.

The 1960s rebellions in the United States were not only concurrent with, but in many ways built upon, the resistance to the European-dominated colonial order by national liberation movements in the Third World. By the mid-twentieth century, these movements proved politically uncontainable, and the US and Canadian states, along with other Western states, responded with socioeconomic as well as political liberalization that remade the university, economy, state, and capital. Like the upheavals across North America, these anti-colonial developments were met with the cultivation of compliant native elites and comprador bourgeoisie in the newly independent Third World (Sivanandan 1982). Where these strategies of incorporation failed, dictatorships, authoritarianism, and state violence took the lead.

In the metropolitan centres of the West, civil rights and expanded access to citizenship opened the doors of the university to previously excluded populations. The mounting demands for socioeconomic transformation resulted in what sociologist Bruce Hare (1995) termed the "desegregation of the visible elite" in the case of the United States. These measures worked hand in hand with the state violence that quelled, exhausted, or destroyed the radical energies of the Indigenous, Black Power, civil rights, and immigrants' rights movements. As will be discussed more fully in the next section, the transformation of the modern university from pillar of white supremacy into champion of liberalism and multiculturalism did not root out but rather reworked its older colonial-racial structures and functions. As such, the biologically determinist and eugenicist racial sciences, the Orientalist and overtly racial paradigms that had earlier been the bedrock of the disciplines, were now severely discredited (Said 1978, 1993; Hall 1997; Chow 2002). If, in Canada, the state's adoption of official multiculturalism became the site for such reworking of the nation's racializing ideologies (Bannerji 2000; Ahmed 2012; Thobani 2007a), the state-driven racial liberalism in the United States that was organized by the university became the key instrument for its engagement with, and management of, the nation's racial politics. Inclusion on the domestic front worked in tandem with imperialism at the global level as US capital expanded its domination across the international order (Melamed 2011; Thobani 2020).

The university hence was a direct beneficiary of these changes. US hegemony in the post-war period made its Ivy League universities among the most coveted in the world; Canada's reputation as a global peacemaker cultivated a different kind of niche market. These institutions funded and now attracted into their hallowed halls intellectuals, scholars, and scientists from across the post-independence Third World, even as the CIA took care of resolutely revolutionary leaders. The development of area studies to inform and expand US and Canadian strategic interests and foreign policy objectives during the Cold War deepened the linkages between the university, state, and capital in what came to be known as the military-industrial complex.

Certainly the development of post-colonial and cultural studies, not to mention global and transnational studies, complicated and contested these developments within the university. The tensions between these fields and area studies were further exacerbated by the speed of neoliberal globalization; the role of states, corporations, and philanthropists as donors; and the vexed contests over cultural authority (Harootunian and Miyushi 2002; Chow 2002). Of particular note here is that the development of these newer interdisciplinary fields was fuelled by the same processes that were intensifying the integration of the post-independence national elites into the global circuits of capital.

Ferguson's (2012) reading of how developments in the new interdisciplines "put specific pressures on the human sciences and the disciplines" (32) draws on Foucault's studies of the contribution of the traditional disciplines to the production of "Man," a novel form of being. The specialized forms of knowledge deployed in the constitution of "Man" as a conglomeration of biological, linguistic, and economic aspects became the academic project, Ferguson notes, with each element of the assembly being advanced in a particular discipline. This was the project interrupted by the fields of Black, Afro-American, Asian-American, and ethnic studies, as well as by Indigenous and Native American studies, as they challenged the constitution of "Man" in modernity's mould of whiteness. The interdisciplines thus contested the hold of Eurocentric epistemologies and pedagogies over the institution and the larger sociopolitical order. In the case of women's studies – which emerged from the various movements for women's liberation of the time – its project was shaped by the production of "Woman" as a monolithic entity, at a tangent with the "race"-related areas of study. The critiques emerging from the interdisciplines thus reflected the politics of their unevenly situated communities of concern. Indigenous and race-related critiques went to the very core of the authority of the white male academia and of the university's very mandate – the production of Western modernity.

The significance of the point that not all the new interdisciplines presented the same kind – or extent – of challenge to white male institutional power should not be overlooked. Read in relation to the race/colonialism-centred interdisciplines, the focus on "Woman" in the feminist interdiscipline, with its elevation of gender and patriarchy as the primary axis of power, took for granted the whiteness and Eurocentrism of the institutional and national order, albeit contesting its domination by white, bourgeois men. As the task of confronting racial-colonial logics was taken up by Indigenous and women of colour feminists, the hegemonic tendency within women's studies gendered the power of whiteness within the university by expanding the representation and authority of white feminists. The newly acquired access to this institutional base allowed white feminists to advance their claim to represent "Woman," to the detriment of the struggles of Indigenous and women of colour. Contesting this development, intersectionality was taken up across the interdisciplines by Black feminists and other women of colour, who spearheaded major conceptual and theoretical breakthroughs. The concept of intersectionality that emerged within Black feminist theory to contest race-blind feminisms (Crenshaw 1991; Combahee River Collective 2014; Collins and Bilge 2016) was soon taken up across women's studies. However, the issues of settler colonialism and sovereignty, abolition and incarceration, racialization of orders and borders were relegated to the periphery. Despite such contesting frameworks being developed within Black, Indigenous, and women of colour feminisms, perhaps even because of them, the most powerful institutional advances – in terms of representation as well as administrative authority – took place on the basis of (de-racialized) gender, that is, by white women.

Certainly women's studies was caught in the culture wars waged against the new interdisciplines by conservative and other defenders of the university's culture of whiteness, its Eurocentric canon and imperialist values. But it was against women of colour scholars that the most virulent expressions of rage were directed, because women of colour and Indigenous women scholars not only contested the power of Man to claim the position of universality but also challenged the power being claimed in the name of Woman by gendering this entity as universal and the Subject of equality. Yet this moment was one wherein other – more pliant – frameworks were also emerging from the centres of power in response to the anti-racist/colonial feminist critiques, dominant among which would prove the inclusionary impulse organized by "equity" and "diversity."

The Equity Regime: "Bastions of Whiteness"

The now burgeoning literature on the experience of women of colour in universities across North America, the United Kingdom, and Australia demonstrates two main points. First, the animosity encountered by women of colour engaged in insurgent knowledge traditions – for which many of us were explicitly hired – emanates from across the university and at multiple levels in its administrative structure. The antipathy is not localizable to any particular discipline, department, or program, even though some may lead in the refining of its modalities of expression. Second, the challenges that arise from such hostility are informed by stubbornly entrenched assumptions (intellectual deficiency, social inadequacy, lack of decorum, incivility, and so on) and practices (silencing, marginalizing, punishing, disciplining) shared across these sites. Recent studies of the institution demonstrate how, for the main, women of colour faculty are constructed as incompetent (Gutierrez y Muhs et al. 2012); subjected to everyday microaggressions (Johnson, Joseph-Salisbury, and Kamunge 2018; Arday and Mirza, 2018; Gutierrez y Muhs et al. 2012; Henry et al. 2017); underpaid and severely underrepresented, especially at decision-making levels (Henry et al. 2017); and their anti-racist labour thwarted by the policies of equity/ diversity that render it non-performative (Ahmed 2012).

In the case of Canadian universities, recent scholarship finds that the equity measures that have been implemented since the mid-1980s have proved largely ineffectual in doing away with racial inequality and discrimination (Henry et al., 2017). Federal equity policies were introduced in the university upon the recommendations of the Royal Commission on Equality in Employment; these recommendations were supported by the Federal Contractors Program, which requires employers receiving public funds to have a representative workforce. Yet, the findings of a recent Social Sciences and Humanities Research Council (SSHRC)–funded study of Canadian universities points out how these measures have not transformed the institution and suggests that racial inequities may even be on the rise (Henry et al. 2017). Despite more than three decades of mandated equity, the SSHRC study concludes:

> Racialized and Indigenous faculty members are numerically underrepresented, and they experience racism in a wide variety of forms, personal and structural, both explicit and extremely subtle. Their work is on the whole poorly valued, as reflected in standard measurements such as salary levels and promotion and tenure, as well as in their ability to engage in research, curriculum development, and the mentoring that will make a difference to future generations … In short, we found that racialized and Indigenous scholars still work in the bastions of Whiteness that our universities have always been. And over and over again, we were told by racialized and Indigenous faculty that they experience the denial of equity in both senses of that term: their experiences of racism are denied, and they are denied full access to the academy. (297–8)

Underscoring the failure of equity policies to advance the status, representation, scholarship, and most important, leadership of faculty of colour and Indigenous faculty within the university, the study dubs equity a "myth" to argue that, for these adversely effected scholars, "the goal of achieving social justice by creating equitable institutions has been consistently promised but persistently denied" (3). That the documentation of such a scandalous situation across the Canadian academic world would spark no urgent response or concerted effort from university administrations, the professoriate as a whole, or even the associations that represent them/us speaks volumes about just how tolerable, if not entirely acceptable, these conditions are to these institutions and representative bodies.

I should note, however, that the findings of the study did not go entirely unaddressed. To be fair, its publication did elicit some responses from certain quarters within some universities. My favourite? Invitations from an equity office to *faculty of colour* to participate in reading groups to discuss the study's findings. Such tepid (absurd?) gestures could hardly be expected to do more than provide such an equity office with an alibi, leaving unabated its whitewashing of the racial divides that were even then deepening within the institution. Canaries in the mine be damned!

Problematizing equity and diversity policies, the SSHRC study called upon universities to live up to their own stated commitments in this regard. This attempt to redress the marginalization and disenfranchisement of faculty of colour and Indigenous faculty was most certainly required; it remains an absolutely necessary objective. Yet, one cannot get away from the actuality that "equity" is a technology of power; it organizes a now deeply ensconced machinery that functions to counter radical anti-racist politics by disciplining them – through bureaucratic structures, categories, and practices of inclusion – to splinter transformative alliances. The crushing of ground-up initiatives to advance the interests of institutional elites and their culture of whiteness feeds and aligns the university directly with the political interests of settler states, nations, and racial capital. Rather than opening up a pathway to racial justice for faculty of colour and Indigenous faculty, the equity regime functions as a zone of containment for our presence, representation, struggles, and aspirations, diverting energies away from transformative possibilities. Equity, then, can be taken as a highly effective institutional mechanism – constructing a zone embodied and peopled by bodies of colour – wherein access to justice is always already deferred and effective pathways to this end always already foreclosed. Indeed, equity *is* the institutionalized derailment of struggles against racial injustice and coloniality within the "woke" institutions of late modernity.

It is useful to revisit the liberalization of Canadian institutions during the 1960s and 1970s in order to map out the conditions that led to the emergence of the equity regime and, more to the point at hand, track its present workings within the university. It will be remembered that Canada was the first country to adopt multiculturalism as state policy during the 1970s. The policy crystallized the shift underway in state, nation, and economy from the earlier overtly racial project of building Canada as a "white man's country" in the post–Second World War period. As noted above, liberalization was the state's response to the radical upheavals of the 1960s, and the emergence of the post-independence Third World. In this moment of global political realignment, the North American university was a key public institution that gave concrete shape and direction to the remaking of national culture, identity, and economic relations.

Increasingly diversified migration from the Third World, along with the Indigenous and anti-racist movements of the 1970s, however, kept up the pressure for change. The Abella Commission was appointed in 1983 to study employment practices and develop measures to advance equality of opportunity and mitigate systemic discrimination for what would become the four officially designated equity groups – women, Indigenous peoples, visible minorities, and people with disabilities. The Commission documented the widespread inequalities within the workforce and across social systems; its report recommended "a mandatory approach by both federal and provincial governments that would require all employers, public and private, to adopt an 'employment equity' program" (Geller 1985, 20). But as Geller noted, although the report identified systemic discrimination on the basis of group membership for the four key constituencies (who made up 60 per cent of the population), the remedies recommended were informed by a liberal conception of equality; that is, they were primarily directed at individual solutions. Hence, even though the report emphasized the need for equal access to education and training, "it accept[ed] an individualistic opportunity to compete model of equality as the goal to strive for" (20). The university's adoption of this individualizing approach in its equity policies contributed immensely to their legitimation; this approach would enable conditional inclusion-as-exclusion with/in the nation's institutions *and* allow them to brand Canada as a multicultural icon in the international field.

Thus redefined, both university and nation-state became expansive entities attracting and catering to lucrative international opportunities and markets for highly skilled labour, along with low wage, deskilled labour. Both could be harnessed to economic growth and the extension of political influence in the new international institutions that were the legacy of the Second World War. Working in the protective shadow of US capital and state, the institutional turn to official multiculturalism helped extend Canadian social capital at the global level by shaping its specific form of whiteness as benevolent and distinguished from the muscular whiteness of the United States. The "real" Canada/ian would continue to be exalted in the state's institutionalization of bilingualism and biculturalism as defining their nationhood, identity, language, character, and culture (Bannerji 2000; Thobani 2007a). Official multiculturalism locked Indigenous and racial Others into essentializing cultural silos that seemingly conflated their positions even as it trapped them into hierarchies of disempowerment and dispossession

(Grande and Anderson, 2017; Thobani 2007a), Equity would siphon off specific sectors of these Others into the service of university and capital.

Malinda Smith (2010) has studied the pragmatic approach to equity that emerged within the university, which began implementing this policy by elevating gender above the other three designated categories. Taking the view that "women" were the most "ready" to enter the institution, equity committees began to promote gender equity and the inclusion of women as the first step. As such, gender became equated with white women by the university, while the other designated groups (Indigenous peoples, visible minorities, and people with disabilities) became constructed as not quite "ready" for inclusion. Equity thus accrued excellence to white women. In practice then, as Smith has argued, "deficit thinking" and "lack" of merit were now associated with the "Other Others," with the result that the privileged "Other" (white woman) made striking gains within the university system. Such a reading of gender as white simultaneously de-gendered the other designated groups, which were implicitly constructed as masculine. Women of colour were thus rendered institutionally illegible in its categories of "gender" as well as "visible minority," with disability all but pushed off the institutional agenda.

A decade later, these equity measures and the spread of multiculturalism transformed discourses of Canadian nationhood so that cultural pluralism and egalitarianism were among the exalted qualities inscribed into the nation's characterization. Jodi Melamed's (2006) study of the post–civil rights development of racial liberalism, which functioned as official "anti-racism," points to a similar dynamic in the United States. Melamed argues that, as this racial liberalism countered the "anti-racism" of movement politics, the resulting shifts in cultural constructs of nationhood secured legitimacy for the US state and advanced the international interests of US capital. Canadian multiculturalism buttressed this US racial liberalism to reshape the economic order, the former extending its reputation as the global peacemaker motivated by its humanitarian ideals. The North American university's identification as the most desirable site for the cultivation of the liberal- and humanitarian-minded "global" citizen demanded in this new age carved out a politically advantageous indispensability for the institution.

The promise of inclusion offered by the Canadian diversity/equity regime to people of colour would prove highly seductive, drawing them into what would become the main modality of their governance by the closing decade of the twentieth century. Sara Ahmed's (2012) study of race, equity, and diversity in the university is highly instructive in revealing how the policies and practices presently mobilized by this paradigm actually function within this institution. Women of colour, Ahmed's study finds, are constructed as the embodiment of "diversity"; their very presence is taken as confirmation of the institutional commitment to "equity." These faculty are hence treated as intrinsically amenable to, and responsible for, "diversity" work. Appointed to committees and set up as the "natural" spokeswomen for these issues, women of colour's efforts to advance anti-racism within the institution are likened by Ahmed to hitting one's head against a brick wall. In other words, equity and diversity function structurally as well as aspirationally to incorporate the labour of women of colour for racial justice by transforming this into "diversity" work. The anti-racist policies and position papers produced through such labour are then treated by the institution as the "doing" of equity, such that anti-racism is rendered "non-performative," that is, these policies do not bring about the change they promise. Instead, the institution treats their very production as confirmation of such change (Ahmed 2012). In the Canadian context, the equity/diversity machinery facilitates the institution's expansion of Eurocentric epistemological traditions, cultures of whiteness, and racial structures of authority. Indeed, these knowledges, logics, and practices are enhanced as racial Others are managed all the more effectively for pursuing a promise that is constantly deferred.

More insidious, institutionalization of equity redirects the concerns and interests of many scholars of colour away from the anti-racist and anti-colonial frameworks and movements that made possible their very access to the university. They would now be rewarded, if one may call it that, for their contributions to refining the political projects that are reliant on ongoing marginalization, if not outright destruction, of anti-racist praxis.

Contemporary Canadian national discourses subtend these discourses of tolerance and inclusion into the past, as diversity and an impulse to egalitarianism are routinely treated as always having been an intrinsic feature of the nation. This way of thinking helps override Canada's historical record of violence by treating it as (temporarily) hijacked by some ill-informed policy or other (residential schools, head tax, immigration restrictions, Japanese internment, and the like). These policies were, goes the view, exceptional, aberrant and highly regrettable. The university's current repetition of pronouncements in favour of diversity and multiculturalism *as* racial redress solidifies this position within the media and economy as irrefutable confirmation that the racial "mistakes" of the past were just that, mistakes, appropriate apologies having been duly registered. A diversified "past" is thus deployed as confirmation of national goodwill. In other words, contemporary multiculturalism recasts the nation's historical record even as it shapes the racial injustices of the present. Multicultural tolerance and race-neutral meritocracy have now come to be incorporated as intrinsically Canadian. Where the Christian/missionary institutions of the eighteenth and nineteenth centuries sought to cultivate Euro-Christian beliefs, values, and practices among Indigenous peoples and to reduce to a minimum the presence of racial migrants, particularly Black and Asian populations, the late-twentieth-century university inculcates multicultural sensibilities among Canadian nationals to encapsulate Indigenous peoples and communities of colour into the nation's proclamations of innocence and goodwill.

Yet even such compliant multiculturalism intensified the pressure on the white professoriate that was struggling to come to terms with the political as well as demographic changes taking place within the institution, as in the country. There was, of course, the outright attack from the right on multiculturalism as "political correctness" and diversity/equity as elevation of mediocrity that could only lead to intellectual stagnation and the death of meritocracy. Such attacks on multiculturalism, equity, and diversity were evidenced in the rise of the Reform Party (which would later merge with the Conservative Party) on an anti-immigrant, anti-feminist, and homophobic platform. The turn to the right during the 1990s would be more thoroughly exploited by the Harper government at a later date, headed by a prime minister who pronounced Canada had no history of colonialism.

The response to multiculturalism from "progressive," including feminist, quarters in the university was slightly more complicated but no less defensive. Carol Schick's (2000) study of a teacher education program at the University of Saskatchewan in the 1990s provides valuable insights into how whiteness was being reimagined by educators through its interaction with multiculturalism. White women participants developed a range of responses to the introduction of multiculturalism into the training program, Schick found. Some resented having to engage this discourse at all and considered it a form of reverse discrimination; others treated cultural tolerance as a moral and ethical issue but not a political or legal one; and some used their feminism to position themselves "beyond" race. Two main techniques allowed the course participants to secure their racial entitlement, argued Schick: first was their "identification with the ideological space of rationality and objectivity" (108); and second was their identification "with the physical space and with the normative designation of who is likely to be found there" (110). Rather than interrogate, let alone confront, white entitlement, these educators engaged multiculturalism in ways that actually enhanced the sense of their own whiteness as entitlement and/ or resentment. The study demonstrated how moral capital was to be claimed in feminist formations of gendered whiteness through engagement with the "difference" of the racial Other. The stakes involved in protecting such gendered racial capital would only rise with the (relatively) increased representation of women of colour in the university during the 1990s and early 2000s. Particularly threatening were those who brought along their anti-racist/anti-colonial knowledge traditions, perspectives, experiences, and practices into the institution.

Global Exchanges

The transformation of the university with the development of the diversity/equity paradigm discussed above had ramifications for national as well as international politics. The extent to which domestic and foreign policies and interests were intertwined became starkly evident with the "War on Terror," which made the university a key battlefront. Equity would now co-exist with the reinstatement of Western cultural supremacy; diversity would stand for a responsible multiculturalism that could sustain the war's Islamophobic discourses.

The neoliberalization of the 1990s harnessed the historically entrenched relations of dispossession, extraction, and exploitation to the accelerated global mobility of capital and finance that was enabled by the digital and technological revolution. The globalization of the media and cultural industries glossed over the deregulation and privatization that resulted in massive cutbacks in social spending, growing unemployment, erosion of rights, and imposition of structural adjustment. Migration flows escalated as the spread of extractive industries and speculative capital built on the environmental and social disasters produced by the earlier era of "development" across the Third World. The promotion of unrestrained free markets also led to phenomenal growth in the international demand for post-secondary education among the growing middle classes in the Global South.

But globalization's very processes of penetration and integration reinvigorated the struggles that would once again destabilize the international order; these would also undermine the authority of national as well as global elites and institutions. The violence instigated by economic restructuring simultaneously fuelled Indigenous, anti-racist, and anti-imperialist resistance, which, while grounded in these specific communities of dispossession, was being reshaped by the new international linkages that were being built on the ground (Million 2013; Caven 2013; Simpson and Smith 2014; Mamdani 2004; Devji 2005).

By the closing decade of the twentieth century, new potential arose for global alliances as solidarities increased within and between anti-colonial and anti–free trade organizing, from the anti-NAFTA Zapatistas and Indigenous movements, including the Memorial Marches for the murdered and missing Indigenous women and girls, to the Palestinian resistance. This potential was enhanced by the anti-imperialist struggles across Africa, the Middle East, and Asia (Islamist as well as secular), and in South and Central America, which were fuelled by growing immiseration and state violence. Across North America and Europe, the momentum for change coming from anti-racist movements was reinvigorated with the rapid demographic changes underway. The conditions for coalitions across borders were also being created in women's and human rights movements at the United Nations (UN) world conferences – including the UN Fourth World Conference on Women (Beijing, 1996), the UN Conference Against Racism (Durban, 2001, among others. These were linked to the Peoples' Summits that organized opposition to the policies of the World Trade Organization (WTO), the International Monetary Fund (IMF), and the World Bank, as well the North American Free Trade Agreement (NAFTA), the General Agreement on Tariffs and Trade (GATT), the Asian-Pacific Economic Cooperation (APEC), and so forth.

Within the university, vital spaces were opened up in the interdisciplines by radical scholars who came from, and maintained their alliance with, these struggles. Rewriting the histories of Man and Woman from their own particular locations, these scholars destabilized the epistemic power of the disciplines still holding onto their enlightenment projects. Critical anti-racist scholars also confronted the integrationist agendas of the interdisciplines. One needed only to read the archives of the residential school system as a tool of genocide and the narratives of the abolitionist Black women activists who challenged the denial of education to their communities alongside Macauley's Minute (the blueprint for colonizing the native mind) to comprehend the internal relationality between these systems, practices, and ideological convergences that had produced colonization as a global structure. When brought into dialogue, critiques of the place of education in organizing these violent processes of dispossession revealed the various ways in which white supremacy was instituted in different locales as a globally integrated structure. Reading globalization in the context of W.E.B. Du Bois's *The Souls of Black Folks*; Fanon's *Wretched of the Earth* and *Black Skin, White Masks*; Steve Biko's *Black Consciousness in South Africa*; Ngugi wa Thiong'o's *Decolonizing the Mind*; Edward Said's trilogy (*Orientalism, The Question of Palestine, and Covering Islam*); Ashis Nandy's *The Intimate Enemy*; Spivak's *Can the Subaltern Speak?*; Linda Tuhiwai Smith's *Decolonizing Methodologies*; and Vijay Prashad's *The Darker Nations*, among the many other such accounts, laid bare the continuities between the (semi)pacified struggles for multicultural inclusion within the university and the condition of coloniality more generally. What unanticipated avenues for political solidarities might emerge by interrogating the historical linkages between education and racial-colonial violence; between the neoliberal university and racial terror; and between the amnesia of the inter/disciplines and ongoing genocide, famine, and starvation? Who could predict the outcome were the possibilities for cross-community and international solidarities to be materialized *within* the university? What possible horizons might be opened up for collectively envisioned life-enhancing futures?

Many of these possibilities were the product of the intellectual and political labour of Indigenous women and women of colour within the university who built cross-border networks as they engaged global and national structures of power. For example, the Canadian state's repeated upholding of Indigenous women's dispossession led them to take their struggles to the UN and work with international human rights groups (McCarthy 2015; Wolfe and Chief Elk 2012; Amnesty International Canada 2004). For another example, women of colour in the North and women in the Global South organized and led delegations to the international women's conferences held under the auspices of the UN; these activists mobilized local and regional anti-racist coalitions to oppose the international financial institutions and trade agreements (Antrobus 2004). Such political activism, and the training, research, and theoretical advances that were promoted, highlighted the continuities in the violence that shaped the lives of Indigenous women, men, and their communities (Maracle 1981; Million 2013, Tuhiwai Smith 2012) as well as the linkages between coloniality, racial terror, and neoliberal restructuring. Such activist scholarship expanded the political scope for solidarities across the colonial-racial divides among, and between, Indigenous women and women of colour.

The attacks of 9/11, however, transformed the geopolitical field and, with it, the possibilities for advancing such activism and solidarities. One significant consequence of the War on Terror was the decline of the anti-globalization movement in the changing context of heightened militarization and securitization; another was the reinvigoration of the university's relation to state and economy through its advancement of the ideologies and technologies of global war. In the US-led invasions and occupations of the War on Terror, the university became a key part of its arsenal as the institution advanced the military-intelligence-technology nexus (for example, academics worked to design torture techniques, served on human terrain teams, trained military and other personnel in cultural sensitivity, developed emergent digital platforms, not to mention expanded research in the arms and extractive industries). The Islamophobic ideologies of the war found a home within the university, with their legitimation and extension facilitated in the inter-disciplines (such as women's and gender studies, sexuality studies), as well as in new fields of study (including anti-terrorism and security studies, de-radicalization programs, and other similar projects). With the United States, Canada, and the United Kingdom taking the lead in the occupation of Afghanistan, and the United States and the United Kingdom leading the Iraq invasion, the settler colonialism of North American nation-states became articulated to the "new" occupations in the Middle East and Central Asia. The war-related fields mentioned above became new growth areas for academic research, teaching, and funding. Infused now with the discourses of terrorism, militarization, and securitization, assertions of Western cultural supremacy proliferated in pervasive denigrations of Islamic "cultural barbarism" across the social sciences and humanities. Multiculturalism came under some fire for nurturing potentially deadly cultures/communities within Western nations. This discourse, however, had not outlived its uses, for multiculturalism was soon resuscitated as diversity from liberal quarters to mitigate the critiques of white supremacy arising from the Black Lives Matter, anti-Islamophobia, and other anti-racist movements in the changed political environment a decade and a half later.

The global war had as significant an impact in the university as it did in national and global politics, given the involvement of the older disciplines as well as the newer interdisciplines in shaping the forms of violence waged by the US-led alliance. Anthropologists, sociologists, and psychologists pathologized Islam and Muslims; legal scholars and political scientists redefined international law; feminists gendered Islamophobia and endorsed the Western nation-states' reconstruction projects to "save" Muslim women and girls, for some obvious examples.

In their study of the "imperial university," Chatterjee and Maira (2014) link US military operations to "debates about nationalism, patriotism, citizenship, and democracy" in the academy as they study the evolving relation between the two (5). Censorship and intimidation gained new ground in the university during this period, even though the institution's clamping down on dissent was often framed as a defense of academic freedom. Chatterjee and Maira argue that "what is really at work in these attacks are the logics of racism, warfare and nationalism that undergird U.S. imperialism and also the architecture of the U.S. academy" (6). Pointing to the "state of permanent war that is core to U.S.

imperialism and racial statecraft," they argue that this war now "has three fronts: military, cultural, and academic," such that "debates about national identity and national culture shape the battles over academic freedom and the role of the university in defining the racial boundaries of the nation and its 'proper' subjects and 'proper' politics" (7). The surveillance of Muslim and Arab-American – especially Palestinian – scholars and students, the monitoring of activist scholars, the censuring of Palestinian solidarity events, and the use of SWAT teams against student protests are among the practices of intimidation that shape the climate of intellectual repression in the university, argue Chatterjee and Maira. This climate of repression was also to be found in the Canadian university, although its iteration of national-racial identity remained entangled in the bid to maintain a distance from the racial politics of the United States (Thobani 2018). Although expressions of Canadian exceptionalism draw upon and distance themselves from articulations of US exceptionalism, the former is no less vested in the valorization of Western cultural superiority, albeit in a liberal incarnation.

The post-9/11 militarized patriotism drew in feminist as well as queer activists and scholars who grounded their hyper-nationalism in gender and sexual politics, in Canada as in the United States (Thobani 2007b; Puar 2007). These reworked gender/sexual politics had to contend with two additional factors in Canada: first, the saturation of national identity with a morality centred on multiculturalism and humanitarianism; and second, Indigenous women's exposure of the violence of the residential school system as well as their activism on the murdered and missing women and girls from their communities (Amnesty International Canada 2004; Palmater 2015; Million 2013).

With regard to the first factor, multiculturalism, the university's diversity and equity machinery began to focus on sexuality in addition to gender – and to the further detriment of race, Indigenous, and disability–based initiatives – to uphold the idea of tolerance and pluralism. Such privileging of sexuality in equity policies resulted in what Smith (2017) calls the "diversification of whiteness," so that the representation of (white) trans and queer scholars was accelerated. The second factor, Indigenous women's activism, led to the appointment of the Truth and Reconciliation Commission (TRC) and, upon the publication of its Call to Action, to the state- and university- led project of "reconciliation." "Indigenization" of national institutions was forwarded as the means of repairing the harms of the residential school system. This commitment to inclusion, Joyce Green has argued, leaves aside "the truth of that little land-theft matter that needs recognition and restitution if reconciliation is to be meaningful for Indigenous peoples" (Green 2020). How the ensuing performances of remorse and acknowledgement function within the university to mobilize narratives of Indigenous trauma while restabilizing settler narratives of compassion has been critiqued by Indigenous scholars (Million 2013; Ladner and Tait 2017; Daigle 2019). The nation's redemption of its innocence through such public expressions of regret for injustices that are treated as past organizes its present waging of injustices; regret for the old colonial practices obscures understanding the violence of the present.

The dislodging of (race-related) multiculturalism and the insertion of (sexuality-based) difference into the diversity/equity paradigm through Islamophobic constructs of the "cultural barbarism" of Muslims was therefore internally connected to the reconciliation addressing the harm done to Indigenous communities by the residential school system. These two developments not only occurred in the same moment, that of the War on Terror, but were integrally interlinked. While the first (Islamophobia and expansion of gender/sexual egalitarianism) justified the new occupations, proxy wars, and imperialist interventions of the global war, the second (Indigenous reconciliation) sutured over the rupture in the national narrative of Canadian exceptionalism that was accomplished by Indigenous struggles, particularly those led by Indigenous women.

The reworking of the Canadian nationalist discourse that I am describing here – remorseful in relation to Indigenous reconciliation, but endangered in relation to Islamic/Muslim barbarism – enabled acknowledgement of past injuries to function as alibi for the new occupations and wars in which the nation-state was embroiled (Thobani 2007a, 2020). The recasting of Indigenous peoples as subjects of trauma exalted the nation's remorseful largesse in supporting Indigenous healing, even while the heroism of the nation was exalted in its wars with Muslims (demonized as premodern cultural fanatics) to save the women and gender/sexual minorities in their communities. Recognition of Indigenous peoples within Canada thus worked to mystify the colonial nature of the Canadian nation-state, while its construct of Islamic barbarism justified its reassertion of colonial/imperial power as necessary to protect the nation and its inclusive values. Whereas Indigenous peoples were to be included into nationhood through "reconciliation" as the projected future, Muslims and Arabs were to be subjugated to the occupation and invasions they had brought onto themselves.

Chatterjee and Maira (2014) are spot on when they point out that the role of the university becomes even more vital to national governance during moments of international crises. The battles they describe in the

US academy over the meaning and identity of the nation had their parallels in the Canadian university. However, unlike the United States, Canada's national politics were being transformed to an unprecedented degree by the Indigenous resurgence during the global war, and the university took the lead in advancing reconciliation as the nationalist project. This reconciliation, as Indigenous scholars have argued, would incorporate (palatable) aspects of Indigeneity, while precluding the possibility of Indigenous sovereignty (Green 2020; Ladner and Tait 2017). The combined state-university management of Indigeneity made this into yet another cultural resource available to the "caring" nation. The Canadian commitment to pluralism could now be evidenced in this new relationship with Indigenous peoples to uphold the narrative that it was this cultural tolerance that made the nation the target of the "real" savage, the intolerant and hate-filled Islamist fanatic. The virulence of the anti-Muslim violence in the early phase of the War on Terror would eventually also inflame anti-Black and anti-immigrant/ refugee racism on the domestic front. To further compound these racial politics, the increased migration generated by the conflicts of the global war accelerated the demographic shifts already underway in both the United States and Canada, further fueling the already growing anxieties about the erosion of white entitlement.

The university is a conduit for these racial-demographic changes in yet another manner: its increased fiscal reliance on the recruitment of international students. This reliance has facilitated yet another migration stream, that of highly educated elites, which is entangled in the politics of white resentment, as evidenced by the Trump phenomenon in the United States and by the election of right-wing parties in Canada's biggest provinces. Debates about UBC being "too Asian," for example, are of a piece with the racial resentments stoked by populist and white supremacist movements. From national security threats to skewed real estate markets, from escalating housing crises to overburdened social services, from increasing tuition fees to white flight, Canadian cities as well as universities are anxiety-ridden sites with the potential of racist irruptions bubbling just beneath the surface of their pluralist veneer.

The stakes in the management of these demographic and political shifts remain high. As the (mythic) divide between the racial politics of the "domestic" and the "foreign" collapsed in the global war, and the nation-state's narratives of its past fell apart in the face of the Indigenous Resurgence, Black Lives Matter, and other anti-racist movements, the university's role in advancing reconciliation and equity as technologies of governance makes it an indispensable institution to state, nation, and economy. It is this function of the university – the reworking of the ideologies, knowledges, and practices necessary to national and international governance – that is the focus of attention in the chapters that follow.

Breaking Through the Zone of Containment

In "Race, Gender and the University: Strategies for Survival," Mohawk legal scholar-activist Patricia Monture (2010), one of the founders of the Researchers and Academics of Colour for Equity (RACE) network, advised Indigenous women and women of colour to draw on Indigenous knowledge practices in their work within the university. Reflecting on her own teaching experience, her counsel was to know who we are, to know the space we are in, and to value the experience and knowledge that we bring to it – no easy task, as those struggling to transform the university know full well. Monture's words are perhaps even more salient now than when she penned them, given the resurrection of white supremacist values and activism on campuses across North America. The sociologist Agnes Calliste, another founding member of the RACE network, underscored the necessity of learning from the earlier struggles of Black working-class women and men. Her studies explored the rigid segmentation of the labour market in Canada and argued for the necessity of attending to the anti-racist struggles of the past in mapping out collective pathways to the future (see, for example, Calliste and Dei 2000).

The authors of this collection follow in the path of such praxis-oriented scholarship; they are located at various, and asymmetrical, levels within the academic hierarchy in Canada and the United States. Drawing upon their teaching and research, as well as on their own experiences in the university, the authors dissect the practices of an institution riven by struggles to uphold its structures of authority and manage the divides that continue to rip open the fabric of the social order, all the while keeping its brand marketable.

The collective analysis and critiques presented in the following chapters give the reader new insights into how the university reworks racial and colonial hierarchies in a cross-cutting manner as it informs the production of identity, politics, and culture in contemporary North America. Addressing the disparate elements of this reworking (epistemologies, administrative practices, curriculum, classroom interaction, and so on) as these intersect to constitute the whiteness of the university gives the collection its unifying thread.

The first chapter, annie ross's "Don't Cry, Fight! vs. Deference to the Corporate State," takes the reader through a meditative – if searing –

contemplation on the "omnicide" that destroys life to produce new forms of Indigenous dispossession; this death drive leaves in its wake a devastation that threatens the future of the planet. Detailing the extent of the linkages between the university and corporate capital, ross holds the university accountable for its assaults on the Indigenous knowledge systems that revere all forms of living beings. She compels the reader to face up to the consequences of the university's training of successive generations to reproduce the institution's own reverence for corporate capital. The university's investment in extraction and appropriation are what drive the "knowledge" produced here, she warns, as she advocates repossession as a means to salvage what may yet be possible to save from the ruins of the life-world. Walking the reader through the rubble of the present, ross's hope-filled argument for opening the university's doors to Indigenous philosophies, theories, and practices, to respect for all life and commitment to multispecies interdependence, shares a vision to allow justice to enter the institution. Rejecting the corporate "personhood" that is legitimized and organized by the academy in favour of "Indigenous bioregionalism," which supports the well-being of "all Living Beings," is the only path to survival, ross argues.

ross's chapter calls the reader to learn to read, to think, and to feel differently – to experience knowledge as a speaking to mind, body, and spirit, as a cultivation of the sensibility of being as collective living. Her chapter gives the reader a wealth of knowledge and critical thought, and teaches the value of lived experience; each sentence demands careful attention to grasp the dire conditions of the present and to appreciate the urgent need to act now if we are to secure the future of the planet and all its life forms.

Chapter two, Audra Simpson's "The State Is a Man," follows with an account of the violence done to Indigenous women across the Americas; her focus is on the death-drive directed towards Indigenous women in contemporary colonial practice. Settler governance, Simpson argues, requires such death, and the state exonerates its nationals from culpability. Moreover, narratives of Canadian innocence acquire renewed legitimacy in state apologies and attempts to "reconcile" the nation's violent past with its (violent) present. Such apology obscures how the "extractive and simultaneously murderous state of affairs" continues to prevail across the country. The experiences of Indigenous women carry the power to cut through such narratives of innocence, but these are not readily available to students in the university. Settler sovereignty demands Aboriginal disappearance from the classroom as from the national space.

Simpson unpacks the public response to Attawapiskat Chief Theresa Spence's hunger strike in protest of then prime minister Harper's refusal to address the terrible conditions in which her people live. Within their societies, Indigenous women's bodies were symbols of political power, Simpson explains; their bodies signalled more than *flesh*, unlike the case with European women. This power of Indigenous women threatens settler sovereignty, and the settler state targets them in order to "kill" traditional governance itself. Simpson contrasts the ridiculing of the chief's hunger strike to the sympathetic response to the murder of Loretta Saunders, an Inuk woman. Saunders was killed by the renters who sublet her flat, and this death evoked public grief among Canadians. Loretta Saunders could pass as white, Simpson argues, so her killing could thus be read as an attack that could happen to anybody. But *this* violence happened to *this* body, to this *Aboriginal woman's body*, is Simpson's point.

These violent events and experiences, like Indigenous knowledges, are kept from students, and Simpson discusses how introducing non-Indigenous students to these topics comes as a surprise to them. If she did not teach her students about these issues, they may never "even learn about them." Such institutional erasure makes the very idea of "reconciliation," of forgiving and forgetting the violence, "absurd" and "insulting," Simpson argues, "because historical, bodily, and heuristic violence, along with theft," can be neither forgiven nor forgotten. Simpson challenges the cultivation of collective amnesia in the university by calling on the reader to see and remember this violence, to understand that this is not forgotten by Indigenous women.

Chapter three, "Colonizing Critical Race Studies/Scholars," interrogates why critical race studies (CRS) has not come into its own as a field of study in Canadian universities. CRS is an integral aspect of anti-colonial, abolitionist, and anti-racist challenges to colonial postmodernity and racial capitalism, yet this field remains a curious absence in the university, languishing on the margins of the inter/disciplines. Reflecting on my experience trying to advance this interdisciplinary field, my chapter identifies and analyzes the practices that thwart the establishment of CRS as a distinct and self-defining scholarly field that is organically tied to the leadership of women of colour and Indigenous women. Blocking the development of CRS is to simultaneously disenfranchise these scholars, I argue as I study the hostility generated from the interdisciplinary fields of women's, gender, sexuality, and social justice studies to ground-up initiatives advancing CRS. My argument is that CRS has such a destabilizing effect on these "progressive" fields that such a counter-hegemonic tradition is intolerable to them.

The institutional base secured by these Eurocentric interdisciplines, and the power it allows them to access, has situated them at the forefront of containing the counter-hegemonic activities and scholarship of women of colour.

My chapter describes how appropriation, dispossession, and demonization are key institutional responses deployed to extend the proprietary rights of gendered/sexualized whiteness over "race," and over the labour of women of colour faculty and students. Treating race as analogous to gender and sexuality, feminist administrators harnessed the punitive power of the institution to secure the whiteness of the interdisciplines through "social justice" studies and to cultivate integrationist approaches and compliant models of "racial studies." The main conclusion I draw from my own experience and research is that the deployment of keystone neoliberal practices in gendered/sexualized forms is constitutive of these interdisciplines *as well as* of the university's technologies of governance.

In chapter four, "Our Canadian Culture Has Been Squeamish about Gathering Race-Based Statistics," Enakshi Dua compares the debates about race-based data collection in national politics, the university, the media, and the alt-right. Although Canada has had a legislative framework for such data collection to address systemic discrimination since the 1980s, anti-racism–driven attempts to collect such data have been met with hostility from the four sites she studies. Interrogating such opposition, Dua finds the idea that Canadian "culture" is "squeamish" about the endeavour is widespread across these sites. Tracking how power is deployed in the production of this particular "truth claim," she demonstrates how core assumptions regarding race, whiteness, and nation are shared among politicians, university administrators, journalists, and ultra-right campaigners. Noting that the collection of such data is a double-edged sword – race-based statistics can be used to produce alibis for racial profiling as well as policies to counter racism – Dua demonstrates how much of the opposition to collection of this data for anti-racist purposes rests on a shared reluctance to tackle the structures that produce white privilege and racial hierarchies. Unpacking how racial power circulates in these debates in her four research sites, Dua identifies an investment in protecting whiteness as their common thread.

Dua's study underscores the obstructionist approach of the university to combatting racial inequality, in violation of the requirement of the Federal Contractors Program (through which universities are funded) to produce this data. Indeed, as she learns from her interviews, administrators and faculty who work on equity issues experience institutional resistance to the implementation of anti-racist policies in nine out of ten universities. Dua's findings lead her to raise the question, If such data can be collected and acted upon to advance gender equity, as is presently the case, why not the same with regard to race? A collective denial of racial inequality fuels the opposition in the four sites, she argues, which advances the claim that race-based data collection serves the nefarious "special interests" of opportunistic anti-racist organizations and activists. Promoting the idea that such data leads to "reverse" discrimination, opponents use the notion of shared Canadian "values" to mask their sense of racial grievance. Dua goes on to demonstrate how the highly reputable publication *University Affairs* served as the venue for the entry of alt-right perspectives into university debates on the topic. Their shared antipathy to race-based data collection normalizes white supremacist discourses and practices, and Dua shows how alt-right politics are shaped by the same racial assumptions that inform liberal discourses in the university.

"How can you *not* know?" Delia Douglas asks in chapter five, "Access Denied: Safe/guarding the University as White Property," as she draws attention to the severe underrepresentation and deplorable treatment of Black women faculty in the Canadian university. Defining the university as a "crime scene" as well as "white property," Douglas interrogates how both are secured through the denigration of Indigenous, Black, and women of colour faculty and their scholarship. The institution continues to protect its whiteness in this manner even as the country's population becomes more diverse. Most students from Indigenous and people of colour communities are unlikely to ever be taught by Indigenous and women of colour faculty, Douglas observes. Instead, these young people will be drawn into reproducing the university's whiteness and its racist exclusions. Cultivating their "unseeing" of the racial segregation that structures this institution schools young people of colour and Indigenous youth into accommodating whiteness and upholding its privileging; as such, these students are trained into subservience to their own racial domination. Moreover, the institution's disavowal of racism within its ranks and structures is conjoined with narratives of innocence that uphold settler practices, Douglas argues, as she links the "regulation of racialized and gendered bodies" to the "regulation of racialized and gendered bodies of knowledge."

Black and other women of colour faculty who make it into the university, Douglas points out, are encouraged to discipline each other to uphold the institution's whiteness. What can be known in the university is controlled by who is allowed to enter the institution, and as Douglas demonstrates, the exclusion of Black women from the ranks of the professoriate keeps their perspectives out of the institution. The cost is the destruction of their talent, creativity, and knowledge, and Douglas calls on the reader to bear witness to this banishment of Black women's scholarship. The conditions of precarity that structure the experience of Black women is further compounded as they are punished for their insurgent scholarship by being confined to adjunct faculty positions, without job security, benefits, or opportunities for advancement. This casualization of the faculty is the subject of the next chapter.

In chapter six, "Invisibility, Marginalization, Injustice, Dehumanization," Sarika Bose examines the accelerated casualization of the faculty in the university. This development has intensified the economic exploitation as well as financial vulnerability of adjunct faculty, imposing on them a regime of marginalization, shame, and humiliation. Drawing on the UN Declaration of Human Rights, Bose argues that the university's treatment of the "subaltern academic" violates their basic human rights, erodes their citizenship, and decimates their human dignity. Without access to research and funding opportunities, and barred from the institution's governance structures, the just-in-time hiring and insecure working conditions of contract faculty contravenes the self-proclaimed "egalitarian" values of the university as well as its promise to train students to become "citizens." Bose shows how deep run the injuries of job insecurity, which include high stress levels and burnout, hopelessness, poverty, and homelessness. The despair of the subaltern academic is not even acknowledged by the university, the effects of which are further compounded by the racialized injustices imposed on adjunct faculty of colour and of Indigenous ancestry. Although this underclass is stigmatized as disposable, it is presently indispensable to the success and profitability of the university.

Academic freedom, considered the cornerstone of university life, is made meaningless in the absence of job security. Bose's study leads her to question how the adjunct faculty rendered "non-citizen" of the institution could possibly train its "citizens" (students) into responsible citizenship. Indeed, students easily recognize the vulnerabilities of these non-citizens and erode their authority in the classroom by inflicting on them their own racial and sexist ideas of human worth. Ending her essay with a call to solidarity, Bose challenges tenured faculty to end their/our contribution to the subalternizing of their/our academic colleagues and to stand with adjunct faculty in their fight for their human rights.

Resisting the militarization of the university in a climate wherein recognition of Indigenous presence and cultural diversity, along with the institution's internationalization, have acquired considerable momentum is the subject of chapter seven, "Refusing Diversity in the

Militarized Settler Academy," by Carol Fadda and Dana Olwan. The US university's expansion of diversity projects to encompass Indigenization coincided with the War on Terror, and although this project is siloed off from internationalization and militarization, Fadda and Olwan demonstrate the connections between these three developments. The "diversity" practices that permeate these fields are signposts to the institution's, as well as the nation-state's, emergent interests, the authors argue.

Drawing on their embodied experience as Arab women (Fadda is born and raised in Lebanon and Olwan in Kuwait/Jordan/Palestine) and on their positionality as students, immigrants, and professors in the United States, the authors present grounded insights into how the "domestic" settler colonialism and racialized exclusions of the US state intersect with its "global" role as an imperialist power in the Middle East. Palestinian dispossession, the Lebanese war, and the first Gulf War taught the authors the realities of US foreign policy and military intervention in the region, and how these are linked to US popular culture. Upon arrival in the United States after the 9/11 attacks, the explosion of anti-Arab racism they encountered there deepened their understanding of the relation of the nation-state's domestic racism to its imperialism abroad. Moreover, the irony of the authors' paradoxical classification as "white" in immigration/citizenship policy and as "diverse" within the university is not lost on them; non-acquiescence, self-representation, and dissent are among the survival strategies they have developed in the institution.

Fadda and Olwan go on to interrogate the function of land acknowledgments, diversity, and study abroad programs in the Middle East in the context of the opening of a new Veterans Resource Center on campus. While Indigenous recognition and promotion of diversity bolster the university's commitment to multiculturalism, these practices accompany the intensification of the displacement, exploitation, and violence of US imperialism abroad. Linking internationalization and study abroad programs in the Middle East to the extension of US national security interests in the War on Terror, Fadda and Olwan argue that campus-based campaigns in support of the academic and cultural boycott of Israel interrupt and expose how settler relations within the United States are connected to those in the Middle East. Fadda and Olwan also highlight how the militarization of the university puts its educational, research, and institutional resources in the service of the war machine. Faculty implication in the militarization and foreign policy agendas of the university and state cannot be easily resolved, the authors argue, as they make the case for faculty to refuse the institution's invitation to "happy diversity" by becoming "blockage points" of non-compliance with the settler and imperialist violence in which the university is embroiled.

In chapter eight, "How Canadian Universities Fail Black Non-Binary Students," Cicely Belle Blain presents their insightful auto-ethnographic account of growing up in a largely white environment. Encountering homosexuality as a primarily white phenomenon, they come to experience Black communities as socially conservative. At a later stage in life, Blain came to learn that theirs was a "reasonably average experience" for mixed race, non-binary Black young people. Mapping out the fraught relation of feminism to queerness and non-binary gender, and of race to slavery and Blackness, Blain argues that gender binary functions as a "sub-tool" of white supremacy

Blain's interactions with undergraduate Black students leads them to conclude that the intersection of race, Blackness, gender, and sexuality leaves these students isolated and alienated, their experience of the university "overwhelmingly negative." It is other Black students who help transform the institution into a place of learning through contesting the Eurocentric education they receive, and through their campus activism. If the institutional environment constrained Blain's own identities, learning, and experience, the Black students offered them, even if only temporarily, the possibility of community. Blain emphasizes how the limited presence of Black students on campus, and the marginalization of Black communities in the city, reduces the possibilities for non-binary Black students to find support and respite from racism. Blain's study of the experiences of non-binary Black undergraduate students makes an invaluable contribution to understanding how anti-Blackness is fostered in the everyday experiences of students.

Chapter nine, "Interrogating White Supremacy in Academia," by Benita Bunjun explores how the classroom space creates silences and erasures, isolation and exclusion. How can this space be transformed into a site for the learning, empowerment, and well-being of students of colour and of Indigenous ancestry? Analyzing student evaluations of her courses, Bunjun finds that white students expect her, as instructor, to create a climate of comfort for them in the classroom and to protect the "whiteness" with which they identify. Paying particular heed to how these students respond to her racialized body in a position of authority, she argues against faculty of colour taking upon themselves the burden to make the classroom a "happy place." Speaking from her "unhappy" location in this space, Bunjun's outrage at the expectation that faculty of colour nurture the whiteness of students and contribute to the erasure of

Indigenous and students of colour as "bodies out of place" rings loud and clear in this chapter.

Bunjun argues these encounters in the "contact zone" that is the university reproduce, and confront, nationalist discourses, racial forms of (un)belonging, and (dis)entitlement. Instructors' attempts to create an alternate space for Indigenous and students of colour for their critical learning about, and reflection on, their own presence, histories, and perspectives is met with defensive postures from white students. The only tolerable bodies of colour, whether instructor or student, are those that service the white subjects who claim unhindered entitlement to the space. Refusal to live up to the "duty" to play the model minority comes with its own peril, Bunjun argues. Yet refusal is necessary if students are to be introduced to the historicity of settler colonialism and the racial dynamics that unfold within the nation-state, much as they do within the classroom. A rejection of this duty is required if students are to be taught to think critically, to think theoretically as well as historically. If such teaching is not undertaken in the classroom, students receive an education that merely reproduces the comforting myths of whiteness.

In contrast, students of colour reported in their evaluations that the demand on them to perform "happiness" and "gratitude" came not only from white classmates but also from other faculty, and from the staff who provide student services. International students also reported difficulties in negotiating Eurocentric knowledge systems that disappear their own histories and the experiences of their families and communities. These students face considerable pressure to adopt Anglo names and suppress their experiences of war, displacement, and migration. The resulting fracturing of their sense of self, and of their links to their ancestral and spiritual lineages, is the price to be paid for their success in acquiring an "international" education. Creating alternate spaces for student learning is critical to their well-being, Bunjun argues, although the irony is not lost on her that international students pay exorbitant tuition fees to learn the very Eurocentric traditions from which their ancestors fought to liberate themselves. Being the "feminist killjoy" in such a classroom requires courage, Bunjun notes, for it entails challenging whiteness, transphobia, ableism, and racism in this space as well as in the larger society in which students live and work. The task is not easy, but its necessity is the message that resonates in all the chapters of this collection.

In the final chapter, "Dreaming Big in Small Spaces," Jin Haritaworn presents an unabashed call for insurgent activism in the university. The racial crisis in the larger social order that is evident in the heightened visibility of white supremacist movements has made the cost of complicity too high, the dangers too great, for Indigenous and scholars of colour to comfort themselves with performances of "liberal outrage." Denunciations of the electoral victories of Donald Trump in the United States and of Doug Ford in Ontario may assuage the liberal conscience, but these only provide cover to the "old" white supremacy and will certainly not bring an end to colonial violence and political attacks on people of colour or on trans rights, they argue. As the ultra-right redefines the meaning of gender, sexuality, and race across North America through repealing sex education, outlawing ethnic studies, and reversing gay rights, education is yet again the "battleground over racialized and gendered lives."

Haritaworn's defence of activist scholarship is a reality check on the political rearrangements of the present and on the utter capitulation of the university to them, even as the institution continues to represent itself as champion of the education that has the power to counter white nationalism. Dissecting this fallacy by naming whiteness as the pressure put on queer/trans/Black/Indigenous/of colour faculty to engage in this Sisyphean labour of the institution, Haritaworn points out how none of this "work" actually confronts the violence done to Black, Indigenous, and people of colour across the social order. Drawing attention to the implication of the professional intellectual in these conditions of violence, Haritaworn calls on scholars to engage in transformative politics, to work from the position of powerlessness. Unmaking the inhospitable institution that organizes their complicity by the offer of inclusion is the urgent task of the present. Haritaworn argues that it is the powerless un/professional, daring to dream of "marvellous futures," who defies the seductions proffered by the institution's complicit elites.

Conclusion

The two events with which I began this introduction – the dedication of the Musqueam Post and the deposing of the UBC president – point to how fraught are the racial politics of the present, which threaten to unravel the colonial logics that structure the North American university. The institution remains housed on stolen lands and mired in Eurocentric epistemologies; its pedagogies incorporate students into neoliberal governance practices. The Indigenous Resurgence, Black Lives Matter, migrant rights, and other anti-racist movements across the United States and Canada have their representation also on the university campus. These linkages make the university, like the society it serves, unstable and volatile.

Having played a leading role in the production of colonial ideologies, settler politics, and racialized subjects, the institution is now embroiled in the cultural refashioning of the whiteness that is being daily contested across North America. The university sinks deeper into the racial quagmire as it advances the refortification of the borders – material and ideological – which uphold the white supremacy that a deeply entrenched global structure of power.

The university hence faces an irreconcilable contradiction. As it intensifies its relation to the colonial/imperial state and nation, to militarized capital, and rebrands itself as a global institution to access the lucrative international markets for education, pressure mounts on the institution to respond to the political consequences of the escalating violence and resulting demographic shifts, which are being further exacerbated by the migrations from wars zones and societies facing environmental collapse. The university's governing elites are faced with unprecedented challenges on a daily basis to their racial authority, overrepresentation in positions of power, and outdated epistemologies, employment practices, and institutional cultures. In other words, even as the university restructures and "diversifies" its activities, hiring practices, and student body, these very shifts intensify the anti-racist/anti-colonial challenges to its investment in the culture of whiteness. Furthermore, increased pressure is now also being applied to the liberal institutions of the nation-state, among which the university still counts itself, by the demands of the white supremacist movements, which, caring not a whit for the niceties of multicultural respectability, are fast ripping off the fig leaf of racial tolerance and inclusion. The university's predicament is indeed of acute proportions.

True, the capacity of the university to manage these formidable challenges – from outward appearance at least – seems to be working for the moment by its two-pronged promise of inclusion: equity/diversity and Indigenizing the academy. Canadian and American universities are still reaping the fruits of an alluring multiculturalism as evident in the levels of student enrolment, particularly of international students from the Global South. Yet, this growth of the university exposes the already significant underrepresentation and marginalization of "domestic," so to speak, faculty and students of colour. The university's current practice of including international students in its "equity" and "diversity" calculations cannot hide its racial politics – not from "domestic" or "foreign" students.

For faculty and students of colour, the hollowness of the promise of inclusion is daily exposed by the university's revamping of "older" forms of racial injustice and colonial erasures into newer formulations as it responds to contemporary movements of resistance within, and outside, the institution. These movements have once again thrown into upheaval the university, which is compelled to respond with modes of power that can placate – if not neutralize – the former's insurgent demands. Examining how the university functions at the centre of these contentious politics, and delineating the strategies being developed as it negotiates the governmentalities of the present, the chapters of this book expose and confront its structures of power and authority. With university after university now lining up to pronounce its commitment to inclusion and diversity, with each institution solemnly promising to do better, it would do well to attend to how such strategies of containment both depoliticize and deradicalize the anti-racist/colonial praxis once again placed on the institutional agenda. Solidarities on the ground are met with strategies of divide and rule.

In closing, I want to thank the authors who have contributed their work to this collection; it has been an absolute honour for me to work with you all in bringing this book to fruition. I also want to express my deep gratitude to annie ross for sharing her artwork for the cover of this book. When we were discussing this image, titled *i, delusional,* annie recounted how this piece responds to the devaluation of Indigenous women's work in the university. Among other things, this image, she explained, is "looking at justice." Once annie spoke these words and purpose, I knew there could be no more powerful image capturing the overall themes of this book. My thanks go also to Meg Patterson, Carolyn Zapf, Janice Evans, and the University of Toronto Press team and the anonymous reviewers for their support and assistance in bringing this manuscript to publication.

As I read and re-read the chapters that make up this book, and then read them yet again, I was overwhelmed by the magnitude of the challenges women and queers of colour and of Indigenous ancestry, scholars and activists, face on a daily basis within the academy. I was also repeatedly awed by the courage of the authors, for undertaking this kind of work puts them, particularly the students and untenured faculty, in peril for speaking out. Audre Lorde's unforgettable words urging us to put all our strength in building our vision kept coming to mind as I was working on this introduction:

> When I dare to be powerful, to use my strength in the service of my vision, then it becomes less and less important whether I am afraid.

The authors of this collection have all dared to be powerful at a moment when the costs of giving up our collective power to resist are incalculable.

NOTE

1 The phrase "difference that makes no difference" can also be found in
   Robert Martin's book *There Are Two Errors in the Title of This Book*.

REFERENCES

Ahmed, Sara. 2012. *On Being Included: Racism and Diversity in Institutional Life*.
   Durham, NC: Duke University Press.
Amnesty International Canada. 2004. *Stolen Sisters: Discrimination and Violence
   Against Indigenous Women in Canada*. Ottawa: Amnesty International.
Anisef, P., P. Axelrod, and J. Lennards. 2015. "Universities in Canada
   (Canadian Universities)." *The Canadian Encyclopedia*, 20 July 2015. https://
   www.thecanadianencyclopedia.ca/en/article/university.
Antrobus, Peggy. 2004. *The Global Women's Movement: Origins, Issues and
   Strategies*. London: Zed Books.
Arday, Jason, and Heidi Safia Mirza, eds. 2018. *Dismantling Race in Higher
   Education: Racism, Whiteness and Decolonising the Academy*. London: Palgrave
   Macmillan.
Bannerji, Himani. 2000. *The Dark Side of the Nation: Essays on Multiculturalism,
   Nationalism and Gender*. Toronto: Canadian Scholars' Press.
Brown, Scott. 2016. "Highlights of the Gupta Documents that UBC
   Didn't Want You to See." *The Vancouver Sun*, 7 January 2016. https://
   vancouversun.com/news/staff-blogs/highlights-of-the-gupta
   -documents-that-ubc-didnt-want-you-to-see.
Brownlee, Jaime. 2014. *Irreconcilable Differences: The Corporatization of Canadian
   Universities*. PhD diss., Sociology Department, Carleton University.
Calliste, Agnes, and George Dei. 2000. *Anti-Racist Feminism*. Halifax:
   Fernwood Books.
Caven, Febna. 2013. "Being Idle No More: The Women Behind the
   Movement." *Cultural Survival Quarterly Magazine*, March 2013. https://
   www.culturalsurvival.org/publications/cultural-survival-quarterly
   /being-idle-no-more-women-behind-movement.
Chatterjee, Piya, and Sunaina Maira, eds. 2014. *The Imperial University:
   Academic Repression and Scholarly Dissent*. Minneapolis: University of
   Minnesota Press.
Chow, Rey. 2002. "Theory, Area Studies, Cultural Studies: Issues of Pedagogy
   in Multiculturalism." In *Learning Places: The Afterlives of Area Studies*, edited
   by Masao Miyushi and H.D. Harootunian, 103–18. Durham, NC: Duke
   University Press.
Collins, Patricia Hill, and Sirma Bilge. 2016. *Intersectionality*. Cambridge:
   Polity Press.

Combahee River Collective. 2014. "A Black Feminist Statement." *Women's Studies Quarterly* 42 (3/4): 271–80. https://doi.org/10.1353/wsq.2014.0052.

Compton, James. 2016. "Reasserting the University Tradition." *Bulletin, Canadian Association of University Teachers* 63 (December): 5. https:// www.caut.ca/bulletin/2016/12/president's-message-reasserting-university -tradition.

Crenshaw, Kimberle. 1991. "Mapping the Margins: Intersectionality, Identity Politics, and Violence against Women of Color." *Stanford Law Review* 43 (6): 1241–99. https://doi.org/10.2307/1229039.

Daigle, Michelle. 2019. "The Spectacle of Reconciliation: On (the) Unsettling Responsibilities to Indigenous Peoples in the Academy." *Environment and Planning D: Society and Space* 37 (4): 703–21. https://doi.org/10.1177 /0263775818824342.

Davidson, Cliff. 2015. "The University Corporatization Shift: A Longitudinal Analysis of University Admission Handbooks, 1980–2010." *Canadian Journal of Higher Education* 45 (2): 193–213. https://doi.org/10.47678/cjhe .v45i2.184441.

Devji, Faisal. 2005. *Landscapes of the Jihad: Militancy, Morality, Modernity.* Ithaca, NY: Cornell University Press.

Ferguson, Roderick. 2012. *The Reorder of Things: The University and Its Pedagogies of Minority Difference.* Minneapolis: University of Minnesota Press.

Findlay, Stephanie, and Nicholas Köhler. 2010. "The Enrollment Controversy." *Maclean's*, 10 November 2010. https://www.macleans.ca/news/canada /too-asian/.

Geller, Carole. 1985. "A Critique of the Abella Report." *Canadian Woman's Studies* 6 (4): 20–2. https://cws.journals.yorku.ca/index.php/cws/article /viewFile/12796/11879.

Giroux, Henry. A. 2014. "When Schools Become Dead Zones of the Imagination: A Critical Pedagogy Manifesto." *Policy Futures in Education* 12 (4): 491–9. https://doi.org/10.2304/pfie.2014.12.4.491.

Grande, Sandy, and Lauren Anderson. 2017. "Un-Settling Multicultural Erasures." *Multicultural Perspectives* 19 (3): 139–42. https://doi.org/10.1080 /15210960.2017.1331742.

Green, Joyce. 2020. "Enacting Reconciliation." In *Visions of the Heart: Issues Involving Indigenous Peoples in Canada*, 5th ed., edited by Gina Starblanket and David Long, with Olive Patricia Dickason, 239–552. Don Mills, ON: Oxford University Press.

Gutiérrez y Muhs, Gabriella, Yolanda Flores Niemann, Carmen G. González, and Angela P. Harris, eds. 2012. *Presumed Incompetent: The Intersections of Race and Class for Women in Academia.* Boulder, CO: Utah State University Press.

Hall, Stuart, ed. 1997. *Representation: Cultural Representation and Signifying Practices*. London: Sage Publications.

Hampton, Rosalind. 2020. *Black Racialization and Resistance at an Elite Canadian University*. Toronto: University of Toronto Press.

Hare, Bruce. 1995. "On the Desegregation of the Visible Elite." *Sociological Forum* 10 (4): 673–6. https://doi.org/10.1007/BF02095774.

Harootunian, H.D., and Masao Miyushi. 2002. "Introduction: The 'Afterlife' of Area Studies." In *Learning Places: The Afterlives of Area Studies*, edited by Masao Miyushi and H.D. Harootunian, 1–18. Durham, NC: Duke University Press.

Harvey, David. 2005. *A Brief History of Neoliberalism*. Oxford: Oxford University Press.

Henry, Frances, et al. 2017. *The Equity Myth: Racialization and Indigeneity at Canadian Universities*. Vancouver, BC: UBC Press.

Johnson, Azeezat, Remi Joseph-Salisbury, and Beth Kamunge. 2018. *The Fire Now: Anti-Racist Scholarship in Times of Explicit Racial Violence*. London: Zed Books.

LaCapra, Dominick. 1998. "The University in Ruins?" *Critical Inquiry* 25 (1): 32–55. https://doi.org/10.1086/448907.

Ladner, Kiera, and Myra J. Tait. 2017. *Surviving Canada: Indigenous Peoples Celebrate 150 Years of Betrayal*. Winnipeg: ARP Books.

Mamdani, Mahmood. 2004. *Good Muslim, Bad Muslim: America, the Cold War and the Roots of Terror*. New York: Pantheon Books.

Maracle, Lee.1981. *I Am Woman: A Native Perspective on Sociology and Feminism*. Vancouver, BC: Press Gang Publishers.

McCarthy, Tom. 2015. "Canada Has Failed to Protect Indigenous Women from Violence, Says UN Official." *The Guardian*, 12 May 2015. https://www.theguardian.com/world/2015/may/12/canada-violence-indigenous-first-nations-women.

Melamed, Jodi. 2006. "The Spirit of Neoliberalism." *Social Text* 24 (4 [89]): 1–24. https://doi.org/10.1215/01642472-2006-009.

– 2011. *Represent and Destroy: Rationalizing Violence in the New Racial Capitalism*. Minneapolis: University of Minnesota Press.

Million, Dian. 2013. *Therapeutic Nations: Healing in an Age of Indigenous Human Rights*. Tucson: University of Arizona Press.

Monture, Patricia. 2010. "Race, Gender, and the University: Strategies for Survival." In *States of Race: Critical Race Feminism for the 21st Century*, edited by Sherene Razack, Malinda Smith, and Sunera Thobani, 23–36. Toronto: Between the Lines Press.

Newstadt, Eric. 2008. "The Neoliberal University: Looking at the York Strike." *The Bullet*, # 165, 5 December 2008. https://socialistproject.ca/2008/12/b165/.

Palmater, Pamela. 2015. *Indigenous Nationhood: Empowering Grassroots Citizens*. Halifax: Fernwood Publishing.

paperson, la. 2017. *A Third University Is Possible*. Minneapolis: University of Minnesota Press.

Puar, Jasbir. 2007. *Terrorist Assemblages: Homonationalism in Queer Times*. Durham, NC: Duke University Press.

Readings, Bill. 1996. *The University in Ruins*. Cambridge, MA: Harvard University Press.

Said, Edward. 1978. *Orientalism*. New York: Pantheon Books.

– 1993. *Culture and Imperialism*. London: Random House.

Schick, Carol. 2000. "'By Virtue of Being White': Resistance in Anti-racist Pedagogy." *Race, Ethnicity and Education* 3 (1): 83–101. https://doi.org /10.1080/713693016.

Schuessler, Jennifer. 2013. "Dirty Antebellum Secrets in Ivory Towers." Review of *Ebony and Ivory: Race, Slavery, and the Troubled History of America's Universities* by Craig Steven Wilder. *New York Times*, 18 October 2013. https://www.nytimes.com/2013/10/19/books/ebony-and-ivy-about-how -slavery-helped-universities-grow.html.

Simpson, Audra, and Andrea Smith, eds. 2014. *Theorizing Native Studies*. Durham, NC: Duke University Press.

Sivanandan, Ambalavaner. 1982. *A Different Hunger: Writings on Black Resistance*. London: Pluto Press.

Smith, Malinda. 2010. "Gender, Whiteness and 'Other' Others in the Academy." In *States of Race: Critical Race Feminism for the 21st Century*, edited by Sherene Razack, Malinda Smith, and Sunera Thobani, 37–58. Toronto: Between the Lines.

– 2017. "The State of the Academy: Issues, Policy and Effects on People." Panel presentation at the conference Racial (In)Justice in the Canadian Academy, UBC Faculty Association, Vancouver, BC, 16 March 2017.

Thobani, Sunera. 2007a. *Exalted Subjects: The Making of Race and Nation in Canada*. Toronto: University of Toronto Press.

– 2007b. "White Wars: Western Feminisms and the 'War on Terror.'" *Feminist Theory* 8 (2): 169–85. https://doi.org/10.1177/1464700107078140.

– 2018. "Neoliberal Multiculturalism and Western Exceptionalism: The Cultural Politics of the West." *Fudan Journal of the Humanities and Social Sciences* 11 (2): 164–74. https://doi.org/10.1007/s40647-018-0227-x.

– 2020. *Contesting Islam, Constructing Race and Sexuality: The Inordinate Desire of the West*. London: Bloomsbury Academic.

Tuhiwai Smith, Linda. 2012. *Decolonizing Methodologies: Research and Indigenous Peoples*, 2nd ed. London: Zed Books.

UBC (University of British Columbia). n.d.-a. "Affiliations." *Indigenous Portal*. University of British Columbia. https://indigenous.ubc.ca/indigenous -engagement/affiliations/.

UBC (University of British Columbia). n.d.-b. "Indigenous Engagement."
    Indigenous Portal. https://indigenous.ubc.ca/indigenous-engagement/.
UBC News. 2016. "Musqueam Post Dedicated at UBC Vancouver Campus."
    UBC News, 6 April 2016. https://news.ubc.ca/2016/04/06/musqueam
    -post-dedicated-at-ubc-vancouver-campus-today/.
Westheimer, Joel. 2010. "Higher Education or Education for Hire?" *Academic
    Matters*, April–May 2010. https://academicmatters.ca/higher-education-or
    -education-for-hire-corporatization-and-the-threat-to-democratic-thinking/.
Wilder, Craig Steven. 2008. *Ebony and Ivy: Race, Slavery, and the Troubled
    History of American Universities*. New York: Bloomsbury.
Wolfe, Lauren, and Lauren Chief Elk. 2012. "Sexual Violence Is Tearing
    Native American Communities Apart." *The Guardian*, 8 September 2012.
    https://www.theguardian.com/commentisfree/2012/sep/08/sexual
    -violence-native-american-communities.

1 Don't Cry, Fight! vs. Deference to the Corporate State: Abrogation of Indigenous Rights and Title, Civil Rights, and Social and Environmental Justice at the Imperialist University

ANNIE ROSS

Opening

Imperialist neoliberal economics, the violent taking, reap and rape, rush to the very last of every living Being – entrenched systemically, psychologically, and culturally – has infiltrated every social institution, such as those in the domains of politics and popular culture, including the university. Neoliberalism is a system that grants corporations impunity to abrogate rights and to commit what may be considered crimes, especially against Indigenous peoples. In speaking of corporate harms against workers – but relevant to corporate harms against Land and all of her Beings, against democratic rights and justice – one could ask, along with Glasbeek, "Why is corporate deviance not treated as a crime?" and also find those forces exempted from guilt because of their membership in the ruling class (Glasbeek 1984). According to Laura Macdonald and Arne Ruckert, neoliberalism can be defined as

> a new form of Social rule under which elite class power and the profitability of capital have been successfully restored. (quoted in Williams and Disney 2015, 4)

Imperialism is the work of systems – governments, corporations, and their military and police forces, factory farms, spreadsheets, and those so individually tied to their foundation of ruin as "development" that they do any and all manner of things to have their way, including indoctrinating (or attempting to) others into their manners, ideologies, and practices. An imperialist university, advancer of neoliberalism, is one in the chain of those who abrogate Indigenous rights[1] and title, social and environmental justice, civil rights, the rights of all living Beings to not only survive, but thrive. Change is mandatory in order to transform the heart from one of violence and wreckage to one of responsible peace and justice-making with our Sacred Planet and all of her Beings. Leo Panitch and Sam Gindin define neoliberalism as a

> state-led economic restructuring oriented to removing, through expansion and deepening of markets, democratically imposed barriers to accumulation. (quoted in Williams and Disney 2015, 4)

Our Sacred Home, and all Wild, Sacred, and Good, has been commodified and is only seen as a monetary exchange, all Her other values denied. Modernity's replacements are pavements; processed, calorie-dense, cruelty-based, nutrition-poor foods; psychological and practical disconnection from a relationship with Natural/Supernatural Beloveds (the real) replaced by the virtual (computer generated); and the vanquishment of mysterious Power Beings and Places with a culture of entrenched, needless, excessive cruelty and endless wars.

Having consumed the biggest, the strongest, and a majority of Earth's Sacred Beings for individual power and obscene wealth, ruin (neoliberalism) has consumed Wild, Sacred, and Good Places, Beings, and sustainable[2] life. Unremediated/able ecosystems, imposed poverty, unmet basic needs and desires of all living Beings, trauma, and erosion/destruction of basic human, constitutional, and environmental responsibilities (meaning, rights as responsibilities to protect all Land, Water, Air, Life) are left behind. Despite our well-fed, housed selves from our privileged university place, little leadership is displayed here to challenge the lawlessness of corporations and militarized police, political expediencies[3] of the imperialist agenda, their making of suffering, dispossession, and violations of democratic rights from the historic era to the present. Too little, if any, work is carried out in training the university community to claim their responsibilities and Spirit power in their lives for a just society; instead, there is "sacrific[ing] integrity and truth for power, personal advancement, foundation grants, awards, tenured professorships, columns, book contracts, television appearances, generous lecture fees and social status. They know what they need to say. They know which ideology they have to serve" (Hedges 2013). Much can be said, globally, about neoliberalism in Indigenous communities. For example, Leslie Gill makes the following point:

> The impunity-backed state terror that fractured countries such as Guatemala, El Salvador, Chile and Argentina while they were ruled by harsh

regimes set the stage for consolidation of neoliberal economic models under civilian governments. (quoted in Williams and Disney 2015, 1)

Neoliberalism's foundations are racism, misogyny, speciesism, and elitism. It is colonialism's plunder in the modern age; its only change in the Americas from 1492 is bigger, more ruinous omnicidal machines – chemical, biological, radiological, nuclear, and other weapons of terror. Its effects are imposed poverty upon Indigenous communities, and with unremediated Land, it creates environmental refugees or people forced to live without drinking water, safe homes, health care, and freedom from contaminations. Neoliberalism is the culture of violence. Wealth and power for the few is at the expense of the health of the commons – those Beings (Land, Water, Plant, Animal, Air, Every One) critical to true security for all. In turn, corporations desperate to transform their "magnitude of harms and incidents," which raise "overarching concerns" (Imai, Gardner, and Weinberger 2017, 8), offer financial incentives to community entities in exchange for public naming opportunities. Here, wealth from impoverished primarily Indigenous communities, further devastated by the corporations "magnitude of harms and incidents," is donated to universities (although who rightfully owns the monetary wealth is a question for debate), who then name buildings, schools, public relations campaigns, and programs in attempts to transform a corporate identity via the school of public opinion. Without consent, all members of the university community are forever branded as well, forcefully aligned with the acts of the corporation, for example, those documented in "The Canadian Brand: Violence and Canadian Mining Companies in Latin America" (Imai, Gardner, and Weinberger 2017). In their "Conclusion: A Call for Action," the authors quote Justice Ian Binnie (formerly of the Supreme Court of Canada) when he said: "One of the most fundamental precepts of our legal system is that if there is a wrong there should be a remedy. And at the moment, these people in the third world have no remedy."[4] Speaking of what Binnie termed "wrong," or how to speak of such tragic realities, the authors state:

> [In this study, we] have limited the data we have collected to violence and criminalization ... [T]here are many more conflicts that result in protests, blockades and legal actions on which we do not report. Therefore, this study should not be taken as a measure of the extent of *conflict* associated with Canadian mining, as the self-imposed limits placed on our data collection in the interest of quality have resulted in the exclusion of many conflicts. We have argued that there is a degree of *proximity* between

violent conflict and Canadian mining companies, and that something more needs to be done to address the situation.

Canada has received criticism from international bodies for its failure to develop mechanisms for holding Canadian mining companies accountable for their overseas projects. In 2013, a group of organizations from Latin America presented 23 case studies involving conflicts with Canadian mining companies in the region to the Inter-American Commission on Human Rights. In 2015, a number of Catholic Bishops issued a document criticizing the practices of Canadian mining companies ... As of October, 2017, five United Nations treaty bodies, beginning in 2002, have urged Canada, specifically, to assume its responsibility to protect against human rights abuse outside its territory, and to provide effective oversight regarding its companies' overseas operations, including through extraterritorial regulation: the Commission on Human Rights (2003); the Committee on the Elimination of Racial Discrimination (2007 and 2012), the Committee on the Rights of the Child (2012), the Human Rights Committee (2015) and the Committee On Economic, Social And Cultural Rights (2016). (Imai, Gardner, Weinberger 2017, 42; emphasis in original)

How is it that resource extractionists, at the forefront of issues regarding Indigenous human rights, claim hero status via the university? Do Indigenous lives and the life of Land and her Beings matter? One could look at a culture of the university, where this author experienced consistent resistance to Indigenous rights as responsibilities discussions; derision and contempt from colleagues and overseers; formal and public questioning of bona fide Indigenous history; silencing of an Indigenous point of view and words that challenge the imperialist worldview; advancement of needless violence; and termination strategies against Indigenous peoples. Ahistorical opinions trump Indigenous knowledge sets, well-researched and accepted facts, and data in support of Indigenous-centric realities, and there is a shutting down of initiatives, deliverables, inviting-in of Indigenous community, unless these have been presented (in this author's experience, by males to other males) to the accepted Eurocentric hierarchy and are considered "safe" for the neoliberal agenda. One male may and does shut down the voices of many women and any Indigenous anything that challenges the oppressive, resource extractive, lawless, neoliberal status quo. There is contempt and intolerance for Indigenous testimony, perspective, and history. Those who profit(ed) from war against Indigenous people attempt to be the only authors of the historical record, placing themselves as the only purveyors of truth and making a dominant culture set of opinions and marginalizations our collective story. Oppressive, ongoing contests between what is and is not considered legitimate knowledge in the university – especially concerning those diverse Indigenous bioregionally centric philosophies, sustainable practices, spiritual and practical realities that offer alternatives to Anthropocene's vanquishments – reveal how entrenched concepts of which type of knowledge is worthy of the institution, which type is "in step" with an academic culture, what is the "fittest" here.

Training in Indigenous-centric bioregionalisms, community-centric activism (the university to the people, the university With our Beloved Land), and grassroots and professional action to change unethical policies, laws, and agreements – training to end all the myriad lawless practices and to actively transform our culture of violence and its unacceptable violations of rights, title, ethics, and laws – is sorely needed. It is ethical and relevant to train all citizens in rights, title, charters of rights and freedoms, democracy, and the inherent belonging of all Beings (possessing the right to life in its most basic, healthy, sustaining form). This training is meaningful, purposeful, important, and worthy work for our Planet's and our own very survival and thrivance. There is no shortage of need for this work and for many workers to carry it out. Our calling, our mission is our responsibility to Home/Land, the lives of all Beings, their viability, to eternity. A healthy planet is an active choice necessitating varied, consistent acts of sacrifice, smarts, creation (physical, emotional, intellectual, and spiritual), and fierce love for all who live.

There may be many paths to becoming closer to our elusive environmental justice, civil rights, and rights as responsibilities for all Beings. Every life has a purpose and work to perform as a part of our collective Earth. One starting mechanism is to simply name behaviours and actions for what they are, as opposed to what they pretend to be. What modern life terms "economic development," in regard to resource extractive industries, has no "eco" or "logic," but instead is a model of destruction, the tearing apart, the breaking apart to the smallest, as is the root philosophy of the atomic bomb. The neoliberal (capitalism on steroids) present (exported around the world at the expense of Home/Lands, Beings, and humans) destroys Indigenous communities, rights, livelihoods, and possibilities for the seventh generation by ruining Land, displacing/exterminating living Beings, and leaving behind, in many cases, polluted waters, air, and land that can no longer support life. The corporate "person" who benefits from universities' priorities is the crony-capitalist, the neoliberal, the destroyer of democracy. There are better ways.

Reconciliation Means Remediation

Loyalty to, belonging with, via concerted effort, Land and her every Being is a foundational variable for all Beings' right to live free from cruelty, pollution, destruction of Home/Land habitat and to be in relationship with all other living Beings, freely, cleanly, without malice or omnicidal and genocidal destructions. In our era of reconciliation, remediation, or putting back together all that has been broken apart by human hands, is our work. Belonging to Place, diametrically opposed to the practical and physical breaking apart of all as "development," is the diligent work of many Indigenous communities in order to act in ways to keep living Beings viable for the seven generations. Every ceremony, every song, every gathering, every meal is the putting back together of all that has been, and might be, broken apart. Practice is the learning and making to ensure the health and happiness of all Beings. A primary difference between Indigenous bioregionalisms and Western empire is here: putting everything all back together versus breaking it all apart. Does our work knit, or does it ruin? Are our dreams made of the sacred nature of Creation (Making within the original instructions of sustainability and responsibility to all life), or are they daytime nightmares of Lands whose every Being has been vanquished?

Positioning Ethics, Responsibilities, Rights

Years ago, when I taught what little I knew about the Dream of the Ghost Dance and the Massacre of Wounded Knee (which took place in 1890), I would have to think of so many other massacres in history's bloody trail; genocides of many Indigenous Nations and countries of the Americas, where Indigenous peoples were and are systematically targeted, killed, removed, and/or had other acts of violence inflicted upon them/us. I include extinctions of all living Beings here, as speciesism (the belief of human supremacy over all life) is a colonial imposition.

As teaching years grew to decades, more crises added to our historic list of Land exploitations and race-based, state-sponsored violence against Indigenous peoples, such as the twentieth-century continuing genocide against the Maya, where entire villages were burned and Beings murdered. Canada has seen many militarized conflicts against Indigenous peoples, domestically and internationally, where Indigenous rights as responsibilities and title, as well as existing enshrined rights, while "guaranteed" to everyone, are denied to Indigenous peoples. We are naming missing and murdered

Indigenous women and girls (MMIWG), Indian residential schools, and Land conflicts from contact to the present, such as settlement of the entire country, vanquishment in favour of empire, as well as Oka (1990), Gustafsen Lake (1995), Ipperwash (1995), Burnt Church (1999–2002), Elsipogtog (2013), Unist'ot'en (2019–present), the US Standing Rock (2016–17), and many other ongoing challenges to Indigenous human rights.

> Indigenous peoples have always asserted our laws and presence on our territories, but I was denied access to my wife and family's territories, Gidimt'en yintah, which was subjected to militarized police operations and an exclusion zone earlier this year. Now, we can't even get a proper and independent investigation into the illegal police misconduct and criminalization of Indigenous people. This is outrageous. (Cody Merriam, quoted in BCLA 2020)

Place names, names of individuals and communities, titles of species dispossessed and extinct forever lay the historical context regarding destructive campaigns against Home/Land and the people at the behest of corporation and empire, linking officious violence and injustice against Indigenous peoples from the beginning of colonization to the present.[5] Empire dispossesses humans and other Beings from Home/Lands and assures destruction of Home for most of the Earth's inhabitants and for the habitats themselves. To the list, we may add ongoing Indigenous Land defence against fracking, species extinctions, pollution, dispossessions, and their terrible others: Mount Polley mine's predicted environmental disaster (2014–present); Dakota Access Pipeline (2016); Sacred Stone Camp[6] and Site C dam (ongoing). Beatriz Manz's analysis (below) of Guatemala's genocide against Maya Indian people, if one changes the names, could fit Canada and other global corporate players:

> [In the 1980s, Guatemala's] state-sponsored violence reached genocidal proportions and led to community ruptures, endemic fear, deepened distrust, and unprecedented levels of daily violence that have continued into the post-war period. Tragically, the war's resolution has not ended the country's volatility and insecurity. Reconciliation is challenging and requires a much deeper structural overhaul. It is problematical for a society that has been created on a rigid, ethnic-based, and highly divisive foundation now to take steps toward reclaiming a non-existent pre-war period of concord. An inclusive and just society, which respects the fundamental human rights of all, is essential yet sorely lacking. Moving in this

direction is hindered by the historic impunity enjoyed by the military and
the powerful, as well as a dysfunctional judicial system in need of reform.
(Manz 2008, 151)

To teach, discuss, and place historical events such as these into the academic discourse is to disobey an oppressive status quo, to refuse collusion with rights-destroying corporate malfeasance, to place Indigenous
(and all other) rights into history's bona fide bloody trail, to bear witness. It is as the historian Angie Debo observed when revealing Indigenous dispossession, murder, and violation of treaty and other legal
rights at the hand of fossil fuel "development" in Oklahoma. Her work
proving abuse against Native peoples was derided, censored, as she
"had to violate history to tell the truth" (Debo, quoted in WGBH 1988).
Similarly, Indigenous historians and others must disobey neoliberal
agendas, especially their need to make secrets out of their acts, must
speak truth to power, and challenge status-quo assumptions about
Indigenous peoples in order to be part of a system change. We are moving away, hopefully, willfully, from ecosystems omnicide, genocide, and
human rights (and the rights and responsibilities of and to all Beings)
abuses to a world of equality, justice, and actualized rights. Performing
extended, grassroots, on-the-ground relationship as research and community; using Indigenous-centric methods, philosophies (responsibility to Home/Land, attention to the effect on the seven generations and
on those long gone to the Spirit world), and testimonio (truth-telling by
direct witnesses and those in the direct line of impact) to read all and
anything; placing all into the context of our social contract to care for
one another in order to understand and present a path to justice and to
be a Bear witness so needed in our collective call for rights action and
justice: this, our Work.

Imperialism and Its Others – Racism, Misogyny, Speciesism, Dispossession

Racism, as defined here, is *the use of abusive power over another*, based
upon arbitrary determinants such as race, skin colour, ethnicity, religion, spiritual beliefs, membership in historically marginalized groups
and groups against whom genocide has been committed, Indigenous
peoples. Racism perpetuates historically successful oppressions and
creates, affirms, and promotes measurable and unnecessary lasting
multigenerational harm against Indigenous peoples. Racism is an end;
a dead end, a death camp, a death squad, a mass grave; violent, especially misogynistic, hatred in thoughts and actions that fuel "manifest

destiny,"[7] corporate power, hierarchical, exclusionary social stratifications, and classism.

Racism is born in wasteful destruction against Mother Earth by those wanting more wealth and power for themselves and is gained via violence in all its forms on a finite Mother Earth from the dispossession of Indigenous peoples and destruction of Home/Land. As long as universities train new generations in massively exploitive industries that leave absolute ruin in their wake (for example, the Mount Polley mine disaster and Quesnel Lake in 2014, the worst mining failure in Canadian history) and align themselves with globalists accused, with compelling evidence, of horrendous racialized, sexualized, and violent crimes[8] in advance of their business models, racism in business and political practices will not only survive, but thrive. Universities are and have been the indoctrinating bodies where the corporation is imagined as a natural person with "rights," while human individuals, human and other species communities of Beings, and their/our targeted communities suffer tremendous rights violations, imposed poverty, illness, hunger, starvation, and violence at the behest of empire, while the perpetrators enjoy impunity.

We are speaking of racism in the university, no outlier, but requisite to believe in and promote oppressive systems such as the open-pit mine. In this author's experience, the struggle of the Indigenous person in the Home/Land is parallel to the struggle Indigenous scholars and issues have in the academy, namely lack of recognition and understanding of our cultural practices, contemporary and traditional Nation-centric education, and expertise; lack of acceptance by those in power and their refusal to meet with or hear anyone in a perceived lower position in the imposed university hierarchy; a barely there tolerance for diverse experiences in grassroots community, labelling as less-than-sophisticated, dumb, and laughable, with derision and contempt for Indigenous practices, ideologies, and manners; an intolerance for rights action outside of the neoliberal agenda; shutting down of the othered voice; threats of termination for speaking to rights as responsibilities, title, and the needs of the most marginalized members of society; inability to see foundational societal need that may be met by the university; demand for conformity to the status quo (a top-down approach); deference to an imperialist corporate state; alignment with resource extractionists who destroy Land, her Beings, Water, and rights; public demands of alliance to the power elite; an ever-shifting, uneven use of policy and procedures that one must divine in order to predict; installation of a "Super Indian," a lone regime collaborator who expects all others to follow him/her, and the maintenance of an oppressive status quo;

time-wasting non-productive meetings in place of action as "proof of action"; manufacture of consent; closed doors to rights and justice movements; and inability to hear and gather testimonio/y as relevant to the cause of Indigenous histories, rights, and justice; among others.

The university and its partnerships are actively promoting economic and ecological injustice and destabilization of communities by not addressing economic, social, and civil rights injustices as a priority. These include (but are not limited to) the following: (1) lack of safe life-giving clean water (ruined by corporate pollutions); (2) importation of sexualized violence via influx of outsiders who impose their actions upon rural communities (man camps, gangs, drugs); (3) poisoning (nuclear, chemical, radiological, biological); (4) imposed poverty and other human rights abuses; (5) food insecurity, purposeful destruction of the commons; (6) inadequate, substandard housing (mould infestations, lack of infrastructure); (7) ruin of health and healthy Nature (Home); and (8) destruction of traditional systems that met the basic necessities of life and the ability to thrive culturally, socially, spiritually, and physically; among others. Universities are collaborators with unjust corporate activities (many of which could meet the definition of criminality), with support from the apathetic and regime associates whose acts destroy the commons, food security, and the right of all species to live and thrive. Continuing a business as usual program of study ensures more of the same at a time when economies and ecologies demand root change and transformation in order for any life to be possible on Earth. Our era of a fading extractive economy or, more accurately, the dominant culture's "rush for the last of every living thing" is neither sustainable, nor equitable, nor desirable. Change is our only avenue for long-term species survival. Our Transformation is to ensure the thrivance of all living Beings – our responsibility to our Beloved Earth.

The late Corbin Harney (traditional Newe Medicine Man) worked to see an end to nuclearism and its others, travelling internationally, speaking, building diverse community, beginning every morning with Prayer Songs for Mother Earth, and healing many through Poo Ha Bah, a spiritual retreat in a California desert. His Home/Land, Newe Segobia, had had imposed upon Her, via the military industrial state, the status as the most bombed place on Earth (the Nevada test site), with over 1,100 nuclear detonations (Harney, personal communication, 1999). During Harney's speeches and interviews, a favourite derision from power elites was, "Which university did you go to? Where did you attend school?" as a means to both discredit and shame him publicly. Harney would reply: "That hill over there, and that one over there." He had told me this as he nodded towards surrounding mountains near Poo Ha Bah, recalling relationships with Animal, Insect, and other *Persons* of that Sacred and bombed Land.

> When the snow falls, it makes a design. Every one is special. The design tells you something. Each flake has a different meaning. (Corbin Harney, personal communication, 2006)

What is the university's reason for being? Perhaps our worthy goal is to learn, share, and teach our collective to critically and creatively think and create, with a sense of conscious responsibility for all Beings, in order to assist in the making of a more just, sustainable, biodiverse healthy world. What is made, via the university, that is life affirming and sustainable for ever continuing seven generations? It surely is not what we think of or mean when we see the styrofoam cup, the logging clear-cut, the omnicide that is the tar sands, and nuclear bombs. At the root of modernity's promised (and failed) utopia, rapacious developments' omnicide is a blind addiction to a sickly and broken status quo, one with an inherent insatiable desire for *more*: more wealth for the very few; more food on our plate, more than anyone could possibly eat – and it is wasted, at the expense and loss of many uncounted Beings (human and otherwise). Material wealth in that mainstream point of view announces and practises that there is never enough, more must be taken, bringing the end of Species, Places, and our Planet.

The university delivers and expects an unquestioning indoctrination into destruction of the commons, the Home/Land upon which and with which a truly secure Nation thrives; it is a punishing, marginalizing, dispossessing "economic" model that destroys all living Beings and their/our Homes. Formally, universities say little or nothing of critical importance about the deadly preparations and manufacture of more fossil fuel use (climate change, pollution, habitat loss, temperature changes that bring death, loss of farmlands, pollutions, a plastic "state" in the Pacific as big as Texas), obscene omnicidal clear-cuts, mega mines, and ocean salmon farms, but are openly in support of modern Indian treaty process and other First Nations termination strategies, all of which clearly have at their root, as has always been, the destruction of Indigenous peoples, Lands, Beings.

Doing little to nothing would be debilitating enough; however, universities take money from corporate polluters, genociders, and omniciders, those who ruin, reap, and rape, build arsenals and export violence onto peoples around the globe in attempts to control the world food supply, water, and empire. Donations are their names, many crimes, and money, used to brand buildings, spaces, research goals, and scholarships, and present honorary degrees to those involved in the manifest destiny of empire, expecting that no one knows or asks what players really did to obtain their wealth and power. The university receives a failing mark in being a voice, an educator, an agent for change towards our potential yet unactualized justice for those oppressed by corporate and government malfeasance, in this country and beyond.

Those who have been through colonialism's (history's) bloody trail, murder, disappearances, and other vehicles of genocide, and the ruin of Land, Water, Air, and all Beings, know that there is little safety in moving an institution entrenched in imperialist modus operandi to one of justice and peace. Those on the receiving end of the politics of oppression know how little protection is to be had from fundamentalists of all labels (conservatives, liberals, whomever, all those eager and willing to silence anyone with whom they disagree) where Indigenous rights are concerned. For this reason, any and all opportunities to break the silence, to challenge the broken status quo, to release the burden of imperialism's harm matters.

The university is hand in glove with the corporate state, maintaining, promoting, and preparing others to occupy the present and future with an oppressive status quo that summarily denies rights, Indigenous title, and has little time and attention for the greatest challenges of our times. Many universities have created active relationships with specific corporate entities, thus branding themselves as partners in massive, devastating, rights-violating resource extraction and exploitative endeavours, which reap fabulous wealth and power at the expense of human life, human rights, the rights of Nature and her Beings, the imposition of poverty upon Indigenous peoples, ruined landscapes, destruction of traditional, sustainable, healthy communities and environments, and marginalization (if not complete vanquishment) of the Lands' ability to take care of living Beings (including humans). Whereas there are corporate players who profit from forcibly removing Indigenous peoples from their/our traditional Home/Lands and those who use violence in all its forms against all life, including humans, to make money and obtain power, those who share in those monies are also profiting from alleged crimes, rights violations, *desaparecidos*, and dispossessions.

Simon Fraser University (SFU; the place of the author's employ) is in the direct line of the Kinder Morgan pipeline, one of the projects whose goals are neoliberal profit at the destruction of the Planet via climate disruptions, rising ocean levels, and the creation of millions of climate refugees (in addition to millions at present);[9] many sustained violations of Indigenous rights and title; importations of sexualized violence; wanton killing of animals; incursions into Indigenous Home/ Land and Places left, necessarily, to all non-humans; and importations of alcohol and drugs onto rural Indigenous reserves and rural settlements via industry's man camps (Honor the Earth n.d.; Horwitz 2014). Although the pipeline runs under the university (being constructed at this writing), the university is embarrassingly silent on climate disruptions, carbon load, over two hundred islands going under water due to rising sea levels, mass migrations of environmental refugees, and the direct link to fossil fuels. One may wonder what mechanism is in place that a well-known Canadian university – where educated persons are in positions of significant power; where charter freedoms are protected, guaranteed, and supported via legal tools (and funds); where there is an educated leadership, some of whom are former lawyer and government ministers – can remain opinion-less, voice-less, leader-less in such times as these. With so much at stake for the Planet and all of her Beings, with so many tasks at hand (for all our Relations), administrative silence – especially within a community of established Indigenous communities, activists, and their allies who are in close proximity – speaks to a deep institutional barrier to environmental justice, equality, and civil rights and justice for all of our Earth's Beings. If our best-trained leaders choose to silence themselves, while voices for justice and Indigenous rights are derided, silenced and censored based upon gender, race, and especially Indigenous Blood, we clearly see empire and history's bloody footprint upon all we may wish to do in protection of all Wild, Sacred, and Good.

> If the university professes to be an exemplar of ethical values, why is its real system embroiled in negating democratic processes, power sharing, and justice for all? Why does it perpetuate dysfunction, aggression, greed, individuality, and social injustice? (Catriona Strang, personal communication, 2019)

> They got it backwards. We should be telling them how to live. And it would help.
> We are the landowners to begin with, from the very beginning. Somebody told us a lie and we got our mind made that they own the land. They own nothing. They don't. They make a law all the time without our input into it. (Corbin Harney, personal communication, 2001)

Indigenous land rights and title, from the first moment of Indigenous human habitation, are responsibilities inherent with/in the Land,

evidenced by first-hand experiences since time immemorial to the
present day. Rights as responsibilities are shared and absolute, held by
Indigenous peoples, the Land, Water, Air, and all living Beings, each of
whom have an inherent, guaranteed, and natural set of rights to exist
in health with viability for the seven generations in an eternal spiralling path, ever renewing and everlasting. It is not enough to somehow
barely survive under duress, but to be able to thrive, as these are the
conditions established from the beginning of time for each species, element, and entity (those Natural and Supernatural).[10]

Critical to Indigenous discourse is the absolute right of all living
Beings to exist and thrive. We have proof of our interspecies existence
and complete human dependence upon other species in our familial
names and identities (which return us to the beginning of pre-, proto-
and present human time), clan identity and history, sources of power
and wisdom (Natural and Supernatural), sacred locations, tangible and
intangible (Spirit) Beings of all types as non-separable from human
reality. All of these Beings hold sacred inherent rights to exist, thrive,
maintain, and continue. All places are filled with Spirit, Supernatural
and also those of the humans and other Beings who have passed away
from tangible physical form. There are no empty lands; there are no
meaningless Beings. All acts, from eating to ceremony, are linked to the
maintenance of all Life. All making is to be linked to the health and
welfare of all Beings, especially among those/our peoples who farm,
gather, shop, and eat to survive. What is made is made in the Spirit
world, on Mother Earth. Making, in Indigenous context, is within this
paradigm of survival, maintenance, and thrivance for all species.

Is not the making of any/everything sustainable, healthy, and clean
our primary goal (in and out of the university) in order for all to live in
health and happiness? Working, thinking, making, doing, within and
maintaining a living, biodiverse, sanctified landscape: is this not our
true security? Modern "development" in most cases runs utterly counter to health, happiness, life (and its viability) with and for our "One
true Mother, Mother Earth."[11] Indigenous people demand and have
demanded recognition of rights carriers such as Water, Mother Earth,
Her Beings, and peoples of Earth, as in the work of present-day Water Is
Life, Tiny House Warriors and many other Indigenous peoples' movements worldwide:

> The Care of the Earth is our most ancient and most worthy and, after all,
> our most pleasing responsibility. To cherish what remains of it and to
> foster its renewal is our only legitimate hope. (Berry 2003)

Why do I continue with the struggle? Why do we continue the struggle? Because we love our water. We love our Land, we love our natural resources. This is why we're in the struggle. (Alfredo Jacinto Perez, Sipakapense Council; quoted in Woodin 2015)

The university is in question here, specifically where it is silent, does nothing, and feigns ignorance in the face of grave injustices. It practises and models excess, and supports dismantling of democracy and ruin via lawless political expediencies at the hands of governments and corporations. Its excess is in training students and its larger community to perpetuate injustices and lawlessness at the hands of governments and corporations, de facto proponents and advocates of racism, classism, and misogyny, sponsored by the state and militia; of environmental injustices, especially in targeted poor and racialized communities; of civil rights violations locally, nationally, and globally; and of violations of the rights of all living Beings (including Water, Soil, Air, and Home/Land).

Imperialism's oppressive business model cannot be sustained, when we, collectively, are at the rush for the last of every living Being to destroy and lay to waste. (There is no trash on a Sacred Land.) One hears of student distrust of universities for teaching them a business model no longer useful in the modern world, a dogma of an infinite, unfeeling, inanimate Earth; of greed, corruption, and individualism as virtue; of violence imposed upon all living Beings and Land as a hyper-"masculinity" of a mythic archetypal violence-based worker/destroyer; and of rights violations as a matter of everyday business, claiming all others outside of the corporation to be less than viable/valuable Beings.

> Around the world, Indigenous peoples are consistently among the most marginalized and most frequently victimized members of global society. Our experience working alongside Indigenous communities and activists … underlines the importance of international human rights standards – and the need for all governments to support and fully implement these standards. (Amnesty International n.d.-a)

Society's culture of violence – from domestic violence, street violence, corporate and state-sponsored violences to the brutality that is factory farms, sexualized violence, drugs, resource extractionists' man camps – are all promoted, normalized, and maintained at the university in the following ways (1–8).

1. Naming, Affiliation, Modelling

– Naming communal public university spaces with the names of corporations, such as Canadian mining companies that are "associated with violence and death," and enjoying an "accountability deficit," meanwhile benefitting from the criminalization of democratic rights, such as the abrogation of the right to free speech and assembly/association.

For example, Canadian mining companies are accused of acts that would perhaps be considered "crimes" in a non-corporate reality in Canadian and/or international courts, and/or under Indigenous laws. Indigenous law, protocols, rights as responsibilities may be understood via deep understanding of Nation-specific reality: histories and practices, meaning and responsibility expressed in the aesthetic panoply (stories, language, arts, culture, sciences, math); identity, genealogies and societal ordering, protocols with extended families and clans, neighbours near and far, trade partners, political allies and rivals; active daily relationship with every and all living Beings in the Natural and Supernatural realm, in the daily and ceremonial realities (such as with Plant Parents and other sources of medicine and nutrition), to include practices intertwined with those passed on and those yet to be born. Indigenous law, which is ceremony and practice, express and ensure that the rights of all living Beings to thrive are fulfilled, with the assistance of humans. Human rights are Natural rights in Indigenous law. We are named after Sacred Beings, Phenomenae, and Places.

crime: 3. Any serious wrongdoing or offense. 4. An unjust or senseless act or condition. (Morris 1971, 313)

nukpantumala: n.sg. crime, vice, evil doings, acts of malfeasance. *Pay imuy – t hinlsatskyaqamuy amutsiviy pu'haqam qatsi qatuvosti.* Because of those who are committing these crimes, today our life has become complicated. *nukpan-tumala* [evil work]. (Hopi Dictionary Project 1998, 337)

To explain, regarding the concept of what we mean when we say "crime," it may be thought-provoking to note, for example, that South Africa's apartheid functioned freely, with its actors enjoying impunity, until it was seen, understood, and named as "a crime against humanity." The Jewish holocaust's horrific reality needed a new lexicon, "genocide," and a Genocide Convention in order to be internationally seen, understood, and (potentially) reconciled (thanks to the work of Raphael Lemkin (2013) and many allies). Jurisprudence, rights, are potential and need diligent, consistent work for our rights to be actualized.

Justice, yet to be fulfilled, is an evolving potential. Recently, the Supreme Court of Canada found that human rights abuse cases against Canadian mining companies can and may be heard in Canadian courts, even when the alleged offenses occurred out of country, as in the cases of miners in Eritrea in eastern Africa and at Nevsun, a Canadian mining company based in British Columbia (see *Nevsun Resources Ltd. v. Araya*; Supreme Court 2020a, 2020b). Also, thirteen Maya plaintiffs, victims of mining violence such as assault, forced evictions, maiming, and rape, were represented in *Angelica Choc et al. v. Hudbay Minerals Inc. et al*, the first case against a Canadian mining company regarding human rights abuse outside of Canada that has been allowed to proceed to trial in Canada (Lexpert Business of Law Magazine 2013; Russell 2020; see also *German Chub Choc v. Hudbay Minerals Inc.* and *Margarita Caal Caal v. Hudbay Minerals Inc.*).[12] Here, community members, despite their poverty and limited access to courts, are finding a way to charge extractionist corporations with human rights abuses. Land Defenders have compelling claims and demands for justice from their targeting, arrest, jailing, kidnapping, abuse, disappearances, lethal attacks, and murder. According to Global Witness (2020), 167 Land Defenders were murdered in 2018, and 212 in 2019. There is much work to do in establishing justice and rights.

> They say we are terrorists, delinquents, assassins and that we have armed groups here, but really they're just killing us. (Joel Raymundo, member of the Peaceful Resistance of Ixquisis movement, quoted in Global Witness 2019, 23)

> It's for our forest and future generations. And it's for the whole world. (Nemonte Nenquimo, quoted in Global Witness 2020, 11)[13]

Formerly, mining companies from Canada claimed, with success, that court cases against them could only be heard in the country in which the alleged crime took place, even though the concept and delivery of a fair trial, equal rights, and equal protection under the law is/was unlikely, if not absent, with great potential for real and present danger of imminent harm to whistle-blowers, the abused, and plaintiffs. These realities made/ke a fair trial doubtful due to "lack of judicial independence and other violations of international human rights norms" (Amnesty International 2020). And, as the majority decision from *Nevsun Resources Ltd. v. Araya*[14] stated:

Modern international human rights law is the phoenix that rose from the ashes of World War II and declared global war on human rights abuses. Its mandate was to prevent breaches of internationally accepted norms. Those norms were not meant to be theoretical aspirations or legal luxuries, but moral imperatives and legal necessities. Conduct that undermined the norms was to be identified and addressed. (Supreme Court of Canada 2020b)

What phrase shall we create, if the word "crime" is too offensive to some, perhaps, in order to describe what we mean by the life-altering, devastating destructive effects of massive resource extraction: the left-over ruin comparable to that left behind by war – inflicted damage that cannot be truly remediated in several generations – eternally moving pollutions, rights violations, injustice, imposed poverty, unmet basic needs, and other harms? What word does the English language use, if not the word "crime," in speaking of "crimes against humanity" and "crimes" (ecocide) against nature?

Goldcorp's Equity Silver mine, in Northern British Columbia, Canada, is a closed mine that will generate acid mine damage [and polluting everyone] for between 500 and 150,000 years. (Rights Action 2008)

GOLDCORP CENTRE FOR THE ARTS, SIMON FRASER UNIVERSITY[15]
About Goldcorp's Marlin mine,[16] it is noted:

The mine began in 1999, a few months after the murder of Monsignor Juan Gerardi. A few years later, Bishop Alvaro Ramazzini, who led a march against the mine, received death threats and had to be put under government protection. There were death threats against other anti-mine activists and a car belonging to one of the leaders was set on fire ... In 2010, two men from the San Miguel community shot Diodora Hernandez in the head ... Jose Tavico Tzunun was killed by two heavily armed men. (Imai, Maheandiran, and Crystal 2012, 30)

Documenting Goldcorp in Guatemala at the closing of the Marlin gold mine after twelve years expresses and "reflects the violence of Canadian mining operations across the world. Canadian mining firms are frequently the cause of intense social conflict over resource extraction – from the murders at Banro's gold mines in the Congo to gang rapes by security personnel at Hudbay's nickel mines in eastern Guatemala" (Abbott 2018). Additionally, looking back at the short life of the massive Marlin mine, one resident said: "The only development they brought stayed with them"; while another commented: "The development that the company brought is sickness" (quoted in Abbott 2018). Despite massive profits to the company, left behind to the Indigenous community members are unremediated, contaminated waters and loss of access to clean waters; chemical contamination (including cyanide[17]); the threat of acid and other chemical runoff and erosion of contaminated soils; and ruined land. In many megaprojects, Western-centric manners are imposed upon the Indigenous communities, where traditional forms of relationships are usurped and replaced with colonial mores, social dysfunction, and broken relationships and social structures, especially regarding the mine. Violence, murder, wider access to alcohol, resultant alcoholism and its associated social ills, and a pervasive, lasting poverty brought about by mining's ecological ruin are the legacy.[18]

Extractive industries and others are accused of erosion/destruction of democratic civil rights, imposing and bringing in violence and tools of violence, and imposing uneven protection and application of the law as well as lack of access to protections afforded by the law – especially against Indigenous peoples. Naming of communal university spaces with the names of corporations accused of violence against Nature and her Beings, Indigenous peoples, rural dwellers, and the poor identifies university employees with vanquishment, dispossession, rights violations, destruction of the commons – the very things many of us have devoted our lives to fighting and working against every day. University administrators, generally, somehow ignore or are unaware of the heinous facts and acts of those who offer funds in exchange for legitimizing their corporate names (in need of redemption) and image by corporate branding. These re-brandings associate the universities' workers with enterprises such as Canadian mining companies (notorious globally, and not in a good way) and other extractionists. In *Angelica Choc v. Hudbay Minerals*, some issues are "gross human rights violations" by the company, including gang rape, murder, and maiming (Amnesty International 2017;[19] Friends of the Earth 2012; Findlay 2019).

In a report on Canadian mining companies in Latin America, the Justice and Corporate Accountability Project (JCAP) summarizes the findings for the years 2000–15:

[We] found incidents involving 28 Canadian companies; 44 deaths, 30 of which we classify as "targeted"; 403 injuries, 363 of which occurred in during protests and confrontations; 709 cases of "criminalization," including legal complaints, arrests, detentions, and charges; and a widespread geographical distribution of documented violence. (Imai, Gardner, and Weinberger 2017, 4)

Two articles published by MiningWatch Canada also examine these issues:

> In Latin America, Canada and its extractive industry are viewed as the new conquistadors; they are thirsty for land and minerals and hungry for power. Canadian mining companies are often positioned at the epicenter of community conflicts in both Indigenous and non-Indigenous communities, and linked with violence, environmental degradation, corruption, and murder. (Pedersen 2015)[20]

> Canada does not have the laws or political oversight mechanisms – let alone the political will – to hold accountable our mining companies. Over the past 15 years or so, there has been a growing number of reports about environmental harms, human rights violations and repression caused by Canadian mining companies around the world. The sheer volume of documented problems show it is not a question of a "few bad apples," but rather a systemic, industry-wide problem – one that will not go away without serious political and legal challenges and reforms ... Impunity and immunity from legal liability are the norm in Canada." (Russell 2016)

WEYERHAEUSER CENTER FOR HEALTH SCIENCES,
UNIVERSITY OF PUGET SOUND

An important question for history is the vanquishment and destruction of the commons perpetrated by what Appleman (1939) called the "Timber Empire from the Public Domain," of which Weyerhaeuser (and many others) gained immensely at the cost of the biodiverse Forest and her Beings, Indigenous peoples, rights and title, and the rights of Land, Waters, and all Beings to live, thrive, and survive. Deforestation, environmental devastation, massive debris, landslides, wastelands, climate disruptions, dispossession, rivers devoid of Wild Sacred Salmon and their dependent Beings, and pollution are some of the industrial abuses and bioregional social and spiritual harm committed by logging companies.

> There can be little doubt that much of the Weyerhaeuser holdings in the Lake States, and later in the South and in the West, was obtained through a circumvention of land law. (Appleman 1939, 205)

Clear-cuts are the most sorrowful and distinctive feature of the Canadian "wilderness," seen and felt both from ground and air. What is remediation for those Lands whose Beings have been left without a Home upon which and with whom to live? What of the imposed poverty on the human communities? We may look to Roberta Keesik of Grassy Narrows, Treaty 3 (signed in 1873), when she said:

> The clear-cutting of the land and the destruction of the forest by Weyerhaeuser is an attack on our people, the land is the basis of who we are. Our culture is a land based culture and destruction of the land is the destruction of our culture. And we know that is in the plans. Weyerhaeuser doesn't want us on the land, they want us out of the way so they can take the resources. We can't allow them to carry on with this cultural genocide. (Roberta Keesik, quoted in Rainforest Action Network 2005, 14)

A 1994 British Columbia (BC) Ministry of Environment report concluded that 485 salmon and trout streams, rivers, and lakes throughout the province had suffered major losses in fish habitat due to industrial logging practices (Werring 2007). To remediate (partially) "a 50 year legacy of impacts," *if* possible, would have taken ten to twenty years, costing $1 billion to $4 billion, in 1994 dollars (Werring 2007). This cost says nothing about the additional waterway ecosystems ruined since, nor about the value of the loss of Sacred Wild Salmon to Earth's many Beings. Where is our literal accounting for the greed, theft, and destruction of the commons? One wonders what the Department of Fisheries and Oceans mandate must be in times as these.

In 2004, one of Weyerhaeuser's clear-cuts above Stillman Creek, Washington, caused "730 landslides [that] filled the Chehalis Watershed with mud and debris, ruining the drinking water for some 3,000 people for more than three months ... [A]s no effective timber industry watchdog exists, such corporate eco crimes go often unreported and unpunished" (Wonders 2010).

Indigenous rights as responsibilities and title are inherent, and dwell in Land and all of her Beings. Infringements upon Indigenous rights, responsibilities, and title regarding Indigenous Land and her Beings in Canada may be referenced by millennia of Indigenous and settler testimonio, as well as in many written forms. Speaking of forests, trees, Kent McNeil (2005) presents details of *Haida Nation v. British Columbia* (Minister of Forests) to consider, in brief, "Aboriginal attachment to the land." About our Relatives (natural resources), McNeil cites two major court cases, *St. Catherine's Milling* and *Delgamuukw*:

> It is the Aboriginal titleholders, not the provinces, that *own* the natural resources, including timber, on their lands. Thus, the provinces cannot access those resources because, in addition to being prevented from doing

so by exclusive federal jurisdiction over Aboriginal title, the provinces do
not own the resources. (McNeil 2005, 450; emphasis in original)

The word "own" is, I think, appropriate because the Supreme Court
clearly regarded Aboriginal title and the right to natural resources
encompassed by it as proprietary (see Supreme Court 1997, supra, note 7,
at para. 113; and the discussion in McNeil 2000, 57–61).

2. Indoctrination into the Dogma of Extremist Capitalism (Neoliberalism and Its Others)

– Teaching, promoting, and encouraging corporate manners and
worldviews, skills, and attitudes necessary to fill roles in extractivist,
cruelty-based, Indigenous vanquishment – practices rooted in racism
and lawless violent dispossession – while simultaneously not providing foundational, basic, easy-to-learn education in enshrined, inherent
rights and justice (civil rights, social justice, Indigenous rights and title,
and environmental justice context).

In this way, universities are indoctrinating future workers in resource
extraction and others to continue rights violations against humans,
Land, and all Species; training future professionals in extractive industries with insufficient (or no) environmental justice context, information on specific law and case studies, testimonio/y, concept of legal
standing, history, and the multitude of sequential and enshrined legal
precedents (international, national, provincial, state, community); and
creating, by design and/or omission, workers blind to their effect in
the world. Apolitical, hopeless, self-medicating humans, a culture of
violence, and perpetuation of acts that guarantee a life-less world are
the result.

SCHOLARSHIP
Scholarships, courses, internships, training, and indoctrination in
extractive industries and their cultures, such as mining, forest destruction (aka, "forestry"), nuclearism, and fossil fuel fracking, extraction,
and transport, are university bound.

The Suncor [read tar sands] Emerging Leaders Award program provides
three scholarships that are valued at up to $10,000 each (payable over four
academic years) and awarded annually to outstanding students entering
first-year Chemical, Mechanical, Civil, or Environmental Engineering
programs at the University of Waterloo. These scholarships are funded
by a generous donation from Suncor in recognition of the outstanding

programs at the University of Waterloo, and to meet the needs of the Canadian oil and gas industry through trained human resources capable of playing leadership roles in the sector. (StudentScholarships.org 2021)

I have had many students in disciplines such as geology, actuarial sciences, and business, for example, hard-working, smart, capable, well-versed in science and math, but who had never heard of Indigenous rights and title, UNDRIP, the Canadian Charter of Rights and Freedoms (as it pertains to Indigenous peoples), speciesisms, Indigenous bioregionalism(s), and famous impactful and relevant Canadian court cases such as *Calder, Delgamuukw, Sparrow,* and *Williams*. Their academic disciplines' graduate students believe they are prepared to work in fields of direct impact with Indigenous communities, the impoverished, the maligned and dispossessed, students considered ready to work without having been exposed to laws, regulations, civil rights, title, and environmental justice issues *that they themselves will be impacting*.

3. Hero Worship of Monster Destroyers[21]

– Creating heroes, leaders, and figureheads by allowing political appointments to university governance boards and positions to be those friendly to massive harms/chaos, many of whom have gained personally from destroying our Earth, vanquishing all living Beings, and creating endangered and extinct Species; and those at the head of dispossession and terminations of Indigenous peoples, who create and created a true *terra nullius*, after they have/had taken all that once was, to become massively and unashamedly financially wealthy – many of them grantees of the Order of imperialist Canada and claiming to be "philanthropists," who return pennies of their ill-gotten gains to universities to salvage their reputations.

One way to describe acts and persons who create destructions (the dreaded chaos) comes from third-Mesa Hopi dialect, "*Koyaanis'unangwa'y* | *ta*: to lack moral constraints, have an evil heart" (Hopi Dictionary Project 1998, 154). If the corporation is a person, then s/he is a "*Koyaanis* | *hoya*: one who is habitually disruptive or destructive."[22] *Koyannisqatsi* is evidenced in wealth extraction that leaves Indigenous peoples and non-human Beings dead, dispossessed, or maimed, in poverty and among ruined lands. *Koyaanis* | *hoya* is the diverting of funds away from basic human needs for the majority of Earth's peoples (for shelter, food, access to clean air, water, soil, health care, and education), leaving a desperate population, many of whom have no choice but to become resource extraction refugees to urban centres where our Beloved Naturals and Supernaturals are ghosts. Ruin, resource extraction, and exploitations create unmet needs and suffering for all of Earth's Beings; destruction of Home and basic human rights; and compromised hopes for many of the world's peoples' ability to simply live with a sustainable present and future (see Gordon 2010).

4. Lies of Omission

– Lack of concerted action in teaching a full history of imperialism in the world, especially in the Indigenous Americas, university-wide and in our collective consciousness, when the university is populated with those able and willing to do this work (of critical note are the historical and consistent ongoing Indigenous termination strategies and antici- patory genocides, species extinctions, and ruin); mute alliance with oppressive regime masters and saying nothing when dispossessed and displaced people are targeted, beaten, arrested, jailed, and murdered, especially for mines, hydroelectric dams, pipelines, and the fossil fuel industry, or when keystone species are vanquished by trophy hunt- ing and ocean-based fish farms; silence, lack of courage, and indif- ference (despite our massive toolbox) by refusing to join the voices of community/ies against resource extraction in our/their Homes in any significant, intelligent, and lasting public manner; and inability or lack of desire to ensure that democratic processes and protections under the law are shared with Indigenous peoples, women, and the oppressed.

The university is involved in training future professionals in subjects with significant relevance to rights actions work (this part is surely excellent), *while omitting* extensive preparation, purpose, and knowl- edge of human rights, environmental justice, martyrdom, liberation theologies, poverty as a consequence of colonization, and the *practi- cal application* of academic disciplines to solve the Earth's justice issues. One example of the worthy use and purpose of these disciplines is seen in the righteous application of forensic sciences to reveal genocide via the state against Indigenous peoples, such as the examination of Gua- temala's mass graves as concrete evidence of Guatemalan genocide (a genocide supported by the United States and denied by both nations). Louise Olivier in "Forensic Evidence Represents a Turning Point for Justice in Guatemala" describes one investigation:

> The CREOMPAZ [Comando Regional de Entrenamiento de Operacio- nes de Mantenimiento de Paz] case brought to light some of the worst state-perpetrated atrocities of the Guatemalan conflict. At the request of

the public prosecutor's office, FAFG [Guatemalan Forensic Anthropology Foundation] forensic experts dug for, recorded, and exhumed the remains of 558 people, including 90 children, in 84 mass and individual graves ... Many of the bodies were blindfolded and their hands and feet bound, suggesting that the base was used as a clandestine interrogation and detention center – and that its victims were summarily executed ... The public prosecutor's office ordered the arrest of 18 retired military officers for war crimes allegedly committed during the country's 36-year internal armed conflict, which took place from 1960 to 1996 and claimed 200,000 lives. Fourteen of those arrested are charged with enforced disappearance, murder, and torture as crimes against humanity. (Olivier 2016)

In other words, disciplines such as these must place their *foundational emphasis* on rights, responsibilities, and justice, with technique as a secondary, not primary, reason for being.

As we go to press, on 28 May 2021, news agencies informed the public of a mass grave at the Tk'emlúps (Kamloops) former Indian residential school. Researchers with ground-penetrating radar found evidence of 215 children's graves. "Unthinkable, undocumented, yet known," is how Mary-Ellen Turpel-Lafond (2021) described the finding, highlighting Indigenous community knowledge of past state-sponsored atrocities that have yet to find place in official history, to be fully understood, fairly spoken of, and somehow reconciled within the power of rights and justice. That mass graves are found in Guatemala, at the sites of Indian residential schools, and in genocidal locations around the world brings urgency to universities to address, through training, community-centred discourse, interdisciplinary education, and advocacy, a rights-based, justice-centric, education.

5. Promoting Indigenous Termination Strategies

– Promoting modern Indian (First Nations) treaty and treaty process and other Indigenous *termination strategies* in Canada and beyond, while ignoring internationally recognized and established Indigenous peoples' rights; suppressing/not promoting university-wide and societal understanding of many of the world's governments' openly violent, oppressive, dispossessive Indigenous termination plans (to include Canada), policies, and practices, and the foundational role of racism, misogyny, and classism therein, and of the use of violence by police, military, and paramilitary forces, and the genocide/omnicide inherent in resource extractions and other corporate plans; creating university relationships with commercial interests whose corporate behaviour is at the root of climate disruptions and environmental refugees to the fossil fuel, mining, hydro, salmon farm and tree-cutting industries, and other primary societal issues.

Modern vanquishment tools violate enshrined and established Indigenous rights and Indigenous title, sovereignty, land, and self-determination, as well as future viability for Indigenous peoples as Indigenous peoples. The injustice of the modern Indian treaty is the injustice of the university; their bureaucratic vehicles are the same: (1) belief in a one god king (a dominant culture power broker with wealth and power at the top of the hierarchy, answerable to none); (2) the myth of the European miracle (Blaut 1993) where the only good and worthwhile comes from European patriarchy, and all others are inferior and wrong, and must be destroyed in the name of progress, civilization, and shareholders; (3) an imperialist corporate economic system based on overconsumption and the concept of trash, greed, and waste; (4) all non-elite members are burdens, "lesser-than" living entities, with various degrees of rights; and (5) human worth and worthy jobs are only in service to corporations, the military, and the dominant nation-state.

Franta and Supran provide an example of university relationships with commercial interests whose corporate behaviour is at the heart of destructions and disruptions:

> Michelle Michot Foss, who offers skepticism about battery production for renewables, is identified as the Chief Energy Economist at the Center for Energy Economics at the University of Texas at Austin. What's not said is that the Energy Institute she founded at UT Austin is funded by Chevron, ExxonMobil, and other fossil fuel interests including the Koch Foundation, or that she's a partner in a natural gas company. (Franta and Supran 2017)

6. Talking a Talk

– Claiming interest and expertise in Indigenous communities while denying Indigenous community relationships, protocols, rights, and responsibilities to all species (thus committing a de facto erasure of cultural practices, political structures, spirituality, relationship with Home/Land, traditional educational practices) and performing cultural vanquishment; repeated use of accepted terminology and phrases to offer "proof" of "Indigenization" and becoming proficient enough to satisfy gatekeepers, thereby earning expert status (a self-appointed role) about all things Indigenous; planning for actions that kill all living Beings, usually starting with the largest and most important species-Beings such as Sacred Wild Salmon and Grizzly Bears, and that destroy ecosystems upon whom communities rely, knowing industrial pollutions will end lives, or, in other words, an anticipatory genocide.

7. Enshrinement of the Status Quo When That Status Quo Is Broken

– Training new generations to promote and partake in an economic system that has left ruin of Land, Water, and living Beings, while dispossessing, disappearing, and relocating Indigenous peoples; instruction and expectation to adhere to neoliberal corporate cultural norms, values, and practices at the behest of empire, a coerced complete acceptance of neoliberalism's lawlessness, brutality, racism, speciesism, and misogynies, which are inherent in the concept of social wealth-based hierarchy (the top 1 per cent) without question or analysis.

Universities train and indoctrinate future professionals in many disciplines, who make accounts for, "discover," validate, create, and maintain massive resource extractions and other acts whose effects are geological in scale and violate international and Indian treaties,[23] as well as national/international agreements (as in the case of the Kyoto Protocol and climate disruptions, Site C dam, and Treaty 8). That universities have responsibilities to teach and support relevant facts regarding history, our laws, treaties, and enshrined democratic principles is necessary for an intelligent and just society.

The expectation is that students, faculty, staff, and all others *will* adopt as normal, expected, and acceptable corporate neoliberal lawless political expediencies in systems, structures, and the so-called economy (violation of civil rights, environmental justice, the rights of all Beings to exist) – omnicidal practices and weapons of mass destruction and terror, all in the practice and maintenance of empire.

For example, engineers, bankers, politicians, lawyers, corporate heads, government workers, and others receive(d) their training in universities; these are the educated, privileged, power-holding individuals behind rights violations at the behest of wealth for the few. State actors practice active deference to the corporate state, who (as a "person") targets, attacks, jails, kidnaps, abuses, and kills activists, peasants, farmers, women, children, and elderlies in advance of personal/corporate wealth. Brutalism and rights violations are actively propagated by the very top members of our hierarchy, where this practice is promoted as a neutral business model.

8. Speciesism, Rights of All Beings

– Promoting and maintaining a flawed system of colonial practices, which does not recognize or esteem the many types of values of Life in its many forms, life/eco systems, and their interdependence, and the many values of all Life destroyed by ruinous systems; and not counting for the lost lives of all Species and the effect of losing Wild, Sacred, and Good upon one another.

Indigenous Responsibilities vs. Modernity's Culture of Violence

Hyper-Rapacious Machines, Arrests, Beatings, Incarcerations, Poverty

Corporations and governments, propped up, supported, and given trained workers by the university, often routinely act outside of established rules, regulations, laws, agreements, and treaties – especially international laws, Indigenous laws, human rights norms, our societal contracts and agreements, regulations, treaties, and in the case of the Mount Polley mine disaster, compliance with established engineering norms and the Mines Act (Hoffman 2015, 151). These alleged and found offenses occur with complete impunity from the federal level to the municipal, using organizations such as law enforcement and armed forces to subjugate Life in all Her forms and Nature's/Land's human and non-human defenders. Concerning the Mount Polley mine disaster and legality, the chief inspector of mines wrote:

> The event has shaken the reputation of the Canadian mining industry, both within Canada and internationally ... Cross-border relationships and treaties are under stress or being revisited. Potential consequences may be felt in terms of future water, fisheries, and other treaties with U.S. interests both in Alaska and across the 49th parallel. (Hoffman 2015, 153)

Corporate purchase of lawyer/technicians and consultants, and the placement and interchangeability of corporate bosses into government is by design. Note that the Business Council of British Columbia, whose executives and board includes representation from Trans Mountain, LNG Canada, Council of Forest Industries, Enbridge, Woodfibre LNG, and Imperial Metals, among others, declares "lobbying activity information" to be in "Aboriginal Treaty and Land Claims Issues."[24] In other words, entrenchment into neoliberal projects and plans ensures projects such as the Site C dam. Taft (2017) wrote of a "deep state" regime in Canada, where specific interests infiltrate all layers of public service in order to advance agendas friendly to specific corporate regimes. It is a commonplace practice to recycle lawyers friendly to modern treaty process (Indigenous termination strategies) into provincial ministerial positions and then to presidents of universities, creating alliances with the very processes and practices that have and continue to violate Indigenous rights, title, and justice.

Corporate greed is neoliberalism's "business" and "development," an out-of-control rapacious machine organized around violence against all Life. The neoliberal culture's destruction of the commons is an organized perverse religion of sorts, founded on an untrue and irrational belief set, that of murder, ignorance, and violence to advance empire. This culture of violence uses murder and utter destruction, and calls it "development"; runs on hatred and rights violations, dismantling democracy; and destroys enshrined laws, policies, agreements, and historic treaties in advance of their exploitations. It is only satisfied after extermination and extinction.[25] Supported in mainstream modern "entertainment" in all forms, it has become an expected requisite of certain types of "jobs," which are destructions vs. *makings*.

> One of the serious illusions we live under in the United States, which is a major part of the whole system of indoctrination, is the idea that the government is the power – and the government's not the power, the government is one segment of power. Real power is in the hands of the people who own the society; the state-managers are usually just servants. (Chomsky 2002)

Hydroelectric dams utterly destroy enormous amounts of Land, bringing utter devastation to humans and other Beings. The Site C hydro dam in BC would flood the Peace River Valley, ruining homes for many humans and non-human Beings. Estimated to cost over $17 billion, it is a tool of a corporate dream, and a nightmare to all others, in violation of Treaty 8, the Canadian Constitution, as well as the United Nations Declaration on the Rights of Indigenous Peoples (UNDRIP; United Nations 2007). The United Nations requests Canada to suspend construction at Site C until there is "free, prior, and informed consent" from all First Nations directly affected (United Nations Committee on the Elimination of Racial Discrimination 2017; Cox 2019).

Hydro dams are thought to be "green"; however, their ruin of Home/Land, production of climate change gas emissions (including methane from natural materials decomposing), destruction of Home bioregion, pollution, and dumping are ruinous and add to already beleaguered

Earth struggling to rebalance Herself. Hydro dams pollute with heavy metals, add to the disaster of climate change, and violate Indigenous rights, environmental justice, and the right for species to simply live and be. Earth's melting ice, glaciers, and disturbed weather patterns are changing water levels, which creates a threatening situation to the dams (and to nuclear power plants).

> Large-scale hydro also causes enormous environmental and social damage, including farmland and habitat destruction, changes to waterways and water tables, and displacement of Indigenous Peoples. Where large areas of land are flooded, mercury in fish increases several-fold, making this traditional source of protein risky to eat. (Suzuki 2018)

Hydro leaves Homeless those human persons and non-human Beings whose Home/Land is coveted by power brokers, and these targeted Home/Lands – clean, sacred supporters of myriad biodiverse species – are left to ruin. Indigenous peoples of these sites, and our binding legal agreements, social contracts, and health of the commons, are racialized, demonized, stigmatized, and vanquished to the point of removal and extinctions. Existing hydro projects need to be remediated from, and while plans for Site C and others go on, lawlessly, universities say and do nothing to stop the impending destruction.

Anticipatory Indigenous Genocide, Racism, Misogyny, Speciesism, Vanquishment, Violence[26]

Violence against land is violence against women.

– Kanahus Manuel[27]

Where genocide is, in part, a systematic, efficient, violent destruction of a targeted group, we are using here the phrase *anticipatory Indigenous genocide* to mean processes such as resource extractions (destruction known by the oxymoronic phrase "economic development") in which killing, destroying, extinction-ing, vanquishing, and dispossessing is requisite to so-called colonial "progress." Picture Alberta's tar sands, where all living Beings are violently dispossessed and murdered, their lives made impossible by the rapacious machine. Tar sands, open-pit mines, and open-pen ocean salmon farms have made and are making entire landscapes uninhabitable, a killing of all life – omnicide.[28] Racism, misogyny, and speciesism against humans and hatred towards other living Beings are requisite for the methods and madness (the nuclear-ist's mutually assured destructions, MAD), as well as the MADness of tar sands, clear-cut logging, ocean open-pen salmon farms, and grand-scale hydroelectric dams.

Trophy and "sports" hunting and poaching of Grizzly Bears, and recreational fishing having precedence over Aboriginal food (survival) fisheries is empire: taking the biggest and best of each Being to clear the Land, making real the colonizers' dream – *terra nullius*. The phrase, once used as a declaration to proclaim Indigenous Home to be devoid of all human life and therefore open to settlement, railroad, and vanquishment, perpetuated an incorrect idea that Land was/is "empty," that Land belonging to no one, and was unused, wasted,[29] a rationale to further facilitate the brutal advance of empire.[30] The true *terra nullius*, however, is in our Sacred Land vanquished from all life forms in the way of extractionists.

High-seas processing boats' interception of fish; destruction of fish breeding grounds by logging, pollution, and mining; climate change; genetically modified organisms (GMOs); and Atlantic salmon farms; among others, created the crash of Wild, Sacred Salmon. Indigenous peoples' compromised ability to have food fish now, starving emaciated Bears unable to feed their young or themselves, hunger of many species and starvation of some is humankind's doing because of those university-trained corporate heads and shareholders, collaborators. A university's focus must include or centre the rights of non-human Beings – in this case, those relied upon for the sustenance of many species, Lands, Waters, and Forests – and the methods, manners, and philosophies to ensure the rights of all Beings to life by our research, teaching, work, and making. Rights are responsibilities, meaning human responsibility is to ensure the thrivance of all species.

Forcing rural and Indigenous peoples into poverty, polluting water sources (no drinking water on too many First Nations reserves for many generations), taking, wasting, and destroying subsistence foods places many in abject desperation, no longer able to have the necessities of life, such as Land, Water, and Air free of pollution, while being at the front line of resource extractions. That the financially richest save, plan, and travel solely to kill via trophy hunts, taking the head and leaving the meat; and that man camps import drugs, violence, alcohol, sex crimes, and murder is a true tearing of our human responsibilities and social contracts. With land opened for clear-cutting and mining, the path to omnicide is complete; the strategic, targeted, ultimate destructions are not remediable in many lifetimes. Human-made wastelands, landscapes of revulsion, and extinctions (human and otherwise) are the major product of capitalist extractivism; to be awake is to suffer colonialisms and empire's imposed sufferings. To be awake means to work in *making*-right thought, right action, right livelihood. Put back together all that is broken apart.

It is no great coincidence that racism and misogyny, as well as sexualized violence, are used by and imposed upon workers and settler resource extractivists, atop communities already impoverished by colonialism's first waves of dispossession. There has never been free, prior, and informed consent for any colonial omnicidal machinations. Economic desperation in certain First Nations communities and disconnection to Land by those living far away in urban centres (who often vote on what happens hundreds of miles away) leads Indian Act chiefs and councils (an imposed colonial system) to approve corporate activities that will further ruin any Land's ability to promote sustainable, Indigenous lives. It is clear that Indigenous lives terminated, compromised, harmed, dispossessed, and removed, while receiving little, if any, security in return, is the same as that for vanquished species of the tar sands, herds of Woodland Caribou, Grey Wolf, Grizzly Bear, Black Bear, Birds, Plants, Insects, Water, Air Land. No thing, no Being can or may live (for now and the next many seven generations) upon and within the tar sands, the open-pit mine, the flooded hydroelectric project site. It is recommended here that any human/corporation working and profiting directly from these destructions, with their families, live upon and take sustenance directly from their handmade landscapes of revulsion for *their* next seven generations. Perhaps then we will see universities commit to knowledge sharing and making regarding planetary interspecies dependencies, acknowledgement for rights and title (of all Beings Indigenous to Place), careers where Land's viability, health, and continuation is of paramount philosophy and method, with systems for counting, measuring, the importance and significance of all living Beings.

Many universities (mine included) train future leaders[31] to imagine, create, participate in, and maintain a broken status quo[32] of anticipatory genocides and omnicides, the destruction of all life in all forms mislabelled as "economic development." That university-trained individuals hold major responsibility for the world's destruction is proof the university has failed its primary mandate to support justice, rights, and democratic principles. That these individuals actively dismantle rights and title, ecology, and cultural practices, and support violent practices and create destruction of the commons fulfils Lemkin's famous definition of genocide:

> It [genocide] is intended ... to signify a *coordinated plan* of different actions aiming at the destruction of essential foundations of the life of national groups, with the aim of annihilating the groups themselves. The objectives of such a plan would be disintegration of the political and social

institutions, of culture, language, national feelings, religion, and the economic existence of national groups, and the destruction of the personal
security, liberty, health, dignity, and even the lives of the individuals
belonging to such groups. (Lemkin 1944, 79; emphasis added)

Many universities participate in and encourage contemporary anticipatory Indigenous genocides, a continuation of Canada's Indian termination plans, coercing consent to bureaucratic erasure of Indigenous
identity and extinguishment of traditional, legally recognized and verified rights and title. Historic treaty is a continuation of governments'
modus operandi of erasing a group of people by act and also via practice and policy. In the Second World War era, Lemkin dedicated his
internal resources to reviewing official German policy in order to reveal
Germany's "policies of systematically destroying national and ethnic
groups, including the mass murder of European Jews" (Holocaust
Encyclopedia, n.d.).

The use of policy to destroy a group may and has been termed "genocide by typewriter" (Hilberg 2003), meaning here: (1) nations create
many varied and detailed policies and public relations campaigns to
destroy a group; and (2) principals of specific nations record their own
history, acts, and philosophies to prove their political "victories" (genocide) against those whom they oppress. Genocidal nations of the world
create/d numerous organizational lists, plans, schedules, tally sheets,
files, and trophies of murdered and missing, *los desaparecidos*, noting
that it is the pen, typewriter, and computer that created and recorded,
and stands as witness to regimes' genocides.

> The National Atomic Museum glorifies weapons of mass destruction
> and the work that creates and sustains them. How can we glorify abso-
> lute violence and expect to have nonviolent, peaceful lives? Why should
> anyone be surprised to find that other nations and peoples are beginning
> to seek what we have never, despite clear legal requirements, renounced?
> How can we sow the wind and not expect to reap the whirlwind? There's
> nothing like glorification of instruments of anticipatory genocide to get
> the public to accept the threat of mass violence as normative, or at least
> something too lavishly supported by authorities to bother protesting. (Los
> Alamos Study Group 2005)

To Break Apart: Omnicidal Machines

When we assemble, speak, and pray for Land and our Beloveds, arrest
is often likely. Written during Emilie Teresa Smith's first night in the
Alouette Women's Correctional Centre, jailed for refusing to plead

guilty to violating an injunction to not block access to the Trans Mountain pipeline project, she asked:

> Who knows her great sadness? And mine? Wondering if we'll win or lose. The Judge, the Prosecutor, the Company, the Government, the Law. When is the law the foundation of our humanity and when does it serve only those most powerful, those rich enough to make the power work for them alone? What are we to do now? How can we stop this destruction, this peril – that seems so far away from this very moment, but is why I am here, after all? Global warming, and pipelines and bitumen. And me …
>
> My heart is pierced through with love, none of it earned by my goodness. It just is: Patti, my beloved boys, their girls, Oscar, the new little one coming, my family and my family-in-law, and my house family, my church, my brothers and sisters in Christ, my co-land defenders everywhere, especially in Latin America, and especially Guatemala, my doggie, the forest, the great sea, the looming mountains, and the wee sparrows. All these are my nest of prayer. And so, I weave them all around me, and sleep comes gently and carries me into the heart of God, where I spend the night free. (Emilie Teresa Smith, 18 August 2018)[33]

When corporation and state destroy democracy as a daily and foundational modus operandi, causing untold suffering and irreparable harm in the world, vanquishing humans and other living Beings, breaking all laws, conventions, ethics, and morals, where is their standing when "standing" is used in the courts to determine who will or will not be heard? What is our prognosis when a state's bottom line is economics based upon ecocide and genocide? How do we as a society indoctrinate others to work for these masters who dismantle our very roots, our social contracts, our agreed-upon *love one another*?

> Industry is a direct attack on our very existence as Indigenous people. (Kanahus Manuel, personal communication, 2017)

Specific corporate industries, whose destructions are geological in effect and scale, promise(d) utopia, a better life for the individual and society, through individual accumulation of material wealth and personal societal power based upon a materialistic hierarchy. As is true for the machine, which first served a useful, sustainable purpose, greed has grown to a point of pathology. Machines are hyper-violent, to the point of creating absolute destruction of all life quickly and irreparably.

Omnicide, the destruction of all life forms at the hand of humans, is not only from nuclearism and the nuclear bomb but also from tar sands, massive clear-cuts, open-pit mines, rising waters from climate disruptions, and fossil fuel extraction and use.

Empires (*read* countries and corporations, their collusions with mining companies, hydro projects, oil and gas, factory farms of immense suffering) use and proliferate paradigms wholly dependent upon complete destruction in the reap and rape that is gathering its wealth and power. *Yuct Ne Senxiymetkwe* (Quesnel Lake), and her watershed, are the Sacred source of life for a vast portion of BC.

> The collapse of the Mount Polley tailings dam will be long remembered as the most destructive assault of Indigenous Title, Rights and Treaty Rights for all First Nations living in the Fraser River Basin. (Grand Chief Stuart Phillip, quoted in UBCIC 2016)[34]

Yuct Ne Senxiymetkwe (The Womb of Mother Earth) is her name (aka, Quesnel Lake watershed). She is the birthplace for Sacred Wild Salmon and many other Lives and Beings. She is a glacial, clear lake, the only inland temperate rain forest in the world, home to Salmon-spawning birth beds, to red-listed endangered Beings such as Mountain Caribou and Grizzly Bear, and as many animals as one may name: Cougar, Brown Bear, Moose, Deer, many types of fish in addition to Salmon, such as Bull Trout, many mammals, lakes, and rivers.

> What happens to our salmon, what happens to our water? If we are not able to use the water, if salmon are infected, it will be devastating to our Nation, our identity. How are we going to pass on our culture and knowledge to our young people? This is what we are calling "honouring our connection to the land" and honouring the stories of our ancestors.
>
> We call this "Heart of Snow Mountains," with sacred water; the water is so strong it is medicine. Our teachings tell us to bathe in the morning, bathe in the evening, to make our songs, prayers, ceremony, which we pass to our youth.
>
> We have to give back not only to the land but to the water. To show respect, to always follow protocols. To treat water with dignity and respect. (Jean William, Secwepemc Elder)[35]

The Imperial Metal Mount Polley mine's containment walls, in place to hold back the mine's generated toxic wastes, chemical, metal, and other pollutants, as predicted by workers, broke, pouring into the surrounding watershed and destroying vast amounts of life.

> On August 4th, 2014 a four square kilometre sized tailings pond full of toxic copper and gold mining waste breached, spilling an estimated 25 billion litres of contaminated materials into Polley Lake, Hazeltine Creek and Quesnel Lake, a source of drinking water and major spawning grounds for sockeye salmon. According to Mount Polley mine records filed with Environment Canada in 2013, there were "326 tonnes of nickel, over 400 tonnes of arsenic, 177 tonnes of lead and 18,400 tonnes of copper and its compounds placed in the tailings pond" in 2012. (The Narwhal n.d.)

Extremely poisonous pollutants ran roughshod, ruining creeks, soils, lands, rivers, and poured deeply into the Womb of Mother Earth's watershed (Hazeltine Creek, Lake Quesnel, and all surrounding areas). According to worker testimony at a Union of BC Indian Chiefs press conference,[36] Imperial Metals employees and engineers' warnings to management, with proof of imminent disaster, brought no relief, and a preventable, caustic deluge was allowed to happen, later confirmed in an official report of the mine disaster: "Concerns regarding steep slope, dam construction material availability, buttress subexcavation, and supervision were identified by employees but not elevated for action by MPMC [Mount Polley Mine Corporation] management" (Hoffman 2015, 7). To summarize from the 2015 chief inspector of mines' report, causes of the event include "absent administration control," "lack of awareness of the risk," and "engineer did not manage risk" (Hoffman 2015, 138), with "no qualified, individual role to take on responsibility for water balance," "no integration of water planning across the entire mine site," "poor water management," "no long term planning," and "no qualified responsible person," among other faults (149).

> Risks as significant as the inadequate foundation studies, variance and absence of beaches, rapidly growing surplus water ... were all discounted, dismissed, or not identified at all. Concerns by workers regarding slope, material availability, buttress excavation, and supervision did not appear to be elevated or reviewed by management. Concerns raised by MEM [Ministry of Energy and Mines] around foundation soils, beaches, and surplus water were also discounted. (151)

Salmon, Grizzly Bears, Plant Parents, and all our Relatives of all species, including humans, were and continue to be harmed to a terribly significant degree in both First Nations and non–First Nations communities throughout Secwepemc territory. Industry, as wars, devastates lands, leaving behind landscapes of sorrow and heartbreak, further testimony to empire's and resource extraction's affliction to destroy all Life. Nevertheless, according to the chief inspector of mines, the "undesired outcomes" from the Mount Polley disaster include "threats to key strategies of British Columbia's mining industry," such as compromise of "our competitive edge" and stream-lined regulatory processes, "health and safety of our workers," protection of the environment, partnerships with First Nations, and development of a skilled workforce (Hoffman 2015, 152). Notably, the only mention of Indigenous people and those Beings who rely upon the Womb of Mother Earth for all variables for existence are only about their relationship (or illusion of one) in support of a de facto lawless industry.

> Two short years ago, the mad rush for higher dividends created the conditions ripe for the apparent gross negligence at Imperial Metals' Mount Polley Mine, combined with the lackadaisical enforcement of the BC Government, led to one of the most infamous instances of flagrant regulatory misconduct and immense devastation to the land, water and air ever seen in this province. In this regard, it is absolutely outrageous that charges have not been laid against Imperial Metals. (Grand Chief Stuart Phillip, quoted in UBCIC 2016)

> Canada has more mine tailings spills than any other country in the world except China and in the face of government and industry inaction, it is a disgraceful distinction. (Phillip and Phillips 2018)

Racism and misogyny are global phenomena and oppressive systems that violate and destroy female, Mother Home/Land, soil, water, and all of her Beings. In our days of empire, obscene levels of targeted violence against females, murders and disappearances in border towns and urban centres, slavery in the "sex" trade, the proliferation of pornography, prevailing female selective abortion and infanticide all have in common the imposed inferiority, commodification, and expendability of the female, linking to empire's targeting and use of female land, female meat (factory farms and meat-dependent diets), the female life-giving force. (Please note, the use of "female" here refers to biological sex primarily, as it is the target point for killers. I also wish to include female-gendered people.) Misogyny's indoctrination begins in the home, imported from work, school, and other institutions, and is supported by and expands into social constructs, laws, policy, and practices; it makes destruction not only socially acceptable but desirable as a bedrock of personal empire (monetary wealth and power over those who have not). There is a wrong-headed idea that the only way to "economic progress" is through the commodification and ultimate annihilation of the female (body, mind, spirit). There is also a lack of political will and social consciousness to challenge a status quo with hatred towards all females as its foundation. It is no mistake that the absolute destruction of the commons is most efficiently achieved through war and acts of war[37] (extra-judicial, state, and/or corporate sponsored). The Mount Polley mine disaster, the destruction of Sacred Wild Salmon, nuclear waste, mining waste, the importation of drugs, alcohol, and sexualized violence are considered acts of war. Each leave levels of devastation in their wake so deep that the home nation cannot recover easily, if ever.

Universities' further support of philosophies and methods of annihilation through indifference and their silence, lack of leadership, and inability to focus clearly to remediate from historic harms is their approval of empire's lawlessness. They also funnel vast amounts of public resources into weapons work, even in times of collective want. The University of California (UC) first made real and proliferated the nuclear arsenal of the United States, the only country in the world to use the bomb in war and against Native peoples of the world. Imagining, researching, making weapons of terror, and adding to nuclear proliferation is acceptable behaviour on the UC campus, but peaceful protest against tuition hikes not.[38] The University of Iowa's College of Engineering directed faculty not to promote climate activist Greta Thunberg's visit via social media. Jason Kosovski, director of marketing and communications in the Engineering College, said: "We cannot use our channels to publicize or promote policy change. We are always free to publicize our research, even if it has policy impacts, but Greta's visit does not fit under the umbrella of university research" (Miller 2019). One wonders, if climate change does not fit "under the umbrella of university research," what does?

Acts of War and Violence at the Behest of Empire

Environmental justice activists, specifically those speaking for the health of Rivers and our elusive relation, *justice*, are targeted and murdered: 185 in 2018, and 212 in 2019 (Global Witness 2020). Many more people are subject to state-sponsored violence, repressions, and dispossession. Among murdered rights holders are Nilce de Souza Maghaes (Brazil, Jirau Dam, 2016), Berta Cáceres (Honduras, Aqua Zarca Dam, 2016),[39] Rosalinda Perez (Guatemala, Tres Marias Dam, 2015), and many other Land, Rights, and Water Defenders (International Rivers n.d.).

One wonders where justice may live when the university remains mute on the ultimate punishment by state actors – murder.

Guatemala's lack of justice compares perfectly with Canada's and the United States' lack of justice for Indigenous peoples attempting to protect their/our very lives, Land, and all of Her Beings. As the British Columbia Court of Appeal said, Land Defenders have "difficulty in receiving a fair trial against a powerful international company" whose resource extraction and other damaging imperialist impositions "align with the political interests" of the state (Canadian Centre for International Justice 2017). We must not find comfort in the mistaken idea that extra-judicial violence at the behest of corporations are Third-World issues, as the very same occurs in Canada and the United States, markedly with Dakota Access Pipeline (DAPL), Elsipogtog, and Unist'ot'en, all fossil fuel corporate impositions upon Indigenous peoples and Lands. Additionally, Guatemala's oppressive regimes are the ongoing brutal reality of overlapping colonizations by US and Canadian industries and governments for power, possession, and profit (Hennessy 2013). Colonization, vanquishment, and destruction in the western hemisphere are against all Indigenous peoples, all Land, and all Beings as their foundational force.

At Elsipogtog, when all possible avenues for relief were denied to Land Defenders in attempts to protect their land and water from SWN Resources (fracking), the community engaged in a direct action of peaceful protest. Snipers pointed assault rifles at the people who lay in the grass, intimidating with the threat of ultimate violence (murder). "A lot of women were attacked in the front line. One woman was praying and was maced in the eyes ... They were shooting our people with rubber bullets – and we were there with just our drums and eagle feathers" (Hennessy 2013). Two Mi'kmaq protectors and Land Defenders, Germaine Bureau and Aaron Francis, were sentenced to fifteen months in prison (Roache 2014), as Canada's Royal Canadian Mounted Police (RCMP) arrests and attacks Land Defenders. One may also recall but two other examples: Ipperwash (and the murder of Dudley George in 1995) and Ts'peten (Gustafsen Lake, with over 400 tactical assault team members, 9 tanks, maiming, and imprisonments).

Dakota Access Pipeline's (Texas's Energy Transfer Partners) multiple, pervasive human rights violations against Indigenous peoples and their allies, recorded on video, film, and via witness testimony, showed the world the organized, pre-planned attacks on citizens in a Western democracy by the very actors with fiduciary responsibility to safeguard rights. Government, police, FBI agent provocateurs (Norrell 2017; Parrish 2017),[40] security forces, and mercenaries are blamed by their victims. Today, there are several federal civil rights lawsuits alleging civil rights abuses. For example, Oregon's Civil Liberties Defense Center (2020) issued a press release concerning ongoing lawsuits titled "Standing Rock Indigenous Water Protector Sues North Dakota Police for Abuse of Civil Rights: Case Joins Several Other Standing Rock Cases Currently Stalled Pending Court Rulings on Defense Motions to Dismiss." Regarding pipeline debates, fossil capitalism, and oil's "deep state," Dayna Scott comments:

> Building a coast-to-coast pipeline to deliver western tar sands crude to eastern refineries will cement our reliance on fossil fuels in a way that is dismissive of the rights and well-being of future generations at the same time that it exacerbates existing environmental injustice in Canada. (Scott 2013)

These actors use tools of war, such as tanks, guns, lethal and "non-lethal" artillery, harassment, and torture; carry out surveillance, violence, brutality, arrest, imprisonment in cages, and sexualized police violence; employ attack dogs; and fire water cannons upon the people in the prairie sub-zero winter in a continual onslaught, as it has always been, to break the heart of the people, force them into submission, and violate established rights and justice at the behest of empire. Violences at Standing Rock are termed acts of war against US citizens by US state and corporate sponsors.[41]

> A United Nations group is investigating allegations of human rights abuses by North Dakota law enforcement against Native American protesters, with indigenous leaders testifying about "acts of war" they observed during mass arrests at an oil pipeline protest. (Levin 2016; see also Amnesty International n.d.-b)

How to Live: A New Model That Is Very Old (in Love with Land and Her Beings)

Land is the origin place of all: history, culture, stories, songs, prayers, ceremony, names, instructions, reasons for existence of all Beings, interrelationships of all who live, the meaning and reality of the past and the future. The concept of zero waste is an ancient Indigenous one. Indigenous reciprocal redistributive economic systems are a practice as old as this Land. These are economic practices to which we must return.

To live with the stomach's needs necessitates the taking of life (plant, animal, water, all Beings). Indigenous Arctic peoples made and make peace with spilling the blood of sea and land mammals, birds, and fish by recognizing humankind's utter dependence, honouring and having active spiritual and practical relationships with Those upon whom life depends/depended, such as Seal, Whale, and Char. Likewise, Indigenous farmers and gatherers made and make peace with those Plant Parents upon whom we depend with ceremony, prayer, and sacrifice.

Vanquishment, Lawlessness, War

In the wake of corporate empire's sense of lawlessness are unliveable lands, environmental devastation, undrinkable waters, violently imposed totalitarian states, erosion of rights, and the destruction of democracy.

Human-centric practices divorced from Indigenous bioregionalisms, such as forest clear-cut devastations, open-pit mining, tar sands, nuclearism and its others, and open-caged farmed Atlantic salmon are achieved through acts of violence, first clearing the land of all her species (and thus the true reason for "hunting") and then de facto proclamation of ownership by governments and corporations of traditional Indigenous Lands. These Lands then become omnicidal landscapes of despair due to the complete marginalization of communities and the commodification of all life at the hand of humans. A system such as this depends upon racism against Indigenous peoples, speciesisms against all non-humans, and a lawless political expediency (to deny rights, title) in order to create and maintain its work of destruction, dispossession, pollution, and degradation.

Endless insatiable greed (the desire for *more* on a finite planet) is, in part, based upon hierarchical ideas of who is worthy and who is not, and upon socioeconomic gender roles and racial divides, divisions cemented in acts that deny justice and rights. To belong to and take part in the destructive philosophy and practice in the modern world is to give oneself over to resource extraction's domination via a lawless political expediency (violating environmental protections, democratic practices and processes, and rights guaranteed to other citizens but denied to Indigenous peoples, for example, Indigenous rights and title). Corporate lawlessness is no accident but rather de facto requisite in order to dispossess Land of all of her Beings and Land herself of her viability (Mother Home/Land, Female). Of course, this lawlessness is manifest from the dreaming and imagining, the engineering, research, and development through to the life of the mine, or the hydro project, or the clear-cut, or the bomb. It allows for a pathological indifference to the suffering of living Beings and to the ruined aftermath and poverty left in its wake when the mine is played out, the forest ruined, and the ocean floor polluted to the point where it may no longer support life and biodiversities. When racism against Indigenous peoples is firmly entrenched in society – in its universities, its grocery stores, its police stations, its schools, its hospitals, its elections – and is used by corporations and agents of the state (military, police, mercenary, and paramilitary), then our economic model, as practiced today, may thrive. For this reason, there is a vested interest among corporations and governments to maintain a status quo of oppression, as opposed to finding and making just methods, ideas, and practices with which to care for our human needs, interdependent as they are with non-human needs of all species and the Planet.

Ongoing Colonial Impositions: Expanding Man-Made Vanquishments; Lands of Dispossession, Ruin, Waste

Colonial impositions are successive, ongoing layerings in the advance and maintenance of empire: outright war, violence by state-sponsored actors (including corporations), dispossessions and removals (including forcible removal of children from families, homes, lands into residential schools, as well as other outside influences that have and do make reserve life unlivable for so many disaffected people, such as today's Ministry of Children and Family Development [MCFD] apprehensions), drugs, alcohol, and the resultant invasive multigenerational poverty as a direct result of corrupt inhumane policy and business practices. Individuals move to cities in flight from imposed states of extreme poverty, where the very foundation of human needs (such as water, for example), are not met: the ultimate form of displacement in advance of domain.

Thus, these individuals cannot thrive and are set in cycles of survival, stress, and despair – not a good place to be creative, productive, innovative, or calm/ing. How can there be a thriving Nature, a true survival that is beautiful and good, when we are set in cycles of survival, stress, and despair with no remediation in sight? It is estimated that a clear-cut will not regenerate for four centuries, assuming it will not be clear-cut again in that time. Universities, reoriented to justice concerns for all species, would see as their charge to create and deliver knowledge, experiences of their students and community members, to create a reimagined economy where we all learn the needs and wants of all living Beings, the needs and wants of all of those elements that support life, and address these as foundational to our work in the world. In other words, in place of the ruinous monster, corporate empire, is an Indigenous-centric, bioregionally responsive, *Belonging to Home/Land.*

True Sacred Wild Pacific Salmon vs. Ocean Atlantic Salmon Farms'
Virus, Atrophy, Cannibalism, Abuse of the Courts to Violate Democratic
Protections and Rights

Well it's a sad fall in my beloved mainland as there are such few salmon that the grizzlies are still out rolling rocks looking for something to eat and the eagles are catching mink and seagulls because there are no dead fish for them to gorge on.

I have never seen anything so sad in my life. Marine Harvest [salmon farm] is gitting just what they want – no more wild salmon.

– Eddie Proctor, 16 November 2017[42]

One of the great blessings of teaching is learning from students, seeing the world through their reality, acknowledging and coming together through learning. I was given a testimony from a young man at the end of term of a very large survey course, and it has stayed in my memory all these years. We had never spoken at length before. Standing among a group of students, he said, with earnest urgency:

My father's been a fisherman on the island forever, just like my grandpa. He was forever too.

I love fish. Did you know Cod are very inquisitive?

My dad says that the government is trying to kill all of the wild Salmon, so the Indian people will starve and have to move away from their lands, and then the government can take all the coastal land and sell it or do whatever they want. (Young Man, personal communication, 2004)[43]

This unforgettable, haunting story from a non-Indigenous person, based upon a family's practice, is concerned with the health and welfare of our human and non-human communities; we, in spite of diversities, are allies in the quest for our own security and viability into the next seven generations, with recognition of our complete and utter dependence upon a clean, healthy, viable ecosystem(s) and her Beings. We also collectively see the devastating negative results of certain policies and corporate and government actions.

Over the years, Young Man's testimony stands as one to return to. His words are continually verified by detrimental actions from the province of BC, the Department of Fisheries and Oceans, and Norwegian salmon farmers, all culpable (at least in part) for declining salmon populations (and ruining rural community and bioregions, as well as Wild Salmon species viability[44]), destruction of ocean floors and her Beings, importing foreign flesh-eating Atlantic fish species to fragile Pacific waters, imperilling rural livelihoods, and – either by will or chance – forcing humans and non-human animals from their true and natural Homes.

COHEN COMMISSION, THE PRECAUTIONARY PRINCIPLE

Governmental collusion in the destruction of the commons upon whom we all depend, culturally, socially, spiritually, and practically across many species, is greatly exemplified by the Department of Fisheries and Ocean's culpability in promoting the destructive, oppressive, democracy-smashing, and community-destroying ocean-based salmon farms.

For many years, scientific evidence of excessive lice infestations and virus/disease originating and promoted by ocean-pen salmon farms damaging Wild Sacred Salmon has been dismissed, ridiculed by corporations polluting the BC coast. Dwindling populations of Wild Sacred Salmon is a nightmare, as so many species of Beings, including humans, depend absolutely and significantly upon Wild Sacred Salmon for our very lives. Additionally, this author and her students witnessed Canadian courts and strategic lawsuits against public participation (SLAPP suits)[45] used by fish farm owners to abrogate freedom of speech and to punitively silence those citizens, artists, and activists seeking remedy from this destructive endeavour that harms ocean floors; Wild and Sacred Pacific Salmon; First Nations and other coastal communities, and their economies and cultural and spiritual practices; the commons; and the food security of many communities (nationally and internationally).

The highest percentages of wild salmon infected with PRV [*piscine ortho-reovirus* (reovirus) *infection*] were found in high-density salmon farmed regions i.e. the Broughton Archipelago (45%) where First Nations are extremely concerned that salmon farms have contributed to the collapse of local wild stocks, Lois Lake (40%) where steelhead farms operate and the Discovery Islands (37%) where the Cohen Commission concluded farm salmon disease could have serious and irrevocable impact on Fraser River sockeye salmon returns. As well, 40% of returning wild adult salmon in the lower Fraser River and 76% of trout in Cultus Lake were infected. In contrast, only 5% of wild fish on the north coast of BC and in the Skeena and Nass Rivers were infected, these regions were the furthest from salmon farms. PRV was detected in all species of Pacific salmon also and trout. (Morton 2017)

In other words, "the percentage of wild salmon infected with piscine reovirus was much higher in wild salmon exposed to salmon farms, than in wild salmon not exposed to salmon farms" (Morton et al. 2017).

Chief Justice Cohen's Commission of Inquiry into the Decline of Sockeye Salmon in the Fraser River[46] used the precautionary principle, which in part is the "duty to prevent harm," even in the absence of data, to err on the side of caution, and to stop an existing practice until more data can be measured. Nevertheless, the BC Department of Fisheries and Oceans granted more fish farm licenses in First Nations and rural communities, despite widespread community opposition. Musgamagw and Namgis First Nations Land Defenders have and are occupying waters around fish farms with the goal to remove them and their destructions.[47] One can clearly see a pattern, a modus operandi, of industry's destructions, which it commits with impunity, and abuse of power engaging state-sponsored actors to harass, harm, and imprison those who oppose violations of their rights and freedoms at the hands of industry. If a corporation is a person, can it not be found guilty of its crimes?

"Trophy" Murder, Vanquishment of the Biggest and the Best

After years of urging the government to ban so-called trophy hunting for bears in their territory, 10 First Nations on B.C.'s north and central coasts [Coastal First Nations Alliance] have declared their own moratorium [absolute ban on trophy bear hunting] but it is not clear if they will be able to enforce it.

– Canadian Press 2012

Wanton destruction and waste of Sacred Wild Pacific Salmon and Grizzly Bears (among all others, as empire attacks) and laying waste their physical remains is to exert a spiritual bankruptcy against all of Nature's Heroes, a de-sanctification of their role as majestic power Beings, teachers, namers, and guardians.

Trophy hunters destroy the biggest and the best of all species. They target Beings for their species, size, and strength, murdering the strongest and most able in that species community, thus emptying Home/ Land in advance of empire. Trophy killers and poachers track and kill those Who are the reason and historical precedent for names, language – actors from the beginning of time to the present day, they who hold affective affinities with humans and other Beings, who are the meaning and reasons for story, prayer, song, clan, house, Home/Land. Poaching, illegal[48] hunting, waste are serious pathologies and crimes against other than human species on Indigenous Lands. Their vanquishment affects all others. Key to their species survival, they are often key to the very survival of all of their relations.

Trophy hunting, like salmon farms, shows clearly the radical philosophical, spiritual, and practical chasm between those entrenched in certain mainstream practices and those following Indigenous responsibilities (to ensure life and thrivance of all Beings into perpetuity) and demonstrates how mainstream acts run counter to and violate Indigenous rights, protocols, meanings, and ways of being in the world. In 2012, a confederacy of First Nations formally condemned trophy hunting for several reasons, including that it is in violation of tribal worldview, practices, and protocols, Indigenous law, and collective ethics.

> For us as First Nations on the coast, it's very intuitive that something like trophy hunting – and the senseless slaughter, for sport, of animals that are a huge part of our culture – is at odds with the future we're envisioning for our communities and our people. (Jess Housty, quoted in Ball 2013)

NFL hockey player Clayton Stoner, in clear violation of Indigenous rights and title, Indigenous Heiltsuk law, and the Coastal First Nations Alliance (nine Indigenous BC Nations), travelled to Indigenous Home/Land and murdered Cheeky, an eighteen-year-old beloved Bear relative, an important community member living in the protected Indigenous Home. Stoner proudly posed with Cheeky's decapitated head for a trophy photo. The NHL had little if anything to say about his violation of the law (both Canadian and Indigenous law), his speciesist abuse of animals, and his sentence upon being found guilty, as professional sports rely principally upon a societal acceptance of meaningless violence.

> We build strong relationships with our relatives in the animal kingdom. To lose a bear like this, especially under these circumstances, really grieved people deeply. (Jess Housty, quoted in CBC News 2016)

SPECIESISM'S COLONIAL HIERARCHIES

Lawless exertion of power over Land, people, and all living Beings runs roughshod over rights, justice, ethics, and the health and viability of the commons like a voracious perpetual motion machine fuelled by greed, hatred, and blood lust. Global modus operandi is the fabled reap and rape, literally, of all Females, Land, animals, humans, and Her others, including Her children of all species. Speciesism is very similar to racism, in that both deny and abridge the rights of all others to Live (the rights to life and health of all species and their Home/Lands). Speciesism is a prejudice against the other; it recreates and maintains a paternal, human-centric, racial, and classist superiority over all others (humans and non-human). Speciesism is a human-centric ideal with an impenetrable dogma in which only certain human beings' financial lives and violent perversions matter, at the cost to all others. It is the highest political and economic form of selfishness and greed, and uses cruelty and violence in its proliferation, negating life forms' personalities, names, reasons for living on Earth, and importance. Speciesism attempts to transform Grizzly Bear. No longer the Clan Leader, the Spirit Guide, Medicine Man, the Vision-Maker, he and she are commodified into merely heads mounted upon a wall. Sacred Wild Salmon are no longer the Sacred Twins, Clan Leader, House-Maker, Life-Giver; they are relegated to the status of "trash" in the way of Atlantic salmon ocean farms.

Speciesism not only denies the sacred nature of Beings; it also destroys cultural and spiritual reality. There is no natural mystery, no gift of possibility, no "what if" faith in a world without Supernatural Beings. Without them, there is nothing to aspire to, thus directly creating *the politics of hopelessness*, a distinct useful political tool of apathy. Why vote, why protest, why learn, why work hard and gain rough hands, why transform the world to justice, if it is all hopeless? For this reason, we embrace thousand-year-old Trees, we bring back Elderberry as Forest Helper, we say, Don't Cry, Fight!

> And, thus, Indigenous Knowledge sets, Traditional Ecological Knowledge, Native Science, Indigenous Philosophy, Indigenous Law, Indigenous Policy (urban, rural, suburban, transnational, bi-national), and Indigenous Governance are needed in the university. (Personal communication from anonymous editor, 2018)

Sacred Beings, Wild Pacific Salmon and Grizzly Bear, are the reasons and initiators for heritage, culture, language, family, mystery, history, Clans, Houses – relationships that matter in this world, in the past world and lifetimes, and into the future. Their abilities to thrive are directly related to humankinds' possibility of survival and are the measure of our true security and viability.

Mowing Ancient Forests (Clear-Cut, Slash and Burn)

Clear-cutting is modernity's avaricious logging method, one that has never been sustainable or desirable. Cleared Land leads to erosions, thereby destroying Homes for many biodiverse species, and affects Land, Air, Water and her Beings for many generations. A clear-cut creates a wasteland from a former paradise; a clear-cut cannot and will not be remediated in a lifetime, and may take up to 4,000 years to return to its former biodiversity and sustainability.

Great Indigenous precedent exists for Tree and Forest protection with the defence against reckless killing of trees by colonizers in 1546, shortly after the Spanish arrival in the Yucatec Maya homeland in present-day Mexico. Maya people practiced acts of resistance against imperialist destructions, led in part by Chilam Anbal against their Spanish colonial oppressors, "speaking for the trees" to protect them from wanton destruction.[49]

ATHLII GWAII (AKA LYLE ISLAND, 1985,
WITH ACTIONS BEGUN IN 1970)

At *Athlii Gwaii*, Haida and their allied peaceful Land Defenders asserted Indigenous rights and title, and the rights of all Beings, in attempts to protect the old growth Forest from being indiscriminately logged. Led by Elders and community leaders, seventy-two people were arrested by the RCMP. Unrestricted clear-cutting and vanquishment of biodiversity's many species and destruction of the Land continues unabated, with provincial government members hand in glove with corporate actors and their financial interests, despite attempts at remedy (land use planning, negotiations, and court cases, to no avail).

Indeed, "much of the BC Cabinet at the time held shares in Western Forest Products" (Pynn 2010). Lumberman/investor Bill Bennett, premier of BC at this time (1975–86), is remembered for slashing social services and labour laws, creating chaos and social ills that led to a general strike (Mickleburgh 2018). In 1996, regarding his investments in the lumber industry, the BC Securities Commission declared Bennett and two co-conspirators guilty of insider trading, and he was "banned from trading in stocks for 10 years and the three [were] ordered to pay a combined fine of $1 million" (Vancouver Sun 2007).

WAR IN THE WOODS (AKA MEARES ISLAND,
CLAYOQUOT MASS PROTESTS)

Tla-o-qui-aht and Ahousaht First Nations, concerned allies, and environmental groups such as Greenpeace and Friends of the Sound worked together in Land defence; over 900 were arrested in 1993 for standing up for our Mother Earth against destruction and ruin. The pattern is familiar: those lawless ones targeting and violently taking Indigenous Land and violating rights for their own financial gain by summarily dismissing rights and ignoring democracy's expected inherent free, prior, and informed consent of those most affected and in the line of impact. Also continuing are familiar violations of justice (civil and environmental), as destroyers of equal protection under the law and remedy through political means (protections non-racialized communities take for granted), dismantling of citizens' and Indigenous rights, destruction of the commons, and vanquishment of species.

What these three actions have in common is the concerns of citizens rightfully standing for the Land within their democratic rights. They illustrate what is wrong with Canada – violence against all who Love Land. Academic departments could be a part of rights actions in many ways, through many disciplines.

Economic Injustices, Open-Pit Mines

Despite massive resource extraction and the wealth and power it brings to empire, individuals and communities in direct line of impact are pushed further into poverty and desperation, where the most basic of human needs are not met by any of modernity's promises and the standard of living for many Indigenous peoples is drastically lowered. Canada's DeBeers Victor Mine in the James Bay lowlands takes billions of diamond dollars in annual revenue, while nearby Home reserve Attawapiskat[50] lacks critical infrastructure, housing, health care, education, and drinking water – those elements foundational to health and well-being. In extreme sub-zero winters, people live in tents or in substandard, crowded housing that is comparable to the worst conditions of so-called "Third-World" countries.

In addition to De Beers's billions in annual revenue for the open-pit mine and extreme poverty for the Indigenous people of neighbouring Attawapiskat, mercury contamination "may be much higher than the government or the company is reporting" (Porter 2017). Mercury poisoning leads to "the creation of methylmercury, a neurotoxin that accumulates in fish and other food sources of the people who live in the area" (Porter 2017). Polluting heritage foods and creating food insecurity is typical for megaprojects such as these, as past experience proves. One may not simultaneously plan and create polluting industries without race-based marginalizations and rights abuses, as practiced today.

In a 2015 report raising a concern about mercury contamination from the Victor Mine, the Wildlands League[51] found that "gaps in reporting by De Beers for monitoring mercury contamination are extensive and persistent"; and rather than clear and open communication, there are "barriers to public access to information about the mine's environmental record," as opposed to openness with the community of impact, shareholders, and the Nation. "Risk assessment of mercury remains shrouded in secrecy"; and Canada's "Ministry of Environment and Climate Change struggles to properly oversee this monitoring program" (Porter 2017).

Compromising Land's power, purpose, and viability via flooding, clear-cutting, and chemical poisoning is systemic and predictable, for example, in the case of *Asubpeeschoseewagong Netum Anishinabek* (Grassy Narrows First Nation), one of many hundreds of cases where industry's temporary rapacious exploitations, with permanent effects, have poisoned Rivers, Lands, and all those Beings who depend upon one another for basic survival. From 1962 until 1970, Reed Paper Mill and Dryden Chemical buried drums of mercury underground and dumped approximately ten tons of mercury into the Waters, Rivers, which were the health, wellness, and economy of Indigenous peoples – Waters who created a thrivance of life. Today, over 90 per cent of the community suffer from mercury poisoning (Gilson 2019), cutting lives short; the mercury affected/s the nervous system and compromises the abilities of the entire community with infirmities and diseases formerly unheard of in Grassy Narrows (for humans – MLS, Alzheimer's, Parkinson's, cancers, and other diseases), poisoning the River systems upon whom all Beings depend, as well as destroying the basis for security, meeting of basic needs, culture, and life itself. Purposeful industrial pollution (is it illegal to dump mercury into rivers?) is an unmitigated peril to health and all life (Bruser and Poisson 2017; see also Amnesty International 2018).

A confidential 2016 report says provincial officials were told in the 1990s that the site of a paper mill near Grassy Narrows First Nation was contaminated with mercury – and that the poison is likely still present. (Bruser and Poisson 2017)

Purposeful industrial contamination destroyed/s the local economy (fisheries, tourism, guide services) and basic, traditional culture, interspecies relationships, and millennia-old and practiced food security. Today, water comes from plastic jugs trucked into the community, as there is no access to safe water for drinking, cooking, or bathing. Grassy Narrows, after many years of Land defence and acts of Indigenous self-determination, was assisted by Amnesty International in 2007 in order to "resist clear-cut logging on their ancestral lands by the forestry behemoth Weyerhaeuser" (Richardson 2007). Despite legal challenges to Weyerhaeuser licenses and lack of Indigenous consultation and consent, common industry stall tactics via the courts allowed forest ruin at the behest of empire to continue unabated. Some grow perversely wealthy, while the communities nearby are left in poverty, ruin, and in this case, irreparably harmed by acts that could and should have never happened. This is what dominant culture terms "economic development."

Attawapiskat, Grassy Narrows, and so many other sites of Canadian imperial history continue on in full view, invisible to the mainstream, so bad actors prevail with impunity. However, there is another model possible: one of illumination, education, communication, and prevention before avoidable destruction of Home/Land, her Beings, rights and title, and democracy; of witnessing, documenting, expressing, and carrying information out to others during events by bad actors; of naming names, visiting and informing shareholders, and demanding ecological justice from government, its agencies, and its citizens; of organizing educational events, arts and research interventions, and showing and presenting a true commitment to Land and Life in all forms. Universities near to or far from Attawapiskat, Grassy Narrows, Standing Rock, Elsipogtog, Burnt Church, Oka, Ipperwash, Gustafsen Lake, and many others need to educate, respond, and create direct action towards ensuring actualization of existing democratic and Indigenous rights and title. This work may be accomplished, for example, by creating and delivering courses, internships, and opportunities for research, creation, and production that directly address remediation from past and present bad acts/actors, with the funding and community support to affect needed change in corporate attitudes, systemic racist systems and policies, "accepted" forms of violence endemic to resource exploitations and "development," abrogation of rights, destruction of title, ruin of Lands, species extinctions, and other chaotic omnicidal mayhem at the behest of empire.

The university must address its role in schooling politicians, government agents, so-called security firms, workers, community members, and administrators to understand the principles of democracy, rights and title, and rights of all living Beings so that these rights are enshrined and each one may work to ensure true actualization of these rights.

Lack of Water, Boil Water Advisories, Polluted Water

Our original healer, Doctor Water,[52] features in all aspects of life, secular and sacred. Assaults against Water are assaults on the physical, emotional, traditional, psychological, practical, and spiritual plane. Humans have neither relief nor remedy from those destroying and polluting our life relative/resource, save for direct action, with varying degrees of what one may term "success." Water, our dear Relative, is defended at Elsipogtog, DAPL, and with issues such as ocean salmon farms and many others.

Even though oil/tar/fossil fuel companies have made billions in revenue, "the First Nations community of Shoal Lake, Man., for example, has been under a boil water advisory for 17 years, despite its location beside an aqueduct that directs safe water to Winnipeg" (Chan 2015). An accounting of drinking water advisories in January 2015 found (a minimum of) "1,838 drinking water advisories in effect in Canada, including 1,669 drinking water advisories in communities across Canada and 169 drinking water advisories in effect in 126 First Nations communities" (Lui 2015, 5).[53]

Fossil Fuels, Climate Disruption, Over 200 Islands Going Under Water

Tar sands and pipelines carrying crude oil from the tar sands and products of fracking mean polluted aquifers, treaty violations, increased carbon load, and the disruption of over two hundred islands, such as the Maldives, to rising ocean levels. The lure of short-term financial gain and personal power leads corrupted or wilfully blinded business and political interests to deny climate change in order to further sell fossil fuels (gas, tar, oil, and their others) and pipelines. The university moving towards this corporate model is its downfall. Corporate donations fuel research into Earth-destroying "technologies," lead to corporate dominance of energy, food, rights (and their destructions), and war. Corporate sponsorships have been the golden carrot few administrators care to challenge, despite our privilege, education, and safety.

Despite massive wealth for companies and growth of empire, Canada's tar sands contribute to climate change's disastrous effects, such as the inundation of islands due to rising sea levels. Mohamad Nasheed, former president of the Maldives,[54] lived through torture and imprisonment for speaking about the threat of rising sea levels due to climate change, a fact of life in at least two hundred islands whose citizens are becoming environmental refugees due to the use of fossil fuels by industry and countries other than the Maldives.

More often than not, massive resource extractions take a place once able to support life and leave behind a landscape of revulsion where traditional means to survive are now impossible, and the new way of life (mining, clear-cutting, fish farms) fills the pockets of the settler colonists (miners, tree cutters, tar sands and fish farm workers), their corporations, and shareholders. The power brokers have little (if any) interest in the rights and health of their communities of impact, nor do they bother to consider their personal and corporate liability and culpability in their destruction, making the life of future generations impossible in these places.

Responsibilities Are Rights and Title (Ongoing Violations of Indigenous Rights and Title – the Politics of Hopelessness)

Indigenous youth suicide incidence is high globally, and mostly involves young males. However, the Inuit of Arctic Canada have a suicide rate that is among the highest in the world (and ten times that for the rest of Canada). The author suggests that suicide increase has emerged because of changes stemming in part from the Canadian government era in the Arctic in the 1950s and 1960s. The effects of government intervention dramatically affected kin relations, roles, and responsibilities, and affinal/ romantic relationships.

– Michael Kral (2012)[55]

Historic and ongoing capitalist colonizations dispossess Indigenous peoples of foundational relationships to Relatives, human and non-human, Natural and Supernatural. Colonial impositions take Land and her Beings, and leave ruin, where none or very few of the traditional Beings may or can survive. Long-standing poverty and other reasons for lack of access to fulfil potential justice and rights create a pervasive politics of hopelessness. Traditionally in Indigenous communities, there are/were/still are Beings, protocols, rights, and relationships with affect, meaning, and possibility; dispossessing of these means there is no recourse, no resolution, no reconciliation.

To Whom Do We Turn? Stop Killing Us[56]

With only one goal in mind – work, get paid big bucks, own a house, a car – all-Canadian luxury, all in for themselves. Once upon a time, our villages were rich in culture where we shared and cared and protected each other and took care of our rivers, traditional territories, all of it. Now they have pushed us so far into their poverty, with many of us still struggling. Look at the reserves; bad water, bad housing. So tell me again what is good about working in these man camps when I am forever adding names to the lists of our women and girls who are missing and murdered, our February 14 Women's Memorial March list. I see the toll it has on our people every minute that I am at work.

– Carol Muree Martin, 2019[57]

Where is there to turn when well-established laws, agreements, and policies are violated, vanquished (in part or in whole), compromised, or simply ignored via practice, policy, and violence? To Whom may one turn when the Canadian RCMP, police, security firms, and mercenaries are purchased and/or used by corporations to exert overreaching authority and unjustly arrest, beat, kidnap, rape, and/or imprison Indigenous peoples on the advance of destructions/extraction and species extinctions? Whom may one call upon when the police and mercenaries commit acts of violence? What court will hear a case fairly when the courts themselves are corrupted?

When courts and their actors are used and abused by corporate powers to violate democratic practices and enshrined principles, and punish citizens with physical violence and imprisonment, especially in regard to Indigenous peoples and persons' *right to life*, to practice a de facto criminalization of Indigenous peoples attempts to save their very lives, and to label as terrorists those who attempt to prevent whole-scale destruction, where is remedy and reconciliation? Universities have a duty to inform regarding Indigenous and democratic rights and to ensure that their teaching, outreach, and community work train and instruct all others in order to actualize justice for all of our communities.

> Groups challenging government policy, particularly surrounding the energy and extractive sectors, have been infiltrated and subject to surveillance by both CSIS [Canadian Security Intelligence Service] and the RCMP ... The recent passage of the *Anti-Terrorism Act*, Bill C-51,[58] raises further concerns about enhanced powers for Canadian intelligence agencies, among other provisions, being used against Indigenous groups and other organizations contesting the government's extractivist agenda. (MiningWatch Canada and ICLMG 2015)

Canada had a National Inquiry into Missing and Murdered Indigenous Women and Girls (MMIWG). This matter is not only a Canadian problem, but one where industry creates/ed lawlessness as a part of their reap and rape mentality, and where women are the primary victims to abusers, such as in man camps, hopeless sections of urban centres where prostitution is a survival strategy or forced upon vulnerable persons (including children and transgendered people), outskirts of reserves and reservations where anti-Indian sentiment runs high, and border towns such as Juarez, Mexico, where hundreds of women have been raped, tortured, and murdered.

In Juarez and Canada, according to one source, it appears the women are targeted for being female, their long dark hair, and dark skin.[59] As with MMIWG, Indigenous women are more at risk of being victims of violent and sexualized crimes in a time where the Land's life is under great threat. Juarez and Canada appear to have much in common, including the lack of government action to investigate cases fully, of interest and ability in capturing and prosecuting criminals, and of justice for families of missing and murdered women and girls (including here all vulnerable folks).

Modernity's problem, the one that will see the end of all species with the destruction of Beings and our Sacred Home (the commons), is advancement of empire at the destruction of the Indigenous Female: Mother Earth as Female (Planetary life-giving Home for all Beings); Home/Land as Mother (regional nurturer, life-giver, so all may Live and thrive); Indigenous Land and her Beings (place of all identity, manners, meanings, personalities and purposes, responsibilities, laws, rights, and justice); and Indigenous as Radical (*Roots*) Place, Home/Land.

Universities, based upon a de facto patriarchal, hierarchical sense of worth and devalued "other," summarily deny access to bureaucratic gatekeepers. Lack of access to decisions and decision-makers, secretive back-door verdicts and dealings, uninformed higher-ups making rulings without communications with directly affected parties, importation of outside "consultants" with little or no experience in place of those in-house with training, skill, and expertise, as well as bringing in consultants to counter Indigenous research, work, and expertise, selecting men (and less-qualified men) and paying them more than women – these are some of the ways the university often erases matrilineal processes, social structures, and protocols. Patriarchy disrupts concepts of shared governance and the importance of balance and agency between all genders. Sexual predation is not addressed. Women, people of colour, seem to not matter, and as former prime minister Steven Harper said about the MMIWG, suffering and violence against women is simply "not high on our radar" (Kappo 2014).

Misogyny may be cultural, societal, global. Please recall that a majority of meat consumed and produced via factory farms is female (Chicken, Cow, Pig). Universities serve cruelty meats at status functions and daily cafeterias, supporting a culture where the female body is an objectified commodity: it is a bacon burger not a female pig and cow; "meat" not lady; "tenders" not female chicken; grossly enlarged breasts as consumables, where a turkey or chicken is no longer a full bird with a life of its own, but merely a breast. The university is clearly in the supply and demand chain for bodies of living Beings (products) whose availability is the agonizing lives of many animals, due to their suffering because of humans, speciesist misogyny, pollutions, additional violence added to a struggling world, and climate disruptions. Reducing Western diets' unnecessary overdependence upon the flesh of others for food[60] (where there are many more just, climate-aware, forest-preserving options) and rejecting overuse of convenience foods would assist in achieving a healthy, life-affirming planet.[61]

Universities recent downward devolution, or lack of fulfilling their potential as justice and rights promoters, makers, and doers, comes from their adoption of a vanquishing neoliberal "me only" corporate model of wealth and power for the few, at the cost of all who Live. Complete assimilation and indoctrination into imperialist methods and ideologies are labelled as Western "success." Neoliberal concepts of success for the few at the ruin of all must be deeply seen and remade to reflect our collective Indigenous Belonging to and with our Home/ Lands. What we count on for what is justice, rights, security, and sustainability does not figure into how public universities "count" on our or their worth:

> Since the BC Liberal government came into power in 2001, the discourse around public post-secondary education has been framed entirely through market metrics: the university is no longer discussed as a public good, as a right, or as a social institution as it may have been in the days SFU was founded, but is instead required to justify itself through a variety of "performance measures": student enrolment, numbers of patents produced, corporate sponsors, etc. While students, staff, and faculty experience these policies as cutbacks, the state is often not actually cutting funds, but rather restructuring and railroading funding so that it comes with "conditions" bearing an uncanny resemblance to the austerity measures endured by countries indebted to the International Monetary Foundation [Fund]. (Brophy and Ticker-Abramson 2011)

Exporting destructions from wealthy countries onto poorer ones, creating and promoting racisms in order to vanquish people from their lives and homes, committing crimes against humans and all Beings and places, hatred for Female, matriarch, life-giver in all of Her forms allows the hatred needed to perform resource extractions. Rape is used as an obscene metaphor for oil extraction; the squeal of a pig being murdered for cruelty meat is the name given to the squeal of oil through a pipe; it is the word used by Vancouver's serial killer to define his Indigenous female victims, whose remains he fed to his abused pigs on his family "farm."[62]

Home/Lands, where Indigenous and rural folks are targeted in order to vanquish the Land (seen and promoted as "less than" the wants of the privileged class); speciesisms, where genocide is committed against all non-human life and species are made extinct; misogyny, where any life-producing entity (Water, Lakes, Land) is derided and easily destroyed; an imposed colonial belief in "trash," something Western societies accumulate and use to pollute other areas – these are examples of the destruction.

Universities are advancers of multinational corporate lawlessness and are blind to social and environmental justice issues and their terrible, and preventable, consequences. If universities, and the privileges they hold, do not use justice as their primary goal and do not serve to promote, create, and maintain their social contract, then why are we here?

Modernity's utopia machine is insatiable, and its fuel is vanquishment and dispossession of Indigenous peoples and all Indigenous Lands' Beings. Alberta's tar sands, Ontario's open-pit diamond mine, British Columbia's ocean-based salmon farms and Imperial Metals disaster, Forest destructions (clear-cuts), trophy hunting, and modern Indian treaty have in common termination strategies and violations of UNDRIP, historic Indian treaty/ies, the Canadian Charter of Rights and Freedoms, Indigenous rights and title, as recognized by the Canadian courts[63] in cases such as *Calder v. British Columbia* (Supreme Court 1973), *Delgamuukw v. British Columbia* (Supreme Court 1997), *Tsilhqot'in v. British Columbia* (Supreme Court 2014), to name only a few of the legal instruments relevant to rights, Land, and justice.

Institutions earn their reputations and maintain their mission and belief systems, in part, via alliances with corporations and corporate practices, corporations who, in hand with government, perpetrate these destructions. Encouraging and training people to contribute to forcing Indigenous peoples off their Home/Lands, forcing them to abandon tradition, sustainability, and access to a free, wild, ever-regenerating self, uses racism as its foundation. The fact that racism, misogyny, speciesism, and their others are requirements for an "economic model" of omnicidal, destructive corporate industry, one that leaves utter destruction as its primary remain and where remediation and reconciliation is not actualized, is evidence of the inner, collective, and shareholder consciousness, which must either ignore or make irrelevant many species' (including humans') right to Life, right to Home.

Lives of the Wild, Lives of the planted and the gathered need new forms of accounting and accountability, in all academic disciplines, for the lives of food bringers (plant, insect, animal, water, mineral).

Rights and Democracy vs. Dispossession and Destruction

Where is this beginning, the rooting place for violence, indifference, hatred, which created/s humanity's endless wars with Land, Water, Air, her peoples, and all living Beings? We speak of racism and genocide; its origins are in what we mean by *cultures of violence*, where all life is regarded as expendable and violence is acted out in acceptable societal norms. That "thing" that allows one to violate Land, to vanquish all her Beings is the root of racism, misogyny; it is the birthplace of domestic violence, war, the tar sands, open-pit mines, the factory farm.

Land Is a Rooted Place of Responsibilities, Rights, and Indigenous Democracy

Do we begin with classical views of the former Greek and Romans and their natural law, or may we go further into history, with the Haudenosaunee Great Law of Peace? May we look to evidence in Indigenous sense of belonging, Land, clans, spiritual beliefs, power, and practice for the multispecies universe and shared rights to ensure survival and thrivance for many generations?

We may rely upon Canada's Charter of Rights and Freedoms and the US Constitution (the Bill of Rights) in our discussions of North America, both of which clearly recognize, support, and ensure enshrined human rights to free speech and assembly, the right to access and practise due process, and equal protection under the law (among many others). All these, vanquished, with empire, extraction, extinctions.

The university is concerned with remaking, promoting, and maintaining a broken, modernist, neoliberal status quo, which uses reap and rape as its defining modus operandi. In my experience, a university's culture demands deference to hierarchy (males of an accepted demographic and sociocultural standing placed in power) and silence in political and rights actions (our source and hope for democracy, rights actions, and justice). It derides and attempts to destroy the very disruptions needed to make positive, life-affirming change. The university culture does not always follow its own implied expectations for academic rigour when empire is the subject and vanquishment of rights is the outcome.

For example, certain students wanted to advocate for their interest in working with tar sands and mining (which is their right and choice, of course) but did not or refused to use peer-reviewed sources in their papers supporting extractive industries (not acceptable for any major in any university). Is this because there is no empirical data supporting tar sands? Is industry, its web pages, and public relations (corporate-fuelled mythomania) one's only source of validation? One student came to me, away from his peers, to testify that his studies never addressed Indigenous rights and title, climate change, pollution, dispossession, species needs and extinctions, global economies, and global environmental refugees, nor any Canadian or provincial laws and court cases relevant to extractionist industries. In other words, the students were being trained as technicians, divorced from the effects of their future work, livelihood, and identity. They were being trained to ignore their power and effect in the world. What future will they have once they understand the effect of their work upon Land and her Beings, globally, such as the woman geologist who witnessed murders in North Mara mine in Tanzania? This question, perhaps, explains the reason why alcohol, drugs, and sexualized violence plague workers of extractive industries.

> Tanzanian opposition politicians have claimed 300 people have been killed since 1999. "For such a high number of violations to have occurred outside a conflict zone in a business context is shocking and exceptional," said Anneke van Woudenberg, the executive director of Raid, a UK corporate watchdog. The owners blame police. "There have been many, many investigations on various allegations, and you can't hold me accountable for the state authority," said the Barrick chief executive, Mark Bristow, when asked about the killings. (Watts 2019)

Not only aiding oppressive systems to continue but creating, promoting, and maintaining them seems endemic in many academic fields:

> It is like they are training technicians, lawyers, to serve the powerful interest.
> We have a real crisis in legal educational institutions that breed the next generation of lawyers. And the lawyers are the architects of corporate power; they are the architects of grinding responsible government into the ground, and turning it into an accounts receivable corporate welfare crony capitalism for these big businesses. And giving these corporations immunities and privileges which we would never have as real individuals. They are artificial entities. (Nader and Hedges 2018; see also Nader 2018)

Propping up and rewarding (via money, notoriety, and power) those who (via corporate structures and police violence) work little and profit greatly (via outright theft and annihilation), beholden, they claim, to invisible nameless and thus irresponsible shareholders whose interests are only financial (the rest be damned) to achieve more personal wealth, achieves rather the destruction of democracy via corporate and government compromise of ethics, laws, treaties, rights, and title. And universities sit idly by, allowing and de facto supporting activist arrests, police brutality and lawlessness, and corporate takeover of the commons. University complacency and university silence is irresponsible, cowardly, ahistorical, and anti-intellectual:

> Humans have always had the struggle of good and evil. The energy cycle is there for infinity. How you choose to use it is what you bring to life – to maintain purposeful wholeness. (Wanpovi (Tewa), in-person conversation, San Ildefonso Pueblo, 2013)

Power Beings of All Species Have an Inherent Sacred Right to Live and Thrive

All Beings have the right to be in relationship with Plant Parents and other Relatives who are our helpers, allies, and true security. Humans have an inherent right to plant, care for, and propagate heritage foods, sacred Plant Parents, food, fibre, beauty, homes for non-humans (the bee garden, the dragonfly nest). Preservation of heritage seed and plant viabilities, personalities, and identities are a part of human responsibility to all species. Air has the right to maintain its clear nature, its original Beingness of swirling, spiritual personality. All Beings have the right to access non-polluted, free-flowing Air, safe from particulate matter, pollutants, nuclear fallout, downwinders (think of flame retardants in mother's milk in the Arctic). Air has the right to move, to carry weather, to perform its ancient works. The university needs to redirect itself, to teach, practise, and promote these basic *rights to make* sustainable, hand-based Land, security, as opposed to promoting corporate global control of GMO monocrops, patents for living Beings, massive chemical pollutions in aquifers and rivers, and other such ills which depredate the viability of Beings foundational to survival and relationship on Mother Earth (think of soil, water, air).

Freedom to share as equal neighbours, responsible to all Beings for their ability to thrive in our Home/Lands, access to clean and viable biodiverse Land, Water, and Air rooted in Indigenous peoples' rights, title, use, and meaning would be attained. Regenerative and transformative powers of all living Beings would be protected, enlivened, and maintained. Indigenous peoples practicing continuation of their Nation-specific ceremony, song, poems, and other political, social, scientific, and aesthetic practices would ensure the continuation of our Natural selves and Earth, which is the original purpose, use, and meaning of what we say when we say "Love Mother Earth."

Respect and observance of traditional territorial relationship (use of all types, ceremonial and secular) and maintenance of traditional *Indigenous redistributive economic systems*[64] would bring equitable, shared, distribution of food and goods, trade and craft items, any and all material wealth. The role of *making* would be a resurgence of the material security of hand-work (craft, art, practice) within relationships with ecosystems, necessitating relationships inside a responsive, interdependent, and reflexive calendar round; knowledge of, and loyalty to traditional use strategies, theologies, mores, and practices within a living role of the good neighbours paradigm in use strategies (no decisions or actions that threaten, malign, pollute, dispossess, or vanquish neighbours; neighbours now are all of us).

PLANT PARENTS

Universities promote and create GMO technologies by accepting industry funds and research direction expressly to mutilate the genetic material of plants and other living Beings for financial profit and control of global food at the behest of empire. GMO reality is human-centric at the expense of all others, a colonial imposition upon the worldview of Indigenous peoples for whom all living Beings share merit, worth, personality, transferrable power, wants, and needs. Family and community small-scale farming collapses under the weight of monocrop corporate agribusiness. Native ecosystems and biodiversity are destroyed by chemicals necessary for GMO to come to harvest. The Spirit Nature of a Supernatural Being, such as Corn, is destroyed. Corn, our Ceremonial Sister, is our bodies, having kept legions of Beings secure for millennia across race, time, species, and nationality.

Indigenous Corn (Her many races), our Ceremonial Sister, is a master remaker, one seed or kernel able to make hundreds more of Herself in one season, a major Power, talent, and identity. She gives her flesh for ours – human, Elk, Bear, Monarch Butterfly, Rabbit, everyone. She has Power to sustain life for many species, the magic to transform one cob into thousands. Monsanto and their/his GMO terminator gene "corn" targeted and ruined Corn's Sacred Ceremonial Everyday Power into the exact opposite of Her true Indigenous identity by removing Her ancient and reliable power of regeneration. Our Ceremonial Sister links many species to one another, species of the past and present into the future, an unbroken link to survival and thrivance. That GMO corn is absolutely unable to reproduce and new seed must be purchased is the killing of Corn's true Indigenous self. It is no coincidence that Indigenous peoples too are manipulated, harmed, and cannot thrive under industrial tar sands, mega mines, and militarized violence. Here we have the contrast:

Indigenous Bioregional Centricity	vs.	**Neoliberalism**
Rights of all Beings to live and thrive	vs.	Human-centricity
Thrivance of Nature Power	vs.	Destruction of Beings' inherent Powers
Interdependence of all living Beings	vs.	Dependence upon corporations
All Beings have inherent rights	vs.	Rights of the elite and the corporation
All Beings have Nature Power	vs.	Commodified lives; value only monetary
Sacred Power of all Beings	vs.	Patents, profits

GMO technologies, corporations who "own" patented GMO seeds, their wealth, and influence have infiltrated certain universities to the point they could be recategorized as "GMO agrochemical universities." Corporate funds from GMO interests not only define research goals and the political points of view necessary for their promotion, consumer acceptance, and world food control; in fact, "corporations have poured money into universities to fund research for decades, but now, the debate over bioengineered foods has escalated into a billion-dollar food industry war" (Lipton 2015).

GMOs take power from farmers, undermine the family farms economic system and food security, destroy rural communities, create dependence upon chemicals for crop yield, destroy biodiversity, and compromise survival for the poor and rural worldwide. GMOs give power over food to corporations, thus controlling who eats and who does not. All Indigenous persons whose families were given the choice between food or historic treaty, starvation or pipeline, death or gold mine are well familiar with empire's strategy.

The University of Saskatchewan (U of S), for example, like many others has close ties to Monsanto, which defines research parameters and research results, relying upon propaganda to sway public opinion and allegiance away from Nature Power to corporate malfeasance via control of our food and our rights to healthy, reproducing food.[65]

Monsanto edited U of S academic articles with no public mention of the corporation's role. As well, the documents indicate the company's executives oversaw the guest list and content of a U of S symposium. Monsanto relies on these academics to spread their message to the public and to regulators, Ruskin [researcher for US Right to Know] said. [U of S professor] Phillips and other professors should declare their Monsanto connections and stop helping corporations "hide their dirty laundry," Ruskin said. "They gin up professors and academics as sock puppets to speak for them." (Warick 2017)

As for the University of Saskatchewan, "tens of thousands of pages of internal documents obtained by U.S. Right to Know[66] via public records requests reveal the close – and often secret – ties between Monsanto, its PR groups, and a group of professors who promote GMOs and pesticides" (Malkan 2020). Additionally, "[U of S professor Phillips is] one of a number of prominent academics in North America who wrote papers advocating for the global use of genetically modified crops. The paper topics were proposed by Monsanto, and the corporation edited the articles and disseminated them via a public relations firm that it had hired – though there was no public mention of the corporation's role" (Desai 2019). Monsanto solicited partner "academics as well as chemical and industry food front groups" to discredit the World Health Organization International Agency for Research on Cancer regarding their categorization of glyphosate (found in the weed-killer Roundup) as a class 2A carcinogen (Malkan 2019).

Utopia's Omnicide: Indigenous Peoples at the Front Line of Corporate Assaults

Edward Teller, labelled one of the twentieth century's greatest minds, father of the hydrogen bomb, famously claimed that understanding the universe is achieved by breaking everything into smaller and smaller pieces. This "breaking apart" (via violent, omnicidal means) is the foundation of modern extractive industries, performed by machines more destructive than nature can remediate, breaking apart Lands upon whose lives humanity and all Beings depend. "Breaking apart" as a foundational philosophy is the variable grabbed onto by historians who claim the "greatest minds" created "the greatest invention" of the twentieth century, the omnicidal nuclear bomb. For Teller, Trinity, Hiroshima, and Nagasaki were not evil enough in intent, purpose, and effect. University-trained, considered an intellectual hero, he advocated for, dreamed of, and birthed the hydrogen bomb, a more spectacularly

violent, maniacal, omnicidal weapon used by the United States to oblit-
erate Pacific Island Nations.

Weave Back Together All That Is Broken Apart
(Remediation, Reconciliation)

A howling communal lament for the reality of university's corporatization bewails, specifically, how the university has changed from its purpose into a corporate instigator and is recruiting, training, supporting,
propping up, creating, and advancing new generations in practices that
further create, enable, and embolden the oppressive status quo based
upon worker exploitations, dispossessions, generation of endless wars
at the advance of empire, species extinctions, and land ruin, which
consistently and increasingly violate basic human rights and needs,
environmental justice, and Indigenous rights and title. To see that the
university is a factory for the advancement of war, obstruction of democratic principles, violation of human rights and the rights of all Beings,
and uneven applications of democratic protections and rights, one only
need look to the example of the University of California's (UC) management of the Lawrence Livermore and Los Alamos National Labs
and their training of scholars in the development, advancement, use,
and testing of nuclear weapons and other weapons of terror or to any
university who chooses silence over rights action.

Sorrow, here, is righteous, in the wake of institutions' increasingly
numb corporatized culture, one that supports and creates an internal
(and expected) desire to do less in life, to instil a sort of non-reflective
mindset of fewer expectations of an individual's ability to have social
purpose and positive collective affect, and to shame and marginalize
activists, grassroots practitioners, and speakers of Indigenous logic sets.

Work to fix a broken status quo (one supported by universities) may
involve work to further acknowledge, enshrine, promote, and protect
all Beings' right to Life, right to live freely, to survive on Wild, Sacred,
and Good; human rights to free speech, freedom of assembly, and freedom of religion; rights to access to due process and equal protections
under the law; and rights to education to create the actions of peace
(which would help). By helping all Beings and all of Nature to thrive,
we assist democracy's viability and certainty.

Reclaim, Remake, Restore Our Ruined Place: Purpose, Duty, Survival

Thoughtful, inclusive, expressive, smartly knowledgeable community work, Beingness, research, teaching, learning, and creation meet

relevancy in striving to actualize and achieve our *potential fulfilment* of social and environmental justice, civil rights, and the rights of all living Beings to live in healthy, sustainable, justice-laden Home/Lands, where all may have an assured survival:

I. Universities need to address basic human and other species needs – those of Land, Air, Water, and all else, and the needs of all living Beings – through all of its programs, institutes, think tanks, curriculum, and research agendas in order to put back together all who have been broken apart, to promote life in its biodiverse, Indigenous forms, and to actively maintain or vacate areas for Earth as a confederation of Wild, Sacred, and Good to thrive.

Every university employee, faculty, student, staff, administration, and community member has an important part to play in order to uphold responsibility to its different constituencies and the rights holders it serves, thus remaking the university to ensure true Home/Land security for all of her Beings by teaching, training, and informing students, community members, ourselves, and our at-large society. In concrete terms, universities need to create, maintain, continually develop, and support curriculum that is not only historical, factual, and responsive but also active and intelligent in presenting justice and rights in context with subjects studied. For example, which university disciplines are responsible for the destruction of the commons, old growth clear-cuts, open-pit mega mines, hydroelectric dams, tar sands? Do their students study their negative effect, worldwide, of these imperialist exports regarding civil rights, environmental justice, and their direct responsibility for dispossession, vanquishment, and rights violations of humans and all other living Beings? Are other academic disciplines embracing their potential for creating a more just world? Our goal is to have practices that consider and respond to the seventh generation forward and behind, the reintegration of multigenerational relationships in all acts of creativity and making (for the Spirit world, the animal world, and the human world) with the practice of hands, mind, and spirit in creation of life-granting and sustaining activities for all species.

II. Official statements from university administrators regarding rights, title, environmental justice, democratic processes, and rights and privileges should be de rigueur and expected, as the eroding of rights occurs daily. Silence on topics such as climate change, food insecurity, modern treaty and the destruction of Indigenous Beings of all species, violence as a cultural norm is proof of culpability and approval of all that is broken, damaging, creating harm. We cannot work for a more just world while we align with corporatists who violate people, Beings, and places, international treaties, laws, and socially agreed and acted upon accepted forms of democratic behaviour, especially when these egregious transgressions are against the poorest, the most marginalized, targeting peoples of colour, and claim to be "engaged with the world"[67] in a just, real, compassionate, and rights-bound manner.

One cannot simultaneously work and advocate for democracy and her others, environmental justice and human rights (Indigenous and all other), the rights of all species, and the rights of Land and Water, while promoting compromise of those same rights through association with corporations who violate these rights as their modus operandi and train future workers in those organizations who are deeply invested in the practice of lawless political expediencies, especially those related to mining, destruction of the commons, human rights abuses, dispossession, and vanquishment.

All subjects, disciplines, schools are indeed tools for right thought, right action, and right livelihood, understanding themselves as rights-based practices, thus participating in fulfilling our potential for justice, democratic principles, civil rights, the rights of all Beings, social and environmental justice in order for all to live, survive, and thrive.

III. Concepts of "success" need to be redefined to include the thrivance of all living Beings to the next seven generations (in an eternally spiralling sense of time) in order to reorient our path and work. Philosophical and practical changes are, in part, what we mean by the phrase, "the only solution is a system change." A university could prepare us physically, spiritually, emotionally, and intellectually in all we actively perform to survive, live, and thrive as interdependent species. Land, Air, Water, and all Species are already doing their work, fulfilling their mission as given to them at the earliest times. Personal success is tied to interspecies community, bioregionally specific thrivance.

IV. To remain up to date and reflexive to changing times, our courses must change constantly to address Earth and society's rapid changes in justice, rights, legal judgements, international rights recognitions, war, environmental refugees, global movements, and dispossessions – all matters relating to Mother Earth and her many equally significant Beings.

V. Reconciliation is Remediation of Life and the Lives of all Beings and their/our Home/Lands.

Remediate and reconcile. Put back together all that is broken apart by humans. Maintain Life in all Her forms. Place health of all bioregions as a priority, along with the ability for all species to thrive. Challenge and remove violence, ruin, dispossession, and war as cornerstones, and replace them with *making* and *maintaining* practically and philosophically, and place our collective resources into this economic model.

Teach, create careers, create a new economy, put in place policy and budgets into remediation from chemical, radiological, nuclear, biological, and other destructions for all Home/Lands. Put back together all Beings of all Lands broken needlessly apart.

Reconcile with Home/Land everywhere by creating practice-based intelligences to make, maintain, and promote Home for all species of all bioregions.

Measure, quantify, and qualify all positive results and make these measures those of success.

Create jobs that focus on *making*, as well as fixing, putting back together all that is broken apart by empire and guarding the irremediable wastelands with the "nuclear priesthood" that Johanna Macey[68] spoke of. Create think tanks to watch over and prevent further contamination from these irremediable lands, and find solutions to such wasted lands, like a monastery of sorts, made up of people whose job is to monitor and keep others away from poisoned lands such as tar sands, nuclear wastelands, grounds contaminated radiologically, biologically, chemically, and otherwise.

Create policies to reflect a social contract for the rights of all Species, Lands, Waters, and Air. End tax subsidies for ruinous practices against Earth such as open-pit mining, clear-cut logging, and ranching, and ensure equitable taxation for all members of society.

Protect Water in all Her Living Life forms. Lakes may no longer be "de-watered" or used as tailings impoundment areas or dumping grounds.

Name, note, create accounting for the loss of all Lives; qualify and quantify the impact socially, culturally, practically, spiritually, and politically upon those in the line of impact and those who rely upon one another to thrive. Quantify and name impacts of incursions upon Indigenous spiritual practices (what is lost when the Sacred Cave, Place of Visions, Grizzly Bear is destroyed, with little to no hope of return?).

VI. Create and commit to measurable conditions for any acceptance of any financial support from any entity – corporate, personal, governmental, and other. Create and use a policy that ensures no monies come from (1) places where "affected communities have organized to press criminal charges against" said corporations;[69] (2) violation of laws, rights, title; (3) violence/vanquishment against humans and living Beings; and (4) dispossession, extinctions, vanquishment, or can, may, or will be accepted and used in any manner by the university.

Commit to never name any public space with the names of oppressors, masters of ruin, rights violators, and other oppressive masters. Donations do come with conditions; we may not work simultaneously for rights while denying those rights by our actions. Naming is our social contract and reflection of our personal and shared values and rights; ownership of public spaces by corporate naming is not a bought privilege.

VII. Assessment tools for courses, research, internships: it is possible to measure, chart, name, and consider courses, research, internships, and mentorships, specifically concerning how exactly specific knowledge and training is or may be applied in the world. Modifying curriculum each semester (which many do already) with an eye to goals and objectives to train students in the challenges all around would help grant students a clear, prior, informed context for their life's work. They will be able to think about their hands and lives in the context of justice, and realize the importance of their lives individually and as part of a greater, interspecies, intertwined, collective Home/Land.

Halt, remake, and replace corporate taking from the poor to give to the rich that leaves desperation and destruction. Train and create careers to remediate from corporate and government wrongdoing, such as careers to reclaim and resanctify our Forests, Watershed, and commons. Remediate contaminations, wastes, droughts, and wasted Water. Create viable economies. Reject violence and destruction. Train in advocacy, rights justice and action, policymaking, and rights and title of all humans, species, Lands, Water, and Air. Create law schools centred on the rights of all Beings and criminalization of crimes committed by lawless political expediencies carried out by elite power brokers.

VIII. Create, offer for free, and maintain a grassroots dictionary of seminal terms, Beings, rights, laws, international tools, and historic events in order to create Indigenous literacies. All folks, especially those who run for office, would have a place to learn seminal terms such as sovereignty, self-determination, and study court cases such as *Delgamuukw*, *Williams*, and international binding agreements between sovereigns such as treaty, and many others. All members of the university community would be bound to at least read the list and the spoken definitions to ensure a teaching and learning so we may come closer to understanding the first peoples and Beings of Sacred Home/Land.

IX. Destruction of the commons stems from an inability to belong to Home/Land, a lack of sense of responsibility for the diverse Lives that diverse humans interact with. Universities must take a more active role in subverting modernity's *politics of hopelessness* to create possibility, to create abstract realities such as a *just society* for present and future seven generations; to build progressive movements such as those that have been historically necessary for civil rights; to create secure communities integrated with the Wild, Sacred, and Good; to formulate collective Indigenous-centric *responsibility to place*; to create policy and justice initiatives reflective of local government and national initiates for all living Beings in order to erase the imposed colonial human-centricity, which is the soul of destruction.

X. Our hope is to reimagine, recreate, and live within (as much as possible) Indigenous bioregionalisms in order to know and be held responsible, as community, to all living Beings to ensure their lives, survival, and their ability to thrive for their seven-hundredth generations. This goal requires learning the names and personalities of all Beings, their distinct, needed, and powerful agency on this Mother Earth, their rights and practices, and how humankind and all species may co-exist and help one another, assisting all Life forms and their needs in order for all to exist. Life, democracy, love, belonging are not come by via passivity, but demand eternal and daily vigilance.

Opening university doors (those traditionally and vehemently shut) to Indigenous philosophies, theories, methods, practices, and living with/in a bioregion within a calendar round in relationship with and for all living Beings would help bring elusive justice towards fulfilment. Indigenous practices encouraged and taught in a classic Indigenous-centric mentorship model, or modified for large classrooms, disciplines, and applied studies, would help create a healthier, more viable, national security to live within working Indigenous paradigms of multispecies interdependence, respect, and work for and with all living Beings, Matriarchy, and dare one say, Spiritual reality, where humans do not occupy the highest level of existence but share with all lives and lifeforms. The university must reject corporate "personhood" towards vanquishment as operating principle, and move towards teaching, being, thinking, and acting towards the health, well-being, actualization of rights, and justice for all living Beings.

NOTES

1 "Rights" here are defined as inherent, fundamental, Spirit-based, and legal realities. Rights are ethical, intrinsic, Indigenous, and also enshrined in legal instruments, enshrined in the Land and her many protected and beloved Beings. We may begin to think of rights as the shared and equal dignity and value of all living Beings to not only survive but to thrive within a thriving, regenerative bioregion, within the boundaries of Mother Earth's finite self, Her needs and wants, and the rights of all others to live, such as the rights of Rivers, the rights of Land, the rights of all species, and the rights of Mother Earth.

2 "Sustainable" may (in part) be defined as the thrivance of all Wild, Sacred, and Good so that all may live. Sustainability ensures segregation of all life away from human-specific harms to leave part of the planet for itself, free from human interference; to continue Earth's inherent interspecies, interdependent responsibility towards one another; to guarantee freedom from chemical, radioactive, plastic, biological pollution and poisoning; and to protect from genocidal, ecocidal, extinctive, and omnicidal acts.

3 "Lawless political expediency(ies)" is defined here, in part, as a *political system of exclusion, indifference, uneven application of the law*; destruction of environmental laws that protected Land, Water, and those Beings; violation of scientific principles/practices in order to advance resource exploitation; abridgement of democratic principles enshrined in the Charter of Rights and Freedoms; resources placed primarily into war-making globally; subsidies for reap and rape economics; wealth and power for the most powerful and most wealthy, taken forcefully from Indigenous Homes, not for Indigenous needs; creation of a *culture of violence*: abuse, carnage against all living Beings, an omnicidal reality.

4 Imai, Gardner, and Weinberger (2017) quote from "An Interview with the Honorable Justice Ian Binnie," *Ottawa Law Review* 44, no. 3 (2013): 571, 589.

5 For the purpose of this chapter, "empire" refers to governments, corporations, their greed sickness, and the power of fatality resulting in multispecies and multigenerational vanquishment from all that is Wild, Sacred, and Good (Land).

6 Sacred Stone Camp was (is) the gathering place for spiritual presence (and resistance to ruin) in the face of land desecration from the Dakota Access Pipeline and fossil capitalism's destructions of Land and Waters sacred to Indigenous Nations, including the Sioux Nations, Arikara, Mandan, and the Northern Cheyenne (G., in-person communication, 2018).

7 "Manifest destiny," in the nineteenth century, is a term that gave voice to the rationalization that non-Indigenous people were divinely predestined to have material wealth and power (at the expense of Indigenous peoples) in the "New World." The sentiment was used by both church and state for missionization purposes as well as dispossessions, wars, murders, massacres, and Indian residential schools. Using organized religion(s) as a justification for genocide and vanquishment, via act, policy, and practice, is the birthplace of empire.

8 Consider the case of Jack Diamond, whose massive rendering plant, West Coast Reduction, was frequently visited by Robert Pickton, beginning in the 1980s, in order to dump biological waste from his family home/pig farm in Port Coquitlam. "It wasn't long before he [Pickton] was so well-known at West Coast that he'd be waved in; no one bothered to inspect his containers … No one ever asked questions or inspected the barrels; regular customers

like Willie could dump whatever they liked … The rendering plant, which has two docking berths for container ships and large bulk tankers, ships its products all over the world. It has made its owner, Jack Diamond, one of the wealthiest men in British Columbia … His wealth allowed Jack Diamond to join the world of horse breeding and make a success of it, to become a member of the Sports Hall of Fame and a philanthropist behind many good causes. He was Simon Fraser University's most generous donor. But what went on in the plant was something not widely discussed, just understood. Very few, if any, of the available articles about Jack Diamond tell you what his company actually did" (Cameron 2011, 51–3).

9 "'Climate change is the greatest security threat of the 21st century,' said Maj Gen Munir Muniruzzaman, chairman of the Global Military Advisory Council on climate change and a former military adviser to the president of Bangladesh. He said one metre of sea level rise will flood 20% of his nation. 'We're going to see refugee problems on an unimaginable scale, potentially above 30 million people'" (Carrington 2016).

10 Mainstream Canadian constitutional and legal affirmations of Indigenous rights (aka, Indigenous rights and title) in Canada are legion, such as in the Royal Proclamation (1763), the British North America Act (1867), numerous court cases, the Canadian Charter of Rights and Freedoms, historic treaty (as opposed to modern treaty, which is also a vanquishment tool), and other legal instruments such as the United Nations Declaration on the Rights of Indigenous Peoples (UNDRIP).

11 "Our One true Mother, Mother Earth" (Grand Chief Stewart Phillip, Union of British Columbia Indian Chiefs, various public rallies attended by the author, 2012–17).

12 For details of these cases, please see Crystal, Imai, and Maheandiran (2014).

13 Nemonte Nenquimo is the president of the Indigenous Land Defender organization *Waorani Pastaza* (Ecuador), who prevailed in their legal battle to stop oil and gas exploration.

14 Nevsun Resources is a mining company based in Vancouver, BC, Canada. "The workers sued Nevsun, saying it was responsible for slavery; forced labour; cruel, unusual, or degrading treatment; and crimes against humanity. They said these were violations of 'customary international law'" (Supreme Court of Canada, 2020b).

15 Activists, professors, students, staff, community members, various organizations, professional and grass-roots groups, and other individuals created the SFU Against Goldcorp and Gentrification in the fall of 2010. Two of their demands were to remove the name Goldcorp from the centre for the arts and to create and develop a policy and code of ethics for donations at SFU.

16 For information on the negative impacts of the Goldcorp Marlin mine in Maya Mam and Sipakapense territory, see ADISMI 2007.

17 For the use of cyanide, see Imai, Mehranvar, and Sander (2017, 120–1).

18 Note that in March 2021, "Osgoode Hall professor Shin Imai has filed suit [in the Federal Court of Canada] against the federal foreign affairs minister contending that Canada has improperly withheld information about its diplomatic interventions on behalf of Goldcorp, a Canadian company accused of human rights abuse at its mine in Guatemala" (Carolino 2021).

19 *Angelica Choc v. Hudbay Minerals.* "The Maya-Q'eqchi' opposed the mining project, and claimed they were not consulted by the Guatemalan government in the transfer of land to private interests. The plaintiffs claim that security personnel employed by Hudbay's local subsidiary shot and killed school teacher and anti-mining activist Adolfo Ich Chamán, shot and paralyzed youth Gernam Chub Choc, and gang-raped 11 Maya-Q'eqchi' women. Because Hudbay is a Canadian company, the plaintiffs seek a remedy for the human rights violations in Canadian courts" (Amnesty International 2017; see also Crystal, Imai, and Maheandiran 2014).

20 For further details on the community resistance to Canadian mining operations in Guatemala, see also Pedersen (2014).

21 Monster Destroyers are those in the oral histories of the legend time who roamed the landscape, eating everything in their path and leaving all to waste. We are referencing here the *Popol Vuh* and oral histories from the Southwestern United States (see Tedlock 1996).

22 As the daughter of a Maya mother/auntie, our close relatives to the north are Hopi. Using Hopi words here fits cleanly this discussion of two separate world systems, Indigenous and modern Western, which are diametrically in opposition to one another in both philosophy and practice. (I am not a speaker of my mother's heritage language.)

 Koyaanis qatsi. Koyannisqatsi: n. sg. life of moral corruption and turmoil (re: life of a group), life out of balance. v. *Suyanisqatsi*: life of harmony; *Koyuunisqatsi* I *lawu* (*lalwa*) vn. i. be behaving in a corrupt manner; *Koyaanus* I *ti* (toti) vi. p. become chaotic in one's life style (neglecting one's family, being adulterous, pleasure-oriented); become corrupt. *Puma pep kiivit – toti.* They became corrupt as village residents.

23 Here, "Indian," in "Indian treaties," means Indigenous peoples of North America. "Indian" is a term enshrined in laws, court cases, and other legal instruments. There are many Indigenous peoples who use the word in self-reference.

24 Business Council of British Columbia (BCBC). Please note the listings of BCBC's executive officers and board of governors (BCBC 2019).

 Please see also Office of the Commissioner of Lobbying in Canada (n.d.) for registration information and lobbying interests of BCBC.

25 Extinctions at the hand of humans created our human-centric Anthropocene era. Human/mankind's insatiable pathological greed, violence, lust, gluttony, and continuous relentless injustices have brought geologic, atmospheric, biospheric, hydrologic (all of Mother Earth's powers and Beings), destructive changes to Mother Earth.

26 What comes first, hatred for Female or hatred against First Peoples? This question is a worthy discussion for a longer paper.

27 Kanahus Manuel, Tiny House Warriors (in-person communications, 2017).

28 The term "omnicide" was first used to describe the effect of weapons of mass destruction, such as nuclear and hydrogen bombs, to describe their power beyond the murder of humans to include the hyper-violent taking of all life forms.

29 In a Natural/Supernatural world, no place may be, can be, or is empty at any time.

30 Universities train and indoctrinate into an economic system based upon consumption and destruction, continuing in colonization's practices that, by plan, policy, and act, create a true *terra nullius*, a place where no living Being may survive (*read* tar sands, open-pit mines, nuclear testing sites), pouncing into Home/Lands with modernity's version of entitlement and manifest destiny.

31 University-trained individuals working in corporations and governments featured in this article include prime ministers Stephen Harper (BA, MA economics, University of Calgary) and Justin Trudeau (McGill University and UBC, literature and education); Stephen J. Kean, CEO of Kinder Morgan (law degree, University of Iowa); Kristalina Georgieva-Kinova, CEO of the World Bank (MIT, London School of Economics); Donald Trump, former president of the United States (BS economics, Wharton School of the University of Pennsylvania); Hugh Grant, CEO of Monsanto (MBA, International Management Centre, Buckingham); David Garofalo, CEO of Goldcorp and Hudbay Minerals (University of Toronto); Alf-Helge Aarskog, CEO of Marine Harvest (degree in fish nutrition, University of Agriculture, Norway); Brian Kynoch, president, executive officer, Imperial Metals (bachelor of applied science, UBC).

32 "Status quo" here refers to an imperialist takeover of Indigenous lands, their destruction, and eventual ruin.

33 Emilie Teresa Smith, priest of New Westminster Anglican Church; public post about her arrest and incarceration as punishment for her environmental and civil rights work in BC, Canada, via social media (18 August 2018).

34 Also: "In May 2016, BC Auditor General Carol Bellringer released a scathing report finding that the 'monitoring and inspections for mines were inadequate to ensure mine operators complied with requirements.'

Further, the UBCIC has yet to see a genuine commitment from the Province of BC to adopt all the Independent Expert Engineers Panel Report's seven recommendations ensuring that such a disaster will not happen again. Consequently, several First Nations and Tourism operators have filed lawsuits against Imperial Metals.

"UBCIC Vice-President Chief Robert Chamberlin, an advocate for the protection of wild salmon, insists 'Too little has been done to prevent another Mount Polley disaster. Where are the stronger regulations and industry scrutiny that are desperately required? These forms of environmental catastrophes represent a clear threat to wild salmon and an unacceptable infringement of Indigenous Rights'" (UBCIC 2016; see also Office of the Auditor General 2016a, 2016b).

35 See *Indigenous Resistance to the Mount Polley Mine Disaster* webinar, with Kanahus Manuel (Secwepemc Matriarch, Tiny House Warriors), Secwepemc Elder Jean William, and Joan Kuyek (founding coordinator of MiningWatch Canada, 1999–2009) that took place on 17 September 2014 (Manuel 2014).

36 Worker testimonio at Union of BC Indian Chiefs (UBCIC) press conference, Vancouver, BC, 2014 (Author's personal witness and notes).

37 "Acts of war" here are defined, in part, as (1) violent impositions by a standing army (and their armed agents) against those with little power, means, influence, or vehicles to actualize their potential, guaranteed rights; (2) unlawful arrest, abuse, torture, and physical and psychological harm against rights-holders; (3) abuse of the courts by corporations and/ or governments (domestic or foreign) to abridge, deny, and abrogate guaranteed rights and privileges of citizens, especially Indigenous peoples; (4) targeting social justice and environmental justice advocates, grass-roots workers, and professionals for arrest, prosecution, violence, and murder; (5) destruction of the commons; (6) imposition of food insecurity by willful acts of environmental destruction, importation of disease, and dispossession; and (7) poverty as a colonial/corporate manufacture.

38 For example, in 2011, John Pike, a university police officer at the University of California, Davis, committed a chemical assault upon students sitting peacefully in an action against tuition hikes, their protected right. Sitting with arms linked together as a sign of non-violence is a well-known strategy and symbol in movements such as civil rights, used by the Quakers and other pacifist organizations. Pike carefully walked past the students and targeted and sprayed their eyes and faces with a chemical weapon (Aggie Studios 2011; ACLU 2012; see also Parvini 2016).

39 On 5 July 2021, Roberto David Castillo, former head of the dam company Desarrollos Energéticos, was found guilty of being a co-collaborator in ordering the murder of Berta Cáceres (see Lakhini 2021).

40 Heath Harmon, Fort Berthold Reservation, was the lover/informant whose gun Red Fawn is accused of possessing (Norrell 2017; Parrish 2017).
41 Testimonio from 7, matriarch at Standing Rock, her home community (personal communication, 2018).
42 Eddie Proctor, lifetime coastal dweller, Echo Bay, BC (social media post, 16 November 2017).
43 Young Man's story haunted me because of its truth. I had lived in the rural North Pacific in the 1980s and was very familiar with fisherpeople and their livelihood. There, it was comfortable to live a near-subsistence lifestyle and to work with community and a Native non-profit organization, becoming further educated about rural community, species co-existence, biodiversity, the Alaska Native Claims Settlement Act (ANCSA), and sustainable practices.
44 Wild is as wild does, although marketing has claimed Atlantic farmed salmon raised in pens, subjected to life-long suffering and cruelty, penned in ocean cages where they live in filth with significant compromise from infectious sea lice, poor nutrition, viruses, and bacteria are somehow "wild," showing clearly the falsehoods perpetuated by this colonial, destructive, imposition on Indigenous and rural communities.
45 Strategic lawsuits against public participation (SLAPP suits) are delivered by corporations against individuals, abusing the courts to abrogate civil rights and threatening any critics with personal financial ruin.
46 For an analysis of the Cohen Commission recommendations, please see Watershed Watch Salmon Society (n.d.); for the full report (3 volumes), see Cohen 2012.
47 Harms via ocean-pen salmon farms include, but are not limited to, ongoing pollution via weapons of mass destruction (chemical and biological); lack of clean-up (remediation, the root of reconciliation); destruction of ecosystems, especially sea floors where waste chokes out bottom-dwellers; land theft (an act of manifest destiny) for siting their industry; violation of Indigenous rights and title guaranteed by the Canadian Charter of Rights and Freedoms, court cases, UNDRIP, and other legal mechanisms; use of police forces against land, sea, and rights defenders; vanquishment of accepted peer-reviewed scientific data, eroding confidence in the scientific model and education as a viable means of discussion and understanding; human rights abuses; abuse of the courts by industry to further erode rights and freedoms; abuse of Canadian law in favour of corporate lawlessness and destruction of the commons; abuse of other species of fish, upon whom sea mammals and birds rely, to manufacture pen food, starving out natural species of sea-dependent Beings; lack of responsibility to Land, Water, and communities of all species; escapement of Atlantic salmon who cannibalize Wild Sacred Salmon; endangering health of all

who consume farmed Atlantic ocean-pen "salmon"; pollution of the BC coast and coastal Pacific Rim with alien species salmon; destruction of Home Indigenous species of Sacred, Wild Salmon and other Beings such as sea lions, seagulls, eagles, seals, and others; lice infestation that severely compromise Sacred Wild Salmon young who travel beside fish farms and are then infected; dumping infected fish blood and waste directly into water and environs; and spreading infections such as lice, viruses, and disease.

48 "Illegal" here means hunting that contravenes Indigenous laws and responsibilities; in violation of Indigenous laws, especially as regards poaching and hunting by non-Indigenous people.

49 For a discussion of Maya resistance to Spanish rule, see Jones (1989). "Indigenous people have had clear understanding of the colonizer's disharmonious and anti-environment theology and practice, and know that if left unchecked, they would lead to an end of the specific Indian nation's way of life, and ultimately, all life on the planet. The Yucatec Maya of 1546, following their calendars and prophecies, sacrificed to maintain their ancient culture and society, and responsibility to Mother Earth" (ross 2002).

50 "'It's really terrible that in Canada we have people in tents and shacks when it's minus 15,' Turmel [NPD interim leader at the time] said after touring the town and meeting several families. There is little new in the plight of the people of Attawapiskat. Aboriginal leaders will tell you there are similar crises on reserves in northern Manitoba and northern Saskatchewan" (Toronto City News 2011).

51 To read the full report, see Wildlands League (2015).

52 "Doctor Water" is the reverent name applied to Water in Natural and Supernatural forms by Corbin Harney, Western Shoshone Medicine Man (deceased 2007). There are many spiritually respectful terms for Water in many Indigenous Nations (Harney, in-person communications, 1999–2007).

53 See also ArcGIS Online (2021) and Council of Canadians (n.d.).

54 See the film The Island President, directed by Jon Shenk (2011).

55 On average, 60 per cent of Canadian First Nations (Indigenous) reserve children live in poverty, suffering an increase from 2005–10, with food insecurity, hunger, poor housing, underfunded schools, and underfunded or non-existent child welfare services.

56 "Stop Killing Us" is a phrase from a home-made banner presented on the occasion of the annual march for Murdered and Missing Indigenous Women at the Carnegie Community Centre, Vancouver. BC.

57 Carol Muree Martin, activist, worker, and advocate with folks from Vancouver's downtown eastside (public social media post, 2019; used here with permission).

58 Regarding Bill C-51 (aka, the Anti-terrorism Act of 2015 under then prime minister Stephen Harper), Grand Chief Stewart Phillip, Union of BC Indian Chiefs, stated: "We believe this bill is less about Jihadists under every bed ... and more about increasing the output of the tarsands, and facilitating the heavy oil pipeline proposals across the country, and will serve to severely undermine the constitutional and human rights of indigenous peoples" (quoted in O'Malley 2015).

59 For more information on the women of Juarez, please see Simmons (2006).

60 Overconsumption and heavy consumption of meat, typical in the Western diet, contribute significantly and are "incompatible with climate goals" (Carrington 2014).

61 "Convenience foods" are defined here as calorie-dense, nutritionally poor, consumable products, those highly processed, GMO, pesticide- and/or chemical-laden foods, which take the place of traditional foods and those edibles close to their source of origination.

62 Please do not read this endnote unless you absolutely must, as it is obscene. "Rape her until she cums black gold" (Facebook comment by a tar sands worker discussing his work and advocating rape against female Land Defenders); on Robert Pickton, one of Canada's serial killers of Indigenous and other women, please see Stevie Cameron (2011); on the link between cruelty meat, factory farms, and violence against women, please see Carol J. Adams (2015).

63 These violations are parallel to similar violations against Indigenous peoples via gold mining and hydroelectric dams in Central America.

64 Examples of this system include (1) gathering goods collectively in order to give them away community-wide; (2) constant gifting and regifting of foods, medicines, plants, handmade goods, cultural properties held in common, and other items; (3) open display of wealth only in order to share wealth; (4) joint use of shared areas with strict protocol to maintain life and thrivance of all Beings; and (5) friendship and relationship protocols that ensure no action is taken that destroys the neighbours' territory (especially in regards to migratory species such as Sacred Wild Salmon).

65 Please note the Obama White House, House and Senate leaders' affiliations with corporate giants that sponsor bills and political campaigns such as non-labelling of their GMO "foods" in order to protect personal profit (Hauter 2016; see also Renter 2013).

66 "US Right to Know is a non-profit organization working for transparency and accountability in our nation's food system." The US Right to Know agrichemical documents "collection includes documents acquired ... through state public records requests, FOIA [Freedom of Information Act] requests, whistleblowers, and litigation" (Ruskin and Gillam n.d.).

67 "Engaging with the World" is the motto of Simon Fraser University.

68 Author Joanna Macy finds the need for a "nuclear priesthood," a "transgenerational nuclear guardianship" made up of people who would live their lives at sites of nuclear and radiological contaminations with the purpose of monitoring and warning others away from certain danger and harm. Macy finds this necessary, as nuclear contamination lasts longer than signage, symbols, or language, and it is our responsibility to warn future generations into imaginable perpetuity. See Brandt (2015).

69 One of the biggest copper mines globally is Alumbrera, Argentina, where "affected communities have organized to press criminal charges against the mine operators (Goldcorp, Xstrata, and Northern Orion) for the damage they have done to the natural environment and especially to water resources" (Rights Action 2008). At the time of this writing, it is unknown as to the outcome of these cases.

Also, "for the first time in Latin America, criminal charges have been laid against a mining company for crimes against the environment. On June 6, 2008, the Federal Chambers of Tucuman brought charges of environmental contamination against Julian Rooney, VP of Bajo La Alumbrera. He was not jailed, but his possessions were impounded. The Alumbrera copper-gold mine is owned by Swiss giant XSTRATA COPPER (50% and operator), Vancouver-based GOLDCORP (37.5%) and Toronto's YAMANA GOLD (12.5%)" (Canadian Mining Journal 2008).

Further, in February 2020, the Supreme Court of Canada ruled that a human rights lawsuit against a mining company (Nevsun Resources) can be heard in Canada (Amnesty International 2020).

REFERENCES

Abbott, Jeff. 2018. "Something in the Water: The Lasting Violence of a Canadian Mining Company in Guatemala." *Briarpatch*, 29 August 2018. https://briarpatchmagazine.com/articles/view /something-in-the-water.

ACLU (American Civil Liberties Union). 2012. "Students Sue U.C. Davis over Pepper-Spraying." *YouTube*, 6 March 2012. https://www.youtube.com /watch?v=OmQnkQbiDeI.

Adams, Carol J. 2015. *The Sexual Politics of Meat: A Feminist-Vegetarian Critical Theory*. New York: Bloomsbury Academic.

ADISMI (Association for the Integral Development of San Miguel and Communities in Resistance in San Miguel Ixtahuacán). 2007. "The Negative Impacts of the Goldcorp/Marlin Mine in Maya Mam and Sipakapense Territory." With Rights Action / Derechos en Accion. Translated by Rosalind Gil. https://static1.squarespace.com/static/5e333dd15d21eb4f38e57e9d/t

/5eed36dcedb2ed6e5ab2c744/1592604380477/07-11-21.GC-GT.Rp-ADISMI
.htm.pdf.

Aggie Studios. 2011. *UC Davis Protesters Pepper Sprayed* (video). *YouTube*, 18
November 2011. https://www.youtube.com/watch?v=6AdDLhPwpp4.

Amnesty International. n.d.-a. "Our Work: Issues: Indigenous Peoples in
Canada." *Amnesty International*. https://www.amnesty.ca/our-work
/issues/indigenous-peoples/indigenous-peoples-in-canada.

– n.d.-b "Standing Rock." *Amnesty International*. https://www.amnestyusa
.org/standing-rock/.

– 2017. "Angelica Choc v. Hudbay Minerals." *Amnesty International*, 7 March
2017. https://www.amnesty.ca/legal-brief/angelica-choc-v-hudbay
-minerals.

– 2018. "Justice for Grassy Narrows." *Amnesty International*, 24 May 2018.
https://www.amnesty.ca/news/grassy-narrows-new-report-strongest
-evidence-yet-mercury-poisoning.

– 2020. "Mining Company Lawsuit Can Be Heard in Canada, Rules Supreme
Court in Historic Decision." *Amnesty International*, 28 February 2020.
https://www.amnesty.ca/news/mining-company-lawsuit-can-be-heard
-canada-rules-supreme-court-historic-decision.

Appleman, Roy. E. 1939. "Timber Empire from the Public Domain." *Mississippi
Valley Historical Review* 26 (2): 193–208. https://doi.org/10.2307/1897743.

ArcGIS Online. 2021. "First Nation Communities Drinking Water Advisories
South of 60." https://www.arcgis.com/apps/instant/minimalist/index
.html?appid=6270f51978984c688dadbc6d382277c0.

Ball, David. 2013. "Coastal First Nations Vow 'Good Fight' to Stop Grizzly
Hunt: Province, First Nations Coalition in Jurisdictional Battle over
Controversial Trophy Hunt." *The Tyee*, 5 September 2013. https://thetyee
.ca/News/2013/09/05/GrizzlyHuntFight/.

BCBC (Business Council of British Columbia). 2019. "Governance: Executive
Committee." Accessed fall 2019. https://www.bcbc.com/about/governance.

BCLA (British Columbia Civil Liberties Association). 2020. "Civil Liberties
and Indigenous Rights Groups Call on CRCC to Immediately Take
Conduct of Investigation into Wet'Suwet'en Land Defender's Police
Complaint." Press Release. *BCLA*, 27 August 2020. https://bccla.org
/news/2020/08/civil-liberties-and-indigenous-rights-groups-call-on
-crcc-to-immediately-take-conduct-of-investigation-into-wetsuweten-land
-defenders-police-complaint/.

Berry, Wendell. 2003. *The Art of the Commonplace: The Agrarian Essays
of Wendell Berry*. Edited by Norman Wirzba. Berkeley, CA: Counterpoint
Press.

Blaut, James. 1993. *The Colonizers Model of the World: Geographical Diffusionism
and Eurocentric History*. New York: Guilford Press.

Brandt, Werner. 2015. "Transgenerational Nuclear Guardianship – Joanna Macy." *Work That Reconnects Network*, 1 December 2015. https://workthatreconnects.org/resource/transgenerational-nuclear-guardianship-joanna-macy/.

Brophy, Edna, and Myka Ticker-Abramson. 2011. "From Utopian Institutions to Global University: Simon Fraser University and Crisis of Canadian Public Education." *EduFactory webjournal* 1: 6–21. https://transversal.at/media/attachments/edufactory-journal-1.pdf.

Bruser, David, and Jayme Poisson. 2017. "Ontario Knew about Grassy Narrows Mercury Site for Decades, But Kept It Secret." *Toronto Star*, 11 November 2017. https://www.thestar.com/news/canada/2017/11/11/ontario-knew-about-mercury-site-near-grassy-narrows-for-decades-but-kept-it-secret.html.

Cameron, Stevie. 2011. *On the Farm: Robert William Pickton and the Tragic Story of Vancouver's Missing Women.* Toronto: Vintage Canada.

Canadian Center for International Justice. 2017. "In Milestone, Court Clears Guatemalans' Lawsuit against Vancouver Mining Company to Go to Trial." Business and Human Rights Resource Centre. https://www.business-humanrights.org/en/latest-news/in-milestone-bc-court-clears-guatemalans-lawsuit-against-vancouver-mining-company-to-go-to-trial/.

Canadian Mining Journal. 2008. "ENVIRONMENT – Argentina Lays Criminal Charges against Alumbrera." *Canadian Mining Journal*, 29 June 2008. https://www.canadianminingjournal.com/news/environment-argentina-lays-criminal-charges-against-alumbrera/.

Canadian Press. 2012. "Bear Hunting Ban Declared by 10 B.C. First Nations." *CBC News*, 13 September 2012. https://www.cbc.ca/news/canada/british-columbia/bear-hunting-ban-declared-by-10-b-c-first-nations-1.1180591.

Carolino, Bernise. 2021. "Osgood Professor Asks Feds to Disclose Alleged Aid to Goldcorp in Human Rights Disputes." *Canadian Lawyer*, 12 March 2021. https://www.canadianlawyermag.com/practice-areas/litigation/osgoode-professor-asks-feds-to-disclose-alleged-aid-to-goldcorp-in-human-rights-dispute/353899.

Carrington, Damian. 2014. "Eating Less Meat Essential to Curb Climate Change, Says Report." *The Guardian*, 3 December 2014. https://www.theguardian.com/environment/2014/dec/03/eating-less-meat-curb-climate-change.

– 2016. "Climate Change Will Stir 'Unimaginable' Refugee Crisis, Says Military." *The Guardian*, 1 December 2016. https://www.theguardian.com/environment/2016/dec/01/climate-change-trigger-unimaginable-refugee-crisis-senior-military.

CBC News. 2016. "NHLer Clayton Stoner Fined $10K for Hunting Grizzly Bear without a Proper License." *CBC News*, 17 January 2016. https://www.cbc.ca /news/canada/british-columbia/clayton-stoner-pleads-guilty-1.3421884.

Chan, Emily. 2015. "At Least 1,838 Drinking Water Advisories across Canada: Report." *CTV News*, 13 March 2015. https://www.ctvnews.ca/health /at-least-1-838-drinking-water-advisories-across-canada-report-1.2278160.

Chomsky, Noam. 2002. *Understanding Power: The Indispensable Chomsky*. Edited by Peter R. Mitchell and John Schoeffel. New York: The New Press.

Civil Liberties Defense Center (Oregon). 2020. "Standing Rock Indigenous Water Protector Sues North Dakota Police for Abuse of Civil Rights." Press Release, 8 April 2020. https://cldc.org/wp-content/uploads/2020 /04/040820-FINAL-Poemoceah-complt-PR_.pdf.

Cohen, Bruce. 2012. *The Uncertain Future of Fraser River Sockeye*. 3 vols. Commission of Inquiry into the Decline of Sockeye Salmon in the Fraser River. CP32-93/2012E. Ottawa: Privy Council. http://www.publications .gc.ca/site/eng/432516/publication.html.

Council of Canadians. n.d. "Safe Water for First Nations." https://canadians .org/fn-water.

Cox, Sarah. 2019. "United Nations Instructs Canada to Suspend Site C Dam Construction over Indigenous Rights Violations." *The Narwhal*, 9 January 2019. https://thenarwhal.ca/united-nations-instructs-canada-to-suspend -site-c-dam-construction-over-indigenous-rights-violations/.

Crystal, Valerie, Shin Imai, and Bernadette Maheandiran. 2014. "Access to Justice and Corporate Accountability: A Legal Case Study of Hudbay in Guatemala." *Canadian Journal of Development Studies* 35 (2): 285–303. https://doi.org/10.1080/02255189.2014.908274.

Desai, Saima. 2019. "Group Hopes Courts Will Force U of S to Release Documents on Ties to Monsanto." *Briarpatch*, 28 February 2019. https:// briarpatchmagazine.com/saskdispatch/view/group-hopes-courts-will -force-u-of-s-to-release-documents-on-ties-to-monsan.

Findlay, Andrew. 2019. "Canadian Mining Companies Now Face Human Rights Charges in Canadian Courts." *The Narwhal*, 7 June 2019. https:// thenarwhal.ca/canadian-mining-companies-will-now-face-human -rights-charges-in-canadian-courts/.

Franta, Benjamin, and Geoffrey Supran. 2017. "The Fossil Fuel Industry's Invisible Colonization of Academia." *The Guardian*, 13 March 2017. https://www.theguardian.com/environment/climate-consensus-97 -per-cent/2017/mar/13/the-fossil-fuel-industrys-invisible-colonization -of-academia.

Friends of the Earth. 2012. "Goldcorp: Environmental Criminal: Canadian Mining Corporation and Its Criminal Record in Guatemala." *Friends of the Earth / Les Ami(e)s de la Terre*, 16 November 2012. https://foecanada

.org/2012/11/canadian-mining-corporation-and-its-criminal-record-in
-guatemala/.

Gilson, Shelby. 2019. "'My Ears Keep Ringing All the Time': Mercury
Poisoning among Grassy Narrows First Nation. *Pulitzer Center*, 29 July 2019.
https://pulitzercenter.org/stories/my-ears-keep-ringing-all-time-mercury
-poisoning-among-grassy-narrows-first-nation.

Glasbeek, Harry J. 1984. "Why Corporate Deviance Is Not Treated as a
Crime: The Need to Make 'Profits' a Dirty Word." *Osgoode Hall Law
Journal* 22 (3): 393–439. https://digitalcommons.osgoode.yorku.ca/ohlj
/vol22/iss3/1/.

Global Witness. 2019. *Enemies of the State? How Governments and Business
Silence Land and Environmental Defenders*. London: Global Witness. https://
www.globalwitness.org/en/campaigns/environmental-activists
/enemies-state/.

– 2020. *Defending Tomorrow: The Climate Crisis and Threats against Land
and Environmental Defenders*. London: Global Witness. https://
www.globalwitness.org/en/campaigns/environmental-activists
/defending-tomorrow/.

Gordon, Todd. 2010. *Imperialist Canada*. Winnipeg: ARP Books.

Hauter, Wenonah. 2016. "The United States of Monsanto?" *Huffington Post*,
14 March 2016. https://www.huffpost.com/entry/the-united-states
-of-mons_b_9440798.

Hedges, Chris. 2013. "The Treason of the Intellectuals." *Truthdig*, 7 July 2015
(original publication 2013). https://www.truthdig.com/articles/the
-treason-of-the-intellectuals/.

Hennessy, Angela. 2013. "Did Canadian Law Enforcement Just Ambush
a Peaceful Mi'kmaq Anti-Fracking Protest? Only If Responding
to Drums and Feathers with Dogs and Snipers Counts." *Vice*, 18 October
2013. https://www.vice.com/amp/sv/article/4w7ymm/did-the-rcmp
-just-ambush-a-peaceful-native-anti-fracking-protest.

Hilberg, Raul. 2003. *The Destruction of the European Jews*. 3rd ed. New Haven,
CT: Yale University Press.

Hoffman, Al. 2015. *Mount Polley Mine Tailings Storage Facility Breach, August
4, 2014: Investigation Report of the Chief Inspector of Mines*. BC Ministry of
Energy and Mines, Mining and Mineral Resources Division, 30 November
2015. https://www2.gov.bc.ca/assets/gov/farming-natural-resources-and
-industry/mineral-exploration-mining/documents/directives-alerts
-incidents/chief-inspector-s-report-page/m-200_mount_polley_2015
-11-30_ci_investigation_report.pdf.

Holocaust Encyclopedia. n.d. "What Is Genocide?" *Holocaust Encyclopedia*,
US Holocaust Memorial Museum. https://encyclopedia.ushmm.org
/content/en/article/what-is-genocide.

Honor the Earth. n.d. "Man Camps Fact Sheet: Chasing Out the Specter of Man Camps." *Honor the Earth.* https://www.honorearth.org/man _camps_fact_sheet.

Hopi Dictionary Project. 1998. *Hopìikwa Lavàytutuveni. Hopi Dictionary: A Hopi-English Dictionary of Third Mesa Dialect.* Tucson: University of Arizona Press.

Horwitz, Sari. 2014. "Dark Side of the Boom: North Dakota's Oil Rush Brings Cash and Promise to Reservation, Along with Drug-Fueled Crime." *The Washington Post,* 28 September 2014. https://www.washingtonpost.com/sf /national/2014/09/28/dark-side-of-the-boom/.

Imai, Shin, Leah Gardner, and Sarah Weinberger. 2017. "The 'Canada Brand': Violence and Canadian Mining Companies in Latin America." Osgoode Legal Studies Research Paper No. 17/2017. http://dx.doi.org/10.2139 /ssrn.2886584.

Imai, Shin, Bernadette Maheandiran, and Valerie Crystal. 2012. "Accountability across Borders: Mining in Guatemala and the Canadian Justice System." *Comparative Research in Law and Political Economy.* Research Paper No. 26/2012. https://digitalcommons.osgoode.yorku.ca /clpe/28/.

Imai, Shin, Ladan Mehranvar, and Jennifer Sander. 2007. "Breaching Indigenous Law: Canadian Mining in Guatemala." *Indigenous Law Journal* 6 (1): 101–39. https://digitalcommons.osgoode.yorku.ca /scholarly_works/802/.

International Rivers. n.d. "Murdered for their Rivers: A Roster of Fallen Dam Fighters." *International Rivers: People, Water, Life.* https:// www.internationalrivers.org/murdered-for-their-rivers-a-roster-of -fallen-dam-fighters/.

Jones, Grant D. 1989. *Maya Resistance to Spanish Rule: Time and History on a Colonial Frontier.* Albuquerque: University of New Mexico Press.

Kappo, Tanya. 2014. "Stephen Harper's Comments on Missing, Murdered Aboriginal Women Show 'Lack of Respect.'" *CBC News,* 19 December 2014. https://www.cbc.ca/news/indigenous/stephen-harper-s-comments-on -missing-murdered-aboriginal-women-show-lack-of-respect-1.2879154.

Kral, Michael. 2012. "Postcolonial Suicide among Inuit in Arctic Canada." *Culture, Medicine, and Psychiatry* 36: 306–25. https://doi.org/10.1007 /s11013-012-9253-3.

Lakhani, Nina. (2021, 5 July). "Berta Cáceres Assassination: Ex-head of Dam Company Found Guilty." *The Guardian.* https://www.theguardian.com /world/2021/jul/05/berta-caceres-assassination-roberto-david-castillo -found-guilty.

Lemkin, Raphael. 1944. *Axis Rule in Occupied Europe: Laws of Occupation, Analysis of Government, Proposals for Redress.* Washington, DC: Carnegie Endowment for International Peace.

– 2013. *Totally Unofficial: Autobiography of Raphael Lemkin*. Edited by Donna-Lee Frieze. New Haven, CT: Yale University Press.

Levin, Sam. 2016. "Dakota Access Pipeline Protests: UN Group Investigates Human Rights Abuses." *The Guardian*, 31 October 2016. https://www.theguardian.com/us-news/2016/oct/31/dakota-access-pipeline-protest-investigation-human-rights-abuses.

Lexpert Business of Law Magazine. 2013. "Ontario Superior Court Decision in Choc v. Hudbay Minerals Paves Way for Defining Responsibility of Canadian Companies with Foreign Operations." *Lexpert Business of Law Magazine*, November/December 2013. https://www.lexpert.ca/article/ontario-superior-court-decision-in-choc-v-hudbay-minerals-paves-way-for-defining-responsibility-of-canadian-companies-with-foreign-operations/.

Lipton, Eric. 2015. "Food Industry Enlisted Academics in G.M.O. Lobbying War, Emails Show." *New York Times*, 5 September 2015. https://www.nytimes.com/2015/09/06/us/food-industry-enlisted-academics-in-gmo-lobbying-war-emails-show.html.

Los Alamos Study Group. 2005. "Hiroshima Survivor, Disarmament Advocates to Attend Gross 'Blast from the Past' Weapons Fete at National Atomic Museum." http://www.lasg.org/ActionAlerts/ActionAlerts2005.htm.

Lui, Emma. 2015. *On Notice for Drinking Water Crisis in Canada*. Ottawa: The Council of Canadians. https://canadians.org/sites/default/files/publications/report-drinking-water-0315_0.pdf.

Malkan, Stacy. 2019. "Monsanto Relied on These 'Partners' to Attack Top Cancer Scientists." *U.S. Right to Know*, 31 March 2019. https://usrtk.org/gmo/monsanto-relied-on-these-partners-to-attack-top-cancer-scientists/.

– 2020. "Corporate Influence at the University of Saskatchewan: Professor Peter Phillips and His Secret 'Right To Know Symposium.'" *U.S. Right to Know*, 11 June 2020. https://usrtk.org/our-investigations/corporate-influence-at-the-university-of-saskatchewan-professor-peter-phillips-and-his-secret-right-to-know-symposium/.

Manuel, Kanahus. 2014. *Indigenous Resistance to the Mount Polley Mine Disaster* (webinar). With Secwepemc Elder Jean William and Joan Kuyek. *YouTube*, 17 September 2014. https://www.youtube.com/watch?v=lUbHMMVzwEY.

Manz, Beatriz. 2008. "The Continuum of Violence in Post-war Guatemala." *Social Analysis: The International Journal of Anthropology* 52 (2): 151–64. https://doi.org/10.3167/sa.2008.520209.

McNeil, Kent. 2000. "Aboriginal Title as a Constitutionally Protected Right." In *Beyond the Nass Valley: National Implications of the Supreme Court's Delgamuukw Decision*, edited by Owen Lippert, 55–75. Vancouver, BC: Fraser Institute, 2000.

– 2005. "Aboriginal Rights, Resource Development, and the Source of the Provincial Duty to Consult in Haida Nation and Taku River." *The Supreme Court Law Review: Osgoode Annual Constitutional Cases Conference* 29. https://digitalcommons.osgoode.yorku.ca/sclr/vol29/iss1/21.

Mickleburgh, Rod. 2018. "1983: The Year BC Citizens and Workers Fought Back." *The Tyee*, 6 July 2018. https://thetyee.ca/Opinion/2018/07/06/Year-BC-Citizens-Workers-Fought-Back/.

Miller, Vanessa. 2019. "University of Iowa Tells Faculty Not to Promote Greta Thunberg Visit via UI Social Media: 'This Event Does Not Fall within the Scope of Something We Can Promote.'" *The Gazette*, 4 October 2019. https://www.thegazette.com/subject/news/education/greta-thunberg-iowa-city-climate-strike-university-of-iowa-facebook-post-social-media-20191004.

MiningWatch Canada and ICLMG (International Civil Liberties Monitoring Group). 2015. "Highlights from *In the National Interest? Criminalization of Land and Environment Defenders in the Americas*." https://miningwatch.ca/publications/2015/9/21/national-interest-criminalization-land-and-environment-defenders-americas.

Morris, William, ed. 1971. *The American Heritage Dictionary of the English Language*. Boston: American Heritage Publishing and Houghton Mifflin Company.

Morton, Alexandra. 2017. "The First Scientific Evidence that Farm Salmon Are Infecting Large Numbers of Wild Salmon." *Raincoast Research*, December 2017. http://alexandramorton.typepad.com/alexandra_morton/2017/11/higher-virus-infection-rates-in-wild-salmon-exposed-to-fish-farms-broughton-archipelago-and-discovery-islands-most-heavi.html.

Morton, Alexandra, Richard Routledge, Stacey Hrushowy, Molly Kibenge, and Frederick Kibenge. 2017. "The Effect of Exposure to Farmed Salmon on Piscine Orthoreovirus Infection and Fitness in Wild Pacific Salmon in British Columbia, Canada." *PLoS ONE* 12 (12): e0188793. https://doi.org/10.1371/journal.pone.0188793.

Nader, Ralph. 2018. "Land of the Lawless: How Power in America Has Turned the Rule of Law into a Mere Myth." *Lapham's Quarterly* 11 (2). https://www.laphamsquarterly.org/rule-law/land-lawless.

Nader, Ralph, and Chris Hedges. 2018. "American Mythology and the Loss of Democracy." *On Contact*, hosted by Chris Hedges (television series). *RT*, 24 June 2018. https://www.rt.com/shows/on-contact/430720-nader-us-mythology-democracy/.

The Narwhal. n.d. "News and Information on the Mount Polley Mine Disaster." *The Narwhal*. https://thenarwhal.ca/topics/mount-polley-mine-disaster/.

Norrell, Brenda. 2017. "The Intercept Exposes FBI Informant Owned Gun in
    Red Fawn Case at Standing Rock." *Censored News*, 11 December 2017. https://
    bsnorrell.blogspot.ca/2017/12/the-intercept-exposes-fbi-informant.html.
Office of the Auditor General of British Columbia. 2016a. *An Audit of
    Compliance and Enforcement in the Mining Sector.* Victoria, BC: Office
    of the Auditor General. https://www.bcauditor.com/pubs/2016
    /audit-compliance-and-enforcement-mining-sector.
– 2016b. "Compliance and Enforcement Lacking in B.C.'s Mining Sector."
    News Release, 3 May 2016. https://www.bcauditor.com/sites/default
    /files/publications/news-releases/MEDIA_Compliance_and
    _Enforcement_Mining_NR_FINAL.pdf.
Office of the Commissioner of Lobbying in Canada. n.d. "Registry of
    Lobbyists: Business Council of British Columbia." https://lobbycanada
    .gc.ca/app/secure/ocl/lrs/do/vwRg?cno=16634&regId=512079.
Olivier, Louise. 2016. "Forensic Evidence Represents a Turning Point for
    Justice in Guatemala." *Open Society Foundation*, 25 March 2016. https://
    www.opensocietyfoundations.org/voices/forensic-evidence-represents
    -turning-point-justice-guatemala.
O'Malley, Kady. 2015. "Bill C-51 Hearings: First Nations Could Be Targeted,
    Pam Palmater Says." *CBC News*, 24 March 2015. http://www.cbc.ca/news
    /politics/bill-c-51-hearings-first-nations-could-be-targeted-pam-palmater
    -says-1.3006731.
Parrish, Will. 2017. "An Activist Stands Accused of Firing a Gun at Standing
    Rock. It Belonged to Her Lover – An FBI Informant." *The Intercept*,
    11 December 2017. https://theintercept.com/2017/12/11/standing-rock
    -dakota-access-pipeline-fbi-informant-red-fawn-fallis/.
Parvini, Sarah. 2016. "UC Davis Spends $175,000 to Sanitize Its Online Image
    after Ugly Pepper Spray Episode." *Los Angeles Times*, 14 April 2016. https://
    www.latimes.com/local/lanow/la-me-ln-uc-davis-pepper-spray
    -20160414-story.html.
Pedersen, Alexandra. 2014. "Landscapes of Resistance: Community
    Opposition to Canadian Mining Operations in Guatemala." *Journal of Latin
    American Geography* 13 (1): 187–214. http://dx.doi.org/10.1353/lag.2014.0018.
– 2015. "Canadian Mining Undermines Democracy in Central America:
    Canada's multinationals Work Hand-In-Hand with Corrupt Governments
    and Threaten Democracy in Post-Conflict Central American Nations."
    MiningWatch Canada (blog), 24 August 2015. https://miningwatch.ca/blog
    /2015/8/24/canadian-mining-undermines-democracy-central-america.
Phillip, Grand Chief Stewart, and Robert Phillips. 2018. "Stewart Phillip and
    Robert Phillips: Mining Reform Is a Tale of Broken Promises." *The Province*,
    27 September 2018. https://theprovince.com/opinion/op-ed/stewart
    -phillip-and-robert-phillips-mining-reform-is-a-tale-of-broken-promises.

Porter, Jody. 2017. "De Beers Victor Mine Fails to Monitor Mercury Risk, Environmental Group Says." *CBC News*, 21 December 2017. https://www.cbc.ca/news/canada/sudbury/de-beers-victor-mine-fails-to-monitor-mercury-risk-environmental-group-says-1.3371451.

Pynn, Larry. 2010. "Changing History: The Legacy of Lyle Island, 25 Years Later." *Vancouver Sun*, 13 November 2010. https://www.pressreader.com/canada/vancouver-sun/20101113/287745630086315.

Rainforest Action Network. 2005. *American Dream, American Nightmare: The Truth about Weyerhaeuser's "Green" Products and Homes.* https://www.ran.org/wp-content/uploads/2018/06/weyerhauser_report_(1).pdf.

Renter, Elizabeth. 2013. "Exposed: List Emerges of Politicians Paid by Monsanto, as Senate Rejects States' Rights to Label GMOs." *Occupy.com*, 20 May 2013. https://www.occupy.com/article/exposed-list-emerges-politicians-paid-monsanto-senate-rejects-states-rights-label-gmos.

Richardson, Benjamin J. 2007. "Protecting Indigenous Peoples through Socially Responsible Investment." *Indigenous Law Journal* 6 (1): 205–34. https://digitalcommons.osgoode.yorku.ca/scholarly_works/803/.

Rights Action. 2008. *Investing in Conflict: Public Money, Private Gain: Goldcorp in the Americas.* Toronto, ON: Rights Action. https://miningwatch.ca/sites/default/files/mininggoldcorpbw042608.pdf.

Roache, Trina. 2014. "2 Mi'kmaq Warriors Sentenced to 15 Months over Elsipogtog Fracking Fight." *APTN National News*, 30 July 2014. https://www.aptnnews.ca/national-news/2-mikmaq-warriors-sentenced-15-months-elsipogtog-fracking-fight/.

ross, annie. 2002. "One Mother Earth, One Doctor Water: A Story about Environmental Justice in the Age of Nuclearism. A Native American View." PhD diss., University of California, Davis.

Ruskin, Gary, and Carey Gillam. n.d. "US Right to Know Agrichemical Documents." University of California San Francisco Library Chemical Industry Documents. https://www.industrydocuments.ucsf.edu/chemical/collections/usrtk-agrichemical-collection/.

Russell, Grahame. 2016. "Canadian Mining Harms around the World: Criminal and Civil Law Reform Needed Now." *MiningWatch Canada*, 13 November 2016. https://miningwatch.ca/news/2016/11/13/canadian-mining-harms-around-world-criminal-and-civil-law-reform-needed-now.

– 2020. "Will Justice Be Possible in Canada or Guatemala for Hudbay Minerals Mining Repression?" *Rights Action*, 22 May 2020. https://rightsaction.org/emails/will-justice-be-possible-in-canada-or-guatemala-for-hudbay-minerals-mining-repression.

Scott, Dayna Nadine. 2013. "The Networked Infrastructure of Fossil Capitalism: Implications of the New Pipeline Debates for Environmental

Justice in Canada." *Comparative Research in Law & Political Economy.* Research Paper No. 27/2013. https://digitalcommons.osgoode.yorku.ca /clpe/274.

Shenk, Jon, director. 2011. *The Island President* (documentary film). San Francisco: Actual Films.

Simmons, William Paul. 2006. "Remedies for Women of Cuidad Juarez through the Inter-American Court of Human Rights." *Northwest Journal of International Human Rights* 4 (3). https://scholarlycommons.law .northwestern.edu/njihr/vol4/iss3/2/.

StudentScholarships.org. 2021. "Suncor Emerging Leaders Award." *StudentScholarships.org.* https://studentscholarships.org/scholarship/8291 /suncor_emerging_leaders_award.php.

Supreme Court of Canada. 1973. *Calder v. British Columbia* (AG) [1973] SCR 313, [1973] 4 WWR 1. https://scc-csc.lexum.com/scc-csc/scc-csc/en/item/5113 /index.do.

– 1997. *Delgamuukw v. British Columbia* [1997] 3 SCR 1010. https://scc-csc .lexum.com/scc-csc/scc-csc/en/item/1569/index.do.

– 2014. *Tsilhqot'in Nation v. British Columbia* 2014 SCC 44, [2014] 2 S.C.R. 256. https://scc-csc.lexum.com/scc-csc/scc-csc/en/item/14246/index.do.

– 2020a. "Case in Brief: *Nevsun Resources Ltd. v. Araya.*" https://www.scc -csc.ca/case-dossier/cb/2020/37919-eng.aspx.

– 2020b. *Nevsun Resources Ltd. v. Araya* [2020] SCC 5. https://www.canlii.org /en/ca/scc/doc/2020/2020scc5/2020scc5.html.

Suzuki, David. 2018. "Large Dams Fail on Climate Change and Indigenous Rights." With David Schindler. *David Suzuki Foundation*, 18 January 2018. https://davidsuzuki.org/story/large-dams-fail-climate-change -indigenous-rights/.

Taft, Kevin. 2017. *Oil's Deep State: How the Petroleum Industry Undermines Democracy and Stops Action on Global Warming – in Alberta, and in Ottawa.* Toronto: James Lorimer.

Tedlock, Dennis, trans. 1996. *Popol Vuh: The Mayan Book of the Dawn of Life.* New York: Touchstone.

Toronto City News. 2011. "Faced with Extreme Poverty, Attawapiskat Reserve Cries Out for Help." *City News*, 30 November 2011. https:// toronto.citynews.ca/2011/11/30/faced-with-extreme-poverty -attawapiskat-reserve-cries-out-for-help/.

Turpel-Lafond, Mary Ellen. 2021. "The Discovery of a Mass Gravesite at a Former Residential School in Kamloops Is Just the Tip of the Iceberg." *The Globe and Mail*, 30 May 2021. https://www.theglobeandmail.com/opinion /article-the-discovery-of-a-mass-grave-at-a-former-residential-school-is-just/.

UBCIC (Union of British Columbia Indian Chiefs). 2016. "UBCIC Supports Actions Recognizing Mount Polley Devastation." News Release, 10 August 2016. https://www.ubcic.bc.ca/mountpolleydevastation.

United Nations. 2007. *United Nations Declaration on the Rights of Indigenous Peoples* (UNDRIP). https://www.un.org/development/desa /indigenouspeoples/declaration-on-the-rights-of-indigenous-peoples.html.

United Nations Committee on the Elimination of Racial Discrimination. 2017. *Concluding Observations on the Combined Twenty-First to Twenty-Third Periodic Report of Canada.* CERD/C/CAN/CO/21-23. Adopted by the Committee at its ninety-third session, 31 July to 25 August 2017. https://undocs.org/en /CERD/C/CAN/CO/21-23.

Vancouver Sun. 2007. "A Lumberman's Life." *Vancouver Sun,* 27 July 2007. https://www.pressreader.com/canada/vancouver-sun/20070727 /282608848413031.

Warick, Jason. 2017. "U of S professor Says There's Nothing Unusual about His Ties to Monsanto: Documents Show Agri-Business Coached Peter Phillips, Edited Academic Articles." *CBC News,* 7 May 2017. https:// www.cbc.ca/news/canada/saskatoon/u-of-s-professor-says-there -s-nothing-unusual-about-his-ties-to-monsanto-1.4100399.

Watershed Watch Salmon Society. n.d. "Cohen Report Card." https:// watershedwatch.ca/resource/cohen-report-card/.

Watts, Jonathan. 2019. "Murder, Rape and Claims of Contamination at a Tanzanian Gold Mine." *The Guardian,* 18 June 2019. https:// www.theguardian.com/environment/2019/jun/18/murder-rape-claims -of-contamination-tanzanian-goldmine.

Werring, John. 2007. *High and Dry: An Investigation of Salmon Habitat Destruction in British Columbia.* Vancouver, BC: David Suzuki Foundation.

WGBH. 1988. *American Experience* (series). "Indians, Outlaws, and Angie Debo." WGBH Media Library and Archives. http://openvault.wgbh.org /catalog/V_DC690F33B85B4DE9B685B2DFEA9E5756.

Wildlands League. 2015. *Nothing to See Here … Failures of Self-Monitoring and Reporting of Mercury at the De Beers Victor Diamond Mine in Canada.* Toronto: Wildlands League. https://wildlandsleague.org/publications /nothing-to-see-here/.

Williams, Ginger, and Jennifer Disney. 2015. "Militarism and Its Discontents: Neoliberalism, Repression, and Resistance in Twenty-First Century US-Latin American Relations." *Social Justice* 41 (3): 1–28. https://www.jstor .org/stable/24361630.

Wonders, Karen. 2010. "Greenwashing Weyerhaeuser." *Cathedral Grove,* 10 October 2010. http://www.cathedralgrove.eu/text/05-Pictures-Politics-10.htm.

Woodin, Hayley. 2015. "Goldcorp's Marlin Mine: A Decade of Operations and Controversy in Guatemala." *BIV,* 4 May 2015. https://biv.com/article /2015/05/goldcorps-marlin-mine-decade-operations-and-contro.

2 The State Is a Man: Theresa Spence, Loretta Saunders, and the Gender of Settler Sovereignty

AUDRA SIMPSON

This chapter[1] makes two very simple arguments: one about settler statecraft and the other about settler imperative. First, Canada requires the death and "disappearance" of Indigenous women in order to secure its sovereignty.[2] Second, this sovereign death drive then requires us to think about the ways in which we imagine not only nations and states but also what counts as governance itself. Underpinning these arguments is a crucial premise: Canada likes to tell an innocent story about itself – that it is a place founded by immigrants and settlers, which somehow escaped the ugliness of history, a place very different from the place south of it, across that border. Canada is not like that other place for many reasons, it tells itself.[3] However, it is especially exceptional now, because it has apologized; it stood and faced its history, and it has "reconciled" the violence of the past with its present. Presumably, with this acknowledgment of wrongdoing, Canada may move on. These emotional gestures, registered at an institutionalized state level, are undermined by an extractive and simultaneously murderous state of affairs. In spite of the present-day discourses from Canadian political scientists and policymakers that imagine a process of equality through the space afforded to Indigenous political orders as the "third order of government,"[4] the evidence suggests that Canada is quite simply a settler society whose multicultural, liberal, and democratic structure and performance of governance seeks an ongoing "settling" of this land. The process of settlement is definitely *contra* equality. I will speak more of the evidence shortly. This settling thus is not innocent – it is dispossession, the taking of Indigenous lands. And it is not over; it is ongoing. It is killing Native women[5] in order to take the land and has historically done so. This killing allows me to qualify the governance project as gendered and murderous.

Relatedly, Jodi Byrd's (2011) *Transit of Empire* structures its intervention using two methodological axes: one of "cacophony," the other of "transit." It is through these axes that history is known, possibility made, and that difference is rendered. With "cacophony," there is the possibility of multiple, sometimes competing and contesting, narratives of truth and, within them, possibility as well. But with multiplicity also comes the riot of noise that requires an ear and decipherment, an audibility but perhaps also a willingness to listen. With these two axes/methodological modalities introduced to us, we see Byrd's analytic commitments unfold. Indigeneity, she argues, operates as a transit, an emptying nodal point or circuit, which allows empire to move geographically, politically, hermeneutically. With this movement, Indigeneity is moved well beyond the body and a global heuristic. "Cacophony" more than acknowledges, in a thin manner, the ways in which force structures the multiplicity of voices and truths that emerge out of the transit of this force; it privileges the lives of multiple narratives and invites us to listen closely for those that may matter to us and remain unacknowledged.

In all the acoustic mess of settlement, one trumpeting discourse is clear: that of "the state." Here, I want to ground Byrd's transit in flesh, because the force that she describes and analyzes through texts, I will demonstrate, moves through bodies, through flesh. The state that I seek to name has a character: it is male, more than likely white – or aspiring to an unmarked centre of whiteness – and definitely heteropatriarchal. I say "heteropatriarchal" because it serves the interests of what is understood now as "straightness" or heterosexuality and patriarchy, the rule by men.[6] The state also seeks to destroy its inverse: women and girls. It does so with a death drive to eliminate, contain, hide, and in other ways "disappear" what fundamentally challenges its legitimacy: Indigenous political orders. However, here is the rub: Indigenous political orders were established first, prior to the project of founding, of settling, and as such continue to point, in their persistence and vigour, to the failure of the settler project to eliminate them.[7] They are subjects of dispossession, of removal, but their polities serve as alternative forms of legitimacy and sovereignties to that of the settler state.

Settler states do *not* narrate themselves in the following manner:

As settler states, we are founded upon Native dispossession, outright and unambiguous enslavement. We are tethered to capitalist modes of production, which allow for the deep social and economic differences that take shape in contemporary "unequal" social relations. We now seek to repair these unequal social relations through invigorated forms of economic liberalism, which will further dispossess and, some would say, consensually enslave those who do not own their means of production or who opt out or fall out of this form of economic life.

More often than not, and here I am thinking of the United States (in its cagey political project), Australia and Canada fancy themselves as multicultural, democratic, economically liberal, committed to free trade among nations, and sometimes to social policies that allow for forms of historical redress that correct or attempt to repair the fundamental and un-narratable violences that brought them into being. Their histories do not live fully within the present, do not enter into a cacophony of discourses, but instead take the form of supposedly good policy and good intentions, of liberal settler governance. Those good policies and intentions perform a kind of historical reckoning through truth and reconciliation commissions, discourses of "healing," and apologies – in general, the performance of empathetic, remorseful, and *fleetingly* sorrowful states. But states are built upon violence and still act violently, either at a bureaucratic level, at an economic level (as we saw with former prime minister Stephen Harper's relentless drive to extract resources from the land),[8] or through a violent indifference (as we saw with that same government's unwillingness to launch an inquiry into the murdered and missing Indigenous women and girls, MMIWG). This unwillingness was absolutely of a piece with Harper's 19 August 2014 statement declaring that the problem of murdered and missing Native women should be understood as a "crime" rather than as sociology (CBC News 2014a). As a crime, the problem appears to have no context, no structure animating it, no materiality besides a legal transgression, thus becoming the appearance of death after a murderous act, with a perpetrator, a victim, and a clear and punishable transgression of a moral and legal code. This "crime" is an individuated, judiciable act – justice can be served. But Harper uttered that statement as the bodies aggregated and became something sturdy, something apparent, something hard to ignore, a cacophony of death, of grief and outrage. Harper said those words even though the density of Native women's bodies, the aggregate of grief, has been called a "phenomenon" of such statistical significance that it warrants reports, warrants explanation. Yet, in response to this phenomenon, sociological fact, or crime, Stephen Harper replied to Peter Mansbridge's December 2014 query on the need for a national inquiry by saying, "It isn't really high on our radar, to be honest" (Mansbridge 2014). This specificity of the murdered and missing Indigenous women and girls is part of the diffuse forms of violence that constitute a state: the intentions, the feelings, and the capacities of its citizens, who can also, as we saw in the case of Loretta Saunders and so many more, kill. States do not always have to kill; their citizens can do that for them.

How do the subjects of such states reach for life in the face of this death? How do they not lose themselves in the cacophony? What does it say for the future? I will consider two cases that stretch beyond a simple, monologic story of governmental sorrow, abandonment, and ineptitude and into an opening of the ways in which we think about citizenships or publics, particularly the way in which these concepts may be in active antagonism with the subjected, with those who are being made vulnerable. The arc of this article will be the following: bodies, sovereignty, and what I see as the necessity of pedagogical practices of thoughtful antagonism and "contention," not "reconciliation."

Bodies

In December 2012, Theresa Spence announced that she would stop eating until the prime minister of Canada and the governor general of Canada – the official representative of the Crown – met with her to discuss treaties, to discuss the deplorable conditions of life in her community, as well as the broader and also deplorable conditions of life in the North. Each of these men, as the embodiments of states, she said, had a hand in the suffering, in the failure to meet their historic obligations to the land and to the people upon the land, who were living in contaminated conditions without clean water and proper housing in legendarily cold and bitter winters. She described the Conservative Party in power as particularly "aggressive" and Prime Minister Stephen Harper as exceptional in his willingness to withdraw the care and compassion that is supposed to mark a twenty-first-century liberal, democratic state.

As with all spectacularized political cases, things were not what they seemed. The hunger strike was not a hunger strike in a strict sense of the term, and to be fair, which many were not at the time, a hunger strike under conditions of ongoing death deserves more interpretive flexibility than Theresa Spence or any Indigenous or racialized woman in Canada would or could be afforded in those moments. But to continue with my other point, it was not a hunger strike in a "classic" sense – it was rendered a "soft" hunger strike in endless newspaper articles, blog posts, vicious comment sections, Twitter flame wars, and on television.[9] We heard in comparative terms that Spence's campaign did not compare to the hunger strike of Bobby Sands or other "successful" strikes – for example, the hunger strikers at Guantanamo, who had to be force-fed; hers did not compare to those other declarations of a willingness to die, because those other strikes nearly ended in death or, in fact, did end in death. Spence was drinking fish broth twice a day and so was "fudging" things (so to speak). And you would think she was actually eating fudge, as irate Canadians "weighed in" continuously on her insincerity, her avarice, her body, and, in particular, her fat. Yet, as the hours turned into days and the days turned into weeks, people caravanned to her camp across from Parliament to assemble around her, to offer strength to her, to visit her, to pray with her. They did not care if she drank fish broth twice a day. They prayed for her continued life, and they celebrated her fortitude. Of this gathering, the Anishinaabe scholar Leanne Simpson (2014) argued in her crucial piece "Fish Broth and Fasting":

> We protect the faster. We do these things because we know that through her physical sacrifice she is closer to the Spiritual world than we are. We do these things because she is sacrificing for us and because it is the kind, compassionate thing to do. We do these things because it is our job to respect her self-determination as an Anishinaabekwe – this is the most basic building block of Anishinaabeg sovereignty and governance. We respect her sovereignty over her body and her mind. We do not act like we know better than her.[10]

Out of respect for Spence's action and for her sovereignty, other Indigenous people stopped eating in solidarity, all repeating her "demand" to meet with the prime minister, to have the treaties upheld, to make something happen in a governmental storm of complete and total indifference to the life of the land and people in Canada. This indifference has a life of its own, of course, and its clearest embodiment and manifestation, Stephen Harper, sowed his own roots as a chief policy analyst for the Reform Party in 1987 – a party that was resolutely opposed to any form of Indigenous right not based on the rights of the individual to acquire and accumulate property. This way of thinking about rights converted historic agreements signed between their country – Canada – and First Nations, agreements that are in fact *treaties*, into "race-based" forms of recognition that were not tenable with the idea of equality-as-sameness, which Harper's particular political party advocated for. Hence, Harper's immediate shelving of the Kelowna Accord upon coming into office. The foregoing is a gloss on a deeper history of Reform/Alliance Party politics that take the form of conservative skepticism (and here I am being generous) towards Indigenous peoples in Canada. But it is enough to say for now that the intellectual and political project of neoliberal capital accumulation, which marked Harper's ascent to the position of prime minister, is what Theresa Spence walked into. During this time of aggressive moves into soil and subsurface soil, of governmental indifference if not abandonment, she stopped eating.

Here, I want to gender this argument and move to her body. Theresa Spence's appearance, her fleshy appearance, was itself a site of ire for commentators online, in Twitter flame wars, and in print journalism. She was too fat! We heard in different ways, over and over again, that she needed to be sincere, to be what she was supposed to be – a person in starvation. Yet, her "excess" flesh, flesh that exceeds the Western, normative body mass index (BMI) of under 25, itself defies the logic of genocide and, in this defiance, settler domination. Why this link between fat, her fat in particular, and resistance or refusal of domination? Because what she is required to do, with or without the starvation, is die. In fact, her very life, like the lives of all Indian women in Canada, is an anomaly because, since the 1870s, Indian women have been legally mandated to disappear – through the Indian Act's previous instantiation of Victorian marriage rules whereby an Indian woman who married a non-Indian man lost her Indian status (her legal rights-based identity) and as such her right to reside on her reserve. With this legal casting out also came the casting out of the possibility of transmitting that status to her children, as well as a loss of governmental power with Indigenous governance itself, the political form that her body and mind signified.

Here, I want to use an example to demonstrate this argument about symbolization, Indigenous political orders, and settler governance. In the case of Iroquois or Haudenosaunee peoples (the peoples who signal North America's first "new world" democracy), this move to make Indian women white, to remove their status as Indians was a blow to the knees, if not a strangulation of Indigenous governance and political order, because Iroquois women appointed chiefs, held property, counselled chiefs, and dehorned them if necessary (removed them from their position of chief). They divorced their men by placing the men's belongings outside of the longhouse. They were the inverse of settler colonial woman: they had legally mandated authority and power, and so they represented an alternative political order to that which was in play or was starting to be in play in the late nineteenth century. Iroquois women embodied and signalled something radically different to Euro-Canadian governance, which meant that part of dispossession, and settler possession, required coercive and modifying, sometimes killing, power to target their bodies. Because, as with all bodies, these bodies were more than just "flesh" – these bodies were and are sign systems and symbols that could effect and affect political life. So they had to be killed or, at the very least, subjected, because what they were signalling or symbolizing was a direct threat to settlement.

Now I want to emphasize that the technique of elimination I am describing here is legal, and the time I am thinking of is the mid- and late nineteenth century, when the legal work of the Indian Act came into play and marriage rendered Indian women the property of their husbands. As such, if Indian women "married out," they were disappeared into a white settler body politic through a limited enfranchisement (here I say "limited," because as new white women, they would not vote in Manitoba until 1918 or in Quebec until 1940). Nonetheless, when their Indigenous political order was overlaid by the Indian Act, the act's gendered rules specifically recognized only some forms of marriage, defining a notion of out-marriage while simultaneously imposing patrilineal descent. At that moment, we see a heteropatriarchal and white settler sovereignty ascend and show us its face. It does so through its work with this legal move to dispossess people of land, of territory, to kill traditional governance forms, and in the Haudenosaunee and other Indigenous cases, to supplant traditional Indigenous governance, sovereignty, and political life. This aim was achieved through the imposition of federal and state law in particular legislative moments,[11] but also through slow processes of forced geographic removals, assimilation projects, and citizenship itself. The move to patrilineal/patriarchal governance in Indian territories was a legal femicide of a sort – not of fleshy bodies but of political form, as women are crucial to the structure of the Iroquois Confederacy.

Yet, this very instrument of Indian women's legal death or redefinition as subjects of white sovereignty is what makes Theresa Spence a "chief." She is an elected Indian Act "chief," 136 years after the act was imposed on Indians in Canada and 82 years after her Cree trapping community of Attawapiskat in Northern Ontario entered into treaty with Canada – Treaty 9 in 1930. The Attawapiskat people were among the last to sign on or be added to this treaty. At that point, this small "hunting band," one that lives at the mouth of James Bay, an important stopping point for travellers, fishermen, and hunters, was brought into the legal life of an emergent state. Within 82 years, the broader political orders of "Cree" in James Bay (who live in both what is now Northern Ontario and Northern Quebec) have suffered at least one serious famine at the turn of the twentieth century due to beaver pelt overhunting, have resisted and then endured the construction of a hydroelectric dam in 1971 (for Quebec), and have then treated again in 1975 with the signing of the James Bay Northern Quebec Agreement (JBNQA).[12] It was at that time that Mathew Coon Come (1996) argued:

> Under this Agreement ... [we were] promised compensation, schools, social services, health care, sanitation, housing, employment and training. We were also assured that our hunters and trappers would be able to continue their traditional way of life. As with other Indian treaties, many important commitments have not been honoured.

What appeared to be an exorbitant payment for their water at that time was actually paltry: now they cannot fish because of methylmercury poisoning; they struggle with obesity because of the sedentary lifestyle required by their forced relocation and confinement to a reserve; and then they had to contest with every bit of energy imaginable – a public relations firm in tow – a second hydroelectric project, "Great Whale" in 1992, which was to provide energy to sell to the United States.

Theresa Spence's people are literally cousins to this devastation[13] and seem to suffer even more. Outside of recent treaty and provincial payments, it is as if they exist outside of time; they suffered the same famines as their kin in Quebec and live in what to all accounts sounds like a surreal, federally recognized zone of simultaneous emergency and abandonment. Since Spence's tenure on the band council, starting in 2010, there have been *three* states of emergency declared for various reasons: because of flooding, because the houses are in such disrepair they are uninhabitable, because of sewage backup – because these conditions are not survivable anywhere but especially not in subzero temperatures. However, Indian Affairs stated: "Only 46 of Attawapiskat's 316 housing units are considered adequate, while another 146 need major work and 122 are placement" (Cheadle and Levitz 2013). Further to this, an Aboriginal and Northern Affairs representative revealed that, of the 316 homes, 85 percent are "unfit for human habitation."[14] The Canadian Press – where they have alighted upon Attawapiskat – have zoned in on federal transfers to the community, totalling $31 million each year and requiring forensic auditing on where the money has gone. Yet, these transfers were made in the shadow of a De Beers Victor diamond mine that started extracting from the land next to Attawapiskat in 2009 – something the people have since protested vigorously, pointing to problems with a community consultation process and the signing of a 2005 Impact Benefit Agreement (IBA), negotiated in secrecy, which did not result in housing, better health-care services, jobs, or an improved recreation facility for the youth.[15] Shiri Pasternak (2015) has argued in her meticulous analysis of the fiscal warfare against

First Nations people and the case of Attawapiskat that these IBAs are another strategy to gain access to Indigenous lands, because they "sanitize a regime of accumulation" in new "frontiers like Attawapiskat" (14). She elaborates: "While IBAs technically constitute a consultation process, since they imply consent from First Nations, these agreements contain confidential and non-compliance clauses that scholars refer to as a hostage situation of 'indentured servants,' who promise to work a certain number of years in exchange for their freedom, no matter how bad the working condition" (21).[16] According to a 2013 Aboriginal Peoples Television Network (APTN) article, this problematic IBA provides Attawapiskat with roughly $2 million a year, 1.5 per cent of De Beers's annual revenue, and De Beers has transferred $10.5 million into a trust fund for Attawapiskat as of January 2011. The mine also generated $448.8 million in gross revenues by the same date (Barrera 2013).

Within this context, Theresa Spence, out of what some may say was desperation or deep strategy, stopped declaring states of emergency in the North and, while down south in their nation's capital, Ottawa, for an Assembly of First Nations General Meeting, decided to declare her own body an exception. She declared her own body a space for the pronouncement of need, of sovereignty, the site of the decision *not* to eat. And to *not* eat solid food until the prime minister, Stephen Harper, would meet with her to talk about the indifference his Conservative government had shown not only to Attawapiskat but also to all communities in the North, to the land, to the people on the land. She then started her fast in a traditional dwelling constructed parallel to Parliament, and her body, her action, became a piece with the "Idle No More" movement – which may be the largest broad-based grassroots social and political movement to unfold in Canadian history.[17] The movement's goals are literally and directly to "stop the [Stephen] Harper government from passing more laws and legislation that will further erode treaty and indigenous rights and the rights of all Canadians" (CBC News 2013b). Further, Idle No More states that it "calls on all people to join in a peaceful revolution which honours and fulfills Indigenous sovereignty and which protects the land, the water, and the sky" (Idle No More 2020).

With those objectives, the movement has taken the form of "actions": flash mobs and round dances in public spaces, peopled at times by hundreds and thousands of participants who drummed and danced peaceably, as well as peaceful road blockages. Although Spence's action was separate from that of the four women in Saskatchewan who first brought the serious implications of the government's Omnibus Bill C-45 to public attention,[18] the two actions drew strength from each other and shared similar concerns. The omnibus bill was a budget bill that would do many things but, of most interest to Native people and others also concerned about the environment, would amend the Indian Act so that reserve lands could be leased without a majority consent of the voting membership; it would also amend the Navigational Protection Act so that major pipeline and power line projects did not have to prove their project wouldn't damage or destroy a navigable waterway it crosses, unless the waterway was on a list prepared by the transportation minister and the Environmental Assessment Act (this omnibus bill also further reduced the number of projects that would require impact assessment under the old provisions). Idle No More describes itself as an ongoing movement that takes exception to the lack of consultation that marked the passage of these acts, as well as the way in which the acts overrode existing treaty agreements and the Indian Act itself, not to mention fundamental issues of consent and the abusive indifference of the federal government to the lives and lands of Indigenous peoples. According to estimates by Idle No More, these amendments removed environmental protection for 99.9 per cent of lakes and rivers in Canada (CBC News 2013b). Because of this removal of legal protections (and probably other very good reasons), the movement joined forces with those who want to simply end the prospect of tar sands extraction in Northern Alberta, being carried out in order to transport and sell oil elsewhere – treating the land like a dead body to be extracted from. It is not surprising that, in that political moment and in the historical context that structures Canada, Theresa Spence's body would be treated with the callous indifference, if not the ire, that it was.

Flesh and Sovereignty

I want to explain the reason for this callous indifference and to do so with recourse to Theresa Spence's body and its relationship not so much to this movement as to death and its failure to die. Spence fasted for six weeks, drinking one cup of fish broth in the morning and one at night. During that time, the Sarah Palin of electoral politics in Canada, then Conservative (Algonquin) senator Patrick Brazeau, declared at a fundraising dinner that he had had the flu and lost more weight in one week than Spence did in six weeks. This jibe prompted a heckler to chime in (and be repeatedly reported in the press), "She's fatter!"[19] Spence's fleshy body was not seen as a sign of resurgent Indigenous life to white Canada. It was not seen as a stubborn, resolute, and sovereign refusal to die, staying alive to *have that conversation* about Crown obligations, about housing, and about historical obligations. Rather, her fleshy body was read as a failure to do what it was supposed to do: perish. Conservative, neoliberal governments require extractive relationships to territory at all times, focusing upon surplus rather than social welfare or care of their supposed citizens (even if the people are differently citizened, as Indigenous people are).[20] Those governments that are Conservative settler regimes require a double move: to extract from land and kill land if necessary – land is metaphorically a resource that gives itself for this purpose. Harper's regime was most open about this way of viewing territory. Some would argue (here I am thinking of Patrick Wolfe's work and those on his tail or trail) that all settler colonial regimes have territory as their irreducible element – a desire for territory, not labour or exclusively labour, for example. Theresa Spence's two bodies, her chiefly one and her womanly one, were especially untenable because they were both Indian bodies. An Indian woman's body in settler regimes such as the United States and Canada is loaded with meaning, signifying land itself or the dangerous possibility of reproducing Indian life and, most dangerously, other political orders – *other* life forms, other sovereignties, other forms of political will. Indian women in the aforementioned example of the Haudenosaunee Confederacy transmit the clan and, with that, family, responsibility, relatedness to territory. Feminist scholars have argued that Native women's bodies were like land to the settler eye, and as such, in the settler mind the Native woman is rendered "unrapeable" (or highly rapeable)[21] because she and land are matter to be extracted from, used, sullied, taken from, over and over again, something that is already violated and violable in a great march to accumulate surplus, to "production."

This explanation helps us to understand the "phenomenon" of the disappeared women, the murdered and missing Indigenous women and girls in Canada. When we account for this way of looking at Indian women, it is not a mystery; it is not without explanation. Their "disappearances" are consistent with this ongoing project of dispossession. And we can see that this project *is* sociology, and it *is* criminal. Sherene Razack (2002), Andrea Smith (2005), Amnesty International (2004, 2009),[22] the filmmakers Christine Welsh (2006) and Sharmeen Obaid Chinoy (2006), as well as countless activists and heartbroken, devastated family members who have marched and petitioned, who have stayed on the police, have all documented, theorized, and written about these deaths, these disappearances, which are explained not only by police ineptitude, by police racism, by gendered indifference, but also by Canada's dispossession of Indian people from land. This dispossession is raced and gendered, and its violence is still born by the living, the dead, and the disappeared corporealities of Native women. The disappearance of Indian women now takes on a sturdy sociological appearance: "missing" in the past decade, gone from their homes, murdered on the now-legendary "Highway of Tears"[23] in Northern British Columbia, off streets or reservations. Indian women "disappear" because they have been deemed killable, rapeable, expendable. Their bodies have *historically* been rendered less valuable because of what they are taken to represent: land, reproduction, Indigenous kinship, and governance, an alternative to heteropatriarchal and Victorian rules of descent. As such, they suffer disproportionately to other women. Their lives are shorter; they are poorer, less educated, sicker, raped more frequently; and they "disappear." Their disappearance thus is not an unexplainable phenomenon; like the "Oka Crisis" of 1990 in Mohawk territory, these not-so-mysterious disappearances are symptomatic of what administrators have called in Canada (and sometimes in the United States) "the Indian Problem." But the Indians' problems – dispossession and settler governance – are not up for examination and scrutiny, as they were with Idle No More and the pushbacks such as Oka, Ipperwash, and Elsipogtog. Theresa Spence's fleshy life, disciplined in a spectacular declaration to not eat in order to effect a political end, was a sovereign exception to the exception in which Indian people find themselves in settler states of occupation, Indigenous dispossession, and, right now, what may be qualified as neoliberal indifference and aggression. The chief's two bodies signalled too much for a settler eye and imagination to see and hear, let alone act upon, and were she to have died, her body would have in fact been the eliminatory logic of the state laid bare and made all too real. In these times, when the drive to death is apparent; when we are sent the memo repeatedly on the relationship between ideological degradation, gender, dispossession, and governance, rendered in the bodies of the murdered and missing women; when Indigenous people are rising up all over, holding hands with settlers in absolute concern, grief, and outrage; the language normatively should not be "reconciliation," since the historical violence of colonialism is not over. It is ongoing (Coulthard 2014).

Grief

I now want to turn to a death that was a grief-filled nerve ending within this state of affairs. Loretta Saunders was a young Inuk woman who was killed in February 2014. I will unpack some of the details of her passing shortly, but I will say for now that this violent murder is actually unexceptional when considered against the larger corpus that I have been talking about. The sociological fact, the crime of "murdered and missing Indigenous women and girls in Canada," is one that was exceptional in that it actually seemed to matter; it seemed to shock Canada. It was saturated with grief and managed to rouse the issue of the murdered and missing women to settler (and Indigenous) consciousness in ways perhaps that it had not done before.[24] However, before talking about the specifics of Saunders's passing, I want to think first about the writings of Darryl Leroux, her thesis advisor, who attempted upon her death to puncture common understandings of the murders and deaths of Indigenous women in order to offer historical and political context to these deaths.

After Saunders's death was confirmed – and it was a "fact" that she was gone – Darryl Leroux (2014) made a careful and simultaneously impassioned plea in the *Huffington Post* for white Canadians to think about the history that they inhabit, the benefits that they incur from Indigenous dispossession – as Indigenous dispossession, as I have just argued, is foundational for Canada (and, of course, the United States). And Indigenous women's vulnerability to harm, to violence, is symptomatic of this dispossession. Before I get further into the crux of this argument, I will just rehearse a few points. When we speak of dispossession, we are speaking of the materiality of land – the land that Indigenous peoples own, care for, are related to, and are moved from by force or by fiat for settlement. Thus, when we think about dispossession, we have to think about it as an ongoing activity that the United States and Canada are very involved in, as these governmental projects also move Indigeneity – as a living thing, a corporeal thing, and also a system of ideas and practices – out of the way. These states have to be involved in this ongoing "moving away" because they fundamentally need the land and its resources to fuel themselves and keep producing themselves, not only as political orders but also as systems that are attached to people who are not Indigenous but who can invoke Indigeneity in different ways to suppose themselves, to construct themselves, as civil, as lawful, as the "not-that" (savage and prior other). This explanation may seem a crude construction from various literatures, but I want to ground my analysis in the need not only for land but also for selfhood and statecraft to legitimatize claims to governance. When we talk about dispossession, when we talk about settler colonialism or imperial colonialism, we are not talking about prior events or even just about events; we are talking about ongoing processes and what the comparative historian Patrick Wolfe has called a sturdy, enduring "structure," and from this perspective, not only an event.[25] Alyosha Goldstein (2014) has recently called for a further nuancing of this idea as assemblage, the feature of a discernable will to eliminate over time, which is borne out in the Canadian case and especially so in relation to gender. Structures move through time and place, and if you pay close attention, you can actually *see* structural activity.

The evidence for this "structure," some of which was in Leroux's articles on the Saunders murder, is a "termination plan," put forth by Harper's regime in September 2013 (Diabo 2014), for the ongoing tar sands project[26] in Northern Alberta, which strips the topsoil of Northern Cree and Ojibway communities in order to extract oil from the stripped earth to pipe it through the United States and ship through, literally through, other Indigenous communities and white communities using the trick of "eminent domain" – a legal manoeuver that Indians in the United States are very familiar with, because it was one of the ways in which land was expropriated from them through an argument that targeted the expropriation as necessary "for the public good." The four-phase Keystone Pipeline,[27] in particular, is a compact between big oil (TransCanada Corporation based in Calgary) and local and federal Canadian and US governments, as state permits were required to start construction. Starting in 2008, private industry worked with public law to expropriate private and Indian land to route crude oil from Hardisty, Alberta, to Regina, Saskatchewan, across the border down to Nebraska, and on to Illinois. Later phases extended the pipelines from Nebraska to Oklahoma and to Liberty County, Texas; phases 3 and 3a extended it into Houston, Texas. Phase 4, called Keystone XL, was rejected by the Obama administration after years of review.[28] Nonetheless, the 1,700-mile pipeline was also to route down to the Gulf of Mexico, where the oil would be reworked for domestic consumption and/or sold to markets in China, solely for the profit of big oil, not for the "public good." Indian land in Northern Alberta is being harvested, as is privately held acreage by white Americans in the Plains. White farmers who till the earth in perfect Lockean fashion are being subjected to the legal concept of "eminent domain" in North Dakota.[29] Their experience duplicates precisely what happened to Indigenous peoples whose land the government and oil companies now claim and are taking from them.

Now let me return to this person, the late Loretta Saunders, and what her passing means in all of this. For those of you who don't know Loretta Saunders, she was a twenty-six-year-old Inuk student from Labrador who was studying at St. Mary's University in Halifax, Nova Scotia. She was writing her honour's thesis on the "phenomenon" of murdered and missing Native women in Canada, and during the course of her thesis research and writing, in February 2014, her lifeless body was found in a hockey bag along the Trans-Canada Highway in New Brunswick.[30] Saunders was pregnant on multiple levels, pregnant with the thesis that she was researching and writing, and quite literally three months pregnant. According to all accounts, she was a great student, working hard, looking forward to starting new chapters in her life. Then she was shockingly killed, suddenly, by a white couple subletting her apartment, when she went to collect the overdue rent from them.[31]

Loretta Saunders's murder really, really upset everyone, registering grief and forms of action[32] in ways not seen before for reasons that are both predictable and yet, not. One, she was, like all of these Native women, killed as part of what looks like a vaporous crime spree that belongs not to one serial murderer but to an entire citizenship. As mentioned earlier, 1,181[33] Native women have disappeared or been killed in the past thirty-odd years. There have been two Amnesty International reports; calls for a national public inquiry; reports into police ineptitude; a municipal inquiry followed by an apology from the Vancouver police chief, Jim Chu, for years of doddering inaction regarding the murdered and missing women in that city; and the specificity and particular heinousness of Robert Pickton's perfectly commodifying site of gendered pain and gendered elimination, the "piggy farm." At the "piggy farm," forty-nine women (he confessed to forty-nine and was charged for six) were murdered and ground like meat. Like the violence done to Saunders's body, found in a hockey bag – a container for the sport that seems to condense meaning and hope, while sublimating white male violence in a civil form, and stands for Canada itself – Pickton's violence does perfectly disgusting and unambiguous work to tell us, to scream at us, "Native women will be killed by this country and its people."

Yet, in spite of these signs, settler governance in those moments could not or would not hear the screams. In March 2014, one month after the Saunders murder, the Conservative-led cabinet refused the call for a national inquiry into these deaths that crash through austere Canadian silence in the form of tears, marches, and outrage, congealing into one discourse of outraged grief: Why are these women being targeted? Who is the perpetrator? What do we do?[34]

When history and sensibility is "the perp," a lot has to get done. And the Saunders case agitated all these things in ways not seen before. The agitation is the one way in which this fairly recent murder scrapes at whatever iota of patience Indigenous people have with the current state of affairs. But I suspect the other reason is that Loretta

Saunders looked like a white girl. She had fair skin, blond hair, light eyes – she could have infiltrated a Ku Klux Klan meeting without notice. Perhaps it was this reason, and we will find it more than likely, but perhaps not. It isn't white skin privilege that upset people – that Saunders is more precious than the darker ones among us – it is that her death demonstrates that *no one* is safe. Her violent passing is teaching us that one cannot "pass"; this structure, this assemblage, those people who articulate themselves through and for this violence will find you and subject you – and can kill you. You, too, can be emptied of your familial relations, your relationship to land, your signifying possibility, as the ongoing project of empire transits, in Byrd's (2011) parlance, or plows through you. One's life, one's land, one's sovereignty, one's body are emptied out in order for other things to pass through. This emptying includes fleshy bodies – it includes Theresa Spence's stubborn and life-sustaining fat – because, if you are an Indigenous woman, your flesh is received differently: You have been subjected differently from others. Your life choices have been circumscribed in certain ways, and the violence will find you, choke you, beat you, and possibly kill you. Darryl Leroux (2014) tried to explain this situation to Canadians in the *Huffington Post*, where you will find the startling comments of Canadians who argued in the comments section (in various ways) that "she was not subjected to this violence because she was Inuk; she was subjected to this violence because she is a woman, because these are killers, and *they* are wholly responsible." Somehow, because the killers were not part of the state, they were imagined as being outside of the history that structures them as well. My favorite comment to Leroux's post was and is the following: "You also just helped explain why the numbers for missing/ murdered native women are so high. You count any woman with any amount of native blood as native." The comment completely misapprehends Leroux's argument about history and territory, and his words about that phenotype. His crucial point is that Indigeneity is not a matter of skin colour and that Loretta Saunders was an Inuk because she belonged to her people, she belonged to her family, and they belong to a specific territory. Here, he argued that Indigeneity is actually this kind of specificity of place and people, and that, in particular, this "white Inuk" belonged to those people, and she was claimed and loved and grieved by them. In the numerous YouTube videos on this case, you can see her distraught family pleading to the public for information; you can see her sister Delilah Saunders with tear-stained cheeks calmly ask for information from the public about her sister, and then wait and ask, and then organize a search for her body. When the news comes to the Saunders family, we see them embrace each other with the relief of knowing simply that her body had been found – frozen, in the hockey bag. They were happy that she had been *found*, because so many of these women have not even been found. Couple their sentiments, which are literally heartbreaking, her murder enraging, with the cacophony of comments from the Canadian public to Leroux's blog posts expressing remorse, because this case is so awful that it is inspiring grief even in the trolls.

Pedagogies of Contention

When I first wrote an earlier version of this article, I presented it in Austin, Texas, for a graduate student conference on "Violence Against Native and Indigenous Identities."[35] This presentation took place in April 2014. Like many other people, I was thinking about Loretta Saunders, about the other women, and Leroux's piece made me think about my students,[36] about my job as a professor, but specifically as a research professor who takes teaching very seriously. As a research professor, I should not work so hard on my teaching. Nonetheless, I take it seriously and push things to the point of almost total bodily collapse every year, when I get a long, painful, and relentless bronchitis. I can barely walk to work, let alone lecture, and I work across the street from my apartment. I say this not to dramatize a point about exertion – we all work very hard – but to talk about what I teach and its crucial capacity to exhaust. What I teach – violence, dispossession, Indigenous political life in the face of death – is high stakes, and I know it. *Where* I teach is high stakes, and I know it – in the United States, a site of complete atrophied disavowal of dispossession and ongoing colonialism, disavowal of Indigeneity itself. The courses push up and expose the structures of that dispossession and disavowal to students, while providing a historical narrative with analytics to help them along. Repeatedly, I hear and read from them, in different ways, "We didn't know this"; and from my Indigenous students, of whom there are more than I ever expected, "This helps to put it all together." From all of them, I hear, "Let's do something!" I don't seek to claim an extraordinary status for Native studies alongside other crucial, non-canonical, and subaltern histories, all with their own very serious and searing urgencies, but let me make the modest claim that the material serves as a "surprise" that topples things, and so, I would say, is crucial. But because of its generally non-curricular nature, if I don't get it right, if I don't ensnare my students with this information, they may never get it, and they may never get it because they may never even *hear* it. This silence is because we live in a place, in multiple places, that simply require the disappearance of Indians in order to make the meta claim of the state – "We are a nation of immigrants" – make sense. This statement is not true. Even though Obama quickly offered the exceptional qualifier – "unless you are one of the Native Americans" – he did not explain the violence of settler colonialism, the ongoing violence of this system, and how it is still happening and itself explains the minoritized, post-genocidal, and yes, exceptional, space of Indigeneity. Unless people have the data about dispossession, the conceptual and analytical toolkit to work with these statements, they may take this claim as a fact, and they may be compelled to see it as something true and also virtuous. When they have the material of Native studies and Indigenous studies to think with, these statements are perceived differently; their own histories are perceived differently; and they will have to think more robustly and critically about what is before them. Why is this matter not a matter for everyone to care about, to teach, to think with, and to act upon? Because the disappearance of Indians keeps things in its place, the narratives, the politics, the distributions of power that allow for land to still be taken, for Indigenous identities to still be violated and stolen; because it is presumed that Indigenous peoples are not here to claim each other, to stand up for each other and for themselves. I have written about this situation in my first book, *Mohawk Interruptus* (A. Simpson 2014), but you will find other examples of this clarity of Indigenous political will in other works in literary history (Monture 2014), ethnography (Nesper 2002; McCarthy 2016), and political analysis and critique (Alfred 1995, 1999, 2005; Coulthard 2014; Bruyneel 2007; Moreton-Robinson 2002, 2007, 2014).

The people I have written about (and belong to), the Haudenosaunee, for example, insist on the life of Indigenous nationhood and sovereignty through time and express this life in actions that are about *not* being American, *not* being Canadian, and in this way they are holding these nation-states in a position of doubt, sometimes interrogation and sometimes refusal. Their political posture is, in short, saying *"I am not playing with you. You are not the only political or historical show in town, and I know it."* I think of Loretta Saunders and of her sister's completely devastating blog that documents her love for her sister, the sadness and rage that she wakes up with, her hopes for the safety of other women, her life after her sister's murder (Saunders 2014);[37] and I think of the death grip that threatens to seize all of us, the death grip that is very much part of a settler show – a show of strength, of callous indifference, of ire that pertains to Indigenous women's bodies. I think of how this show attaches itself even to those of us who might

154 Audra Simpson

think we are safe. Simultaneously, I think of Loretta Saunders's thesis advisor, who tried to translate the very things he was surely teaching her, learning from her, to Canadians through the *Huffington Post* article. Is this the cacophony of discourses that vie for a kind of truth-telling? Force qualified as violence moves through us, trying to empty us out, transiting through moving to the flesh that is the subsurface of "identity" as peoples possessing bodies with living histories of relatedness to territory that are constantly being violated, harmed, ignored – allowing some of us to be devalued to the point where we are denied bodily integrity, denied philosophical integrity, flattened, sometimes killed. The force of this onslaught is ongoing and multileveled. I think now, after writing my first book and thinking through the politics of Kahnawà:ke, which is at times extremely difficult but so very alive and vibrant, which resists and refuses this kind of process at every turn, that the desire for reconciliation by the Canadian government is a curious one. I am not sure that it is possible or even fair to attempt to "reconcile" with something that is so violent, so relentless, unless all people stand fully before the sorts of stories I have just assembled – stories that circulate in our communities, stories of the loss, the gains, the names – and think then about what peace means. The settler state is asking us to forgive and to forget, with no land back, no justice, and no peace. I find this request for forgiveness by a killing state to veer towards the absurd if not the insulting, in spite of its conciliatory intent. This feeling is because historical, bodily, and heuristic violence, along with theft, are among those things that are really impossible to forgive – let alone forget.

Acknowledgments

This article is dedicated to the late Loretta Saunders and the MMIWG who have been stolen from their territories and their loved ones. The article was first written for the "Violence Against Native and Indigenous Identities" conference at the University of Texas at Austin in 2014, and I thank Lakota Pochedley for the invitation to Austin and the occasion to write new work for that specific event. Expanded and revised versions were presented at the Native and Indigenous Studies Association meeting in 2014, as well as at the University of Winnipeg, Ryerson University, Carleton University, McMaster University, Concordia University, Clark University, and the University of California, Los Angeles (UCLA). I thank Isabelle St. Amand and Martin Loft for inviting me to keynote "Revisioning Americas" in Kahnawà:ke, as well as Tracey Lindberg and Malinda Smith for inviting me to keynote the Critical Race and Anticolonial Studies Conference in Edmonton, Alberta, where an earlier version of this piece was presented in 2014. I am grateful to these audiences for their engagement. Any mistakes are my own.

NOTES

1 An earlier version of this article was previously published in *Theory & Event* 19, no. 4 (2016). Slight changes have been made to reflect updated literature.

2 For the reach of global, imperial, and comparative analysis of settler colonialism, see Cornellier and Griffith (2016). See also Goldstein and Lubin (2008).

3 See Regan (2011) for an account and analysis of Canadian self-perception, especially as international peacekeepers and in relation to the United States.

4 See *Report of the Royal Commission on Aboriginal Peoples: Vol. 2. Restructuring the Relationship* (Ottawa: RCAP, 1996), 270.

5 And it is over-incarcerating Native men. See Razack (2014) for a book-length analysis of the over-preponderance of deaths in custody; most are men.

6 This concept is argued in various ways by Aileen Moreton-Robinson (2014).

7 See Kevin Bruyneel (2007) and Audra Simpson (2014) for related arguments.

8 Trudeau cancelled the controversial Enbridge Northern Gateway project that would have transported oil from the Alberta tar sands to the coast of British Columbia just nine days after assuming office. He is, however, supportive of the Energy East and Trans Mountain pipeline projects, because they are thought to offer a "cleaner" solution than pipelines that transport crude and are underway with more process and consultation with First Nations. The younger and presumably innovative and inclusive Trudeau was widely regarded at the point of his election as a departure from the Conservative Party leader Stephen Harper, who held office for nine years but was unable to achieve construction of the pipelines (see Hislop 2016).

9 For an excellent summary of this type of comment, see Huffington Post Canada (2013).

10 In her piece, Leanne Simpson (2014) recasts the action of Theresa Spence in ceremonial terms and as a simultaneous enactment of the consequences and critique of Indian Act colonialism. She argues: "Colonialism has kept Indigenous Peoples on a fish broth diet for generations" (155).

11 Treaty-making ended, for example, in the United States in 1871, and the Indian Act was imposed in Canada in 1876.

12 The James Bay Northern Quebec Agreement affects the Cree in what was once James Bay and is now referred to as "Eeyou Istchee."

13 Shortly after Theresa Spence's hunger strike, an article appeared on *CBC News* that is rich in its invitation for critical commentary (Milewski 2013). According to this article, the Quebec Cree avoided their Attawapiskat cousins' fate basically by controlling the process of "economic development" through techniques of political resistance until their terms were met. The article emphasized that the Quebec Cree are not "opposed to development," but simply want to control it and to receive revenues from it. Time does not permit me to deconstruct the underlying principles of this discourse, but later versions of this project no doubt will.

14 For details on the audit and Theresa Spence's response, see CBC News (2013a).

15 See the film *The People of the Kattawapiskak River* (Obomsawin 2012) for a documentary treatment of the housing crisis as well as a crucial account of the community's independent funding of their hockey rink.

16 In footnote 101 of her article, Pasternak (2015) provides a genealogy of IBAs as an accumulative technique and traces them back to *Haida Nation v. British Columbia* (*Ministry of Forests*) 2004 SCC 73. In a nutshell, although there must be consultation with First Nations if Aboriginal Rights will be contravened, the cunning of IBAs is that they imply consent and do not require it fully. In her analysis, Pasternak draws on Caine and Krogman (2010).

17 Admittedly, this claim is difficult to prove, as the Idle No More movement was and perhaps still is amorphous and prone to spontaneous public actions and thus difficult to "calculate." Other "to the streets" actions and protests have been significant in demographic scale, notably the Winnipeg workers' strikes of 1919 (see Heron 1998) and the gendered consumer activism of the "Homemakers" organizations throughout the 1930s, who organized in vigorous protest against rising milk prices (see Guard 2010). I am grateful to Jarvis Brownlie for pushing me on this claim.

18 The Omnibus Bill-C45 was first brought to public attention by four women in Saskatchewan: Jessica Gordon, Sylvia McAdam, Sheelah McLean, and Nina Wilson, as well the woman who first started the hashtag "Idle No More" (and thus created intensive discussion and actions), Tanya Kappo. Theresa Spence was similarly acting in protest to what she called (and her people call) the "aggression" of the Conservative government in Canada. In their callous indifference to the lives and lands of Native people in the North, housing in her community is abominable and water undrinkable. This situation is endemic to many reserves in the North. For a detailed legal history of Spence's action, placed within the larger context of

Indigenous dispossession and Canadian lawmaking, see Pasternak (2015).
For a multivocal edited account of the Idle No More movement, see Kino-
nda-niimi Collective (2014).

19 The exchange as reported by Huffington Post Canada (2013) went like this:
"I look at Miss Spence, when she started her hunger strike, and now?"
Brazeau quipped. A spectator then cried out, "She's fatter," sparking
laughter.

20 For an ethnographic account of this different citizenship, see Audra
Simpson (2014).

21 See Andrea Smith (2005), as well as Jacki Rand (2008), specifically chapter
six, which links a degraded status of Kiowa women to settler capitalism.
Heidi Stark (2016) offers a crucial analysis of the gendered construction of
Indigenous women as territories of lawlessness in the twentieth century:
"Indigenous women's bodies were constructed as inherently deceptive,
cunning terrains, lawless frontiers, virgin territory, in need of conquest
and civilization, that were to be strictly controlled through law because of
the perilousness these lawless spaces posed." There is reference to sexual
violence as well in Ned Blackhawk (2006) and James Daschuk (2013), but
these works do not make the claim regarding gender and territory that
Smith, Rand, and Stark do.

22 Six Nations Mohawk lawyer and University of Windsor law professor
Beverly Jacobs was the lead researcher for Amnesty International's
Stolen Sisters Report. A conversation with Jacobs titled "I Want
Canadians to Care" was posted on the Amnesty International Canada
blog, *Human Rights Now*, on 1 October 2014 (https://www.amnesty.ca
/blog/%E2%80%9Ci-want-canadians-to-care%E2%80%9D-a-conversation
-with-bev-jacobs).

23 Highway 16 stretches across Northern British Columbia. Eighteen women
have been murdered between Prince Rupert and Prince George, rendering
that stretch the "Highway of Tears" (Obaid Chinoy 2006). On 12 September
2012, it was reported that Bobby Jack Fowler murdered one of these
women in British Columbia and died in an Oregon jail in 2006.

24 I will explain some of this thinking shortly, but let the attention paid to
Loretta Saunders's death, shocking because of what Doenmez (2015)
calls a "fatal symmetry," not override the sustained memorialization and
activism of the families and other loved ones of the Indigenous women
and girls or the grass roots community activism and documentation. Every
14 February is a day of remembrance for the women and girls, and sees
memorial marches all throughout Canada. Please consult the website *It
Starts with Us* (http://www.itstartswithus-mmiw.com/) for a No More
Silence database that documents the missing women. This site works in
partnership with Sisters in Spirit through the Native Women's Association

of Canada. Defunded by the Conservative government, the Sister's in Spirit initiative documented the root causes of violence and harm in Native women's lives.

25 The paradigmatic piece in Patrick Wolfe's work is found in Wolfe (2006).

26 For an excellent summary of the oil or tar sands projects in Northern Alberta, and the "catastrophic climate change that … [Keystone XL] would induce," as well as American lobbying efforts against it, see Lizza (2013).

27 The fourth phase was not approved by the American state department in November 2015. This rejection was challenged and revoked during the Trump presidency through the issuing of a Presidential Permit (thus bypassing the need for review of environmental impacts). On his first day in office, the forty-sixth US president, Joseph Biden, revoked the Presidential Permit for the proposed Keystone XL pipeline. See Lefebvre and Gardner (2021).

28 Obama gave a statement cancelling the Keystone XL pipeline on 6 November 2015 (Obama 2015).

29 See Conca (2014) for an account of the successful opposition in the courts to TransCanada's attempt to assert eminent domain in Nebraska.

30 In her master's thesis, "Already Disappeared: Interrogating the Right to Life of Indigenous Women in Canada," Caroline Doenmez (2015, 13) has called the shock of Saunders's writing about what would befall her a "fatal symmetry"; Doenmez analyzes the Canadian government's "failure to protect" in the case of Saunders, alongside analyses of the treatment meted out to Cindy Gladue and Tina Fontaine.

31 For details of Saunders's murder and the sentencing of Blake Legette and Victoria Henneberry, the couple who killed her, see Rhodes (2015).

32 Loretta Saunders's murder is the only individual murder that occasioned a march on Parliament (CBC News 2014b).

33 These numbers are based on Royal Canadian Mounted Police (RCMP) data, which cover a thirty-three year period, 1980–2012. This total is flawed, as it does not include cities where the RCMP do not have jurisdiction, like Vancouver and Toronto (Doenmez 2015, 14–15). In 2006, Sisters in Spirit, a government-funded grassroots initiative, started tracking numbers of MMIWG. They collaborated with the Native Women's Association of Canada (NWAC) and, by 2010, had recorded 600 MMIWG, also backtracked thirty years. Sisters in Spirit was defunded in 2010. An overview of these different databases and grass roots initiatives can be found on the *It Starts With Us* website (http://itstartswithus-mmiw.com/about/).

34 The Inquiry into Missing and Murdered Indigenous Women and Girls was launched on 3 August 2016. Its Final Report was published in September 2019 (see https://www.mmiwg-ffada.ca/).

35 The conference "Violence Against Native and Indigenous Identities: Unearthing and Healing Our Communities" took place at the University of Texas in Austin, Texas, on 28 March 2014.

36 It was my former student Lakota Pochedley who invited me to the University of Texas in Austin, as she was then a graduate student there and had gone on after completing a thesis under my supervision at Columbia.

37 Loretta Saunders's sister Delilah documented her story in a heartbreaking blog, *A Homicide Survivor's Journey through Grief* (Saunders 2014).

REFERENCES

Alfred, Gerald Taiaiake. 1995. *Heeding the Voices of Our Ancestors: Kahnawake Mohawk Politics and the Rise of Native Nationalism.* Toronto: Oxford University Press.

– 1999. *Peace Power and Righteousness: An Indigenous Manifesto.* Toronto: Oxford University Press.

– 2005. *Wasáse: Indigenous Pathways of Action and Freedom.* Peterborough, ON: Broadview Press.

Amnesty International. 2004. *No More Stolen Sisters: A Human Rights Response to Discrimination and Violence against Indigenous Women in Canada.* London: Amnesty International.

– 2009. *No More Stolen Sisters: The Need for a Comprehensive Response to Violence against Indigenous Women in Canada.* London: Amnesty International.

Barrera, Jorge. 2013. "Attawapiskat Councillor Accuses De Beers of Trickery as Showdown Looms on Diamond Mine Ice Road." *APTN*, 15 February 2013. https://www.aptnnews.ca/national-news/attawapiskat-councillor-accuses-de-beers-of-trickery-as-showdown-looms-on-diamond-mine-ice-road/.

Blackhawk, Ned. 2006. *Violence over the Land: Indians and Empires in the Early American West.* Cambridge, MA: Harvard University Press.

Bruyneel, Kevin. 2007. *The Third Space of Sovereignty: The Postcolonial Politics of U.S.–Indigenous Relations.* Minneapolis: University of Minnesota Press.

Byrd, Jodi. 2011. *Transit of Empire: Indigenous Critiques of Colonialism.* Minneapolis: University of Minnesota Press.

Caine, Ken J., and Naomi Krogman. 2010. "Powerful or Just Plain Power-Full? A Power Analysis of Impact and Benefit Sharing Agreements in Canada's North." *Organization & Environment* 23 (1): 76–98. https://doi.org/10.1177/1086026609358969.

CBC News. 2013a. "Attawapiskat chief slams audit leak as 'distraction.'" *CBC News*, 7 January 2013. https://www.cbc.ca/news/politics/attawapiskat-chief-slams-audit-leak-as-distraction-1.1318113.

– 2013b. "9 Questions about Idle No More." *CBC News*, 5 January 2013. https://www.cbc.ca/news/canada/9-questions-about-idle-no-more-1.1301843.

– 2014a. "Harper Rebuffs Renewed Calls for Murdered, Missing Women Inquiry." *CBC News*, 21 August 2014. https://www.cbc.ca/news

/canada/manitoba/harper-rebuffs-renewed-calls-for-murdered-missing
-womeninquiry-1.2742845.
– 2014b. "Loretta Saunders Vigil Draws Hundreds to Parliament Hill." *CBC News*, 5 March 2014. https://www.cbc.ca/news/canada/nova-scotia
/loretta-saunders-vigil-draws-hundreds-to-parliament-hill-1.2561062.
Cheadle, Bruce, and Stephanie Levitz. 2013. "Attawapiskat Spending Audit Reveals Lack of Basic Accounting." *HuffPost*, 7 January 2013. https://www
.huffingtonpost.ca/2013/01/07/attawapiskat-spending-audit-theresa
-spence_n_2425725.html.
Conca, James. 2014. "TransCanada Tries to Seize U.S. Land for Keystone Pipeline." *Forbes*, 24 February 2014. https://www.forbes.com/sites
/jamesconca/2014/02/24/foreign-company-tries-to-seize-u-s-land-for
-keystone-pipeline/.
Coon Come, Matthew. 1996. "Remarks to the Canada Seminar." Harvard Center for International Affairs and Kennedy School of Government, Harvard University, Cambridge, MA, 28 October 1996. http://www
.nativeweb.org/pages/legal/coon_come.html.
Cornellier, Bruno, and Michael R. Griffiths. 2016. "Globalizing Unsettlement: An Introduction." *Settler Colonial Studies* 6 (4): 305–16. https://doi.org
/10.1080/2201473X.2015.1090522.
Coulthard, Glen Sean. 2014. *Red Skin, White Masks: Rejecting the Colonial Politics of Recognition*. Minneapolis: University of Minnesota Press.
Daschuk, James. 2013. *Clearing the Plains: Disease, Politics of Starvation, and the Loss of Aboriginal Life*. Regina: University of Regina Press.
Diabo, Russell. 2014. "Harper Launches Major First Nations Termination Plan as Negotiating Tables Legitimize Canada's Colonialism." In *The Winter We Danced: Voices from the Past, the Future and the Idle No More Movement*, edited by the Kino-nda-niimi Collective, 51–64. Winnipeg: ARP Books.
Doenmez, Caroline Fidan Tyler. 2015. "Already Disappeared: Interrogating the Right to Life of Indigenous Women in Canada." Master's thesis (Human Rights), Columbia University.
Goldstein, Alyosha. 2014. "Introduction: Toward a Genealogy of the U.S. Colonial Present." In *Formations of United States Colonialism*, edited by Alyosha Goldstein, 1–32. Durham, NC: Duke University Press.
Goldstein, Alyosha, and Alex Lubin, eds. 2008. *South Atlantic Quarterly* 107 (4). https://read.dukeupress.edu/south-atlantic-quarterly/issue/107/4.
Guard, Julie. 2010. "A Mighty Power against the Cost of Living: Canadian Housewives Organize in the 1930s." *International Labor and Working Class History* 77 (1): 27–47. https://doi.org/10.1017/S0147547909990238.
Heron, Craig, ed. 1998. *The Workers Revolt in Canada, 1917–1925*. Toronto: University of Toronto Press.

Hislop, Markham. 2016. "How the Trudeau Government Tore Up the Rulebook on Pipelines." *Canadian Business*, 21 July 2016. https://www .canadianbusiness.com/economy/how-the-trudeau-government -tore-up-the-rulebook-on-pipelines/.

Huffington Post Canada. 2013. "Patrick Brazeau Suggests Theresa Spence Gained Weight during Protest." *HuffPost*, 31 January 2013. https://www .huffingtonpost.ca/2013/01/31/patrick-brazeau-theresa-spence_n_2589799 .html.

Idle No More. 2020. "Vision." *Idle No More* (website). https://idlenomore.ca /about-the-movement/.

Kino-nda-niimi Collective. 2014. *The Winter We Danced: Voices from the Past, the Future and the Idle No More Movement*. Winnipeg: ARP Books.

Lefebvre, Ben, and Lauren Gardner. 2021. "Biden Kills Keystone XX Permit, Again." *Politico*, 20 January 2021. https://www.politico.com/news/2021/01 /20/joe-biden-kills-keystone-xl-pipeline-permit-460555.

Leroux, Darryl. 2014. "White Skin Didn't Save Loretta Saunders from Colonial Violence." *HuffPost*, 22 May 2014. https://www.huffingtonpost.ca/darryl -leroux/loretta-saunders-indigenous-_b_5007672.html.

Lizza, Ryan. 2013. "The President and the Pipeline: The Campaign to Make the Keystone XL the Test of Obama's Resolve on Climate Change." *The New Yorker*, 9 September 2013. https://www.newyorker.com /magazine/2013/09/16/the-president-and-the-pipeline.

Mansbridge, Peter. 2014. "Interview with Stephen Harper (Full Text)," *CBC*, 17 December 2014. https://www.cbc.ca/news/politics/full-text -of-peter-mansbridge-s-interview-with-stephen-harper-1.2876934.

McCarthy, Theresa. 2016. *In Divided Unity: Haudenosaunee Reclamation at Grand River*. Tucson: University of Arizona Press.

Milewski, Terry. 2013. "How Quebec Cree Avoided the Fate of Attawapiskat." *CBC News*, 14 May 2013. https://www.cbc.ca/news/politics/how-quebec -cree-avoided-the-fate-of-attawapiskat-1.1301117.

Monture, Rick. 2014. *We Share Our Matters: Two Centuries of Writing and Resistance at Six Nations of the Grand River*. Winnipeg: University of Manitoba Press.

Moreton-Robinson, Aileen. 2002. *Talkin' Up to the White Woman: Indigenous Women and Feminism*. Queensland, AU: University of Queensland Press.

– ed. 2007. *Sovereign Subjects: Indigenous Sovereignty Matters*. New South Wales, AU: Allen & Unwin.

– 2014. *The White Possessive: Property Power and Indigenous Sovereignty*. Minneapolis: University of Minnesota Press.

Nesper, Larry. 2002. *The Walleye War: The Struggle for Ojibway Hunting and Fishing Rights*. Lincoln: University of Nebraska Press.

Obaid Chinoy, Sharmeen, dir. 2006. *Highway of Tears*. N.p.: Sharmeen Obaid Films. DVD.

Obama, Barack. 2015. "Statement by the President on the Keystone XL Pipeline." The White House, Office of the Press Secretary, 6 November 2015. https://obamawhitehouse.archives.gov/the-press-office/2015/11/06 /statement-president-keystone-xl-pipeline.

Obomsawin, Alanis, dir. 2012. *The People of the Kattawapiskak River*. Ottawa: National Film Board of Canada. DVD.

Pasternak, Shiri. 2015. "The Fiscal Body of Sovereignty: To 'Make Live' in Indian Country." *Settler Colonial Studies* 6 (4): 317–38. https://doi.org /10.1080/2201473X.2015.1090525.

Rand, Jacki. 2008. *Kiowa Humanity and the Invasion of the State*. Lincoln: University of Nebraska Press.

Razack, Sherene. 2002. "*The Murder of Pamela George*." In *Race, Space and the Law: Unmapping a White Settler Society*, edited by Sherene Razack, 123–56. Toronto: Between the Lines Press.

– 2014. *Dying from Improvement: Inquiries and Inquests into Indigenous Deaths in Custody*. Toronto: University of Toronto Press.

Regan, Paulette. 2011. *Unsettling the Settler Within: Indian Residential Schools, Truth Telling and Reconciliation*. Vancouver, BC: UBC Press.

Rhodes, Blair. 2015. "Loretta Saunders Murder Was 'Despicable, Horrifying and Cowardly.'" *CBC News*, 28 April 2015. https://www.cbc.ca/news /canada/nova-scotia/loretta-saunders-murder-wasdespicable-horrifying -and-cowardly-1.3052465.

Saunders, Delilah. 2014. *A Homicide Survivor's Journey through Grief* (blog). https://homicidesurvivor.wordpress.com/.

Simpson, Audra. 2014. *Mohawk Interruptus: Political Life across the Borders of Settler States*. Durham, NC: Duke University Press.

Simpson, Leanne. 2014. "Fish Broth and Fasting." In *The Winter We Danced: Voices from the Past, the Future and the Idle No More Movement*, edited by the Kino-nda-niimi Collective, 154–7. Winnipeg: ARP Books.

Smith, Andrea. 2005. *Conquest: Sexual Violence and Native American Genocide*. Boston: South End Press.

Stark, Heidi K. 2016. "Criminal Empire: The Making of the Savage in a Lawless Land." *Theory & Event* 19 (4). https://www.muse.jhu.edu /article/633282.

Welsh, Christine, dir. 2006. *Finding Dawn*. Ottawa: National Film Board of Canada. DVD.

Wolfe, Patrick. 2006. "Settler Colonialism and the Elimination of the Native." *Journal of Genocide Research* 8 (4): 387–409. https://doi.org/10.1080 /14623520601056240.

3 Colonizing Critical Race Studies/ Scholars: Counting for Nothing?

SUNERA THOBANI

The black woman has learned from the behaviour of her master and mistress that if accommodation results in patronizing loosening of her bonds, liberation will be more painful.

– Hazel Carby, "On the Threshold of Woman's Era"

Institutionalizing such fields as Ethnic Studies still contains an inevitable paradox: institutionalization provides a material base within the university for a transformative critique of traditional disciplines and their traditional separations, and yet the institutionalization of any field or curriculum that establishes orthodox objects and methods submits in part to the demands of the university and its educative function of socializing subjects into the state.

– Lisa Lowe, "Immigrant Acts"

Introduction

As a meeting that I attended while I was writing this chapter began to wrap up, an administrator approached me to inquire whether I might consider joining a committee working on issues of concern to women faculty. I responded that I had participated in a meeting of that very committee a few years earlier when I had urged committee members to address a number of issues of concern to women of colour faculty, particularly the racial wage gap. The suggestion did not go down well, I explained, as I was not invited back to committee meetings. To this, the administrator retorted, "Well, it is the Women's Committee, not the Equity Committee." The message was not difficult to decipher: women of colour faculty do not count as "woman" in a top tier Canadian university – that is, unless we are prepared to negate our lived experience in the service of upholding the whiteness of the category "woman."

Another incident soon followed to remind me of the command that women of colour erase our own experience and knowledge to uphold the racial power structure of the institution. In this instance, I was presented with a document that was the official response to my repeated complaints of being bullied and harassed. Among other measures, the document stipulated the forfeiture of my right to file an official grievance under the university's "Respectful Environment Statement" as well as its policy on "Discrimination and Harassment," the latter covering the grounds included in the Human Rights Code. Granting me partial and conditional relief from an unbearably toxic work environment, the terms of the document also offered an undetermined form of "mediation" in response to my request – earlier agreed upon verbally – for an independent investigation of my work environment. The document was revised after I refused to sign it. The story of what led to this situation is sordid and long; it is for another day. The point I want to underscore here is that, as a woman of colour faculty, I could not take my human rights, so to speak, as unconditionally protected in, or by, this institution.

The first incident reveals the paradoxical feminist ejection of women of colour from the category "woman," even as this politics promises gendered inclusion; the imposition of the category "woman" here instantiates the negation of the being of women of colour in the very moment that it offers recognition. This encounter also speaks to the ready administrative transmutation of "race" into the bureaucratized category "equity." The second incident demonstrates the institutional will to strip away the status of "human" from the unruly woman of colour by bargaining individual access to the hard-fought-for legal protections against such erasure. Moreover, the institutional sanction of the racial toxicity in its workplace culture is evident in the deployment of such punitive compulsion. Reading the two experiences together – uncannily, they occurred in the same period of time – demonstrated to me that women of colour faculty are neither "woman" nor "human" within the Canadian university, and that our claim to rights and protections is contingent on perceived good behaviour. These rights can be dispensed with where and when the governing elites of this institution deem it expedient.

I make no claim here to my experience being exceptional. There is now a body of scholarship that demonstrates otherwise. Moreover, a number of trusted colleagues and legal experts whom I consulted with regard to the above-mentioned document assured me that the stipulation that had disturbed me so was neither unusual nor of concern. Indeed, an administrator who attempted to make the document a condition for the review of my promotion file assured me that signing it would be for my own protection. For women of colour, the cost of inclusion in this institution is non-membership in its system of rights.

Part study of institutional practices, part auto-ethnography, and part political memoir, this chapter is an interrogation of the techniques of power deployed in, first, the disciplining of women of colour faculty; and second, the colonization of our insurgent knowledge traditions in the Canadian university. Even as the sorts of practices I am describing here shape the experience of many – one might even say most – women of colour faculty, not much attention has been directed to how such punitive governance practices regularly emanate from "progressive," in this case feminist and queer, institutional sites. It will be my argument that this "progressive" site is constitutive of the university's governing mechanism and practices. Like the encounters they attempt to regulate, these practices are informed by the university's embeddedness in racial-colonial logics – at the level of representation and epistemology – that are presently manifest in neoliberalizing forms of management. It is my contention that these practices are now at the forefront of the appropriation, redefinition, and neutralization of insurgent knowledges and justice-oriented praxis that emanate from the work of unruly women of colour and Indigenous women faculty.

Critical Race Studies: A Curious Absence

The centrality of the university to the production, and institutionalization and dissemination, of the racial-colonial discourses that shape national and international relations and conflicts is the subject of increasing attention (Wilder 2013; Ferguson 2012; Chatterjee and Maira 2014; Arday 2018). Accounts of campus battles over the "free speech" of white supremacists; censures of pro-Palestinian Boycott, Divestment, Sanctions (BDS) activism; and tolerance for Islamophobic, anti-Black, and anti-Asian racism on North American campuses now appear regularly in the media. Yet, even as such white supremacist organizing on campus and liberal support for imperialist wars have redefined the political landscape of the Canadian university, none of the "progressive" interdisciplinary fields or the "older" academic disciplines have made it their priority to centre the study of race or promote anti-racist/colonial epistemologies and pedagogies within their respective fields. Despite the efforts of women of colour scholars – many of whose careers in the social sciences and humanities are dedicated to these topics and whose work draws on traditions broadly defined under the rubric of critical race studies (CRS) – such work languishes on the margins of the conventional disciplines and the now equally conventional "new" interdisciplines. In other words, CRS has yet to come into its own as a distinct, self-defining field of scholarship in the Canadian university, even as the racial politics of the last two decades have irrupted in violence the world over.

My own experience within the university leads me to consider such treatment of CRS, and of the women of colour engaged in this field, as neither benign oversight nor unfamiliarity with the subject matter as suggested in the recent spate of statements of support for Black Lives Matter emanating from across the institution. Rather, I identify an active hostility at work towards CRS, primarily for its destabilizing effects on the institution and its hierarchies of power. The scholars working in this interdisciplinary field are perceived within the institution as a threat that heralds the unravelment of its established fields of study and, by extension, of the hold of elites over the institution itself. Hence, bodies of knowledge linked to CRS, like the racialized bodies that embody its lived experience, are routinely constructed as disruptive in institutional practices. The analysis of these conditions presented in this chapter draws on my earlier research into Canadian nation-state formation (Thobani 2007) and my research into the global War on Terror (Thobani 2020); my decade and a half of teaching in the fields of women's/gender/sexuality studies as well as CRS; my activism in women's and anti-racist movements; and my participation in countless academic workshops, conferences, and public lectures at universities across Canada.

My early scholarship was shaped by anti-colonial, critical race, and Third World feminist theoretical traditions, yet when I entered the university in Canada, first as a graduate student and later as a member of the faculty, there was no obvious institutional location or support for these traditions. This is not to say that anti-colonial studies and CRS did not have a presence in Canadian universities at the time. They most certainly did. Indeed, a number of Indigenous scholars and scholars of colour with stellar reputations were spearheading this work. A handful of endowed chairs could also be found at a few universities, as could a smattering of courses on particular specializations within CRS. On occasion, national and international conferences were held on these topics. Yet, scholars engaged in this work were typically located within the established disciplinary and interdisciplinary departments and programs that were themselves being critiqued for their Eurocentric epistemologies, pedagogies, and paradigms; valorization of whiteness and colonial governmentalities; and dismissive approaches to race and coloniality. Undertaking the challenging work of CRS at the margins of these inter/disciplines hence undermined the former's scholarly relevance and constrained its impact. These conditions also undermined the status within the institution of the scholars engaged in this work.

The case was somewhat different with regard to First Nations studies, for although the university's larger indifference to this field was obvious, Indigenous scholars had carved out an institutional base that was strongly rooted in the struggles of their communities. Yet the institutional framework for Indigenous inclusion was predicated on multicultural discourses, not on recognition of treaty-based obligations (Gaudry and Lorenz 2018; Grande and Anderson 2017). Moreover, this Indigenous inclusion also reflected the shifting treatment of "race" and "culture" within American anthropology, which then designated Indigenous peoples as having cultures that should be preserved, in contrast to Black people who were defined as racially deficient and hence in need of "racial uplift" (Baker 2010). These divides of "culture" and "race" instituted in Western classificatory systems, including Orientalist designations, were widespread in the Canadian university as constitutive elements of the multiculturalism that shaped the overarching national discourse.

Multiculturalism both obfuscated and justified the university's "race-blind" approaches to its knowledge production; the idea that multiculturalism proved that the nation-state itself was "beyond race" legitimized the social as well as political "redundancy" of this phenomenon. I remember being advised early in my academic career that including the study of Indigenous issues in *Exalted Subjects* would make the book feel outdated. Yet it was clear to me that it was the relation of CRS – arising as it does from the historical consciousness and experience of racialized-colonized peoples, from their "being-for-themselves," as Fanon (1974) put it – to revolutionary praxis that made the field unwelcome.[1] For despite the numerous limitations in the development of this field in other sites, the United States being a salient example, and despite the encroachment of racial liberalism that seeks to impose respectability and quietism on CRS praxis, the field continues to defy institutional containment. Moreover, CRS inevitably has to contend with, however problematically it has done so, the "internal" racial-colonial hierarchies, asymmetrical positionalities, and formations of power that were instituted across the colonial order. This made CRS a productive site for advancing the knowledge that spoke across the "internal" racial hierarchies among what are now dubbed "BIPOC" communities. The debates and conflicts within CRS that resulted from these divides are robust, even when deeply acrimonious and divisive. These debates and conflicts are what keep the field resistant to the siloing off of specific racialized communities and national formations in the grand colonial strategy of divide and rule. In short, the field is yet to be truncated into the mould of the "progressive" interdisciplinary traditions that are not only steeped, but now invested, in Eurocentric rationalities and Western worldviews.

My understanding of feminist politics was forged within such debates in these traditions. Indeed, I was recruited for a faculty position precisely in order to develop anti-racist intellectual projects and to expand women's and gender studies' links to women of colour communities. I had previously served as the first woman of colour president of the National Action Committee on the Status of Women (NAC), Canada's largest feminist organization during the 1990s. That was a moment when anti-racist women's organizing was pushing mainstream social movements to their limits. My involvement in NAC was shaped by a shared commitment in the organization's Women of Colour Caucus to bring anti-racist praxis to the centre of the organization, and through this, to feminist politics across the country; this commitment had brought caucus members together on NAC's executive board.

Not surprising, my tenure as NAC president began with a series of racist responses – from inside as well as outside the organization. The period was also one of a growing backlash and rise of a populism then led by the Reform Party that was pushing national/ist politics further to the right. Employment equity was under attack, as were anti-racist feminist projects, abortion rights, and feminist anti-violence work. Homophobic and anti-immigrant discourses were becoming pervasive in public debates, and feminists of colour – construed as both latecomers to the nation and imposers of "identity politics" and "political correctness" – were a favourite target for public anger. Moreover, racial conflicts were also deepening within feminist organizations at this time. Within NAC, although individual white feminists were unequivocally committed to support the women of colour, no organized anti-racist caucus of white feminists emerged during my tenure.

My experiences at NAC made me acutely aware of just how deep ran the racial-colonial divides in the Canadian women's movement and how entrenched was the feminist investment in the idea of Canadian exceptionalism. As my tenure at NAC became more and more fractious, I became convinced of the need for an independent, cross-country organizing base for women of colour to advance anti-racist politics and to build alliances, particularly with Indigenous women, that remained outside the dominance of white feminism. Building this political vision and the base for dialogue and shared knowledge production, along with advancing the organizational capacity of women of colour to counter the growing backlash, were the objectives I carried into the university.

My project then was to establish a centre or institute that would foster the conditions for such research and scholarship; a space for exchange, debate, and coalition building; and a site that could function as a think tank to intervene in the political debates of the day and promote anti-racist political activism.

I began this work in the university along two tracks: the establishment of a cross-country research network, which eventually developed into Researchers and Academics of Colour for Equity (RACE); and the building of a base for CRS at the University of British Columbia (UBC), particularly through the remaking of a pre-existing centre into RAGA, the Centre for Race, Autobiography, Gender and Aging. Working with like-minded women of colour colleagues, we organized a national conference at UBC in 2001 to profile critical race and Indigenous feminist scholarship. At the consultation which followed, participants discussed the challenges we faced in our research and scholarship, as well as our experiences in our workplace. The magnitude of the challenges faced by participants – from lack of institutional support to marginalization, harassment, and intimidation – convinced the gathering of the need to establish an organization that would advance our scholarship, strengthen our research networks, and provide support to colleagues under attack at their respective institutions. It was thus that RACE, a network that was the first of its kind in Canada, was born.[2] At UBC, we initiated CRS related activities – workshops, symposia, film screenings, student panels, and conferences – to strengthen the linkages among scholars of colour and of Indigenous ancestry. This work eventually led to my appointment in 2008 as the director of RAGA, whose mandate was now redefined to begin the task of laying the groundwork for a CRS program.

It is the work related to these ground-up initiatives, and the institutional responses they elicited, that are addressed in the following sections. A number of points need clarification before I proceed any further. First, I do not claim here that the colleagues with whom I worked in the two initiatives subscribed to a singular theoretical or political approach to CRS, or to the extent of its remit. As is the case in all such interdisciplinary fields, we drew upon, and were advancing, a range of epistemological approaches to the study of race and colonialism. We did, however, share a commitment to advance a CRS program that was led by, and tied to the advancement of, the leadership of Indigenous women and women of colour faculty and students.

Second, the events and incidents discussed throughout this chapter are not presented in chronological order so as to protect the anonymity and confidentiality of colleagues, students, and administrators with whom I worked in a period that covered over a decade and a half. Moreover, I do not refer to any individual by their actual academic rank, title, name, or other identifying markers. Instead, individuals are referred to by their institutional role. Individuals holding positions of managerial authority – regardless of level and rank – are referred to as "administrators"; this designation is only to apprise the reader of their access to institutional power. I take this term from Bill Readings (1996), who defined the "administrator" as the "new hero of the university"; he also noted that this managerial class of the "university in ruins" may or may not be drawn from within the professoriate. My use of this particular term also emphasizes the point that I do not consider the institutional responses to my work as arising from the ill intent of any particular individual or as locatable only at the interpersonal level in terms of conflict, personality clashes, or communication styles. Indeed, I take the encounters I study here to be rooted in long-standing epistemological and political struggles, that is, in the conflicting political visions, objectives, and interests that have made the university the contested site that it remains. Put more bluntly, I consider the events, encounters, and conflicts discussed here as reflective of larger historical struggles and contemporary battles over the meaning, function, and future of the university. These conflicts are rooted in the foundational matrix of the institution, as well as in the larger economy and polity in which the university functions to produce, organize, and legitimize structures of racial power, with its intersecting social relations and hierarchies.

The section that follows presents a very brief discussion of some of the epistemological, representational, and political issues at stake in the establishment of CRS as a self-defining field, as much as such "autonomy" is possible within a neoliberalizing Canadian institution. I then move to discuss a number of representative incidents that reveal the inhospitable conditions that make such CRS work (im)possible. For reasons that become clear in this section, such work has profoundly destabilizing effects on the institutional status and political projects of the "progressive interdisciplines," including, in this case, women's and gender studies, sexuality studies, and anti-oppression/social justice studies, which are generally taken for granted as transparently "egalitarian" sites within the institution. The institutional practices I identify as at work in the incidents I describe provide a valuable glimpse into how racial-colonial logics are extended into neoliberal governance practices that are lived out in the daily operations of the university. Ultimately, as I discuss in the conclusion, it was the practices emanating from these "progressive" spaces that destroyed the possibilities for the building of an autonomous institutional base for CRS.

Three main practices are identified here in the "progressive" responses to the transformative potential of CRS. First is the appropriation of the creative intellectual labour of women of colour as "belonging" to feminist, gender, and sexuality studies. This proprietorial assertion is a vital element in the rights of whiteness that are so routinely asserted in the university, assertions that are constitutive of "whiteness" itself "as property" as theorized by Cheryl Harris, and by Delia Douglas in this collection. My reading of this appropriative gesture shows how it subjugates the women of colour who develop this work as it upholds the primacy of gender and sexuality scholarship. Second, the appropriation functions through an institutional reworking of race as analogous to, and interchangeable with, gender and sexuality, such that the whiteness dominating women's, gender, and sexuality studies becomes extended over the field of CRS. This imposition of equivalence to override the innovative frameworks and intellectual activities developed by women of colour scholars allows feminist and queer scholars to engage in a hostile takeover that is represented as a benevolent gesture, an act of solidarity. The takeover aligns the institution's colonizing tendency with its neoliberal technologies of governance to advance a "post-racial" order in the very moment that race is recognized as a salient factor. Third, the punitive measures for resistance to the university's racial status quo include demonization of women of colour alongside other institutional punishments. Dehumanization, bullying, harassment, and infliction of stress and trauma through fostering toxic work environments are often the forms such punishment assumes. The coming together of these three practices – appropriation, subjugation, and punishment – results in the institutional disenfranchisement of women of colour scholars that confirms the proprietary rights of whiteness. Anti-racism praxis is thus met with the punitive force of the institution, presently spearheaded in the university's "progressive" sites with their thin veneer of "inclusion."

Whiteness in the Canadian University: Not Us, Not Here

Even as Canadian institutions are embedded in the production of racial-imperial hierarchies at the national as well as international level, their technologies of governance function largely through the denial of race as an axis of power structuring the nation-state itself. The official discourses of multiculturalism, diversity, and equity, and more recently, that of "reconciliation" are integral to this form of governance. A typical example is a survey on racism that begins by conflating "prejudice" with "racism" and finds that "Canadians think racism is on the rise in

the world but not here."[3] This "not us, not here" approach only ruptures, and even then only momentarily, in the most egregious and
politically sensational cases that come to be treated as uncharacteristic
and aberrant (the mass shootings of Muslims, police violence, a prime
minister in Blackface, for recent examples).[4] At moments of political
upheaval – such as that generated globally by the Indigenous Resurgence, Black Lives Matter, and other anti-racist protests – statements of
good intent and promises to do better at inclusion are proffered. This
treatment of racial and colonial violence as aberrations and unintended
underscores how obfuscation of these relations of power is the rule in
Canadian institutions, notwithstanding the everywhere visible signs of
Indigenous dispossession, racial segregation, and structural racisms.

Such claims of racial innocence, what Jiwani (2007) calls "discourses
of denial," are repeatedly deconstructed by critical race scholars who
have demonstrated how the constitution of whiteness is articulated to
the language of cultural tolerance that grounds Canadian nationalism
(Jiwani 2007; Ladner and Tait 2017; Razack, Smith, and Thobani 2010;
Bannerji 2000; Thobani 2007; Dua 2007; Maracle 1988). Within the university, CRS scholars disrupt the reproduction of the "not us, not here"
narrative by centring the histories, epistemologies, and perspectives
of Indigenous peoples and people of colour. As such, this scholarship
opens up possibilities for tracking and transforming the "race blind"
form of whiteness that now organizes the racial hierarchy. More relevant than ever in this racial configuration is Sylvia Wynter's (2006)
observation regarding Eurocentric epistemological traditions, that
"you cannot solve the issue of 'consciousness' in terms of their body of
'knowledge.'" Moreover, as Wynter's engagement with these Western
traditions also shows, the question of race, specifically Blackness in
her work, is inseparable from that of gender and sexuality. One consequence of such attention to the complexities entailed in the production
of race is that it inevitably leads to the questioning of the white feminist
and queer suppression of the experience and knowledge of women and
queers of colour, a condition requisite to the former's claim to speak in
the name of all "Others."

Another key aspect of the organization of Canadian whiteness in
the university is its rupturing of the internal connection of CRS to the
intellectual-political leadership of women of colour and Indigenous
women. This leadership has been crucial to the historical advancements
in knowledge about, and resistance to, colonial-racial forms of dehumanization, violence, and injustice. Some examples include Indigenous
women's linking of the residential school system to ongoing sexual
violence, and of the link between such violence and the destruction of

Indigenous sovereignty (Maracle 1988; Simpson, chapter two this volume; Million 2013). Black feminists developed the concept of intersectionality to draw attention to the centrality of race in the production of gender, class, and sexuality (Crenshaw 1991; Hill Collins 1998). Women of colour scholars studied the production of the Canadian nation through the racialization of migration and identified the processes that continue to situate Black, Asian, and other "immigrant" women at the bottom of its hierarchies (Das Gupta 1996; Calliste and Dei 2000; Ng 1996; Bannerji 1995); they also identified how the gendering of immigration and citizenship policy produces racial/ethnic enclaves, as well as "immigrant" and "refugee" communities as threats to the nation's welfare and security (Dua 2007; Razack 1998; Thobani 2007). Yet, these intellectual breakthroughs and their opening up of critical political space have not reshaped feminist herstories or the whiteness that structures "progressive" interdisciplinary fields in Canadian universities.

Certainly, the project of building a base for CRS was not without peril. The fraught dynamic of inclusion and exclusion that shapes the interdisciplines is also a challenge faced by CRS, as is the pressure of institutional co-optation (Ferguson 2012). Yet, despite such challenges, as Gates (1991) argued some decades ago in his defence of developing African American studies, "the choice is not between institutions and no institutions. The choice is always, What kind of institutions shall there be?" (110). Gates was arguing in defence of constructing a canon for the nascent field. He was taking on the opposition from the academic right to what it considered a displacement of the Western canon through "politicizing" knowledge; Gates was also countering the view from the left that building African American studies could only advance institutional co-optation.

At a later date, Ferguson (2012) would argue that it was precisely the entry of the new interdisciplines into the university, including race and ethnic studies, that "denote the moments in which minority difference entered full historical narration" (32). Prior to this development, it was "Western Man" who stood at the centre of the intellectual labour of the disciplines. Ferguson defines the challenge that was faced by radical scholars as how to be "in" the institution but not "of" it. Mike Murase likewise noted that the development of ethnic studies and Asian American studies "marks the first organized effort within the formal education system to reinterpret the history of Third World peoples" from the perspective of Asian Americans in the United States and to "disseminate the life stories of millions of non-white people in America" (quoted in Ferguson 2012, 32). Such debates, and the opposition to their entry into the academy, intensified in the culture wars of neoliberalism, and as I demonstrate below, now emanate from the powerful institutional base established by the white-dominated, Eurocentric-oriented, progressive interdisciplines in the Canadian university.

Much as the perils of incorporation of CRS into reformist institutional agendas cannot be minimized, neither can the risks arising from reproduction within the field of theoretical approaches that essentialize race, or that are fixated on the rights-based framework of the nation-state to obfuscate the global structure of colonial-racial post-modernity. Although CRS coheres around deconstruction of the multiple productions and normalizations of "race" and "colonialism," whether in biologically determinist, culturally relativist, social constructionist, or bio/necropolitical terms, the danger of essentialization remains real enough. However, the centring of the experience, knowledge, and forms of being that are organically tied to the global struggles of peoples of colour and Indigenous peoples give CRS its disruptive quality. In the United States, this field has made major strides in the university in the programs and departments that make up its various permutations, including African American and Black studies, critical ethnic studies, Asian American studies, Latinx studies, and Native American/Indigenous studies, all indelibly shaped by the work of women of colour and Indigenous women – scholars, activists, artists, writers, orators.

The suppression of debates and scholarship about race facilitates the reproduction of the Canadian institution's whiteness; this also forces CRS scholars into an ongoing struggle to cling onto the footholds so precariously carved into the margins of the existing academic structure. It is therefore not surprising that recent studies find scholars of colour and Indigenous scholars to be among the most underrepresented in the social sciences and humanities (Henry et al. 2017), fields that study the social world, its histories, politics, cultures, political economy, and so on. This relegation of CRS scholarship to the very edges of the fields that produce knowledge about a world in which our communities of concern are disenfranchised, dispossessed, and brutalized cannot but contribute to these very forms of violence.

In addition to the issues discussed above, a number of other no less salient concerns that arose from my work in the women's movement, most particularly in NAC, influenced my work upon getting a faculty appointment. First was the internationalist dimension of the anti-racist analysis and political activism of the NAC Women of Colour Caucus; second was the gaping divide between Indigenous women and women of colour in the crosscutting movements of the period; and third was the investment of the mainstream women's movement in the idea of Canadian exceptionalism. These interconnected factors compounded the task of building political solidarity between women of colour and Indigenous women, a task already overburdened by the dominating presence of white feminisms over women's organizing. It would take me too far afield to discuss these factors at length here; suffice it for me to briefly outline why these concerns mattered in my work in the university.

The anti-racism of the women of colour in the NAC caucus was heavily influenced by the anti-colonial/imperialist praxis that had historically developed in the global context of Euro-American empires. Moreover, many of us came from working-class communities. It was therefore from these community-based and collective perspectives that the caucus engaged mainstream feminist politics; now working within a national organization, our political priorities developed in a manner that linked settler colonialism in Canada to our own histories of colonialism as a global structure. We defined neoliberalism as the latest iteration of this structure, which tied Indigenous dispossession to migration, structural adjustment policies, as well as the privatization of the welfare-state system. The political solidarities we sought to advance were therefore envisioned in this expansive global-historical context; our critique of the racial-colonial logics of the Canadian nation-state linked this to the imperialist domination of the nation-state system imposed upon the Third World. The work of our caucus was, by its very nature, opposed to the nationalist tendency that ran so strongly through the Canadian feminist movement. The political positions and campaigns of the caucus were hence grounded in a critique of the Canadian state that spoke to its domestic as well as its foreign policy interests. These expansive approaches were met – inside the feminist organization as well as in its allied social movements – with accusations of inadequate comprehension of Canadian politics, and even of feminist politics, soon followed by a deepening hostility towards what was considered our focus on issues irrelevant to "Canadian" women.

With regard to the divide between the women of colour and Indigenous women's movements, the NAC caucus was in no doubt about the power of white feminism as an overdetermining force in our attempt to build relations of solidarity. The following example illustrates the challenges presented to us by this overwhelming character of white feminist politics; it concerns the "national constitutional debates" of the early 1990s regarding the political, cultural, and legislative relationship between "English" Canada and "French" Quebec, and of both to Indigenous nations. This debate took place within the feminist movement, likewise focused on the relationship between the Quebecois and Canadian women's movements and their relationship to Indigenous women's movements. As was the case with the "progressive" position being developed at the time towards a resolution of this "national question," the feminist debate within NAC centered upon, and advanced, the "three nations" position – that is, the recognition that "Canada" was founded not by two nations, British and French, as was reorganized by the Report of the Royal Commission on Bilingualism and Biculturalism, 1967–1970, but by three nations, British, French, and Indigenous. This "resolution" gestured towards Indigenous inclusion into Canadian nationhood, an important development in the wake of the Oka crises and ongoing Indigenous activism, but it did so through reiteration of the foundational racial-colonial logics of the settler colonial nation-state. Encoded into this resolution was the whiteness of the Canadian national project through reinstatement of its British-ness and French-ness, while the recognition of the "third nation" incorporated Indigenous nations, communities, and peoples into this homogenizing and Eurocentric construction of nationhood.

Moreover, this redefined Canadian nationhood erased the presence, struggles, and concerns of women of colour in the country, making illegible their histories of colonization, enslavement, indentureship, and migration. This domination of the gendered national debates by white feminists, no doubt committed to advance a progressive, inclusionary politics based upon their recognition of Indigenous women/peoples, preserved their own idea of the gendered nation that eliminated space for women of colour in its politics. Relegated to the status of latecomers in these proprietary politics, any attempt by women of colour to participate in these debates was to risk being constructed by white feminists as opponents of the gains made by Indigenous women. To speak of the histories of the colonial-racial subjugation of women of colour was to risk coming into visibility through the lens of racist opposition to recognition of Indigenous claims. These debates made clear to many women of colour that building political solidarities with Indigenous women had to be done on a basis other than its mediation through such gendered Canadian nationalism. Certainly, the divisions were significant in the political perspectives of women of colour with regard to this, and other, issues, which I have no intention to gloss over. All I can do here is point to the complex racial-colonial divides, hierarchies, and politics that had to be navigated in the work of the NAC Women of Colour Caucus.

The solidarity among the women of colour in the caucus – to the extent that we built it during my tenure – was based upon, and constantly fought over, the commonalties in our experiences of struggle and our shared objectives, not on essentializing approaches to racial or ethnic difference, or on the basis of cultural nationalism. Building solidarity across the asymmetrically situated communities of colour from which caucus members came, and in the process, working to transform the mainstream women's movement was the larger objective that held this project together. Developing a broad yet deep enough political consensus on particular issues and campaigns was the means of possibility for advancing our work. This political project-in-common was sustainable only through robust debate, constant attempts to bridge our divides, and nurturing our relationships in the caucus space where we could retreat from the organization's whiteness. Essentializing political approaches would of course emerge on a recurring basis, but these were, and had to be, contested in our working relationships. The stakes in holding our coalition together were clear to caucus members; we learned to navigate the pitfalls we encountered as we also contested the essentialization of whiteness and naturalization of nationalism within Canadian feminism.

As I look back at that experience, albeit short-lived, I consider the space created within the caucus for women of colour and Indigenous women to engage with, debate, and confront our asymmetrical positionalities and divergent political perspectives as having been vital to our collective political development. Relatively independent of the white feminist presence that dominated the organization, the caucus also provided us a space to engage with the larger organization from a position of (relative) strength, a crucial factor in the changes we did make at the time. It was thus from such an always already-fleeting commonality of purpose within the caucus that members built our solidarities with white feminists. When the caucus eventually fractured, it was on the grounds of political disagreements that could no longer be reconciled, and not on the basis of essentialist ideas about racial/ethnic/cultural incommensurability. This experience was the immediate context that also informed my CRS-related work within the university.

The Institutionalization of Feminist Power: Counting for Nothing?

As mentioned above, my initial appointments in the university were in women's and gender studies (WAGS), a well-established interdiscipline by that time. This field has since expanded into women's, gender, and sexuality studies, and then again into social justice studies. These developments are generally viewed positively within the university, even though there is the perennial hand-wringing over the loss of "woman" as the central focus of concern. The reasons for these developments are varied. Robyn Weigman (1995), for example, attributed the first shift to the feminist disappointment at the failure of women's studies to hasten the liberation that was its promise. She argued that many feminists took the turn to theory, and to expand their focus to include gender/ sexuality, as the means to realize this potential, whereas Wendy Brown (2008) identified the non-singularity of the foundational category and concern of women's studies as rendering the feminist project itself impossible. The extent to which these shifts were driven by women of colour's contestation of the whiteness of the feminist project, and of WAGS within the university, remains significant; this cannot be left unattended.

Women of colour scholars in Canada were underrepresented in WAGS during the 1990s, more so perhaps than even in the older disciplines, while the presence of Indigenous women faculty was almost non-existent. These representational disparities were addressed within the field by periodic attempts at "inclusion" by hiring adjunct faculty and by celebrations of "diversity" that closely echoed the rhetoric that was a mainstay of state multiculturalism. The earlier critiques developed by women of colour and Indigenous women of the whiteness of feminist/ women's studies programs, centres, and movements; of their Western values and exclusionary hiring practices; of their Eurocentric epistemologies and curriculum had little impact on the development of WAGS itself. These critiques were – more often than not – met with defensive postures and offensive attacks, the former leading to much agonizing about the difficulties of recruiting qualified women of colour, the latter to admonishment of their infantile investment in an "identity politics" that threatened to derail the feminist project, defined as beyond race. Although I had studied these critiques and, having learned important lessons from my own work in women's organizations, was viscerally aware of the white feminist backlash against the anti-racist politics of women of colour, I was nonetheless unprepared for the depth of the hostility to anti-racist work within the Canadian university. No doubt the shift in racial politics brought about by the War on Terror intensified this hostility, and as I was soon to learn, also heightened the stakes within this "liberal" institution that became once again situated on the front lines of disciplining, neutralizing, and containing radical intellectual work as well as the women of colour scholars who produced it.

Women's lived experience is, of course, a privileged site within feminist methodologies; the theorization of the political as grounded in the personal has been a cornerstone of WAGS since its inception, as was standpoint theory (Pateman 1988; Harding 2004; Ahmed 2000). Illustrating how power circulates in the everyday gendered encounters that were dismissed in other academic fields as trivial and unworthy of attention, feminist theory pivoted on the insight that gender oppression is folded into the most mundane aspects of daily life in the private as well as the public spheres. It is therefore ironic that women of colour's interrogations of how racial power, including that of white women, functions in our everyday lives were, and continue to be even now, dismissed by white feminists as born of resentment, anger, or downright vindictiveness (hooks 1981; Lourde 1984, Mirza 1997).

The problem of whiteness that women of colour were struggling with was hence deeply entrenched in WAGS, much as it was across the institution and the larger social order. The conditions within UBC during this period were to later become the subject of a report commissioned by the President's Office, *Implementing Inclusion: A Consultation on Organizational Change to Support UBC's Commitment to Equity and Diversity* (Iyer and Nakata 2013). It is notable that this report found the university was failing to meet its own mandate as articulated in its strategic plan, *Place and Promise: The UBC Plan*, which envisioned the institution as "vital" to the "social and economic well-being" of British Columbians, as a "place for dialogue on the issues of the day" (Office of the President 2012, 3). *Implementing Inclusion* identified race as a major factor in the failure of the university to deliver on its promise; the report drew attention to the glaring underrepresentation of Indigenous scholars and scholars of colour in leadership positions and linked this inequality to the culture of institutional whiteness that was pervasive within the university. Stating in no uncertain terms that there existed a "lack of representation of racialized groups in senior positions and on committees … lack of safe spaces for racialized groups, and the persistence of Eurocentric norms in the evaluation of scholarship and work performance" (Iyer and Nakata 2013, 14), the report was blunt in its observation that "UBC's leadership and therefore its key decision-makers are predominantly white" (14). The conditions identified in this report were hence part of the institutional context for my CRS-related work, and the failures later identified by the report shaped the environment in which this work was received.

Unaware though I might have been of the full extent of the problem of race across this institution as later documented by the report, I was certainly not immune to its consequences. I was learning quickly how it was not just the "lack of representation" that was the problem; more concerning was the active destruction of anti-racist initiatives and leadership of women of colour that was taking place within the university. In my own case, for example, I was informed by administrators at a periodic review that my record of service was insufficient for consideration for promotion. Although research, publications, and teaching count for much more in tenure and promotion calculations, it was "service" that was made the issue in my case. I had served on every university committee to which I had been assigned; I had also provided extensive details about the activities and projects I had undertaken to promote CRS on campus and across the country, which included the organization of workshops, symposia, and national conferences for faculty and students of colour; development of research networks to promote anti-racist scholarship; expansion of the university's links to communities of colour; and mentoring undergraduate and graduate students of colour. These activities, I explained to the administrators, served not only the UBC community but also the larger academic community in the country. This work was, after all, what I had initially been appointed to undertake. The response of these feminist administrators? "This counts for nothing," one stated, and the other concurred. This "assessment" of my work was echoed in eerily similar terms in the experience described to me at a workshop by an Indigenous colleague. Her work, she explained, was constantly devalued and undermined by her colleagues. "They tell me I am nothing, and I keep doing all this work. But they keep telling me I am nothing, so I want to know on what basis am I nothing," she told me. This colleague's experience, as well as my own, is documented by other women of colour scholars who have described how they are "presumed incompetent" at leading US universities (Gutiérrez y Muhs et al. 2012).

Unpacking exactly what it is that "counts for nothing" proved to be a productive exercise. It revealed the enormity of the issues at stake in such feminist and institutional dismissal of the work of women of colour and Indigenous women scholars. The stakes are nothing less than control by feminist scholars and administrators over their "everything" within the institution, that is, over their universalization of their whiteness to further their gendered access to institutional power. Their control relies on the neutralization of the anti-racist deconstruction of the category "woman," and of "gender" politics as essentially white. This containment of anti-racist praxis necessitates the destruction of the autonomous leadership of women of colour and Indigenous women that resists the dictates of white tutelage. Subjugation of women of colour and Indigenous women scholars is thus indispensable to the self-representation of the white feminist scholar as the heroic subject of this institution.

I experienced another equally instructive encounter on an ad hoc committee formed to organize an event for International Women's Day (IWD). Committee members discussed various themes for the event; my suggestion was to highlight the issue of murdered and missing Indigenous women and girls (MMIWG), given how serious this violence was in the city. The suggestion was eagerly accepted. At the next meeting, committee members were informed that a white feminist was to be invited to speak on this issue. How, where, when, or who made this decision was not clear. The possibility that an IWD event on MMIWG would be organized to provide a platform to a white feminist had not even occurred to me when I made the suggestion, and I immediately objected. The event should feature Indigenous women, scholars, and activists working on the issue, I argued. No support was expressed for this position. Once the vote was called, I requested the discussion, as well as my opposition, be recorded in the minutes. This request was denied, and I was informed the minutes would only record the vote, not the discussion or my name as the dissenting vote.

Soon after, the copy of a letter written to the committee chair on behalf of Indigenous women activists in the city who opposed the planned IWD event was passed on to me anonymously. The letter's authors objected to the event on the basis that, as Aboriginal women, they had led the organizing for the murdered and missing women and opposed white feminists' "profiting" from their pain and activism. The letter stated in no uncertain terms the intention of the signatories to organize a protest should the IWD event go ahead as planned. The next committee meeting proceeded with no mention of this letter. I raised the matter, at which committee members accused me of "pushing" them "to take sides" on the issue. They argued that they were committed to "dialogue" and supported the expression of a "plurality" of views on the matter. They then went on to accuse the authors of the letter of "bullying" them. As for the protest mentioned in the letter, the chair ended the discussion by stating that those who wanted to attend the IWD event would do so, and those who wished to join the protest were free to do that. In any case, the event was later cancelled when a sponsoring partner withdrew their support.

This attempted transformation of an event to support Indigenous women's activism against settler violence into an opportunity to honour a white feminist was an appropriative act, but such appropriation was here underwritten by the feminist access to institutional authority. A committee established to celebrate international women's activism was thus remade into an occasion for the extension of white feminist control over the representation of Indigenous women and their activism. The construction of Indigenous activists as the aggressors who spurned feminist benevolence, and of white feminists as the victims of such aggression, shaped this white feminist narrative of ingratitude. The resulting production of "victimized" gendered whiteness – "pushed" by women of colour and "bullied" by Indigenous women – redefined what were quite basic anti-racist organizing principles into injury to white feminists.

The cultivation of gendered white victimization to shut down anti-racist feminist praxis would become more pronounced over time. The practice surfaced soon enough in another encounter and in an equally disruptive manner, this time in connection with the research-related activities of students of colour and of Indigenous ancestry. Given the paucity of CRS-related courses on campus, students of colour and Indigenous students interested in this scholarship initiated the formation of a research network that was housed at the RAGA centre. I served as one of two mentors for the group. Students from the network had, in line with the centre's policy, booked the space for one of their regular meetings. I was away when the meeting took place, but upon my return was immediately summoned by an administrator to her office. Apparently, she had received a complaint from a white student who reported being denied access to the centre. This student, the administrator informed me, did not feel "welcome" at RAGA and wondered whether the centre "belonged" to her too. I was told in no uncertain terms to change the centre's policy so that white students could use the space as and when they so wanted. Upon inquiry, I learned from the student of colour network coordinator that, as their scheduled meeting got underway, the white student had come to the centre and demanded she be allowed to use the space. The coordinator explained that the network had booked the space and that the white student was welcome to use the centre during the hours allotted to her (all students were given scheduled access to RAGA workstations upon application). Upon receiving these details, I did not change the centre's space use policy. My decision, however, was read by the administrator as uncooperative and hostile.

The sheer absurdity of the directive that the space use policy of a centre focused on race be changed to accommodate the *sense of entitlement* over the space of a white student by overriding *the right* of students of colour was apparently lost on the administrator. In this case, gendered whiteness was construed as vulnerable to exclusion and victimization by students of colour. The white student's experience of the presence of students of colour as an obstacle to her assertion of her entitlement was upheld by the white administrator, who both confirmed and enhanced the student's sense of racial power. In this textbook case of white racial bonding, the administrator's validation of the student's preposterous demand likewise constructed the students of colour as the source of aggression (their presence made the space "unwelcome"). My refusal to give in to the administrator's attempt to push me to violate the most basic tenets of anti-racist practice, let alone the university's own workplace protocols and student support policies, ended up constructing me as belligerent and non-compliant. White ownership of the (publicly funded) university space was thus normalized so that the mere presence of students of colour, even when they followed regulations, was deemed intolerable. Indeed, the mere presence of bodies of colour was taken to render the space unwelcoming.

These incidents I recount here not because I consider them exceptional or the most egregious that I have experienced in the university, or have had described to me by colleagues. I recount them because they demonstrate how institutionalized feminist power functions in such routine acts of racial inclusion (whiteness) and racial violation (non-whiteness). This use of institutionalized power to decimate the rights of women of colour is also illustrated in the next example.

I had arrived a few minutes early at a student supervisory committee meeting and found an administrator already seated at the table. As I took my chair, a colleague who also served on the committee arrived. After we exchanged pleasantries, this colleague turned towards me and, out of the blue, said, "If you feel like they're ganging up on you, you should not doubt this. I have seen it happen." Taken aback (I took her comments to refer to an earlier meeting in which we had both participated), I asked her why she thought this was the case. Her answer was short and straightforward. "Racism," she stated. The administrator seated at the table said not a word about this exchange; "equity" was part of their portfolio. My experience of attending meetings during this period was that of being set upon by a gang of schoolyard bullies; the administrator was well aware of these brutalizing encounters, as I had described them to her in detail.

Such refusal to act against racism and bullying I encountered time and time again, but of course this "failure" actually sanctioned the power of colleagues to demean and punish women of colour faculty, and students, who refused the institutional imperative to nurture whiteness. Once, I informed an administrator that my work conditions had deteriorated quite severely due to what I considered retaliation for my CRS-related initiatives. The administrator responded by asking me whether I might be interested in participating in a campus-wide discussion about equity and race. I pointed out that my message referred to specific violations of workplace policies and procedures. This clarification was met with silence.

The administrative refusal to take the most basic action to ensure implementation of the university's *own* workplace policies, not to mention anti-racism legislation, is commonplace, as I heard again and again from women of colour and Indigenous women faculty at numerous workshops and conferences held across the country. In my own case, I came to understood this refusal as either a total lack of concern among the institution's leadership regarding the punitive treatment of women of colour faculty, or its explicit endorsement. This belief has only deepened as I have watched administrators against whom complaints were made by women of colour faculty and students at a number of universities be promoted to higher – and more powerful – positions. Interestingly enough, more often than not, these higher level positions include equity and diversity portfolios.

Implementing Inclusion, the report mentioned above that was commissioned at UBC, identified the university's equity/diversity policies and activities as concentrated in six main areas: "education and training, scholarship, communication, accommodation, proactive initiatives, and compliance" (Iyer and Nakata 2013, 3). Underscoring their finding that the university's structure was "not sufficiently supportive of these [equity] initiatives and even presents a barrier to positive change" (4), the report's authors flagged race as a particular concern. It is notable that, during my tenure at the RAGA centre, we were organizing activities in four of the six areas identified in the report. RAGA was regularly profiling the research as well as leadership of scholars of colour and of Indigenous ancestry in all its activities. In other words, the RAGA centre was addressing the very gaps identified by the report as contributing to the university's failure on meet its own stated objectives. Yet, despite RAGA's success in these areas – *perhaps because of it?* – the centre was all but destroyed two years later. Predictably enough, the university's response to the *Implementing Inclusion* report was to ignore its actionable findings on race. Instead, the very practices that had been identified as "failed" were reinvigorated to appoint yet more white administrators to oversee what the institution defined as its "renewed commitment" to "inclusion." The report's *race specific* recommendations were thus recalibrated to the institution's *race-blind but gender/sexuality specific* approach to equity and inclusion. In other words, the report was put to work to make the university even whiter, an instance of what Ahmed (2012) calls the "non-performativity" of anti-racism policies and Smith (2010) calls the "diversification of whiteness."

From my present vantage point, I can see that the incidents I describe here were shaped by the patterns of racial inequality, abuse, and microaggressions that were being identified and documented by many women of colour faculty in Canada, the United States, and the United Kingdom during the same period (Henry et al. 2017; Gutiérrez y Muhs et al. 2012; Ahmed 2012; Johnson, Joseph-Salisbury, and Kamunge 2018). In my case, each act of resistance against the assertion of white racial power led to my being constructed as the aggressor, unreasonable, and difficult to work with, in short, what is described in the scholarship as "the angry woman of colour." The refusal of women of colour to serve in the role of the grateful supplicant to feminist benevolence continues to be met with demonization.

In my case, things eventually came to a head. To cut a long story short, an external review made the recommendation that, based on the significant accomplishments of RAGA, an Institute for Critical Race Studies be established at the university. The recommendation was not supported by WAGS, then being transformed into a Social Justice Institute to include sexuality, race, and social justice studies. To my knowledge, this was the first time such a recommendation had been made at this university, and as I continued to advocate for the implementation of this recommendation, I experienced what I can only describe as a barrage of hostility that undermined my very ability to do my job. The hostility was expressed in numerous ways, including denial of assistance the university was required to provide following a workplace injury; undermining of my academic freedom by an administrator who met with my students to discuss with them the contents of the course they were taking with me without informing me; allocation of challenging teaching schedules; evaluation of my teaching by an administrator with whom I had reported a conflict; being passed over for merit for the duration of this conflict, despite having received it periodically in the past; and repeated harassment at meetings. The mistresses' tools are wielded with no less ferocity than those of the master.

It is useful to recall Ferguson's (2012) argument that the university functions as a site for the transmutation of insurgent expressions of minority difference into assimilationist modes as I unpack here the two main arguments that were presented to me by administrators as well as colleagues in opposition to the establishment of a CRS Institute. The first was that "race" was already included in WAGS, and in the Social Justice Institute, so there was no need for a CRS Institute; and second, the transfer of sexuality studies into the social justice framework was a model for how CRS could likewise be incorporated. In response, I pointed out that both WAGS and sexuality studies remain rooted in Eurocentric epistemologies and white cultural traditions, and that these interdisciplines have extended the power of whiteness to claim proprietorship over all matters related to gender and sexuality, an argument many CRS scholars have also made. In contrast, CRS is a counter-hegemonic project that contests colonial logics as well as the power of whiteness, the production of race and the global racial hierarchy, the Eurocentrism embedded within the inter/disciplines, and the institutional structures and work cultures of the university. Moreover, in this case, the social justice framework was developed from within WAGS and sexuality studies to advance these traditions, not from within the CRS framework. This is what made the appropriation of the groundwork laid by RAGA a hostile takeover. Both arguments were to no avail.

The integration of race into the social justice framework as analogous to, and interchangeable with, gender and sexuality effectively subjugates CRS to the whiteness that dominates gender and sexuality studies and thereby neutralizes the former's transformative potential. Such absorption also ruptures the organic relation between CRS, antiracist praxis, and the leadership of women of colour. In other words, this absorption of race into social justice studies transforms race into the "difference that makes no difference," to borrow the phrase from Stuart Hall.[5]

The predatory impulse driving the will to appropriation that I am describing found expression in the most incredulous manner at committee meetings. In one such meeting, a white administrator stated to a group of women of colour faculty, students, and community activists who had developed the CRS initiative that race "belongs" to her, and would remain in the Social Justice Institute despite our overwhelming opposition. To this remark, a woman of colour community activist retorted, "This is a total mind-f…"

The study of race does not, of course, "belong" to any one disciplinary or interdisciplinary field to the exclusion of others. Indeed, I have already noted how some of the most important CRS scholarship in Canada was developed by scholars located within the established disciplines as well as the newer interdisciplines. Moreover, arguments for the redundancy of a stand-alone CRS are easily refuted, even by a quick glance at the histories of WAGS and sexuality studies. Many of the older disciplines, including anthropology, sociology, law, history, philosophy, and so on, now routinely offer courses on gender and sexuality. Has this made WAGS or sexuality studies redundant? I have yet to hear feminist or queer scholars argue that all gender-related courses and programs in departments other than WAGS or social justice be shut down because "woman," feminism, and gender "belong" to WAGS, or "queer" and "sexuality" to sexuality studies. Indeed, feminists earlier pushed for and welcomed initiatives to expand the study of gender and sexuality into the older disciplines. In short, the argument that race "belongs" to WAGS/sexuality studies/social justice is no more than a colonizing attitude, a bid to assert control over insurgent traditions and discipline them into neutered pedagogies of minority difference to service whiteness. The white feminist/queer takeover of a CRS initiative in the making ensured the latter's subservience from its very inception, a subservience structured in advance by the concentration of decision-making power over the "anti-racist" mandate, content, and pedagogies of this "CRS" in the hands of white administrators and colleagues.

CRS is not a facsimile of WAGS or queer studies. Moreover, the idea that CRS, and women of colour scholarship in general, is either oblivious or hostile to gender and sexuality can only be sustained by deliberate erasure of the work of the pioneers of CRS and intersectionality. Hong and Ferguson (2011) have pointed out:

> Much of what we call "women of colour feminism" can be seen as queer of colour critique, insofar as these texts consistently situate sexuality as constitutive of race and gender. Further, not coincidentally and not unimportantly, lesbian practice and identity were central to many of the most foundational women of colour feminists, including Audre Lorde, Cherrie Moraga, Barbara Smith, and the Combahee River Collective. We thus narrate queer of colour critique as emerging from women of colour feminism rather than deriving from a white Euro-American gay, lesbian, and queer theory tradition. (2)

Struggle against the institutional erasure of this history – and the politics it founded – is what I take to be the "nothing" that my work amounted to in the estimation of the feminist administrators who shaped my work environment.

As I responded to the arguments against an independent CRS Institute at meeting after meeting, I tried to imagine a comparable scenario wherein feminist scholars had come together, laid the foundation for a feminist studies program, only to be informed by male colleagues and administrators that this work counted for nothing and that it would be they – with no expertise in or commitment to feminist studies, values, and practices – who would establish, develop, and control feminist studies. I found myself unable to even imagine such a scenario, which is equally inconceivable with regard to queer studies. Yet, in the case of CRS, the white-dominated feminist/queer consensus that emerged in opposition to the establishment of an institute found expression in the all-too-familiar racial-colonial – now merged with neoliberal – practices of appropriation, disenfranchisement, and demonization.

Ultimately, the possibility of building a CRS Institute at UBC was destroyed. During this period, however, I was continually struck by how closely the institutional practices I was identifying in the encounters recounted above paralleled the forms of governance I was tracking in my research on neoliberalism, Islamophobia, and the War on Terror. The rise of white supremacist politics in the global war and the rhetoric of white victimization also mirrored the narratives of victimized gendered whiteness cultivated by the women faculty, students, and administrators in the events I have described. These connections cannot be developed further in this chapter; let me just note that the place of the university in reworking the ideologies and practices that feed and sustain contemporary white supremacy cannot be overlooked in studies of the Canadian university.

Social Justice Made Me Do It!

The herstory of WAGS in Canada has been traced back to the activism of second wave feminism in the 1960s and 1970s. This origin story is well ensconced; what it leaves out is the field's conviviality with the politics of whiteness as well as its contentious relation with the intellectual thought and political praxis of women of colour and of Indigenous ancestry. For these latter communities, WAGS quickly became a site regulating their access to the institution itself, its whiteness now supplemented by the inclusion of a feminism that confirmed the university's new-found reputation as "progressive" and "inclusionary." The critique of this feminism's whiteness began with the establishment of WAGS in Canada, as in the United States, in anti-racist and anti-colonial feminist scholarship (Carby 1986; Lourde 1984, hooks 1981; Davis 1981; Maracle 1988; Monture-Angus 1995; Bannerji 2000; Razack, Smith, and Thobani 2010). Evasion of this critique allowed the domination of "race-blind" feminist approaches that reproduced the singularity of the category "woman" and "queer" to become entrenched not only in WAGS and social justice studies but across the university's administrative structure and work culture. The concurrent working of multiculturalism as official "anti-racism" allowed the interdisciplines, including WAGS, to highlight and incorporate culturalizing expressions of minority "difference" (see Ahmed 2012; Razack, Smith, and Thobani 2010; Thobani 2007). However, these "race-blind" and "culturalizing" approaches were made unsustainable by the heightened anti-racist activism of women of colour and of Indigenous women in Canada during the 1990s. This activism, evident in NAC and in other national organizations, including the Native Women's Association of Canada, the National Organization of Immigrant and Visible Minority Women, and the Congress of Black Women, contested the priorities, frameworks, and objectives of Canadian feminisms. The destabilizing effects of these anti-racist and Indigenous feminist politics on Canadian feminisms is the context in which the feminist redefinition of race as analogous to gender has been institutionalized within the Canadian university. Represented as a gesture of "solidarity," this form of feminist inclusion organized its expansion of white institutional power in a gendered form in the university. The subjugation of race to gender and sexuality in the new social justice paradigm now situates this at the forefront of containing and neutralizing women of colour's anti-racist insurgent challenges to institutional power.

I conclude this essay with a brief discussion of how a number of key colonizing practices, namely appropriation, subjugation, and demonization, function to expand white proprietorial rights in feminist and queer vernaculars within the university. Moreover, as these practices advance contemporary forms of neoliberal governance, their punitive dimension makes a mockery of the "academic freedom" said to be sacrosanct within the university. Yet, most critical studies on the neoliberalization of the university pay little heed to how its signature practices now emanate, and are perhaps even more effectively deployed, from the "progressive" interdisciplines of gender and sexuality studies.

The proprietary rights asserted by white faculty and students over institutional space, knowledge production, and administrative positions as described in this chapter derive as readily from feminist networks as from the old boys' networks within the university. It is not uncommon to hear feminist colleagues describe WAGS departments and centres as their "home" in the university. Every time I encounter this familial attachment to the institution, I cannot help but wonder what these colleagues' relations to their actual homes are like. The UBC campus space, of course, sits on the traditional territories of the Musqueam people, yet its production as white space, as "home," reasserts the nation's foundational practice of appropriation. To describe the campus workspace as "home" is to assert an intimate and personal relationship to the institution, to experience it as a nurturing space, to claim a "natural" entitlement to the space. Compare this sentiment to the white administrator's and student's reactions to the use of this space by students of colour and Indigenous students as an encroachment that renders the place itself threatening.

Race and space are both fluid, Neely and Samura (2011) note, as they argue that "racial and spatial processes can be seen as co-constitutive and dialectical in nature" (1934). How spaces are organized is closely intertwined with how race is produced, for the use and control of space is intimately connected to the racialization of bodies. Both involve struggles over meaning, resources, and access, and both are also interactional and relational, Neely and Samura point out. These aspects of space-making as race-making are evident in the encounters discussed above, wherein the publicly funded university space functions as a race-making operation through dispossession and disenfranchisement to uphold white entitlement.

Women of colour faculty, students, and community activists launched and led the initiative to build a CRS program; but upon the positive valuation of its accomplishments by an external review committee, it was white feminist and queer administrators and colleagues who claimed their right of ownership over this work. Such setting of the terms and conditions by white feminist and queer scholars for how, where, and when "race," and those who work in this field, are to be allowed to enter the departments that are their "home" is an assertion of racial power. That such practices violate the most elemental of anti-racist practices, the most basic tenets of CRS, not to mention the university's stated ideals of academic freedom and academic excellence, is somehow not "known" within this institution. Likewise, while critical scholars identify the extension of proprietorial rights as a cornerstone of contemporary neoliberal economic and political arrangements at the global level, they seem to "not know" that these are reiterations of bedrock racial-colonial practices of power.

Feminist access to such power is mediated through the stranglehold WAGS has over the category "woman," the field of gender studies, and also over the politics of equity within Canadian institutions. Malinda Smith has studied how "gender" was privileged in the early "equity" measures adopted in the university during the 1990s (Smith 2010). Although four groups were officially designated in federal equity legislation (women, Indigenous peoples, visible minorities, and people with disabilities), in practice, it was "gender" that was privileged. We live with the consequences of that moment of conflation of "equity" with "gender," and "gender" with "white woman."

It must be remembered here that the Black and other women of colour critique of the privileging of white women in the feminist category "woman" was already established at the time that the university's turn to inclusion made white women the subject of its equity policies (Davis 1981; Carby 1986; Lorde 1984; Amos and Parmar 1984; Mohanty, Russo, and Torres 1991). Not surprisingly then, institutional privileging of this gendered subject made white women the biggest beneficiaries of equity measures. Accessing these benefits in turn enabled them to take charge of the equity/diversity machinery of the university.

This expanded feminist access to the university was reliant on the construction of women of colour as not yet ready for inclusion, a construction that required the active erasure of the latter's scholarship and leadership. Excellence was here tied to gender, and through this, to white women; the labour of women of colour "counted for nothing." These institutional practices deepened within the university, appending "not yet" to the "not here, not us" denial of the salience of race in its institutional culture and practices. Gender equity thus became the gift that keeps on giving racial injustice, an economy of exchange now replicated with the inclusion of sexuality in the equity/diversity machinery. Smith (2017) has very insightfully dubbed these developments in "equity" and "inclusion" policies as advancing the "diversification of whiteness."

Ahmed's (2012) influential study of just how destabilizing the mere presence of women of colour can be within the university demonstrates how the designation "angry" transforms us into phobogenic objects. The projection of "anger" onto the anti-racist feminist transforms her into "the problem," Ahmed argues. This projection, I have found, also functions as an alibi for the feminist enactment of institutional power to neutralize the "threat" perceived as arising in the scholarship of women of colour. The resulting transfer of responsibility for her treatment from institutionalized racial injustice onto the individual woman of colour to demand subservience masked as excellence accomplishes at least three things. First, the shift allows the systemic and structural nature of racial injustice to remain ongoing in the crucial moment at which it is contested; second, the institutional retribution that inevitably follows the demonization of the woman of colour makes a spectacle of her so that others can be intimidated into compliance; and third, such punishment functions as a disincentive to others to work with insurgent anti-racist praxis. In short, these moves punish dissent; eject the woman of colour scholar from the sites of competence, rationality, and objectivity; and use her commitment to anti-racist *praxis* to relocate her in the space of anger, irrationality, and unreasonableness.

As this book goes to press, Republicans in the United States are attempting to ban critical race theory from being taught at US universities. The practices I have discussed in this chapter, namely appropriation, fortification of the power of whiteness, and punishment of dissent are hardly anomalies within the larger society. My argument is that it is from their feminist/gendered articulation, and institutionalization, within the university that these practices travel into the larger social order. The "vision," if one may call it that, for the feminist/queer inclusion of "race" under conditions of subjugation to the disciplinary power of the "solidarity" envisioned within "social justice" disrupts and contains the insurgent praxis that is the *raison d'être* of CRS. In the present moment of global racial volatility, such subjugation cannot be disentangled from the white supremacist politics that are redefining the political landscape across North America. The exchanges and encounters that uphold whiteness occur routinely, in full view of, and with the sanction of, administrators *in contravention* of the university's own workplace policies as well as its stated commitments to educational excellence. These practices make the university, now as in the past, a key site for the institutionalization, extension, and transmission of white racial power.

NOTES

1 I am working with an expanded definition of critical race studies in this chapter, not as this field has been defined within legal studies as critical race theory.
2 RACE was founded to promote "critical race feminist scholarship and praxis in several ways, including by: organizing the only annual critical race conferences in Canada; building stronger research and mentoring networks among faculty of colour and Indigenous scholars at the local, national, and regional levels; and fostering stronger links between academics, community-based researchers, and social justice practitioners" (Razack, Smith, and Thobani 2010, preface).
3 For a summary of the survey results, see Rocha (2018).
4 For examples of some of the egregious cases that rupture the "not us, not here" thinking, see The Current (2018), Rankin and Winsa (2013), and Page (2018).
5 The phrase "the difference that makes no difference" can also be found in Robert M. Martin's book *There Are Two Errors in the Title of This Book*.

REFERENCES

Ahmed, Sara. 2000. *Strange Encounters: Embodied Others in Post-Coloniality*. London: Routledge.
– 2012. *On Being Included: Racism and Diversity in Institutional Life*. Durham, NC: Duke University Press.
Amos, Valerie, and Pratibha Parmar. 1984. "Challenging Imperial Feminism." *Feminist Review* 17: 3–19. https://doi.org/10.2307/1395006.
Arday, Jason. 2018. "Understanding Racism within the Academy: The Persistence of Racism within Higher Education." In *The Fire Now: Anti-Racist Scholarship in Times of Explicit Racial Violence*, edited by Azeezat Johnson, Remi Joseph-Salisbury, and Beth Kamunge, 26–37. London: Zed Books.
Baker, Lee D. 2010. *Anthropology and the Racial Politics of Culture*. Durham, NC: Duke University Press.
Bannerji, Himani. 1995. *Thinking Through: Essays on Feminism, Marxism and Anti-Racism*. Toronto: Women's Press.
– 2000. *Dark Side of the Nation: Essays on Multiculturalism, Nationalism and Gender*. Toronto: Canadian Scholar's Press.
Brown, Wendy. 2008. "The Impossibility of Women's Studies." In *Women's Studies on the Edge*, edited by Joan Wallach Scott, 17–38. Durham, NC: Duke University Press.

Calliste, Agnes, and George Dei, eds. 2000. *Power, Knowledge and Anti-Racism Education*. Halifax: Fernwood.

Carby, Hazel. 1986. "'On the Threshold of Woman's Era': Lynching, Empire and Sexuality in Black Feminist Theory." In *"Race," Writing and Difference*, edited by Henry Louis Gates, Jr., and Kwame Anthony Appiah, 301–16. Chicago: University of Chicago Press.

Chatterjee, Piya, and Sunaina Maira, eds. 2014. *The Imperial University: Academic Repression and Scholarly Dissent*. Minneapolis: University of Minnesota Press.

Crenshaw, Kimberle. 1991. "Mapping the Margins: Intersectionality, Identity Politics and Violence against Women of Colour." *Stanford Law Review* 43 (6): 1241–99. https://doi.org/10.2307/1229039.

The Current. 2018. "Police Shootings of Unarmed Black Men Are a Canadian Problem Too, Says Author." *CBC Radio*, 23 March 2018. https://www.cbc.ca /radio/thecurrent/the-current-for-march-23-2018-1.4589415/police-shootings -of-unarmed-black-men-are-a-canadian-problem-too-says-author-1.4589507.

Das Gupta, Tania. 1996. *Racism and Paid Work*. Toronto: University of Toronto Press.

Davis, Angela. 1981. *Women, Race and Class*. New York: Random House.

Dua, Enakshi. 2007. "Exclusion through Inclusion: Female Asian Migration in the Making of Canada as a White Settler Nation." *Gender, Place and Culture: A Journal of Feminist Geography* 14 (4): 445–66. https://doi.org /10.1080/09663690701439751.

Fanon, Frantz. 1974. *The Wretched of the Earth*. Translated by Constance Farrington. New York: Grove Press.

Ferguson, Roderick. 2012. *The Reorder of Things: The University and Its Pedagogies of Minority Difference*. Minneapolis: Minnesota University Press.

Gates Jr., Henry Lewis. 1991. "The Master's Pieces: On Canon Formation and the African-American Tradition." In *The Politics of Liberal Education*, edited by Darryl J. Gless and Barbara H. Smith, 95–117. Durham, NC: Duke University Press.

Gaudry, Adam, and Danielle Lorenz. 2018. "Indigenization as Inclusion, Reconciliation and Decolonization: Navigating the Different Visions for Indigenizing the Canadian Academy." *AlterNative: An International Journal of Indigenous Peoples* 14 (3): 218–27. https://doi.org/10.1177 /1177180118785382.

Grande, Sandy, and Lauren Anderson. 2017. "Un-Settling Multicultural Erasures." *Multicultural Perspectives* 19 (3): 139–42. https://doi.org/10.1080 /15210960.2017.1331742.

Gutiérrez y Muhs, Gabriella, Yolanda Flores Niemann, Carmen G. González, and Angela P. Harris, eds. 2012. *Presumed Incompetent: The Intersections of*

Race and Class for Women in Academia. Boulder, CO: Utah State University Press.

Harding, Sandra, ed. 2004. *The Feminist Standpoint Theory Reader: Intellectual and Political Controversies*. New York: Routledge.

Henry, Frances et al. 2017. *The Equity Myth: Racialization and Indigeneity at Canadian Universities*. Vancouver, BC: UBC Press.

Hill Collins, Patricia. 1998. "It's All in the Family: Intersections of Gender, Race and Nation." *Hypatia* 13 (3): 62–82. https://doi.org/10.1111/j.1527 -2001.1998.tb01370.x.

Hong, Grace Kyungwon, and Roderick A. Ferguson. 2011. "Introduction." In *Strange Affinities: The Gender and Sexual Politics of Comparative Racialization*, edited by Grace Kyungwon Hong and Roderick A. Ferguson, 1–24. Durham, NC: Duke University Press.

hooks, bell. 1981. *Ain't I a Woman? Black Women and Feminism*. Boston: South End Press.

Iyer, Nitya, and Shirley Nakata. 2013. *Implementing Inclusion: A Consultation on Organizational Change to Support UBC's Commitment to Equity and Diversity*. Vancouver, BC: University of British Columbia. https://equity.ubc.ca/files /2010/06/Implementing-Inclusion-Equity-Diversity-Consultation-Report -April-2013.pdf.

Jiwani, Yasmin. 2007. *Discourses of Denial: Mediations of Race, Gender and Violence*. Vancouver, BC: UBC Press.

Johnson, Azeezat, Remi Joseph-Salisbury, and Beth Kamunge, eds. 2018. *The Fire Now: Anti-Racist Scholarship in Times of Explicit Racial Violence*. London: Zed Books.

Ladner, Kiera, and Myra J. Tait, eds. 2017. *Surviving Canada: Indigenous Peoples Celebrate 150 Years of Betrayal*. Winnipeg: ARP Books.

Lourde, Audrey. 1984. *Sister Outsider: Essays and Speeches*. New York: Crossing Press.

Maracle, Lee. 1988. *I Am Woman: A Native Perspective on Sociology and Feminism*. Vancouver, BC: Press Gang Publisher.

Million, Dian. 2013. *Therapeutic Nations: Healing in an Age of Indigenous Human Rights*. Tucson: Arizona University Press.

Mirza, Heidi Safia. 1997. *Black British Feminism: A Reader*. London: Routledge Press.

Mohanty, Chandra. T., Ann Russo, and Lourdes Torres, eds. 1991. *Third World Women and Politics of Feminism*. Bloomington: Indiana University Press.

Monture-Angus, Patricia. 1995. *Thunder in My Soul: A Mohawk Woman Speaks*. Halifax: Fernwood Press.

Neely, Brooke, and Michelle Samura. 2011. "Social Geographies of Race: Connecting Race and Space." *Racial and Ethnic Studies* 34 (11): 1933–52. https://doi.org/10.1080/01419870.2011.559262.

Ng, Roxana. 1996. *The Politics of Community Services: Immigrant Women, Class and the State*. Halifax: Fernwood Press.

Office of the President. 2012. *Place and Promise: The UBC Plan.* Vancouver, BC: University of British Columbia. https://strategicplan.sites.olt.ubc.ca/files /2009/11/UBC-PP-Layout-Aug2012.pdf.

Page, Julia. 2018. "Quebec City Mosque Shooter Obsessed with Mass Murderers Since Adolescence." *CBC,* 16 April 2018. https://www.cbc.ca/news/canada /montreal/quebec-city-mosque-shooting-bisonnette-sentencing-1.4621689.

Pateman, Carole. 1988. *The Sexual Contract.* Stanford, CA: Stanford University Press.

Rankin, Jim, and Patty Winsa. 2013. "Unequal Justice: Aboriginal and Black Inmates Disproportionately Fill Ontario Jails." *Toronto Star,* 1 March 2013. https://www.thestar.com/news/insight/2013/03/01/unequal_justice _aboriginal_and_black_inmates_disproportionately_fill_ontario_jails.html.

Razack, Sherene. 1998. *Looking White People in the Eye: Gender, Race and Culture in Courtrooms and Classrooms.* Toronto: University of Toronto Press.

Razack, Sherene, Malinda S. Smith, and Sunera Thobani, eds. 2010. *States of Race: Critical Race Feminism for the 21st Century.* Toronto: Between the Lines.

Readings, Bill. 1996. *The University in Ruins.* Cambridge, MA: Harvard University Press.

Rocha, Roberto. 2018. "Quebecers among Canadians Most Likely to Believe Racism Is Decreasing." *CBC,* 23 November 2018. https://www.cbc.ca /news/canada/montreal/quebecers-among-canadians-most-likely-to -believe-racism-is-decreasing-1.4887461.

Smith, Malinda. 2010. "Gender, Whiteness and 'Other' Others in the Academy." In *States of Race: Critical Race Feminism for the 21st Century,* edited by Sherene Razack, Malinda Smith, and Sunera Thobani, 37–58. Toronto: Between the Lines.

– 2017. "The State of the Academy: Issues, Policy and Effects on People." Panel presentation at the conference *Racial (In)Justice in the Canadian Academy,* UBC Faculty Association, Vancouver, BC, 16 March 2017.

Thobani, Sunera. 2007. *Exalted Subjects: Studies in the Making of Race and Nation in Canada.* Toronto: University of Toronto Press.

– 2020. *Contesting Islam, Constructing Race and Sexuality: The Inordinate Desire of the West.* London: Bloomsbury Academic.

Weigman, Robyn. 1995. *American Anatomies: Theorizing Race and Gender.* Durham, NC: Duke University Press.

Wilder, Craig Steven. 2013. *Ebony & Ivy: Race, Slavery and the Troubled History of America's Universities.* New York: Bloomsbury.

Wynter, Sylvia. 2006. "ProudFlesh Inter/Views: Sylvia Wynter." Interviewed by Greg Thomas. *ProudFlesh: A New Afrikan Journal of Culture, Politics and Consciousness* 4. https://monoskop.org/images/6/65/Proud_Flesh _InterViews_Sylvia_Wynter_2006.pdf.

4 "Our Canadian Culture Has Been Squeamish about Gathering Race-Based Statistics": The Circulation of Discourses of Race and Whiteness among Canadian Universities, Newspapers, and Alt-Right Groups

ENAKSHI DUA

For most of the last twenty years, the issue of collecting race-based data in universities and other sites has been a contentious issue in social and political debates in Canada. In the 1980s, Canada developed a legislative and policy framework for the collection of race-based data.[1] Despite such a framework, the federal government's commitment to the collection of race-based data has been both tenuous and eroded since the inception of these policies. Complicating public debates is the differential ways race-based data have been deployed. On the one hand, similar to other kinds of statistical data, the collection of race-based data has been central for governmentality. Thus, the debates on the collection of race-based data include the collection of race-based data in censuses and the ways race-based data have been used by police boards. On the other hand, the collection of race-based data has been tied to anti-racist strategies that call for policies to address discrimination, such as effectively monitoring discrimination, identifying and removing systemic barriers, ameliorating historical disadvantage, and promoting substantive equality.

The project of collecting race-based statistics to identify systemic barriers has particularly been met with institutional, political, and social resistance. However, there has been little research on the reasons for this resistance. My first experience with the reluctance to collect race-based data was when, as part of less than a handful of racialized faculty in the Faculty of Arts at my university, I advocated for employment equity policies that would address the underrepresentation of racialized faculty. The response by colleagues and senior administrators was to claim that there was not, in fact, an underrepresentation of racialized faculty. Upon asking that we examine the data on the percentage of visible minorities, a senior administrator responded that such data did not exist. Perhaps because it was mandated by government policies, the administrator, after an awkward silence, quickly added: "It is a difficult issue – it is not in the culture." While the awkwardness was telling, what was significant was the reference to "culture." The deployment of the notion of "culture" is certainly loaded with racialized signifiers of inclusion, whiteness, and nation, particularly in an interaction between a "white" administrator and a racialized woman (see Gilroy 1991; Goldberg 1993).

In 2011, while carrying out research on the extent to which universities collected race-based data (Dua and Bhanji 2012), I came upon two statements that deployed "culture" to refer to the collection of race-based data. On 2 September 2006, the vice-principal of Queen's University, Patrick Deane, in an interview about the collection of race-based data at Queen's, was quoted as saying: "Our Canadian culture has been squeamish about gathering race-based statistics" (quoted in Brown 2006). In February 2007, Jared Taylor, the leader of the US-based neo-right group American Renaissance, gave a speech in Halifax (Canadian Press 2007). In the speech, which focused on the "problems" of "racial diversity," Taylor turned his attention to the question of collecting race-based data. While altering the statement to refer to the use of statistics for governmentality, Taylor drew on the metaphors of "Canada" and "culture," also claiming that "Canada is too squeamish to collect crime statistics by race" (Taylor 2007a). Notably, the phrase "Our Canadian culture has been squeamish about gathering race-based statistics" would not only connect the two projects of race-based data collection, but would also resonate and be deployed by politicians, newspapers columnists, and anti-racist groups, and by other neo-right groups, such as Immigration Watch Canada.

Two aspects of this statement are significant. First are the implicit truth claims about the collection of race-based data that are embedded in the phrase "Our Canadian culture has been squeamish." As Foucault has pointed out, truth claims are located in the deployment of power (Foucault 1980). Thus, the question emerged, What ways is power being deployed in the production of such a claim? Second, and as important, is how this statement was produced and reproduced among several seemingly disparate groups, resonating across different spaces of the university, federal politics, newspapers, and significantly, alt-right groups. As Foucault suggests, a truth claim is linked "by a circular relation to systems of power which produce it and sustain it, and to effects of power which it induces and which redirect it" (Foucault 1980,

113–14). Thus, other questions emerged: How are universities, civil society, and alt-right groups[2] related not only in the social construction of truth claims about the collection of race-based data but also, concomitantly, linked in the circuits of power that are mobilized through these truth claims? And, as important, what kinds of power are induced through such circulations?

The influence of the alt-right[3] in mainstream politics in the United States, Canada, and Europe has led to an increased urgency to understand the ways in which seemingly isolated groups and their related discourses have become hegemonic. University campuses have been a crucial site of far-right activities. Groups such as Rebel Media, Toronto Proud Boys, Alt4Can, Discord, 4chan, and others have reportedly been expanding their activities from online forums to university campuses. Indeed, as noted in several newspapers articles, these groups are organizing, postering, arranging talks, attacking progressive faculty, and questioning academic freedom on campuses (for example, see Porter 2017).

Notably, much of the research on alt-right groups implicitly assumes that these groups, and their associated discourses, are isolated from civil society. In the context of alt-right activities on campuses, university administrators have claimed that the white supremacist rhetoric on campuses comes from outside of the university. This view was evident when, during a three-day conference on reconciliation with the Indigenous community at St. Thomas University in Fredericton, New Brunswick, a poster appeared on a Maliseet-language welcome sign: the poster featured a drawing of a man and a woman who appear to be white, with the slogan "We have a right to exist," and directed readers to white nationalist and alt-right websites. In response, Jeffrey Carleton, a spokesperson for the university, was quoted on the Canadian Broadcasting Corporation (CBC) saying: "I've been here for almost 15 years. I'm only aware of one or two occasions in that time period where there were what could be considered, or called today in the popular vernacular, alt-right posters on campus" (quoted in Gill 2017). His words thus led the CBC journalist to conclude that this event was an isolated one: "[Carleton] said he doubts the signs were posted by St. Thomas students and said the school doesn't have an alt-right problem" (Gill 2017). However, as the production and circulation of the phrase "Our Canadian culture has been squeamish about gathering race-based statistics" suggests, a closer analysis of discourses on the collection of race-based data indicates that the discourses produced by alt-right groups are not exclusive to these groups.

This chapter has two interrelated goals: First is to explore the resistance to the collection of race-based data when it is collected for anti-racist initiatives. In so doing, I examine debates on the collection of race-based data in four sites – universities (for example, faculty administrations, faculty associations, and equity offices), government initiatives, newspapers, and neo-right groups. Second is to explore the similarities in the arguments and discourses that circulate in each of the four sites. Employing a multi-method methodology, I combine document analysis, media analysis, and interview data to examine the discourses of race-based data collection. I first analyze documents on the collection of race-based data in select Canadian government organizations, parliamentary debates, the Ontario Human Rights Commission, fifty Canadian universities, and anti-racist groups. I then assess the resistance to collecting race-based data within universities by drawing on interviews from ten Canadian universities. Following this work, I examine newspaper debates on the collection of race-based data between 1990 and 2018. As part of my research, I undertook digital searches of newspapers at three points of time – 2014, 2017, and 2018 – using several key words to ensure a broad search. Last, I conducted research on four alt-right websites – *American Renaissance, Council of European Canadians, Elliot Lake Blog,* and Jordan Peterson's YouTube Channel.[4] Through the results of this multi-method research, I illustrate the set of public discourses on the collection of race-based data. Moreover, I illustrate how truth claims about the collection of race-based data circulate between universities, newspapers, government debates, and the alt-right.

My exploration of the tensions around collecting race-based data raises the complex and challenging question of how the collection of race-based data is embedded in the circulation of racialized power. In 2008, the Canadian Race Relations Foundation observed: "In Canada the discourse on, and practice of, the collection of data based on race, ethnicity and/or nationality is an evolving area of focus and has been fraught with much debate; and has met with resistance within and among communities, governments, public institutions and other sectors"; the report continued on to identify one of the key barriers to the collection of race-based data as "a 'white middle class' that may feel threatened by the process" (Canadian Race Relations Foundation 2008, 5). Indeed, as this chapter illustrates, the resistance to the collection of race-based data is tied to the protection of whiteness. It is this politics of whiteness that links universities, governments, newspapers, and alt-right groups to the circuits of power. Thus, my study raises significant questions about how alt-right groups are constructed though civil society, and how, in turn, they construct civil society. Additionally, it raises the provocative question of how universities are part of the circulation of racialized power.

Resistance to the Collection of Race-Based Data in Universities: "Where You Can't Name Exclusions and Racism"

Considerable research has illustrated that racism in universities takes place through broad and insidious structures, which include everyday practices such as curriculum, hiring, policies and procedures, and the operations of administrations (Dua and Lawrence 2000; Smith 2013; Henry et al. 2017). This research has located practices of racism within the institutional politics of whiteness in the academy, illustrating that racism is not the result of isolated actions of disparate people but rather is tied to the structure of universities and, indeed, to the very mission of the university as an institution. In this context, anti-racist activists have promoted equity policies that address inequities within the academy. As research has documented, such advocacy has faced both administrative and collegial resistance (see, for example, Dua 2009, 2017b). While scholarship has demonstrated resistance to the formation of equity policies, research on the resistance to the collection of race-based data is scarce.

In order to explore the resistance to the collection of race-based data, twenty-five in-depth interviews in ten universities were carried out.[5] The sample of universities was chosen to reflect a diversity of regions, large and small urban centres, and rural and urban places in the distribution. This sample also represented the range of approaches to equity. In choosing who to interview, attempts were made to include personnel in a variety of positions in each university: administrators, directors of equity and human rights offices, equity/anti-racist officers, and faculty members who served on equity committees. Up to three participants were interviewed at each university: a senior administrator mandated to address equity, an equity officer, and a member of an equity committee. Because of the spatial distance between institutions, many of these interviews were conducted by telephone. As there has been little research on equity and/or anti-racist policies in the academy, open-ended questions were deployed to allow interviewees to identify the history and effectiveness of each policy mechanism.

Notably, the Federal Contractors Program requires that universities – similar to all Canadian employers that receive more than $100,000 of government funds – carry out a periodic census of their workforce and that they make this census available to their employees. In a survey of fifty Canadian universities, Bhanji and I found that only sixteen of the fifty Canadian universities surveyed made data available on visible minorities (Dua and Bhanji 2012). Moreover, fewer presented this data in a disaggregated form, such that meaningful patterns could be made concerning hiring and employment trends within the academy. This number sits in stark contrast to the number of universities that made such data available for gender representation: forty-two of the fifty.

In interviews with equity officers, anti-racist activists, and senior administrators at ten Canadian universities, I explored the resistance to the collection of race-based data. My interview data found a strong pattern – nine of the ten universities did not have data available on the percentage of racialized minorities in student and faculty ranks. In addition, those interviewed reported that, despite long-standing requests for data collection, and despite an obligation to collect and make such data available to the institution's workforce, university administrators have been reluctant to implement anti-racist policies. Similarly, when asked if their university collected race-based data, participants from nine of the ten universities reported a lack of data. For example, one interviewee explained:

> There is, again as far as I know, no data on race and hiring and among the faculty in general. There is data on women and their advancement in the professoriate. So, we do have that kind of data. But we have lack of data of racialized groups.

Notably, it was not just the broader university membership that lacked access to this data, but also equity officers and administrators who are mandated to address issues of employment equity and anti-racism. One participant, an equity officer, reported:

> A lot of time I get the sense that I don't even have access to data that I would think should be available. But my experience, and this is stuff I heard from the [name of university] senate committee too, it is very hard to get data out of the university. Even when asked, they often do not provide it.

An administrator admitted:

> And just because we really don't have any information, trying to get a handle on the demographics, that's hard.

Another equity officer reported that such data is not available for student demographics either, thus not allowing for an assessment of whether racialized students are getting access to the university. Similarly, interviewees reported that data is missing on pay equity, thus not allowing for arguments that racialized faculty are underpaid compared to "white" faculty who have similar qualifications. One participant, an administrator, pointed out:

> I have never seen data on raises and hiring at [name of university]. I don't even know if they gather it. That's not something that we get in any of annual reports of data, especially on salaries. We might have data on students, but I actually don't know. I've heard we're supposed to have it for students, but I'm not sure. That is if we have a kind of breakdown by gender and race of our student body across the faculties, which should be interesting, if we did.

In the one university where such data was available, an equity officer noted that the data was difficult to find, wondering if this barrier was strategic:

> Well, first of all the [name of university] website is very difficult to navigate because offices have unusual names. You really have to know, you really basically have to be given a link to data to find it, unless you have days to troll through various places.

A consistent theme in the interviews was the ongoing struggle to convince university administrators to collect and/or release race-based data to either members of equity committees or to the university community. Indeed, the interviews confirmed that there have been consistent demands for data on the numbers of visible minorities among faculty, staff, and student complements. An equity activist noted:

> One of the goals has been to demand data on issues of race on campus and to advocate for that. I understand that has been a difficult struggle for a very long time.

The struggle to collect race-based data not only took place with university administrators but also, as equity activists reported, within faculty associations and national bodies representing university faculty, such as the Canadian Association of University Teachers (CAUT). An equity activist recalled her efforts during her ten-year tenure at her university:

At [name of equity committee] I was involved with, my colleagues pushed our union to first reveal the data, because initially when I started we did not even get the data, so we needed to get them to disclose the data that they were collecting through the FCP [Federal Contractors Program]. But then, subsequently, when they started to issue these reports, to get them to reveal disaggregated data.

An equity activist who had served on the CAUT Equity Committee reported:

At CAUT that was one on our main ask for the two-years that I was there, because I resigned. It was absolutely an ask for them to collect the data and to push them. Remember that all of the faculty associations are their members, so it is a good place to collect data. The push back was always "this is not our job"; however, subsequent to our ask they did do a collection (on another DG [designated group]). So even though they said it was not their job, they actually publish data on women and Indigenous faculty. So there was a protocol in place, but this was a huge ask for CAUT. Honestly the biggest wall and the biggest barrier continues to be that CAUT still refuses to collect data even though they are using Stats Can data to make it look like they are involved in data analysis on racialized faculty across Canada.[6]

The resistance by faculty associations and the CAUT points to how this resistance is part of a broader understanding of race-based data collection.

Those interviewed noted that such data was a central part of developing anti-racist policies such as employment equity and other strategies to address the barriers that have resulted in underrepresentation. An equity activist noted:

So part of the reason we really wanted this was not just because of the sake of having it, but because any policy ask or development, the starting point in the policy cycle, we need to make the argument through having data.

As another equity activist pointed out, the dependency on statistical data is tied to the need for such data to validate claims of racism:

Because the thinking is that we need to provide evidence of exclusion, and that it is not enough to say there is exclusion, to have the stories and the narratives, they want evidence, and evidence is very much quantitatively based on this social science-y model framework. I went to a conference where I met someone who did data analysis for the Privy Council in the Prime Minister's Office. He said the same thing – he only finds quantitative data convincing. And I think it is doable if they just collected the data, because the data is clear, it is clear what is going on.

A third equity activist unequivocally stated:

What gets measured gets done. Without statistics nothing gets done. Thus, for anti-racist activists the importance of race-based data is tied to strategies of effectively monitoring discrimination, identifying and removing systematic barriers, ameliorating historical disadvantage, and promoting substantive equality. The inability to get access to this data creates serious barriers in their ability to develop effective policies.

Why there is such reluctance becomes the crucial question. In the nine universities where race-based data was not collected, those interviewed were asked to explain why there was such resistance. They pointed to the interpellation of racism, resistance to anti-racism, and whiteness. Two consistent related themes emerged to explain the resistance. First, lack of data served to inhibit the development of anti-racist policies. An equity activist noted:

The biggest barrier is racism! Right? To ask for, to basically be asking to put resources to collecting data, you are asking for accommodation and attention being paid to race, and racialized faculty, and racialized exclusion of racialized faculty ... [T]his is not seen as pressing.

Another, an equity activist, also reported being denied data to allow them to put forward equity initiatives:

But it's more of a sense that others have asked for data and haven't gotten it, and that it's a struggle to get the kind of information you need, in order to make equity policies.

Second, and concomitantly, those interviewed reported that, without such data, others in the university could claim there is no racism. Thus, resisting the collection of race-based data allowed for the position that those racialized as minorities are adequately represented and, consequently, that there is no need for anti-racist policies. One participant, an equity officer, explained:

But I think the alibi is really important ... [W]hat I often heard is that there are racialized faculty, there are *x* amount, look at engineering or whatever, these people are doing fine.

Another equity officer reported her experience, in which the inability to access such data allowed her faculty association to make similar arguments and prohibit the development of anti-racist employment equity policies:

There is a telling incident that I can report to you. It took place when I was the equity officer in my faculty association. My mandate was to promote equity – as a black woman I was asked to join the executive to work on anti-racism. Working with an equity committee, we tried to push for the executive to broaden our employment equity policy from gender to race. When we brought the proposal to the executive, the president of my faculty association declared that there was no need for such a policy – the president declared she had seen university data that showed that visible minorities were fairly represented – we had met our goals. I was shocked. When we asked for this data, we were refused. I spent the next three months unsuccessfully trying to get this data. I was stonewalled at each step. I ended up not being able to get the data. I doubt the data would have shown that racialized groups are fairly represented in my university. But without this data, the president's claims could not be challenged. She did not want an employment equity policy that included visible minorities and used unseen data to stop this. Without data we were unable to challenge her, and our initiative died before it could go to bargaining.

This strategy was successful, as many of those interviewed reported that a lack of data prohibited analyses that allow for the documentation of underrepresentation and, subsequently, the development of equity policies.

Notably, a number of those interviewed also deployed the metonym of "culture" when talking about the resistance to collecting race-based data. An equity officer commented:

So a culture of more openness around data, I think, would go a long way towards opening up equity conversations on campus.

Another equity officer noted:

There needs to be a culture shift on collecting data ... This will only happen if someone on the top is pushing for data.

Those interviewed unpacked the metonym "culture" in referring to the debates on collecting race-based data. Importantly, in unpacking "culture," those interviewed noted the ways in which the deployment of culture was tied to the ways in which dominant "culture" dislocated racism. One equity officer noted:

> Let's unpack the challenges a bit more. What culture do these challenges reflect? How does racism fit into that?

Moreover, those interviewed noted that the "culture" of resistance within universities was tied to the lack of legitimacy accorded to anti-racism among Canadian politicians and civil society. A senior administrator noted:

> Anti-racism had fallen out of favour because of the change of government, everything got wiped out.

Another noted that the federal government placed little priority on enforcing the collection of such data:

> Universities have an obligation, under the Federal Contract Program to report, but this government doesn't require the reports ... [W]e recently went [to the federal government], and we asked for the data, and they said, "Oh, we don't require universities to provide that information anymore. Some of them are still providing it, but we don't do anything." They [the federal government] don't care ... It's dreadful, so we were absolutely shocked to hear this, it's the law of the land apparently, but it has no meaning to the government whatsoever.

Another attributed the lack of data to prevent documentation of racism to a larger social project to prevent social change:

> Having reliable information only gives us social scientists ammunition to undermine the government.

In addition to locating the collection of race-based data within a "culture" of resistance to addressing racism, those interviewed placed this resistance within a politics of whiteness:

> I am going to say it very clearly. Whiteness is our biggest challenge. The *culture* of whiteness, the endemic *culture* of racism, the polite liberal let's not name racism is what our biggest challenge and barrier ... These are

white supremacist institutions, and they are run by and through that logic, or in service of that thinking ... Those are the challenges. I worry that they are incredibly hard to tear down – and that is the thing we are up against. The administration is very clever. Because that *culture* also filters down into our faculty associations. There is no check on that at our local levels. (emphasis added)

Indeed, those interviewed identified the resistance to collecting race-based data as being a part of the ways Canadian universities are complacent in the politics of whiteness:

I mean this place is embedded in a white supremacist state which funds the university and diversity ... What I mean by white supremacist is not that people are here burning crosses and marching, not yet though we are also on that trajectory across our campuses and in the US, what I mean is good liberal well-meaning people who are quote unquote lefty allies ... I can give examples ... Look where we are? Near communities of colour, marginalized from the university, excluded in the city, where is there access to this university? Even with special programs to bring these students in, we don't set it up so they succeed ... And the filter to our graduate programs is severe.

Such politics of whiteness make any initiative that addresses racism not only difficult to take on but also a target of resistance – resistance that silences any attempt to document racism. As an administrator stated:

The push back when we want to make concrete changes is unbelievable ... To counter that, as Sara Ahmed puts it, you are the problem. To name the problem you become the problem. And when you name the problem as race you become a racist problem. Whiteness does a lovely job of turning back our concerns about racism into our racism. That's a piece we all need to think and talk about. And that's where you can't name exclusions and racism. Right? And yet there is an innocence ... whiteness works in this insidious way ... where you don't need to wear a hood or carry a cross to get the effect you want, to get the exclusion to recentre your whiteness, none of that is required, you just need to go about your daily business, it is business as usual in the university, which maintains and retains those exclusions.

My exploration at universities located the resistance to collecting race-based data within a politics of whiteness – a politics that prevented the documentation of racism in order to deny its existence. The politics of whiteness was one that worked through everyday practices of the university to the extent that naming racism became a problem. As one participant stated, the politics of whiteness was not made up of "white supremacist, hoods, crosses and marches" but, rather, practices that incorporated progressive institutions such as faculty associations and liberal notions of equality. Notably, those interviewed pointed to the connections between the politics of whiteness within the university and those within civil society, as they located the resistance to the collection of race-based data within "culture"; broader social processes, such as government policies; and the social importance placed on anti-racism. As I discuss in the next section, newspaper writers' views on the collection of race-based data were also grounded in a project of denying racism. The coverage I analyzed made explicit the claim that naming racism is a "problem" – anti-racism was constructed as a threat to white subjects, universities, and the nation as a whole.

Newspaper Debates on the Collection of Race-Based Data: "The Scourge of Invisible Racism"

In this section, I trace newspaper coverage on the collection of race-based data. I employ two analytic frames of discourse analysis to analyze this material: First, drawing on Foucault's emphasis of genealogy, I trace the temporal trajectory of the discussion, showing how similar positions and metaphors are deployed through time. In doing so, I pay attention to the use of language, metaphors, and the manufacturing of meaning out of pre-existing linguistic resources in constructing discourses on the collection of race-based data. Second, I draw on Billig's (1987) rhetorical analysis, through which he points to the importance of understanding argumentative contexts. Thus, I outline the ways positions are put forward and how these positions are juxtaposed implicitly and/or explicitly against counterarguments. In particular, I look at how dominant discourses on the collection of race-based data are juxtaposed against anti-racist interventions.

In tracing the coverage of the collection of race-based data, I found that public debates gained resonance in the early 2000s, when the collection of race-based data became a source of social and political tension. Three crucial moments took place in the coverage of race-based data: First, in October 2002, the *Toronto Star* published a series of articles that employed data to document racism in police practices, raising both the issue of how such data was collected and how it could be deployed. Second, anti-racist activists a few years later began to pressure the Toronto District School Board and Canadian universities to collect race-based data to demonstrate inequities. Third, in 2010, the Harper federal government cancelled the part of the Canadian census that collected detailed information on racialized groups.

Before 2015, the vast majority of the articles and columns on the collection of race-based data were published in three newspapers: the *Globe and Mail*, *National Post*, and *Toronto Star*. After 2015, articles began to appear in other newspapers ranging from the *Hamilton Spectator* to the CBC's internet dailies. In addition, several of these articles and columns have been preserved on a number of websites, ranging from right-wing sites such as *Plagiarized News and Views*, *Elliot Lake News and Views*, and *Immigration Watch Canada* to the technology website *Neowin* and the progressive website *Science for Peace*. The archiving of these articles points to the significance placed on the collection of race-based data as well as on these particular articles. Importantly, it also points to the circulation of arguments presented in these articles in concomitant discourses.

Race-Based Data to Challenge Racial Profiling: "There Is No Racism"

The media coverage of race-based data collection gained prominence when the *Toronto Star* (hereafter referred to as the *Star*) published a series of news articles on race and crime in Toronto, pointing to racism in policing practices.[7] While this series began with an attempt to illustrate that the Toronto Police Service engaged in racial profiling, much of the subsequent coverage denied such practices of racism. In the emerging rhetoric of denial, the issue of race-based data became central, leading to truth claims that would become central in subsequent coverage – that race-based data is suspect because it reflects the agendas of anti-racist groups.

The series began with an article entitled "Singled Out" (Rankin et al. 2002b). In this article, the *Star* presented an analysis of a set of data on policing and crime that illustrated Black Canadians in Toronto were overrepresented in several offence categories, including drug possession and traffic violations. Based on these findings, the *Star* concluded that Toronto police were engaged in racial profiling: "The findings provide hard evidence of what blacks have long suspected – race matters in Canadian society especially when dealing with police" (Rankin et al. 2002b).

Beginning the next day, "Singled Out" was challenged through several subsequent articles that denied racism; these challenges circulated and produced further discourse. For example, over the next three days, the *Star* published "Analysis Raises Board Hackles" (Toronto Star

2002a) and "Police Union Blasts Star" (Porter 2002), both containing denials of racism. In "Singled Out," then chief of police Julian Fantino vehemently claimed: "We do not do racial profiling ... There is no racism"[8] (Rankin et al. 2002b). Likewise, in the second article, the president of the Police Association stated: "No racial profiling has ever been conducted by the Toronto Police Service" (Porter 2002). The denial of racism was echoed by several local politicians. For example, Mel Lastman, the mayor of Toronto, stated: "I don't believe that the Toronto police engage in racial profiling in any way, shape or form. Quite the opposite, they're very sensitive to our different communities" (Toronto Star 2002a).

Significantly, the series brought the project of collecting race-based data to the forefront of public attention. First, it located the collection of race-based data within a politics of anti-racism, suggesting that the lack of data on "race" and crime was due to pressure by communities of colour to not document criminality. In "Singled Out," the Star claimed: "Nowhere in Canada has debate over keeping, and analyzing, race-based crime data been as angst-ridden as in Toronto – a city boasting of its multicultural identity with a motto declaring diversity its strength." It noted that the Police Board was prohibited from collecting race-based crime data and thus did not analyze it. Fantino was quoted as saying: "We don't keep (that) data. We're not supposed to" (Rankin et al. 2002b).

In 1989, the Toronto Police Board had, indeed, banned collecting statistics linking race and crime. The ban went into effect after Fantino, then a staff inspector, reported to a race relations committee that Black people accounted for most of the crime occurring in the Jane-Finch area. As the Star reported in "Singled Out," "the community erupted in outrage, underlining the taboo that surrounds collection of these statistics" (Rankin et al. 2002b). Fantino told the Star that "good relations have included a commitment to avoid collecting race-based crime statistics that might cast some groups in a negative light." The Star pointed out that the collection of such data was contentious, as "it was feared that such information would be used to reinforce racist stereotypes and label certain ethnic communities as criminal." While "Singled Out" illustrated that data on race and crime challenged such stereotypes, and pointed to the misuse of such data by the police, the ensuing discussion failed to raise these crucial points. In their stead, a truth claim was constructed, which stated that the official bodies were unable to collect and analyze such data due to pressure from anti-racist groups. Notably, in tracing the circulation of discourses, as we shall see in the next section, alt-right advocate Jared Taylor would come to use the ban on collecting race-based police data as the basis for constructing an argument for white supremacy.

Furthering the claim that the collection of race-based data was shaped by anti-racist politics, subsequent news articles raised questions about the reliability of race-based data when used to document discrimination. The ensuing debate raised questions about the reliability of anti-racist uses of quantitative and qualitative data – arguments that would circulate in future newspaper coverage. The Toronto Police Board contested the empirical findings in the original articles by the *Toronto Star*. In response, the board commissioned two studies by independent researchers. The first was undertaken by Edward Harvey, a sociologist, and Alan Gold, a prominent criminal lawyer (Gold and Harvey 2003; Harvey 2003). The second, "Do the Toronto Police Engage in Racial Profiling," was undertaken by Ron Melchers, a criminologist at the University of Ottawa (Melchers 2003). Despite being commissioned, both studies were defined as "independent" analyses of the data. Both studies dismissed the *Star* reports. Harvey and Gold claimed that the *Star* analysis was "junk science" and that the articles were "completely unjustified, irresponsible and bogus slurs" (Gold and Harvey 2003). Harvey and Gold go on to claim that the data in "Singled Out" was "cleaned up" (Harvey 2003, 10), suggesting it was "fed," affecting the findings. In a subsequent document, Melchers (2006) claimed that "the use of statistics in discrimination cases is less a search for truth than it is for advantage, and statistics are remarkably pliable, easily contrived or distorted even when there is no intent of deceit, but only unconscious subversion. The adversarial use of statistics in discrimination cases has grown to become a sub-discipline in its own right, often not a very distinguished one" (68). These studies both circulated two key truth claims: first, that the data employed to document racism was untrustworthy, as anti-racist analysis would manipulate such data to falsely document racism; and second, that qualitative data on the perception of racism was suspect. Indeed, both of these claims would underlie subsequent newspaper coverage. Moreover, the suggestion that race-based data was "fed" would reappear at critical moments in subsequent coverage.

In constructing the discourse of denial, another particular rhetorical strategy emerged: the deployment of headlines to tie the denial of racism to racist stereotypes. For example, an article in the *Star*, "Gun Violence. There Is No Racism. We Do Not Do Racial Profiling" (Toronto Star 2002e), used a headline that deployed gun violence to deny racism, even while the article contained information documenting racist practices. Following the publication of a subsequent article on 26 October 2002, "Black Crime Rates Highest" (Rankin 2002a), the *Star* was challenged on the use of headlines to misrepresent its arguments. Next day the Star reran the article with an apology that stated: "A story on Page A1 yesterday about a racial breakdown of violent crime arrest data said the black population has the highest rate of arrest in Toronto. The headline accompanying the story inaccurately labelled that as a 'crime' rate, which The Star's analysis of Toronto police data did not measure. The Star regrets the error" (Rankin 2002a). Despite this apology, the headlines, which deployed stereotypes that associated Black Canadians with criminality and denied racism would continue to be a crucial rhetorical strategy.

Subsequent coverage drew on these claims. For example, in "Sometimes Race Is Simply a Fact," Christie Blatchford (2002) in the *National Post* repeated the truth claim that racialized people prevent the documentation of crime, as she argued for the need for the police to release "the racial characteristics of suspects." In the column, which was archived on right-wing websites such as *Plagiarized News and Views*, *Elliot Lake News and Views*, and *Immigration Watch Canada*, as well as on the progressive site *Science for Peace*, Blatchford states that "racial profiling isn't all bad," arguing that "it should also go without saying that parents of all races would far, far rather have their sons stopped by police officers trying to find the people responsible ... and momentarily angered or even humiliated."

Notably, this column placed the debate on racial profiling into a discursive understanding of the nation. The words "it should go without saying that parents of all races" further erased concerns of racialized Canadians by drawing these subjects into the "national culture" of the racialized project of fighting crime. It implicitly centred white subjects as the normative citizen. Solidifying the placement of racial profiling in racialized imperatives, Blatchford deployed the metaphor "the elephant in the room" to frame the debate, explicitly claiming that evidence of criminality was silenced and linking this silence to the inability of "Canadians" to articulate their views on racism. This approach further located the tensions within notions of normative citizenship. Blatchford raised another claim that would circulate in discourses of race-based data collection – that data prevented politically incorrect discussion about "race." In 2006, Ron Melchers reiterated this claim in a report to the Directorate Royal Canadian Mounted Police, using Blatchford's metaphor: "This is the elephant in the room. One simply cannot dismiss off hand, as is done in various reports of human rights commissions, commissions of inquiry and by anti-racial-profiling disparities in offending behaviours" (Melchers 2006, 76–7).

*Race-Based Data Collection in Education: "Blame Games Fed
by Ancient Grievances and Guilt"*

Two years after the *Toronto Star* series on racist policing practices,
newspaper writers turned their attention to anti-racist initiatives on
the collection of race-based data in primary and secondary schools
(particularly in the Toronto District School Board) and in Canadian
universities. Higher rates of expulsion for Black and racialized students after Ontario's Tough Safe Schools Act and concerns about the
failure of public schools to address the needs of racialized students,
combined with lower rates of university enrolment and the underrepresentation of racialized faculty, led to a call for data. As we shall
see, the coverage of these initiatives drew on both the metaphors
and the truth claims that had circulated in the debates on criminality,
rearticulating the discontent with race-based data. Importantly, the
coverage of race-based data in education explicitly placed the collection of race-based data within a politics of whiteness – drawing on
metaphors of whiteness to raise the implications of race-based data
for white subjects.

On 17 November 2004, the Toronto District School Board (TDSB)
requested staff to collect race-based data.[9] The purpose of the data
collection was to identify disparities in student achievement, develop
strategies and interventions to address the disparities, and monitor
the results. Zanana Akande, former president of the Urban Alliance
on Race Relations and an ex-principal, stated: "We've pushed for these
statistics to be collected precisely because of concerns there are many
students the system is not serving well" (quoted in Brown 2006). In the
university context, several universities (University of Guelph, Queen's
University, Ryerson University, and the University of Toronto) undertook task forces on racism[10] that concomitantly documented systemic
barriers faced by racialized faculty and students, and called for the collection of race-based data.

Such calls for data were supported by the Ontario Human Rights
Commission (OHRC). On 28 June 2005, the OHRC released a new
policy entitled *Policy and Guidelines on Racism and Racial Discrimination*,
which addressed the importance of collecting data.[11] In this policy, the
OHRC stated that "appropriate data collection is necessary for effectively monitoring discrimination, identifying and removing systematic
barriers, ameliorating historical disadvantage and promoting substantive equality" (OHRC 2005, 42). Moreover, it named all individuals and
organizations in Ontario as being responsible for upholding human
rights within their respective environments, stating that "there is a

positive duty to take corrective action to ensure that the *Code* is not being, and will not in future be, breached" (42)[12]

These initiatives were taken up by newspapers columnists. On 22 November 2005, Margaret Wente published a column entitled "Race Is the Elephant in the Room," drawing Blatchford's metaphor of the supposed inability to discuss "race" and criminality into the issue of collecting race-based data in schools and, concurrently, the topic of employment equity. She wrote:

> Toronto schools are also taking it in the neck for racial profiling. That's because young black males make up a disproportionate number of the students who are penalized for discipline and behaviour problems. Anyone with the slightest experience in Toronto's schools knows these problems are real. *But saying so is not an option.* Instead, the school board has promised the Ontario Human Rights Commission that the schools will be more sensitive ... Next fall, schools will begin to gather race-based discipline statistics in order to detect bias. Want to guess what's going to happen? ... The human-rights commission has also ordered Toronto's schools to start gathering race statistics on their staff. That's because a black teacher from Nigeria complained that he had always wanted to be a principal, but after 20 years had never been promoted. In spite of this systemic racism, I've met several extremely able, black school administrators. (Wente 2005; emphasis in original)

Significantly, Wente goes on to make the claim that such data will lead to increased racial tension. She concludes her column by stating:

> I used to feel quite smug about *the lack of racial tensions in Canada*. It was a mark of our superiority to the United States, I thought. We managed these things so much better up here. No underclass for us. No inner-city ghettos, gangs and guns, or *blame games fed by ancient grievances and guilt*. How wrong I was. How very wrong. (emphasis added)

In her conclusion, Wente connected the collection of race-based data to employment equity and to increasing racial tension, suggesting that both place Canada on a slippery slope. Notably, this claim would soon also be made by Jared Taylor.

In 2006, Louise Brown wrote an article for the *Toronto Star* entitled "Schools Scramble to Take Colour Count" (Brown 2006) that began with the sentence: "Just how white is Ontario's ivory tower?" In this article, Brown explicitly tied the issue of the collection of race-based data to whiteness. Noting that Queen's University, the University of

Toronto, and the TDSB were all collecting race-based data of their students, Brown once again deployed the metaphor of the "elephant in the room." Brown suggested that the collection of such data implies that "it seems race is no longer a four-letter word in the world of learning." Drawing on the truth claim of the inability to openly discuss matters of race, Brown suggested that it is possible in the context of anti-racism. Further, she quoted Queen's vice-principal Patrick Deane, who said: "Our Canadian culture has been squeamish about gathering race-based statistics because no one wants to see ethnic makeup reduced to numbers on a page." However, Brown indicated that there are limitations in the collection of race-based data in universities. Echoing earlier claims that anti-racist groups use race-based data to make unsubstantiated arguments, she suggested that such data illustrate that there may not be "a problem." On this point, Brown also quoted Patrick Deane, who said that "unless you get this kind of information, *you don't really know if you have a problem*" (emphasis added), noting that the data from the Queen's University survey of the first-year class show that representation in the university is "respectable in a national context." Brown went on to suggest the need "for demographic detective work." Thus, she asked the rhetorical question, "How white is the ivory tower?" It is important to note that this article was available on *American Renaissance* until 2019, as well as on other internet-based forums such as *Neowin*, listed under "schools-scramble-to-collect-race-stats."

The truth claim that anti-racism in universities poses challenges to whiteness continued to be a discourse that circulated in Canadian newspapers. Margaret Wente's (2006) "'Culture of Whiteness' in the Ivory Tower? Not" denounced the claims that racism exists in universities. Deploying the metaphor of "culture," Wente responded to a report on systemic racism at Queen's University (which also called for the collection of systemic data) by claiming that Asians "are quite well represented." Wente further suggested that anti-racist initiatives at Queen's University are suspect: "None of this has solved the *racism problem*," she wrote, echoing a trope that would reappear in alt-right coverage. Furthermore, deploying a racialized "our" that centres white subjects, Wente alleged that anti-racist initiatives threaten universities as she declaimed: "Pity *our* universities. When somebody produces this type of rubbish, nobody dares to denounce it – least of all the (mostly white) administration. That's left to cranky old white men like noted historian James A. Leith, professor emeritus" (emphasis added).

Not surprisingly, the next article on the collection of race-based data would return to the suspect character of such data. On 17 November 2008, Rosie DiManno echoed the arguments of the Toronto Police Board,

Margaret Wente, and Ron Melchers, writing: "Statistics are troubling. They carry a weight of certainty that is not always deserved" (DiManno 2008). With this statement, DiManno furthered the truth claim that race-based statistics are deployed to distort reality – "allowing for claims of racism where there are none." DiManno began by reiterating Melchers: "Crime statistics are particularly misleading. The numbers, and what they purportedly reveal, are only as good as *the data fed into a computer.* Often that data is incomplete or deceptive" (emphasis added). In addition, DiManno rearticulated the truth claim that whiteness and Canada are under threat by suggesting that race-based data are used by anti-racist groups to further "special interests" and threaten the fabric of Canadian society:

> Finessing statistics is a skill, especially when the purpose is exploitation of numbers by *special interest groups.* And such groups will pounce on indices that suit their agenda or appear *to legitimize their biases, their bigotry, under cover of broad societal concerns* … *Immeasurable harm* can be caused by collecting – and interpreting – statistics for the purpose of devising public policy, even when the intentions are benevolent. Race-based statistics cannot possibly be reliably benign or helpfully instructive. While the purpose of gathering such information may be educational or altruistic, the objective is a correction of adverse trends in certain identifiable groups; *the unintended consequences will also be predictably poisonous.* (DiManno 2008; emphasis added)

The truth claim that Canada is under threat from anti-racist initiatives and, concomitantly, "racial diversity" continued to be articulated. On 10 March 2010, Margaret Wente published "The Scourge of Invisible Racism," an article that denounced the findings of systemic racism by the Task Force on Anti-Racism at Ryerson, which included efforts to transform the curriculum (Wente 2010). Wente began the article by posing the challenge of changing demographics within the nation: "If you think Canada's cities are diverse today, just wait. *We're speeding toward the age of the visible majority.* By 2031, according to Statistics Canada, nearly two-thirds of Toronto's population will be non-white" (emphasis added). Wente continued to comment on the threat of anti-racism:

> *Sensitivity to perceived discrimination is so acute these days that it can lead to perverse results.* One instructor at the University of Toronto was told not to criticize foreign-born students for their poor language skills, even if they were unintelligible. Some aboriginal students say they shouldn't be evaluated by the same standards as everyone else, because they have different

ways of knowing ... Yet ... students will be working in an English-speaking, Eurocentric world. So they might as well get used to it. (Wente 2010; emphasis added)

In December 2010, Ricardo Duchesne published the article "Progressives Are Running the Universities" in *University Affairs*, one of the two national magazines for university faculty (Duchesne 2010). Duchesne, a faculty member at the University of New Brunswick and a founder of the alt-right website *Council of European Canadians*, wrote this article in response to others that argued for anti-racist initiatives. Duchesne's article is notable as it was the first on this topic by an alt-right writer to be published in a mainstream newspaper – and thus it served to further connect the alt-right into the circulation of mainstream discourse on race-based data. In the piece, Duchesne claimed that racism is "a catch-all explanation for many of their everyday difficulties." Furthermore, he explicitly stated that anti-racism is threatening universities, arguing that it is leading to the decline of rigorous European frameworks: "They don't care much for *Western high culture*. Their research and teaching interests *stand in direct opposition* to the Greek discovery of rational argumentation, the Roman legacy in jurisprudence ... the rise of Galilean and Newtonian science, and indeed the invention of Liberalism and Democracy" (emphasis added). In this editorial, Duchesne rearticulated the underlying argument in Brown, Wente, and DiManno, writing: "It is well known that progressives have been able for decades now to exercise their control through domination of hiring committees and *the imposition of politically correct speech codes designed to exterminate dissent*" (emphasis added). Notably, these claims would be echoed by newspaper writers and become central to alt-right discourse.[13] Significantly, Duchesne's column is the only article written by an alt-right writer (aside from Jordan Peterson, as discussed below) on anti-racism in universities or on the collection of race-based data that has been published in a mainstream venue in the period under study. It is notable that it was a university venue that allowed for the entry of the alt-right writers into mainstream newspapers.

Race-Based Data and the Canadian Census: "Cut Costs and Dissent at the Same Time"

The tensions around collecting race-based data would resonate within the Conservative federal government. In 2010, the Conservative government cancelled the mandatory long-form census and replaced it with a new short-form census that was voluntary. A major difference between the new short-form census and its predecessor was the elimination of questions about ethnicity and cultural heritage.[14] The cancellation of the "long form" again raised significant issues around race-based data collection. The newspaper coverage both supported and contested the cancellation of the long form.

A number of conservative organizations had been undertaking a public campaign against the census. In 2009, Don Rogers, a member of the Canadian Action Party,[15] led the campaign "Count Me Out" against the census, recommending ways to avoid the online census by counselling Canadians on how to provide minimum cooperation. His list included damaging the forms or writing answers upside down. The National Citizens Coalition, which claims a membership of between 40,000 and 45,000, campaigned against the mandatory long-form census. The National Citizens Coalition employed the threat of jail time to elicit support for its position. The Fraser Institute supported the change.

While much of the public campaign against the census was based on how it was an incursion by the state into the privacy of citizens, Peter Coleman, president of the National Citizens Coalition, claimed in a letter to *Maclean's* magazine that the long form constituted a state subsidy to special interest groups and thus was not in the national interest:

> It is curious that most of the groups/organizations clamouring to protect the long census rely upon that census data in some form or another. It is nice to receive free statistics at the expense of taxpayers, but our government should not be compelling this cooperation with the threat of jail time nor should we be bankrolling the whole endeavour. If organizations and special interest groups want data, they should pay for it. (quoted in Wherry 2010)

Members of the federal government gave shifting reasons for the cancellation of the long form. At first, Minister of Industry Tony Clement stated that this change was made on the advice of Statistics Canada (Campion-Smith 2010). On 13 July 2010, in a news release, Industry Canada reflected the position of the Canadian Action Party and the National Citizens Coalition, stating that the reason for the cancellation of the long form was to "respect the privacy wishes of Canadians" (Industry Canada 2010). Clement would later state that the change to voluntary forms was made because of privacy-related complaints, and he acknowledged that the decision was made without consulting organizations and governments that work closely with Statistics Canada (CBC News 2010b). Subsequently, in a House of Commons Industry Committee special hearing on 17 July 2010, Clement claimed the form was cancelled because those who refused to fill it in would risk jail time (CBC News 2010a).

The majority of articles examined in this research contested the cancellation of the long form. These articles either contested the Conservative government's reasons for cancelling the long form or focused on the place of the census in governmentality – arguing for its importance for government policies and thus the functioning of the government. A smaller number of articles focused on the implications of the cancellation of the long form for racial equity. Frances Woolley pointed out, for example, that the implementation of employment equity would be difficult without such data, citing labour lawyer Peter Engelmann: "Statistical evidence is a very important component of proving systemic discrimination" (Woolley 2013). A number of anti-racist groups argued that the decision was motivated by a wish to destroy a useful tool for social advocacy by making it harder to identify and count racialized persons. As one group stated, the cancellation of the long form "cut costs and dissent at the same time" (Voices-Voix 2015).

Significantly, the cancellation of the long form raised questions about the ways in which the collection of race-based data was part of the citizenship rights of racialized groups. As these writers pointed out, the cancellation of the long form represented the marginalization of racialized groups – not only from social citizenship but also from state citizenship. The African Canadian Legal Clinic, for example, tied the cancellation of this form to curtailing demands for anti-racist policies. They pointed to the government's failure to collect and/or produce race-based data and claimed it to be contrary to article 2(1)(c) of the United Nations (UN) Convention on the Elimination of Racial Discrimination and article 2 of the UN Convention on the Rights of the Child (African Canadian Legal Clinic n.d.). Thus, the African Canadian Legal Clinic drew attention to the responsibility of the state to collect data to address racial inequities and flagged the implications of the cancellation of the long form on citizenship for racialized groups.

In the public campaign "The Right to be Counted," the Canadian Council on Social Development (CCSD) argued that "by excluding some groups from the 2011 census, the federal government is saying some Canadians simply don't count as much as others. The Charter protects the right to be treated equally, and that includes the equal right to be counted" (CCSD 2011). Thus, the exclusion of those questions from the short-form census effectively "discriminated against Canadians from different ethnic and cultural backgrounds, as well as aboriginals and people with disabilities" (Canadian Press 2011). The CCSD filed a federal court challenge to the cancellation of the long form. In the hearing, the lawyer who represented the Canadian government, Robert MacKinnon, countered the marginalization of racialized groups from citizenship by arguing that there is "no legal or constitutional requirement to collect any cultural, religious or ethnic data on the census" (Canadian Press 2011). This ruling overrode the legal and policy frameworks that had previously been put into place. Thus, the cancellation of the long form legally altered the state's responsibility to racism.

Pressing for Race-Based Data: "When White Is Black. And Black Has a Target on Its Back"

Between 2012 and 2017, the pressure by anti-racist groups to collect race-based data continued. In 2012, a complaint was launched by Ottawa resident Chad Aiken[16] against the Ottawa Police Services Board. As part of a settlement agreement, the Ontario Human Rights Commission required the Police Services Board to begin collecting race-based data on traffic stops. The Ontario Human Rights Commission, the Canadian Race Relations Foundation, and the Commission on Systemic Racism in the Ontario Criminal Justice System continued to advocate for the collection of race-based data.[17] In 2017, Renu Mandhane, chief commissioner of the Ontario Human Rights Commission, stated to the Standing Committee on Canadian Heritage:

> The government must take concrete steps to identify and eliminate systemic discrimination, including mandating the collection of human rights-based data across government services. For over 20 years, the government has required federal departments to conduct gender-based impact assessments. Our final recommendation is to require impact analysis based on race. (Standing Committee 2017; see also Standing Committee 2018)

Throughout 2017, several government organizations announced plans to collect race-based data, including the Toronto Children's Aid Society and the Ministry of Education, which launched a policy requiring all Ontario school boards to collect race-based data. The Ontario government announced they would collect race-based data on its larger ministries as well. Several universities also began to collect race-based data for employees.

These initiatives received attention. Their announcements coincided with coverage of the collection of race-based data expanding from the three newspapers to other outlets. Despite the expansion in the collection of race-based data, the critiques of race-based statistics continued – and they continued to deploy many of the same tropes. In 2015, Rosie DiManno reproduced her earlier claims in an article entitled "A Thorny History of Race-Based Statistics." There, she argued that race-based data could not be trusted, violently connecting the collection of such data to threatening white subjects with unfair accusations of racism. She opened the column with the words: "What goes around comes around. But sometimes it returns upside-down. *When white is black. And black has a target on its back*" (emphasis added). Placing a racialized "we" in the cover of ambiguity and a racialized "they" to refer to racialized groups, DiManno stated:

> We've put ourselves into a moral and intellectual bind. The reason: *We* don't trust facts. More crucially, we don't trust how facts can be manipulated ... Because we can't control how information will be computed by another person's brain – whether *they'll misunderstand, whether they'll take offense where none was intended, whether they'll hurl accusations of racism* (or sexism, Islamophobia, anti-Semitism, etc.) – *we* tread delicately, self-censoriously. (DiManno 2015; emphasis added)

Not only would these claims continue to circulate among alt-right writers, but two weeks after publication, DiManno's column was reposted to Steven Bannon's alt-right site *Breitbart News* in an article entitled "Canada's Left Wants Racial Crime Statistics to Push #BlackLivesMatter Narrative" (Kraychik 2015).

On 4 November 2017 in the *Globe and Mail*, Margaret Wente responded to Universities Canada's "Action Plan for Inclusive Excellence." "Equal outcomes have replaced equality of opportunity," she wrote, which again invoked the threat of including racialized groups in employment equity at Canadian universities. In the article, Wente asked:

> How do Canada's universities stack up against the world's best? The answer is: Meh. Maybe a handful rank among the global top 100. How many Nobel winners have we produced lately? Better not to ask. But excellence is not the point of universities these days. Diversity is the point – not diversity of thought or intellect, but diversity of race, gender, ethnicity and sexual orientation. To achieve this goal, our universities have announced a major new initiative to collect and publish detailed demographic data on faculty, staff and students. The idea is to ensure that women, Indigenous people, academics with disabilities, and other underrepresented groups achieve equality of numbers. This is a new goal. The old goal was academic excellence. (Wente 2017)

On 2 April 2018, Wente followed up with another column attacking anti-racism, claiming that it would threaten Canadian unity. In an article entitled "The Intolerance Industry Is Working Overtime in Canada," she claimed:

> Our universities are full of tenured professors who make a comfortable living denouncing the sins of the ruling class and organizing conferences on the evils of White Privilege ... *We should also think carefully about how to tackle the challenges posed by our remarkable diversity. Should we split each other into a bunch of identity groups squabbling over the spoils?* Or should we stress *our common values* and do our best to make sure that everybody has a fair shot? Must we claim, as lots of people do, that Canada is rotten with every kind of "ism" and phobia? Or can we acknowledge that we really are a pretty fair and just society that's trying to do better? Maybe I'm prejudiced. But I believe the way forward should be rooted in pride and confidence, not accusations and shame. (Wente 2018; emphasis added)

As we have seen in this section, the resistance to race-based data articulated in newspapers is similar to that in universities – where race-based data is sometimes employed to demonstrate claims of systemic discrimination and sometimes to deny racism. Similar to how it appeared in the discussion of universities in the last section, the resistance to the collection of race-based data for anti-racism in newspapers was tied to whiteness, culture, and nation. Newspaper writers articulated a number of additional truth claims about race-based data: first, that race-based data were untrustworthy and used by anti-racist groups to manipulate "public perception" of racism; second, that claims of racism were dismissible as "ancient grievances and guilt" and, concomitantly, that requests for race-based data were embedded in special interests; and third, that the "elephant in the room" was that anti-racism silenced the "real" discussion posed by the inclusion of racialized groups – a discussion that would illustrate the limits of inclusion. Together, these additional truth claims frame the collection of race-based data as a threat to white subjects (by placing "a target on their back"), creating racial tensions, undermining the quality of universities, and threating the "fabric" of the nation. Crucial in this discussion is the racialized deployment of terms such as "us," "our," "we," "culture," and "Canada" to discursively displace the interests of racialized subjects from the nation. Indeed, such displacement from social citizenship was formalized when the collection of race-based data in the census was cancelled. Significantly, as can be seen explicitly in DiManno's column, the construction of these truth claims simultaneously reversed the "victims" of racism – racialized subjects were constructed as oppressors and those who are racialized as "white" as victims. These truth claims operate as powerful affective technologies, and this strategic reversal is one that is predominant in alt-right discourse.

Particularly striking in the newspaper coverage about collecting race-based data was the scarcity of articles or columns that challenged the dominant rhetoric, especially as it related to the collection of this data in education and for anti-racism. This overwhelming silence was noted when Sam Boshra, an independent Montreal-based economist and editor for EconomicJustice.ca, published a column in the *Globe and Mail* on 8 October 2014. Boshra noted that the Broadbent Institute released a report on family income that failed to include a racial breakdown, commenting: "That the purportedly progressive Canadian think tank did not see fit to mention the glaring omission … is disappointing" (Boshra 2014). Indeed, until the Ontario government's announcement that they would collect race-based data in its larger ministries, the lack of engagement by progressive or liberal voices (other than the articles by Scott Wortley, Frances Woolley, and those on the defense of the collection of race-based data in the Canadian census) was significant, as it suggests a consensus with dominant rhetoric. Importantly, the silence of "white liberal" voices allowed the truth claims put forward by conservative writers to become hegemonic. Furthering the hegemony of this discourse, as I have noted above, several of these articles continue to be available online, including on alt-right websites – pointing to a continued circulation of these truth claims.

Right-Wing Articulations: "Whatever 'Racism' May Be, They All Agree that It Is a Very Bad Thing, and that Canadian Society Is Riddled with It"

In this section, I examine the ways in which narratives produced by mainstream newspapers are interpolated with those that circulate on alt-right websites. As noted earlier, in order to identify the circulation of discourses regarding the collection of race-based data, I conducted digital searches and a search of four alt-right websites – *American Renaissance, Elliot Lake Blog, Council of European Canadians,* and *Jordan B Peterson Clips.* These four sites were chosen as each intersected with newspaper coverage on the collection of race-based data and its associated discourses. I examined these sites for evidence of how the claims articulated in universities and in newspapers circulated specifically on alt-right sites and how claims on these sites concurrently shaped narratives in newspapers. I have paid particular attention to how similar narratives, metaphors, and claims are produced through and travel between sites.

As the last two sections have illustrated, both in universities and in newspaper coverage, the resistance to collecting race-based data has been located within a politics of denying racism – a politics that is concomitantly embedded in a politics of whiteness. As this section demonstrates, there are significant similarities in the discourses produced through newspapers and those produced through alt-right sites. These similarities point to how the racial politics of alt-right groups are embedded in civil society, and how they, in turn, construct civil society. Similar to the newspaper articles examined in the previous section, alt-right sites claim that anti-racism silences the challenges posed by "inclusion," leads to racial tension, threatens white subjects, and undermines national unity and the quality of the university. Moreover, the alt-right writers use strikingly similar metaphors and narratives to those of the newspaper writers when they make the same truth claims.

Ten months after the publication of Wente's (2005) column in which she claimed race-based data could lead to an increase in racial tension, and four months after the publication of Brown's (2006) article that resonated concerns about the collection of race-based data, US-based neo-right group and webzine *American Renaissance* turned its attention to the question of collecting race-based data, using it as an opportunity to make claims against racial diversity and linking it to the rhetoric of "white genocide." Jared Taylor is a self-proclaimed journalist as well as founder and editor of *American Renaissance*, which describes itself as "the Internet's premier racial-realist site" (American Renaissance 2021). Taylor went on to develop ties to Richard Spencer, Jason Kessler, and multimillionaire William Regnery through what they have defined as "an ascendant social movement" (Daniels 2018). Taylor, along with Kessler, helped to organize the "Unite the Right" rally in Charlottesville, Virginia, in August 2017.

In September 2006, Taylor invited David Divine, Dalhousie University's chair of Black Canadian Studies, to debate the question of whether racial diversity is a strength or a weakness. Upon learning of Taylor's ties to white supremacist groups, Divine declined to participate in the debate. In March 2007, Taylor appeared in a debate with Peter March, the Saint Mary's University philosophy professor who had become well known for posting controversial cartoons of Islam's Prophet Muhammad on his office door. The ensuing debate received attention from CBC (CBC News 2007) and CTV (Canadian Press 2007). Since its delivery, this speech has been made available on the alt-right websites *American Renaissance* and *Elliot Lake Blog*, and received attention from alt-right websites such as *Ontrayan*. The speech was subsequently posted on YouTube (Taylor 2010b).

In his comments,[18] Taylor circulated the same truth claims that were made in the newspaper coverage discussed earlier. First, drawing on Patrick Deane's statement "Our Canadian culture has been squeamish about gathering race-based statistics," Taylor claimed that "the elephant in the room" prevented "Canadians" from articulating their views on racism, to the extent that "Canadians" were unable to document the dangers of criminality. Thus, altering Deane's phrase, he declared: "Canada is too squeamish to collect crime statistics by race, but the United States is not."[19]

Second, echoing Margaret Wente's (2005) claim that anti-racism leads to racial tensions in Canada, Taylor (2007a) stated: "So it appears that racism is a very considerable scourge in Canada." He deployed tropes of race and violence, and made explicit Wente's claims by asserting that the inclusion of racialized minorities threatened Canada. He continued on to say: "At its worst, racial diversity can lead to race riots, racially motivated murder and assault"; and he concluded: "How do you even begin to assess whether racial diversity is a strength or a weakness unless you gather the information. Do different groups have different rates of *illegitimacy*? *School failure*? *Poverty*? If they do, does it make [any] sense to add to those racial groups through immigration?" (Taylor 2007a; italics and underlining as appears in the transcript of the speech).

The claim that racial diversity threatens Canada not only circulated in earlier newspaper coverage but was also further echoed in coverage after March 2007. Notably, in 2010, Margaret Wente used the word "scourge" to refer to invisible racism. Deliberately conflating racism with conflict, Taylor went on to suggest that racism threatens Canada: "Whatever '*racism*' may be, they all agree that it is a very bad thing, and that *Canadian* society is riddled with it. Obviously, if there was no racial diversity in Canada, there could be no racial discrimination" (Taylor 2007a, italics and underlining as appears in the transcript of the speech). He concluded that racial diversity "pose[s] a serious threat to the social fabric of Canadian society." As we have seen, this claim was repeated by Rosie DiManno (2008) in her statement that "the objective is a correction of adverse trends in certain identifiable groups; the unintended consequences will be predictably poisonous." Similarly, Margaret Wente (2010) wrote: "If you think Canada's cities are diverse today, just wait. We're speeding toward the age of the visible majority."

Third, Taylor repeated the claim that anti-racism threatens whiteness. For example, in the blog post "Is Burlington TOO White," Taylor commented: "A mid-sized CANADIAN city received a complaint from a foreign-born **BLACK woman**, and her committee of other meddling foreigners, that one of Canada's five top-rated cities to reside in ... is (gasp) apparently much 'TOO WHITE' for her satisfaction" (Taylor 2010a; bold, caps, and underlining as appears in the transcript). Drawing on Wente's (2005) claim about the danger of "blame games fed by ancient grievances and guilt," Taylor noted that one of the dangers of racial diversity is that "racism – whatever that may be – is a moral failing that afflicts only *Whites*" (Taylor 2010a). Taylor followed this speech with several blog posts and books that focused on positioning anti-racism as a threat to whiteness (see, for example, Taylor 2014), claiming it resulted in "white flight" from urban spaces and even white genocide. The central trope of whiteness-under-threat was one that would continue to circulate in mainstream newspapers, being most clearly articulated by Rosie DiManno's (2015) statement "When white is black. And black has a target on its back."

Finally, Taylor rearticulated claims about the domination of left-wing groups – claims that would continue to circulate in subsequent newspaper coverage. Arguing that the production of left-wing policies, which he conflated with anti-racism, "causes damage to the country," he claimed that "it defies common sense" and declared: "You don't want it openly discussed."[20] As illustrated in the previous section, the threat of anti-racism to the national project was a common theme in newspaper coverage – in Wente's (2005) and Brown's (2006) articles, which claimed that universities are "respectable in a national context"; in Duchesne's (2010) column in *University Affairs* that decried the loss of a rigorous European framework; and in Wente's (2018) article titled "The Intolerance Industry Is Working Overtime in Canada." Each of these articles pushed forward the claim that anti-racism posed a threat to whiteness and the nation – a view that is also central to alt-right activities.

Importantly, these claims would not only continue to circulate in newspapers but also in dominant alt-right rhetoric. The rhetoric of the threat to whiteness could clearly be seen in posters that appeared on Canadian campuses. Examples include posters claiming "We Have a Right to Exist," placed under a picture of a young white man and woman; "It's Time to Make Canada Great Again," superimposed over the symbol of the Canadian flag; "It's Okay to Be White"; "It's Now Racist When White People Do It"; and "Equality Is a False God." Such posters have been reported at almost every Canadian university campus, including York University, the University of Toronto, the University of Calgary, the University of Manitoba, and the University of New Brunswick.

DiManno's construction of the "white" victim plays a central rhetorical claim in speeches by alt-right speakers on university campuses. Ben Shapiro, a conservative commentator and former editor-at-large of *Breitbart News*, gave a talk during the Canadian Freedom Summit 2017 at the University of Toronto. Similarly, *Rebel Media* personality Lauren Southern has been invited to speak by student groups at York University, the University of Toronto, and Canadian Christian College. A central refrain in all of these talks is that anti-racism is racist towards those who are racialized as "white." For example, in his YouTube video "Identity Politics and the Marxist Lie of White Privilege" (Peterson 2017), Jordan Peterson circulates earlier claims that "white privilege is a racist concept on its face, with skin colour as the main determinant of value and truth." He goes on to deploy the trope of "culture" to assert whiteness, asking the question, "Is white privilege not just majority privilege … [I]s it not just part of bringing your own culture … Is that not what your culture is for?" Notably, this YouTube video had almost 900,000 views as of August 2018, ranking it as the third-most popular of Peterson's videos.

As with Taylor, Peterson's claims have been taken up in newspapers. For example, on 9 March 2018, Rex Murphy echoed Peterson, Taylor, and Wente to claim:

> White privilege is a contemptible construction. It explicitly invokes skin colour as the only vector of judgment. It insists on "whiteness" as a flaw, a failing, and, as it almost always is, when yoked with "male" is the verbal equivalent of a spit. It is pure stereotype, ugly and angry. It is seen as a necessary term in identity politics, the politics of faction – ethnic, racial and religious. (Murphy 2018; see also Murphy 2015)

Another central truth claim among alt-right writers is that universities are dominated by left-wing faculty who attack the tenets of bodies of thought that are central to whiteness.[21] In 2015, Robert Kraychik in the *Breitbart* article cited earlier, referring to DiManno's article and echoing Taylor to claim the threat of racism to whiteness, also claimed that left-wing groups use race-based data to make false claims: "While racial agitation is not new to Canada, it is certainly enjoying a resurgence in recent years. In order to best frame Canada as a bastion of white supremacy, cesspool of systemic discrimination, and purveyor of white privilege, the left wants cold hard data to misinterpret" (Kraychik 2015). Similarly, in a speech posted to his YouTube channel on 13 November 2017, Jordan Peterson claimed: "Women's studies, and all the ethnic studies and racial studies groups, man, those things have to go and the faster they go the better." He continued: "It would have been better if they had never been part of the university to begin with as far as I can tell." Similar to the rhetoric found in newspaper coverage, Peterson denounced anti-racist scholarship as suspect, claiming "it is interesting where these ideas came from because usually the scholarship is so awful" (Peterson 2017). The claim that critical race studies, feminism, and Marxism is a threat to white subjects has led to the alt-right's phrases "social justice warriors" and "the thought police" – both deployed as examples of threats to whiteness. Indeed, criticisms of anti-racist and critical scholarship by right-wing groups seem to be discussed on a daily basis in print media and on talk shows.

As this section illustrates, discourses of the denial of racism and the threat anti-racism poses to both whiteness and the nation are central to alt-right writers. Echoing the rhetoric of the dangers of anti-racism and a concomitant inclusion of racialized minorities, these groups portray "white" people, Canada, and universities as all being under threat. Alt-right groups repeat and extend the claims made in newspapers that white subjects have a "target on their back" and claim that anti-racism is, in fact, the "real racism." As a result, this claim becomes an effective defense against anti-racism – further allowing anti-racist thought to be dismissed as "bad" scholarship and to be associated with oppressive practices. Such truth claims operate as technologies of affect, where the rhetoric on the threat of anti-racist politics and practice contributes to a discourse of whiteness. Importantly, as we have seen, the claims made by alt-right groups are not exclusive to them, but rather are remarkably similar to the truth claims that circulate in newspapers. While articulated differently in universities, newspaper coverage, and alt-right websites, the similarity of claims made across these three areas is striking. Moreover, the phrases and claims that appear in one location circulate across the others, reinforcing each other and resonating across spaces.

Conclusion: "One of the Crucial Properties of Contemporary Racism Is Its Denial"

My investigation into the tensions surrounding the collection of race-based data in three sites allows for a unique consideration of the ways racialized power operates in Canada. First, it illuminates the larger project of denying racism and discrediting anti-racism. Teun A. van Dijk (1992) argued that "one of the crucial properties of contemporary racism is its denial" (87). As this study illustrates, it is through the denial of racism that contemporary forms of racism are maintained;

this denial is deployed to ensure that barriers experienced by racialized groups are not eliminated, and thus the positions of those racialized as "white" remain entrenched. My study demonstrates why the collection of race-based data has been so contentious: evidence of racism and support for anti-racism challenge the ability to deny racism's very existence. Second, my investigation into the tensions around the collection of race-based data not only clarifies the discursive commonality across university constituencies, newspapers, and alt-right groups but also exposes the fact that these seemingly disparate groups share a politics of denying racism. Importantly, this project suggests that understanding the alt-right's dispute with anti-racism requires grasping how such contestations are ubiquitous in civil society. Third, my research raises implications for understanding the relationship of universities to both discourses of racism and the alt-right. Each of these findings brings forward important consequences for theorizing racism in the contemporary period and elicits a number of theoretical implications for understanding the complexities of racism in the current period.

By illuminating the ubiquity of the discursive denial of racism, this study points to the complex process through which contemporary racism was produced in the post-war period. In an analysis of everyday talk, press, and parliamentary debates, van Dijk (1992) noted that racialized discourses are riddled by contradiction: on one hand, they are governed by general norms of tolerance and acceptance towards "others," while on the other hand, they are governed by feelings of resentment and frustration about those "others." He argued that general norms of tolerance required that racialized articulations must be managed, pointing out that one of the major strategic ways "white" speakers and writers engage in such forms of impression management is through the denial of racism. Building on van Dijk, this chapter elucidates that the "general norms of tolerance" are embedded in two contradictory forces: first, a nation-state that has been and continues to be imagined and institutionalized through whiteness; and second, a socio-legal context that allows the Canadian state to make claims of ensuring equality.

As this study shows, the denial of racism is located in a politics of whiteness. Earlier, I defined whiteness as a racialized system of power that benefits those racialized as "white" while simultaneously marginalizing others – a system of power that is constituted through both individual practices and institutional processes that are culturally, socially, politically, and institutionally produced and reproduced. As much research has powerfully illustrated, in Canada, whiteness was institutionalized through a national project of "a white man's country," an imaginary that shaped British colonial and Canadian

post-Confederation settlement, citizenship, and naturalization policies, and which, in turn, reinforced barriers for full participation in economic, social, and political citizenship (Bolaria and Li 1988; Dua 1999;
Thobani 2007).

The institutionalization of whiteness not only constitutes a system
of power but, importantly, also shapes the investments of those racialized as "white" in maintaining both the national imaginary as well as
its structures of power (Gilroy 1991; Dua 2000; Hage 2000). The mobilization of truth claims employed through racialized uses of "us,"
"our," "culture," and "Canada" strategically displaces the interests of
racialized subjects from the nation and constructs racialized subjects
as "other." Crucial to these truth claims is the affective mobilization
of whiteness. As Sara Ahmed (2012) has argued, texts that circulate in
the public domain work to align subjects with collectives by attribut-
ing "others" as the "source" of feelings (2). As she points out, "such
others threaten to take away from what 'you' have, as the legitimate
subject of the nation, as the one who is the true recipient of national
benefits. The narrative invites the reader to adopt the 'you' through
working on emotions: becoming this 'you' would mean developing a
certain rage against these illegitimate others" (2). This affective politics
can certainly be seen in the phrase "having a target on *your* back" –
a rhetorical device that mobilizes the affect of both victimization and
rage, and concomitantly evokes investments in the power of whiteness.

However, as this study confirms, the project of "white" nationalism can be contested and undermined by the opportunities offered
by state policies for remedying or eliminating racism. Scholarship has
illustrated that such anti-discrimination policies have a complex history. In the aftermath of the Second World War, the association between
overt racism and Nazism led the post-war governments in Britain
and the United States to adopt anti-discrimination laws and policies.
These policies asserted the guarantee of equality, a commitment to the
elimination of discrimination, and an official ban on blatant expressions of "hate" (Balibar 2005; van Dijk 1992; Thobani 2007).[22] Notably,
Canada's legal commitment against discrimination, racism, and hate
speech developed in the 1940s and continued until the development of
the Charter of Rights and Freedoms in 1982.[23] Thus, the post-war state
represented the end of racism and the emergence of a new period that
heralded equality. While the presence of racism was acknowledged, it
was represented as a holdover from the past – and one that the post-
war state had mechanisms to address.

Despite these policies, as many scholars have noted, anti-discrimination
legislation has been ineffective in challenging racism. Scholarship

identifies three interrelated contradictions in anti-discrimination policies: First, anti-discrimination policies depict racism as constituting a form of individual violation of rights and the exercise of racial power as individual and exceptional, and thus, as irregular. As a result, anti-discrimination policies erase the everyday and systemic character of racism and its centrality in the exercise of hegemonic power (Goldberg 2002; Dua and Bhanji 2012). Second, as critical race legal theorists illustrate, the doctrinal categories of the legal system – with their erasure of racialized hegemonic power – reinforce hierarchical social relations and social structures rather than eradicate them (Williams 1998; Crenshaw, Harris, and Lipsitz 2013). Thus, while anti-discrimination legislation offers important legal gains, ultimately, such reform has been averse to those racialized as minorities. As Patricia Williams (1998) has powerfully illustrated, the operation of anti-discrimination law has benefitted whites more than Blacks. Third, given these limitations, anti-discrimination legislation offers a powerful ideology, as it has merely led to the "legitimization of the basic myths of American meritocracy" (Solomos 1990; Crenshaw, Harris, and Lipsitz 2013) or, in the context of Canada, the benign multicultural nation (Razack 2008; Mackey 2002).

In addition to the ideological consequences of anti-discrimination policies, this study confirms that, in the context of white settler nation-states, anti-discrimination policies operate in a contradictory and complex nexus of racialized power, and they become contested sites of power. As we have seen, anti-racist activists deploy anti-discrimination policies to further anti-racism. As a result, anti-racist activists have advocated for the collection of race-based data in order to mobilize for anti-discrimination policies. On the other hand, as we have seen, it is the very *possibility* of employing anti-discrimination policies that mobilizes the politics of denial, and thus makes this denial a rhetorical tool for the circulation of power. The primary effect of the denial of racism is to ensure that the state does not act, thereby leaving a white settler nation-state intact. Thus, the truth claims that circulate around the collection of race-based data conceal a complex operation of power. They mobilize the denial of racism to maintain whiteness. Moreover, the power that circulates in the management of negative articulations of race is complex, as it is a power that does not operate to prohibit negative articulations but rather operates to *allow* such articulations. It is this politics of whiteness that produces, induces, sustains, and redirects racism. As a result, the denial of racism is tied to the very reproduction of whiteness, which, in turn, is constitutive of the reproduction of racism.

By illuminating the ways in which alt-right discourses on racism and their contestations of anti-racism are not significantly different from those in universities and in newspapers, this study also puts forward important insights for theorizing the relationship of the alt-right to civil society. In both academic scholarship and media coverage, the alt-right is framed as a growing phenomenon, and its increase is treated as unprecedented. For example, Giroux (2017) states: "What makes it new is its virulence, its naked expression and its ties to those who govern." Many contend that the rise of the alt-right has been enabled by the internet. Jesse Daniels (2018) notes that the technology industry conceives of the internet as a "place ... much like the imaginary American frontier in a Hollywood western, that should remain free from control by governments of the industrial world." Operating with this politics, technology companies have built an infrastructure where "race is built into digital technologies" (Noble 2018; Nakamura and Chow-White 2011).

Others have attributed the rise of the alt-right to a crisis in white identity – a manifestation of the white men (and women) who are angry about their increasingly precarious economic position. This perspective places a crisis of "white" identity in the context of neoliberalism – either the extension of neoliberalism and its concomitant restructuring of work and wages or the crisis of neoliberal capital accumulation that has resulted in the increasing power of financial capitalism (Giroux 2017; Charles 2018). Notably, this argument reiterates the Marxist analysis of racism as the consequence of a false ideology that uses racialized identities to divide the working class.[24] Drawing on the perspective that racism is a false ideology, scholars theorizing the alt-right have argued that its rise is a "tool" to manipulate the white working class. For example, Charles (2018) states that an "awareness of group membership is the most powerful political tool. It can be used to manipulate people's emotions, their behaviour and choice." Both of these perspectives obscure the relationship of the alt-right to the broader structures of whiteness. First, they obscure the history of whiteness and the importance of ubiquitous investments in whiteness for shaping the rise of the alt-right. Second, as we have seen, they selectively isolate the alt-right from a broader politics of whiteness. As a result, the racism of the alt-right is positioned as irregular and exceptional, and in opposition to the politics of liberalism, indeed, allowing it to be characterized as illiberalism.

In contrast, by tracing the commonality of a discursive understanding of the collection of race-based data in university constituencies, newspapers, and alt-right groups, this study locates the alt-right's politics of racism within the ubiquitous politics of whiteness in civil society. The instances discussed above, where writers in Canadian newspapers articulated remarkably similar language to make claims about the collection of race-based data, racism, and the threat posed to white subjects and the nation, illustrate that the notion of a difference between progressive, liberal, conservative, and right-wing politics of whiteness is a nebulous one.[25] As white subjects of all political stripes mobilized truth claims in order to deny racism and to obstruct the implementation of anti-racism, the rhetoric of the racialized "us," "our," "culture," and "Canada" strategically displaced the interests of racialized subjects from the nation. Crucial in these truth claims was the affective mobilization of whiteness. Moreover, as this study illustrates, these truth claims and phrases (particularly regarding the threat anti-racism poses to white subjects) travelled between sites, linking universities, newspapers, and the alt-right in circular relations to systems of discursive power. Thus, this study points to the critical importance of placing alt-right groups within the ubiquitous and long history of a white settler nationalist project, as well as within the investments those racialized as "white" have in it. Surprisingly, despite the commonality in discourses of whiteness, very few scholars have investigated the connections between alt-right groups and a larger politics of whiteness, either in civil society or within universities.

Finally, my study not only points to directions for re-theorizing the alt-right; it also extends ways of theorizing the relationship between the alt-right and universities. As I noted in my introduction, much of the coverage of alt-right activities on campuses places universities not only as being outside of alt-right politics but also as victims of them. Indeed, scholars often represent universities as the forerunners of progressive values and victims of right-wing attacks. For example, Mitchell (2018) stated that the alt-right "corrupt the very foundations of American universities as places of reasoned debate." While frighteningly true, the underlying assumption that the university and its constituencies are the vanguard of progressiveness obscures the question of why universities are important sites for the alt-right white nationalist agenda.

As this study suggests, universities are crucial to the circuits of power of whiteness, a link that speaks to the importance of universities for alt-right activities. On the one hand, as Said (1978), Mohanty (2003), Spivak (Danius, Jonsson, and Spivak 1993), and others have illustrated, the dominant canons of knowledge within universities operate to produce a "white" hegemony. Thus, some university faculty, newspaper writers, and the alt-right share a commitment to ensuring that European-identified canons are conserved – a project that has implications for data collection, hirings, curriculum, and the kinds of students that are produced. On the other hand, universities have been an important site for anti-racist knowledge production – knowledge production that illuminates the structures and practices of both whiteness and racism. As with the collection of race-based data, the production of anti-racist, feminist, and left scholarship threatens the project of denying racism. As Zhou (2017) notes, "universities have become the straw men for what people like to think is wrong with American higher education. Many Republicans believe that colleges are simply too liberal and want to mandate certain kinds of content – and hiring practices."[26] If we employ an analytical frame that simultaneously highlights the importance of universities in maintaining dominant canons and recognizes them as sites where anti-racist knowledge is produced, we can then understand why universities are a central site of alt-right activities as well as a target of criticism from newspaper writers.

NOTES

1 In 1984, the Abella Report, formally known as *Equality in Employment: A Royal Commission Report*, recommended collecting race-based data for employment equity initiatives (Abella 1984). Subsequently, several mechanisms were put into place to mandate the collection of race-based data. First, Parliament mandated the collection of data through its agencies, notably, Statistics Canada and Census Canada. One of the primary mechanisms through which data on race was collected was through the country-wide census, which is distributed by Statistics Canada. Second, in addition to the census and household survey, the federal government began collecting race-based statistics for the purpose of administering its employment equity program, which requires the implementation of an employment equity census or workforce questionnaire for any organization providing contracted services to the government. The main vehicle for the collection of such data is the Federal Contractors Program. Finally, provincial governments were mandated to collect data through, for example, Ministries of Education and Human Rights Tribunals.

2 The label for white supremacist groups has varied over the period of study. The terms "neo-right," "alt-right," and "far-right" have all been employed. In order to reflect the use of terminology over the period of study, I will use the term that was employed in that particular time period. However, it is important to note that the politics of these groups in the period of study are similar, despite different terminology being used to refer to them.

3 I would like to thank Nael Bhanji for collecting the early material for this chapter.

4 After the events on 6 January 2021, when the alt-right attacked the United States Capitol, Google (as well as Twitter and Facebook) removed

material posted by some alt-right groups. As a result, material from three of the cited sources, *American Renaissance*, *Elliot Lake Blog*, and *Canadian Immigration Report*, have been removed. Consequently, the links for these sites are no longer live. For the purposes of citation for this chapter, I have provided the links. However, it is important to note that these links take the reader to a message that the site has been removed.

5 These interviews were carried out in 2014 and 2015 as part of a Social Sciences and Humanities Research Council (SSHRC)–funded national project on racism in Canadian universities, in which the effectiveness of anti-racist policies was evaluated (see Dua 2017a, 2017b).

6 In 2018, CAUT began to publish race-based data.

7 Some examples of the articles in the series include Toronto Star (2002a, 2002b, 2002c, 2002d); Porter (2002); and Rankin (2002a, 2002b).

8 The police union launched a $2.7 billion class action libel lawsuit against the *Star*. It was eventually dismissed by the Supreme Court of Canada, which upheld a previous decision by the Ontario Superior Court.

9 Notably, since the 1960s, the TDSB had collected data on student achievement; however, after the amalgamation of the Greater Toronto Area (GTA) in 1998, it stopped collecting such data.

10 At the University of Guelph, the Presidential Task Force on Anti-Racism and Race Relations was formed and released a report in 1998 (see Presidential Task Force 1998); the report *Systemic Racism towards Faculty of Colour and Aboriginal Faculty at Queen's University* was released in April 2004 (see Henry 2004).

11 The policy replaces the OHRC's 1996 *Policy on Racial Slurs and Harassment and Racial Jokes.* While the policy is not binding on the courts, its purpose is to set standards for how individuals, employers, service providers, and policymakers should act to ensure they comply with the Ontario Human Rights Code.

12 Several other organizations also called for the collection of race-based data. Organizations such as the National Secretariat Against Hate and Racism in Canada (NSAHRC) endorsed "the responsible collection of race-based data for the purposes of identifying and eliminating discrimination and disadvantage as it affects Aboriginal peoples and racialized groups" (NSAHRC n.d.). The Canadian Race Relations Foundation (2015), in the "The Case for the Collection of Race-Based Statistics," also endorsed the call for such data. The African Canadian Legal Clinic (n.d.) called for "Disaggregated Data Collection (Race-Based Statistics)."

13 Ricardo Duchesne continues to write white supremacist discourse on his website *Council of European Canadians* and in articles such as "The Great Fear – Why Do Whites Fear Their Own Ethnicity?" (2014, reposted 2018) and "Only Whites Can Teach Western Civilization" (2018). He has also

written *Canada in Decay: Mass Immigration, Diversity, and the Ethnocide of Euro-Canadians*, published in 2017 by Black House Publishing, London.

14 The long-form census was reinstated in 2016.

15 Don Rogers served five terms as a Kingston city counsellor, during which he led campaigns for increased policing and law and order.

16 Officers pulled Aikens over in 2005 while he was driving his mother's Mercedes-Benz.

17 For reports on the collection of race-based data from these organizations, see Ontario Human Rights Commission (2009), Canadian Race Relations Foundation (2015), and Commission on Systemic Racism in the Ontario Criminal Justice System (1995).

18 This speech has several, slightly different versions. I am using the speech that appeared on Taylor's website in 2014.

19 The statement "Our Canadian culture has been squeamish about gathering race-based statistics" would resonate and be employed by other alt-right groups. CIReport (2012) says that "Canadian media is decidedly squeamish when it comes to reporting non-white crime." CIReport also claims that journalists are being denied such information and reliable data.

20 Similarly, see the titles of the blog posts "Canadians Duped on Multiculturalism" (Taylor 2011), "Multiculturalism: A Dividing Force" (Elliot Lake News 2007), and "White Americans: An Endangered Species" (Taylor 2007b).

21 The attack on universities has been tied to the use of coercive legislation and the threat of withholding federal funds to demand more right-wing ideology on campus. Stephen Harper cut back funding to university research and implemented tight control over government scientists in their communication with media. Ontario Premier Doug Ford has announced that he will implement a policy that withholds funding to universities that do not allow alt-right speakers on campuses. In the United States, Republican lawmakers and affiliated groups have increasingly sought similar coercive legislation. In 2017, in Wisconsin, after years of GOP attacks on tenure, legislators demanded the cancellation of a class on "Whiteness" and threatened to cut funding if their orders weren't followed.

22 Solomos (1990) has attributed these policies to the influence of the United Nations General Assembly, which adopted the Universal Declaration of Human Rights in 1948. The Universal Declaration established an international standard of non-discrimination on the basis of race, colour, language, national origin, and a number of other grounds. It was adopted by the General Assembly on 20 November 1963.

23 In Canada, the development of anti-discrimination policy has included both provincial and federal policies. In 1945, Ontario introduced the

Racial Discrimination Act, which was followed by Saskatchewan's Bill of Rights in 1947. In the 1960s, the federal government introduced the Bill of Rights. In the 1960s and 1970s, the provinces and territories started to consolidate these statutes into comprehensive human rights codes. Fair accommodation and fair employment practices laws were enacted throughout Canada in the 1950s, followed by equal-pay legislation for women and the Federal Contractors Program.

24 For an exploration of the limitations of conceptualizing racism as a false ideology, see Hall (1996), Gilroy (1991), and Dua and Bhanji (2012).

25 As we have seen, the silence around challenging these narratives points to an astounding hegemony of this racialized imaginary of the nation.

26 The public concern that Canadian universities are dominated by left-wing professors may have led to studies examining the political orientation of university faculty. For example, a study by Reza Nakhaie and Robert Brym (2011), published in the journal of *Canadian Journal of Higher Education*, illustrates that the majority of professors identify as centrist.

REFERENCES

Abella, Rosalie Silberman. 1984. *Equality in Employment: A Royal Commission Report*. Ottawa: Minister of Supply and Services Canada.

African Canadian Legal Clinic. n.d. "Disaggregated Data Collection (Race-Based Statistics)." Policy Paper. https://studylib.net/doc/8102332 /policy-paper---african-canadian-legal-clinic.

Ahmed, Sara. 2012. *On Being Included: Racism and Diversity in Institutional Life*. Durham, NC: Duke University Press.

American Renaissance. 2021. "About Us." https://www.amren.com/about/.

Balibar, Étienne. 2005. "The Construction of Racism." *Actuel Marx* 38 (2): 11–28. English version translated by Cadenza Academic Translations. https://www.cairn-int.info/article-E_AMX_038_0011--the-construction -of-racism.htm.

Billig, Michael. 1987. *Arguing and Thinking: A Rhetorical Approach to Social Psychology*. New York: Cambridge University Press.

Blatchford, Christie. 2002. "Sometimes Race Is Simply a Fact." *National Post*, 29 October 2002, A0 and A08.

Bolaria, B. Singh, and Peter S. Li. 1988. *Racial Oppression in Canada*, 2nd ed. Toronto: Garamond Press.

Boshra, Sam. 2014. "Why Canada Avoids Asking about Race, and Why That's a Problem." *The Globe and Mail*, 8 October 2014. https://www .theglobeandmail.com/report-on-business/rob-commentary /why-canada-avoids-asking-about-race-and-why-thats-a-problem /article20987894/.

Brown, Louise. 2006. "Schools Scramble to Take Colour Count." *Toronto Star*, 2 September 2006, A1.

Campion-Smith, Bruce. 2010. "StatsCan Recommended Move to Voluntary Census, Tony Clement Says." *Toronto Star*, 16 July 2010. https://www .thestar.com/news/canada/2010/07/16/statscan_recommended_move_to _voluntary_census_tony_clement_says.html.

Canadian Council on Social Development (CCSD). 2011. *The Right to Be Counted*. Public campaign.

Canadian Press. 2007. "Halifax Racial Diversity Debate Went Ahead." *CTV News*, 6 March 2007. https://www.ctvnews.ca/halifax-racial-diversity -debate-went-ahead-1.232039.

– 2011. "Court Asked to Add Ethnicity, Religion to Basic Census." *CBC News*, 23 November 2011. https://www.cbc.ca/news/politics/court-asked -to-add-ethnicity-religion-to-basic-census-1.1069697.

Canadian Race Relations Foundation. 2008. "A National Policy on the Collection of Race-Based Statistics." Last modified 14 July 2015. http:// www.crrf-fcrr.ca/en/component/flexicontent/292-policies-and-research /23598-a-national-policy-on-the-collection-of-race-based-statistics.

CBC News. 2007. "SMU Says No Racism Debate on Campus." *CBC News*, 5 March 2007. https://www.cbc.ca/news/canada/nova-scotia/smu-says-no -racism-debate-on-campus-1.661200.

– 2010a. "Clement Amends Census Changes." *CBC News*, 11 August 2010. https://www.cbc.ca/news/politics/clement-amends-census-changes -1.948445.

– 2010b. "Clement to Face MPs on Census." *CBC News*, 24 July 2010. https:// www.cbc.ca/news/politics/clement-to-face-mps-on-census-1.924192.

Charles, Aurelie. 2018. "Our Individual Responsibility to Face Down the Rise of the Far Right." *The Conversation*, 23 January 2018. https:// theconversation.com/our-individual-responsibility-to-face-down-the -rise-of-the-far-right-86503.

CIReport. 2012. *Whitewashing Criminal Justice in Canada*. CIReport.ca.

Commission on Systemic Racism in the Ontario Criminal Justice System. 1995. *Report of the Commission on Systemic Racism in the Ontario Criminal Justice System*. Toronto: Queen's Printer. https://www.publicsafety.gc.ca /cnt/rsrcs/lbrr/ctlg/dtls-en.aspx?d=PS&i=3040651.

Crenshaw, Kimberlé, Luke Charles Harris, and George Lipsitz. 2013. *The Race Track: Understanding and Challenging Structural Racism*. New York: The New Press.

Daniels, Jessie. 2018. "The Algorithmic Rise of the 'Alt-Right.'" *Contexts* 17 (1): 60–5. https://doi.org/10.1177/1536504218766547.

Danius, Sara, Stefan Jonsson, and Gayatri Chakravorty Spivak. 1993. "An Interview with Gayatri Chakravorty Spivak." *Boundary* 2 20 (2): 24–50. https://doi.org/10.2307/303357.

DiManno, Rosie. 2008. "Race Stats Confine Black Youths." *Toronto Star*, 17 November 2008. https://www.thestar.com/news/crime/2008/11/17/race _stats_confine_black_youths.html.

– 2015. "A Thorny History of Race-Based Statistics." *Toronto Star*, 17 August 2015. https://www.thestar.com/news/gta/2015/08/17/a-thorny-history-of -race-based-statistics.html.

Dua, Enakshi. 1999. "From Subjects to Aliens: Indian Migrants and the Racialisation of Canadian Citizenship." *Sociologie et Societé* 31 (2): 145–62.

– 2000. "The Hindu Woman's Question: Canadian Nation-Building and the Social Construction of Gender for South Asian-Canadian Women." In *Anti-Racist Feminism: Critical Race and Gender Studies*, edited by George Dei and Agnes Calliste, 55–72. Halifax: Fernwood Press.

– 2009. "On the Effectiveness of Anti-Racist Policies in Canadian Universities: Issues of Implementation of Policies by Senior Administration." In *Racism in the Canadian University: Demanding Social Justice, Inclusion, and Equity*, edited by Frances Henry and Carol Tator, 160–96. Toronto: University of Toronto Press.

– 2014. "Not Quite a Case of the Disappearing Marx: Tracing the Place of Material Relations in Post-Colonial Theory." In *Theorizing Anti-Racism: Linkages in Marxism and Critical Race Theories*, edited by Enakshi Dua and Abigail B. Bakan, 63–92. Toronto: University of Toronto Press.

– 2017a. "Mechanisms to Address Inequities in Canadian Universities: The Performativity of Ineffectiveness." With Nael Bhanji. In *The Equity Myth: Racialization and Indigeneity at Canadian Universities*, edited by Frances Henry et al., 206–38. Vancouver, BC: UBC Press.

– 2017b. "Shifting Terrains: A Picture of the Institutionalization of Equity in Canadian Universities." With Nael Bhanji. In *The Equity Myth: Racialization and Indigeneity at Canadian Universities*, edited by Frances Henry et al., 171–205. Vancouver, BC: UBC Press.

Dua, Enakshi, and Nael Bhanji. 2012. "Exploring the Potential of Data Collected Under the Federal Contractors Programme to Construct a National Picture of Visible Minority and Aboriginal Faculty in Canadian Universities." *Canadian Ethnic Studies* 44 (1): 49–74. https://doi.org/10.1353/ces.2012.0001.

Dua, Enakshi, and Bonita Lawrence. 2000. "Challenging White Hegemony in University Classrooms: Whose Canada Is It?" *Atlantis* 24 (2): 105–22.

Duchesne, Ricardo. 2010. "Progressives Are Running the Universities." *University Affairs*, 20 December 2010. https://www.universityaffairs.ca /opinion/in-my-opinion/a-response-to-racism-in-the-academy/.

– 2017. *Canada in Decay: Mass Immigration, Diversity, and the Ethnocide of Euro-Canadians*. London: Black House Publishing.

– 2018. "Only Whites Can Teach Western Civilization." *Council of European Canadians*, 28 May 2018. https://www.eurocanadian.ca/2018/05/only -whites-can-teach-western.html.

Elliot Lake News. 2007. "Multiculturalism: A Dividing Force." *Elliot Lake News*, 14 March 2007. https://elliotlakenews.wordpress.com/2007/03/14 /multiculturalism-a-dividing-force-2/ (site removed).

Foucault, Michel. 1980. *Power/Knowledge: Selected Interviews and Other Writings, 1972–1977*, edited by Colin Gordon. New York: Pantheon Books.

Gill, Jordan. 2017. "Alt-Right Propaganda Posted on Maliseet Welcoming Sign." *CBC News*, 30 September 2017. https://www.cbc.ca/news/canada /new-brunswick/alt-right-poster-st-thomas-university-maliseet-sign -1.4315282.

Gilroy, Paul. 1991. *"There Ain't No Black in the Union Jack": The Cultural Politics of Race and Nation*. Chicago: University of Chicago Press.

Giroux, Henry A. 2017. *America at War with Itself*. San Francisco: City Lights Books.

Gold, Alan D., and Edward B. Harvey. 2003. "Executive Summary of Presentation on Behalf of the Toronto Police Service." Toronto: Toronto Police Service. http://www.torontopolice.on.ca/publications/2003.02.20 -review/presentationsummary.pdf.

Goldberg, David Theo. 1993. *Racist Culture: Philosophy and the Politics of Meaning*. Malden, MA: Blackwell Publishers.

– 2002. *The Racial State*. Malden, MA: Blackwell Publishers.

Hage, Ghassan. 2000. *White Nation: Fantasies of White Supremacy in a Multicultural Society*. New York: Routledge.

Hall, Stuart. 1996. "Race, Articulation and Societies Structured in Dominance." In *Black British Cultural Studies*, edited by Houston A. Baker, Mantia Diawara, and Ruth H. Lindeborg, 16–60. Chicago: University of Chicago Press.

Harvey, Edward B. 2003. *An Independent Review of the Toronto Star Analysis of Criminal Information Processing System (CIPS) Data Provided by the Toronto Police Service (TPS)*. Toronto: Toronto Police Service. http://www .torontopolice.on.ca/publications/files/reports/harveyreport.pdf.

Henry, Frances. 2004. *Systemic Racism towards Faculty of Colour and Aboriginal Faculty at Queen's University*. Kingston, ON: Queen's University. https:// www.queensu.ca/provost/sites/webpublish.queensu.ca.provwww /files/files/SystemicRacism.pdf.

Henry, Frances, et al. 2017. "Race, Racialization and Indigeneity at Canadian Universities." *Race, Ethnicity and Education* 20 (3): 300–14. https://doi .org/10.1080/13613324.2016.1260226.

Industry Canada. 2010. "Statement on 2011 Census." News Release, 13 July 2010. Government of Canada. https://www.canada.ca/en/news /archive/2010/07/statement-2011-census.html.

Kraychik, Robert. 2015. "Canada's Left Wants Racial Crime Statistics to Push #BlackLivesMatter Narrative." *Breitbart News*, 31 August 2015. https://www.breitbart.com/politics/2015/08/31/toronto -star-laments-lack-of-racial-crime-data-it-helped-purge-decades-ago.

Mackey, Eva. 2002. *The House of Difference: Cultural Politics and National Identity in Canada*. Toronto: University of Toronto Press.

Melchers, Ron. 2003. "Do Toronto Police Engage in Racial Profiling?" *Canadian Journal of Criminology and Criminal Justice* 45 (3): 347–66. https://doi.org/10.3138/cjccj.45.3.347.

– 2006. *Inequality before the Law: The Canadian Experience of "Racial Profiling."* Ottawa: Directorate Royal Canadian Mounted Police. http://publications .gc.ca/collections/collection_2013/grc-rcmp/PS64-31-2006-eng.pdf.

Mitchell, W.J.T. 2018. "The Trolls of Academe: Making Safe Spaces into Brave Spaces." *Los Angeles Review of Books*, 5 January 2018. https://lareviewofbooks.org/article/the-trolls-of-academe-making-safe-spaces-into-brave-spaces.

Mohanty, Chandra Talpade. 2003. "Under Western Eyes: Feminist Scholarship and Colonial Discourses." In *Feminism without Borders: Decolonizing Theory, Practicing Solidarity*, 17–42. Durham, NC: Duke University Press.

Murphy, Rex. 2015. "'White Privilege' on the March." *National Post*, 15 May 2015. https://nationalpost.com/opinion/rex-murphy-white-privilege-on -the-march.

– 2018. "The Contemptible Concept of 'White Privilege' Is Just Ugly, Angry Racism." *National Post*, 9 March 2018. https://nationalpost.com/opinion /rex-murphy-the-contemptible-concept-of-white-privilege-is-simply -racism-ugly-and-angry.

Nakamura, Lisa, and Peter A. Chow-White. 2011. *Race after the Internet*. New York: Routledge.

Nakhaie, M. Reza, and Robert J Brym. 2011. "Ideological Orientations of Canadian University Professors." *Canadian Journal of Higher Education* 41 (1): 18–33. https://doi.org/10.47678/cjhe.v41i1.2181.

National Secretariat Against Hate and Racism in Canada (NSAHRC). n.d. "Position on the Collection of Race-Based Data." *Indigenous Bar Association*. http://www.indigenousbar.ca/pdf/race-baseddata%20_3_.pdf.

Noble, Safiya Umoja. 2018. *Algorithms of Oppression: How Search Engines Reinforce Racism*. New York: New York University Press.

Ontario Human Rights Commission (OHRC). 2005. *Policy and Guidelines on Racism and Racial Discrimination*. Toronto: OHRC. http://www.ohrc.on.ca /en/policy-and-guidelines-racism-and-racial-discrimination.

– 2009. *Count Me In! Collecting Human Rights-Based Data*. Toronto: OHRC. http://www.ohrc.on.ca/sites/default/files/attachments/Count_me_in %21_Collecting_human_rights_based_data.pdf.

Peterson, Jordan. 2017. "Identity Politics and the Marxist Lie of White Privilege." *YouTube*, 13 November 2017. https://www.youtube.com/watch?v=PfH8IG7Awk0.

Porter, Catherine. 2002. "Police Union Blasts Star." *Toronto Star*, 22 October 2002, A6.

242   Enakshi Dua

Porter, Tom. 2017. "The Alt-Right's Next Target? Liberal Canada." *Newsweek*, 3 October 2017. https://www.newsweek.com/how-alt-right-groups-are -attempting-spread-white-supremacism-canadian-campuses-675742.

Presidential Task Force on Anti-Racism and Race Relations. 1998. *Final Report of the Presidential Task Force on Anti-Racism and Race Relations*. Guelph, ON: University of Guelph.

Rankin, Jim, et al. 2002a. "Black Arrest Rates Highest." *Toronto Star*, 26 October 2002. https://www.thestar.com/news/gta/raceandcrime /2002/08/26/black-arrest-rates-highest.html.

– 2002b. "Singled Out." *Toronto Star*, 19 October 2002. https://www.thestar .com/news/gta/knowntopolice/2002/10/19/singled-out.html.

Razack, Sherene H. 2008. *Casting Out: The Eviction of Muslims from Western Law and Politics*. Toronto: University of Toronto Press.

Said, Edward W. 1978. *Orientalism*. New York: Vintage Books.

Smith, Malinda S., ed. 2013. *Transforming the Academy: Essays on Indigenous Education, Knowledge, Relations*. Canadian Federation for the Humanities and Social Sciences. Edmonton, AB: University of Alberta.

Solomos, John. 1990. "The Politics of Anti-Discrimination Legislation: Planned Social Reform or Symbolic Politics?" In *Racism and Equal Opportunity Policies in the 1980s*, 2nd ed., edited by Richard Jenkins and John Solomos, 30–53. New York: Cambridge University Press.

Standing Committee on Canadian Heritage. 2017. "Evidence: Renu Mandhane." Meeting 72 (16:39). 42nd Parliament, 1st Session, 20 September 2017. https://www.ourcommons.ca/DocumentViewer/en/42-1/CHPC /meeting-72/evidence.

– 2018. *Taking Action against Systemic Racism and Religious Discrimination Including Islamophobia: Report of the Standing Committee on Canadian Heritage*. Presented to the 42nd Parliament, 1st Session, February 2018. https://www .ourcommons.ca/DocumentViewer/en/42-1/CHPC/report-10.

Taylor, Jared. 2007a. "Is Racial Diversity Good for Canada?" *Elliot Lake News*, 11 February 2007. https://elliotlakenews.wordpress.com/2007/02/11 /is-racial-diversity-good-for-canada/ (site removed).

– 2007b. "White Americans: An Endangered Species." *Elliot Lake News*, 25 September 2007. https://elliotlakenews.wordpress.com/tag/2007/09/25 /us-white-people-an-endangered-species/ (site removed).

– 2010a. "Is Burlington TOO White?" *Elliot Lake News*, 1 July 2010. https:// elliotlakenews.wordpress.com/2010/07/01/is-burlington-too-white/ (site removed).

– 2010b. "Jared Taylor vs. Peter March – Racial Diversity in North America (1/6)." *ConsciousWhite*, 15 March 2010. https://www.youtube.com /watch?v=ETWxAN84Lh4.

– 2011. "Canadians Duped on Multiculturalism." *Elliot Lake News*, 17 February 2011. https://elliotlakenews.wordpress.com/2011/02/17 /canadians-duped-on-multiculturalism (site removed).

– 2014. *Paved with Good Intentions: The Failure of Race Relations in Contemporary America*. New Century Books / American Renaissance.

Thobani, Sunera. 2007. *Exalted Subjects: Studies in the Making of Race and Nation in Canada*. Toronto: University of Toronto Press.

Toronto Star. 2002a. "Analysis Raises Board Hackles." *Toronto Star*, 20 October 2002. https://www.thestar.com/news/gta/raceandcrime/2002/10/22 /analysis-raises-board-hackles.html.

– 2002b. "Police Board Wants to See Data on Race Profiling." *Toronto Star*, 25 October 2002.

– 2002c. "Racial Data a Hot Potato," *Toronto Star*, 26 October 2002. https: //www.thestar.com/news/gta/raceandcrime/2002/10/26/racial-data-a -hot-potato.html.

– 2002d. "Statistics Only Lend Weight to Experience." *Toronto Star*, 23 October 2002, B1, B3.

– 2002e. "There Is No Racism. We Do Not Do Racial Profiling." *Toronto Star*, 19 October 2002, A14.

van Dijk, Teun A. 1992. "Discourse and the Denial of Racism." *Discourse & Society* 3 (1): 87–118. https://doi.org/10.1177/0957926592003001005.

Voices-Voix. 2015. *Dismantling Democracy: Stifling Debate and Dissent in Canada*. Justice and Corporate Accountability Project (JCAP), 16 June 2015. https:// justice-project.org/wp-content/uploads/2017/07/dismantling democracy_voicesvoix.pdf.

Wente, Margaret. 2005. "Race Is the Elephant in the Room." *The Globe and Mail*, 22 November 2005. https://www.theglobeandmail.com/news /national/race-is-the-elephant-in-the-room/article740250/.

– 2006. "'Culture of Whiteness' in the Ivory Tower? Not." *The Globe and Mail*, 2 May 2006. https://www.theglobeandmail.com/news/national /a-culture-of-whiteness-in-the-ivory-tower-not/article729199/.

– 2010. "The Scourge of Invisible Racism." *The Globe and Mail*, 10 March 2010. https://www.theglobeandmail.com/opinion/the-scourge-of-invisible -racism/article1365629/.

– 2017. "Equal Outcomes Have Replaced Equality of Opportunity." *The Globe and Mail*, 4 November 2017. https://www.theglobeandmail.com /opinion/equal-outcomes-have-replaced-equality-of-opportunity /article36825364/.

– 2018. "The Intolerance Industry Is Working Overtime in Canada." *The Globe and Mail*, 2 April 2018. https://www.theglobeandmail.com/opinion /article-how-intolerant-are-canadians-really/.

Wherry, Aaron. 2010. "This Issue Need Not Provoke an All-or-Nothing Allegiance." *Maclean's*, 21 July 2010. https://www.macleans.ca/politics /ottawa/this-issue-need-not-provoke-an-all-or-nothing-allegiance/.

Williams, Patricia. 1998. *Seeing a Color-Blind Future: The Paradox of Race.* New York: Noonday Press.

Woolley, Frances. 2013. "How Employment Equity Will Take a Hit from Dodgy National Data." *The Globe and Mail*, 8 May 2013. https://www .theglobeandmail.com/opinion/how-employment-equity-will-take-a -hit-from-dodgy-national-data/article11783704/.

Zhou, Stephen. 2017. "Canadian Campuses See an Alarming Rise in Right-Wing Populism." *CBC News*, 15 January 2017. https://www.cbc.ca/news /canada/manitoba/opinion-campus-right-wing-populism-1.3932742.

5 Access Denied: Safe/guarding the University as White Property

DELIA D. DOUGLAS

There are days, [and] this is one of them, when you wonder what your role is in this country and what your future is in it. How precisely you're going to reconcile yourself to your situation here, and how you are going to communicate to the vast, heedless, unthinking, cruel white majority that you are here. I'm terrified at the moral apathy – the death of the heart – which is happening in [this] country. These people have deluded themselves for so long that *they really don't think I'm human.* [emphasis added]

– James Baldwin, speaking in 1963[1]

Introduction: What's Going On?

I am mindful of the fact that this conference on Racial (In)Justice in the Canadian University is taking place at the University of British Columbia (UBC), which is located in Vancouver on the ancestral, traditional, unceded territories of the Musqueam First Nation and the Coast Salish peoples. I am mindful of the fact that our presence and participation at UBC, an institution of *higher* learning, means that we inhabit unceded territory and are therefore simultaneously implicated in a crime scene and a scene of instruction.

Although James Baldwin is referring to his relationship to the United States, the opening epigraph inaugurates the tone and tenor for the ensuing discussion of racial (in)justice in Canadian universities. Following Baldwin's thoughts, I consider the fraught politics of belonging in the context of dispossession, ongoing settler colonial violence, and the violence of anti-Blackness born of enslavement. This discussion begins from the position that the subject of systemic racism and the particular experiences of Indigenous and racialized minority women in Canadian universities remain on the margins of discussion and action. I build on Cheryl L. Harris's (1993) groundbreaking work "Whiteness as Property." I consider how the university operates as white property in terms of its physical location, organization, culture, population, and pedagogy. I argue that the sustained lack of urgency is part of an actively maintained white naïveté that degrades social relationships and bolsters inequality. I maintain that these patterned exclusions and willful refusals to address the politics of race and racism demonstrate what happens when capitalism, white supremacy, settler colonialism, heteropatriarchy, and the academy collide. I contend that we must confront the integral role that Canadian universities play in the reproduction and maintenance of ongoing settler colonialism.

Where We Live Now

Canada's overall population is becoming more diverse; the country's population growth leads all of the G-8 countries, and its inhabitants represent over 250 ethnic origins.[2] For example, in 2016 approximately one out of every five individuals identified as a "visible minority," with Chinese, South Asians, and Blacks accounting for 61 per cent of Canada's overall "visible minority" population (Statistics Canada, 2017b, 2017c).[3] Notably, Indigenous and members of racialized minority groups remain on the margins of the economy; both have higher unemployment rates and are underrepresented in public administration and other industries that are among the higher paying and secure sources of employment in this country (Block, 2017; Friesen, 2011; Statistics Canada, 2011, 2017a).

In addition, Indigenous and racialized minorities constitute the youngest and fastest growing members of the population, and they will soon comprise the racial majority in several of Canada's major cities in the coming years (Scoffield, 2013; Statistics Canada, 2017b, 2017c). Yet, these young people will rarely, if ever, encounter faculty who are not white. Rather, they will continue to meet universities across the nation that reproduce, rather than interrupt and transform, the exclusionary cultures of whiteness and racism that shape their experiences in so many ways (see, for example, Eisenkraft, 2010; Gutiérrez y Muhs, Niemann, González, & Harris, 2012; Henry, Dua, James et al., 2017; Smith & Bray, 2018).

We Are Living in the Long Emergency ...

Despite over thirty years of an employment equity policy, related diversity talk, and national narratives of inclusion, the proportion of some of the four equity-seeking groups (women, "Aboriginals," "visible minorities," and persons with disabilities) within Canadian universities remains deplorably low.[4] Like the United States and the United Kingdom, Canadian post-secondary institutions remain overwhelmingly white in terms of administration, faculty, curriculum, and culture. With few exceptions, equity has meant gender equity, with the majority of hires being white, able-bodied women (Henry, Choi, & Kobayashi, 2012; Henry, Dua, James et al., 2017; Ramos, 2012; Smith & Bray, 2018; Canadian Association of University Teachers [CAUT], 2018a, 2018b). Crucially, Indigenous scholars remain the most underrepresented of the federally assigned four equity groups, accounting for 1.4 per cent of all university professors (CAUT, 2018a). Moreover, while Canadian universities have seen a slight increase in the number of academic staff who are racialized minorities, members of this equity group continue to have high unemployment rates in general, with female racialized minorities suffering even higher rates of underemployment. Correspondingly, Indigenous and racialized minority professors earn considerably less than male and female members of the dominant racial group, with racialized minority women the most inadequately represented amid the full-time workers in the university (Ramos, 2012; Smith & Bray, 2018; CAUT, 2018a). Furthermore, it is important to note that there are substantive differences among the representation of racialized academics in Canadian post-secondary institutions. For example, the increase in Black academic staff has been markedly slower than their representation in the general labour force (CAUT, 2018a). In addition, of the approximately 64,000 university faculty, Black women comprise about 300 of the roughly 1,000 Black faculty (Henry, Dua, James et al., 2017). Consequently, despite established equity policies, profound employment and pay inequities persist in Canadian universities; few have acknowledged how the pattern of privileging some equity groups over others has resulted in racial and racist outcomes that maintain the current state of racial inequality and the attendant structures and logics of settler colonialism.

As I was preparing this essay, I asked myself: How can you *not* know?

This discussion is motivated by the scholarship of those who have demonstrated how the creation and maintenance of settler colonialism involves the pairing of declarations of racial innocence with the violence of disavowal (Tagore & Herising, 2007). Toni Morrison's (1988) presentation "Unspeakable Things Unspoken" provides an imaginative discussion of the erasure of a Black presence from American literature that is helpful to my understanding of how white racial domination exists alongside national narratives that simultaneously promote the "ideology of racelessness" (Backhouse, 1999, p. 14) and publicly celebrate multiculturalism and diversity. Morrison (1988) states: "We can agree, I think, that invisible things are not necessarily 'not-there' ... [C]ertain absences are so stressed, so ornate, so planned, they call attention to themselves; arrest us with intentionality and purpose" (p. 136). Pursuing the matter further, Morrison communicates her skepticism as to the practicability and sustainability of erasure through her query of the "intellectual feats" and "strategies of escape from knowledge" that must be performed by writers who seek to deny her presence in a world formed by her existence (p. 136).

Following Morrison, I maintain that assertions regarding the irrelevance of race and racism, combined with the renunciation of Canada's history of racial violence, "call attention to themselves," compelling us to question avowals of virtue and racial harmony. The promotion of the tradition of racelessness and mythologies that disappear the brutality of conquest and colonization engender a consciousness in which white British and French settler colonial subjects recognize themselves as the rightful inheritors of status, identity, and power in Canada (Razack, 2002; Schick, 2014). In short, practices of erasure and denial combined with the championing of multiculturalism thwart recognition, enabling white Canadians in their effort to not see or think seriously about racism or even about the probability of racism.

Finally, my discussion is guided by the words of the late anti-apartheid activist Steve Biko (1978), who stated that "the most potent weapon in the hands of the oppressor is the mind of the oppressed" (p. 78).

The Academy: An "Economy of Violence"[5]

Cheryl L. Harris's (1993) formative text "Whiteness as Property" points out a number of features that are relevant to this discussion. In particular, she outlines how "the origins of whiteness as property lie in the parallel systems of domination of Black and Native American peoples out of which were created racially contingent forms of property and property rights" (p. 1714). In the era following conquest and enslavement, whiteness developed into a position of racialized privilege, as white racial identity safeguarded political, economic, and social stability. As Harris explains, the value and the stature assigned to whiteness as property were organized according to a racial hierarchy. In her words, the reverence of whiteness as a prized trait is

> so embedded that it is rarely apparent, the set of assumptions, privileges, and benefits that accompany the status of being white have become a valuable asset that Whites sought to protect and that those who passed

sought to attain – by fraud if necessary. Whites have come to expect and rely on these benefits, and over time these expectations have been affirmed, legitimated, and protected by law. (p. 1713)

Harris (1993) locates the relationship between whiteness and property as tied to "the right to exclude" those who are not racialized as white. Harris explains how, in addition to a person having access to various forms of prestige associated with being identified as white, whiteness operates as a "form of status property" by demonstrating how the "reputational interest in being regarded as white" has long been afforded considerable value, which is tied to identity and personhood (p. 1734). Insofar as property involves entitlements of possession and use, colonizers created and enforced property laws that forcibly removed Indigenous peoples from their land and differentiated between enslaved and free. In this context, whiteness represents a property interest that is based on white supremacy, not simply difference; becoming white was based on marginalization, segregation, and racial subordination (Glenn, 2015; Tuck & Yang, 2012). In addition, Harris (1993) describes how property takes many forms, such as land and other perceptible criteria, as well as a range of constituents such as intellectual property, jobs, privileges, and symbolic capital.

As structure, settler colonialism achieves stability through dispossession, extermination, and forcible manipulation (Glenn, 2015). As Eve Tuck and K. Wayne Yang (2012) explain, settler colonialism involves the reconfiguration of land "into property and human relationships to land are restricted to the relationship of the owner to his property" (pp. 5–6). This system of ownership converts people, ideas, and land into property that can be possessed, purchased, and sold, since proprietorship enables one to do whatever one deems appropriate with one's property to ensure profit.

I contend that the organization and pattern of exclusion of Indigenous and racialized minority faculty safeguards Canadian universities as white property. The sociocultural exclusivity, communicated through the social networks, loyalties, practices, and spatial arrangements, is both constituted by and constitutive of the ongoing project of settler colonialism. For example, the university's organization as white property assumes many forms, some of which are economic, cultural, and social. As an archetype of global capital, the university is implicated in the maintenance of wealth and resource inequalities. Canadian universities uphold the structure of settler colonialism through geographic domination, a coercive system of labour, and what Dolores Calderon (2014) terms "settler colonial narratives" or "grammars" of erasure and disavowal (p. 314). Consequently, the issue of whose bodies are included and excluded, and whose are mistreated and celebrated, is significant. It is precisely because knowledge production is a crucial apparatus through which the needs and interests of the settler colonial state are advanced that I maintain the university's regulation of racialized and gendered bodies is linked to its regulation of racialized and gendered bodies of knowledge (Hong, 2008; Patel, 2015; Razack, 2002).

Hiring: The Wages of Whiteness[6]

What's up with whiteness? Why are white scholars, white men, employing the bodies of white women, hiring as if they were cloning or socially producing white people like themselves?

– Malinda S. Smith, 2007

Hiring is key to the renewal of a department and its future. Of the four designated groups identified by the Federal Contractor's Program, gender equity has received the most attention; this one-sidedness has resulted in the "diversifying of whiteness" (Smith, 2016) because the majority hired have been white women. This pattern of hiring, namely the exchange of positions between white women and men, is tantamount to what Malinda S. Smith (2016) describes as the "social injustice of sameness." That the majority of *successful* candidates have been white is not seen as the result of systemic discrimination; rather it is assumed that the preponderance of white administrators, Canada Research Chairs, and professorships is "just the way things turned out"; these individuals were selected simply because they were the "the best." The unspoken sentiment is that whites are the best. It is precisely because these racially structured environments are not named as such that the university's practice of racial segregation continues in plain sight, hidden behind the ostensibly objective criteria of "excellence," "competence," "best fit," and "best qualified." These semantic strategies represent a privileged disregard that authorizes the institutionalization of white exclusivity; the repeated hiring of whites is one example of how the Canadian landscape is currently being racially and spatially organized to normalize and maintain white racial power (Hong, 2008; Schick, 2014).

In the context of Canada's policies of multiculturalism and employment equity, the white racial hegemony of the academy illustrates the contradictions, challenges, and tensions that confront those who are identified as *non-white* in settler colonialism. For example, if merit and competence are the stated criteria for selection, then the underrepresentation of Indigenous and racialized minority scholars over nearly four decades represents an absence that should "call attention to [itself]; [and] arrest us with intentionality and purpose" (Morrison, 1988, p. 136). The lack of acknowledgment and urgency regarding the white racial composition of universities signals a sanctioned *unseeing*; in settler colonial society, national narratives have continually imagined and advanced white subject positions as *true* citizens, making absent land dispossession, occupation, enslavement, the dehumanization of Indigenous peoples, and the marginalization and discrimination of racialized minorities. The construction of a racialized and engendered national identity based on white innocence and benevolence has been integral to secure and sustain the privilege and power associated with whiteness (Glenn, 2015; Tagore & Herising, 2007; Tuck & Yang, 2012). Consequently, the hiring of whites is at once a symbolic and material manifestation of the university as white property (Harris, 1993); the racialization of this space represents what Carol Schick (2014) characterizes as "a performative act that accomplishes white supremacy and white identity; it also demonstrates and confirms the white racial knowledge of *how* to do this" (p. 100).

Moreover, these patterned exclusions are significant precisely because it is white scholars and administrators who continue to make decisions about the relevance of race and the (in)significance of racism. As Audrey Kobayashi (2007) summarizes, the culture of whiteness is reflected in "the overwhelming power of white academicians which keeps the status quo in place in terms of the content and the standards of the university, in terms of research, in terms of who has access to positions." The resultant privileges and confidence that whites take for granted are evidence of the wages of the academic empire (Du Bois, 1935/1998). Thus, it is not surprising that few whites have had the courage to speak out and challenge these structured exclusions (Henry & Tator, 2007; hooks, 1994; Smith, 2007). In sum, the fidelities and the ways of being and thinking are not unintentional; settler colonialism sanctions the institutionalization of white exclusivity (Kobayashi, 2007; Schick, 2014).

Correspondingly, the hierarchies that exist among equity-seeking groups are revealed in the persistent denial of systemic racism and the white racial hegemony that circumscribe Canadian universities. Because white women have largely benefitted from gender equity, they have become the new gatekeepers, demonstrating a racial allegiance that protects and sustains settler colonial interpersonal relations, intellectual hierarchies, and the university as white property (Henry & Tator, 2007; Lomax, 2015; Smith, 2007). Thus, the systematized exclusion and subjugation of Indigenous and racialized minority scholars and administrators not only communicates an image of unity among whites; it is also one of the ways white women (and men) come to understand and express themselves as the *real* citizen subjects in Canada's settler colonial society (Harris, 1993). Sherene Razack's (2005) analysis of the ways in which white supremacy is embodied is instructive. She writes: "The sense of self that is simultaneously required and produced by empire is a self that is experienced *in relation* to the subordinate other – a relationship that is deeply gendered and sexualized" (p. 343).

With few exceptions, white women's understanding and response to their position within white supremacy, heteropatriarchy, and capitalism has been to advance the colonial structure of racial power rather than subvert it. As Audre Lorde (1984) explains, "white women face the pitfall of being seduced into joining the oppressor under the pretense of sharing power" (p. 118).

Building on Lorde's observation, I would add that white women are not the only ones to be enticed. It must be said that the settler colonial structure of the academy is not only supported by those who are racialized as white; there are Indigenous and racialized minority scholars who are complicit in supporting the ideas, practices, and social arrangements of institutionalized white supremacy, heteropatriarchy, and capitalism that govern the academy. Shaped by histories of violence and its legacies, the construction and dissemination of discourses of race, gender, and sexuality that arose marked not simply difference, but humanness and inferiority. In this context, it is not surprising that we are encouraged to see each other as rivals and to treat one another as adversaries and competitors.

Moreover, the underrepresentation of Indigenous and racialized minority women in particular is an example of how people do not enter and participate in the institution as equal subjects; their absence and the dominant culture of the university means that there are few opportunities to become part of many networks (Ng, 1993). Thus, it is a mistake to view "inclusion" as a process wherein those on the "margins" are able to simply "fit" into the criteria/systems/organizations defined by the "centre." The goal is not to have those in power remain at the centre and "welcome" those who have previously been excluded into existing structures and organizations (Dewar, 1993). At present, white men and women control the present (and future) of Canadian universities; their presence and standing signals discernment and competence. At one level, this process is one of the structures of professional control: "It is through this structure of rank and the procedures by which people are advanced from one to another that the professions maintain control over the nature and quality of work that is done and the kinds of people who are admitted to its ranks and to influential positions within it" (Smith, 1991, p. 242). Consequently, the structures, practices, norms, and values of the university encourage, and in many instances expect, Indigenous and racialized minority scholars to surveil and discipline each other to act in ways that protect and embolden settler colonial society. However, as long as the university remains organized to maintain the needs of the dominant, we will be reduced to battling over position and stature to our detriment (Patel, 2015).

This discussion leads me to pose the following questions: Who is – who can be – a knower, a holder, and/or knowledge producer? And what is it that they can know? I contend that whoever is granted entry into the "hallowed halls" of higher education is inextricably linked to what can be known. I am mindful that the link between embodiment and knowledge production is neither simple nor straightforward, but the lack of urgency over three decades demands that we consider the meaning and significance of the absence of certain bodies and the related absence of certain bodies of knowledge (Hong, 2008).

Canadian universities have responded to shrinking budgets and nearly four decades of retirements by increasingly turning to corporations for financial support and making sure they have a steady supply of contingent faculty to maintain their workforce. In this context, Indigenous and racialized minority faculty are valuable to capital and settler colonialism in so far as the presence of one or two is used to signal the absence of racial bias and racism. Consequently, the corporate neoliberal university has created an economic and moral environment that is at once an economy of value and an economy of violence, since one's worth in the system is determined by one's perceived and conceived abilities, potential, and anticipated contribution to the university and to society at large (Bakare-Yusuf, 1999; Cacho, 2012; Lomax, 2015). Thus, the fact that those who have benefitted the most from the introduction of employment equity have primarily been white women (and to a lesser extent racialized minority men) reveals how race and gender are legible measures of corporeal value.

For us Black women, given the legacy of white supremacist discourses that identify us as subhuman, our absence, I maintain, holds a particular cultural and political significance because it is readily taken as evidence of our *presumed incompetence* (Gutiérrez y Muhs et al., 2012). Hence, we are typically not seen as knowers, or knowledge holders and producers, and neither as authorial figures. The marginalization and exclusion of Black women from the *ivory* tower denies both faculty and students the opportunity to see the world through our perspectives, and the rejection of us as educators and scholars preserves intellectual hierarchies and spatial separation (Lomax, 2015).

In sum, hiring practices contribute to the (re)production and maintenance of the university as white property; the enduring underrepresentation of Indigenous and racialized female minority scholars (there are more racialized minority men) illustrates how universities are organized to protect and reproduce white expectation – a space to extend domination and assert racial authority (Harris, 1993; Patel, 2015).

The Colonial Cultural Logics of Curricula: The Violence of Disavowal

In addition to the management of racialized bodies in the hiring process, the construction of the university as white property is enacted through the contents of the curriculum. Another key locus of cultural struggle, curricular content shapes social relations by offering images and narratives about who (we think) we are and how we understand ourselves to be. Curriculum reflects departmental cultures through mentoring, allocation of teaching and research assistantships, and selection of courses, and socializes students to norms while simultaneously undermining and discouraging certain approaches and areas of study. With respect to our Eurocentric curricula, the absence of some subjects gives the impression that one's experience is not worthy of study, that one has not contributed to society (Agnew, 2003; Smith, 2007).

At present across the country, with a few exceptions, Black, African, and Caribbean studies comprise a course or two but are not a core part of the curriculum. For example, the University of Toronto does not offer graduate courses on Black life at the graduate level; the School of Global Affairs at the University of Toronto does not have programs and courses that focus on the continent of Africa (Habtemariam & Hudson, 2016). UBC has an African studies program, but it offers a very limited curriculum. Notable exceptions are Dalhousie University, which recently created an interdisciplinary minor in Black and African Diaspora Studies; and York University, which introduced a Black Canadian Studies Undergraduate Certificate in the fall of 2018. The erasure of the continent of Africa and the diaspora is significant because it suggests that the history of enslavement is at best only relevant to people of African descent and not central to the making of modernity.

Nearly three decades removed, Roxana Ng's (1993) observation about the status of race in course content persists, as greater consideration has been given to gender and sexuality. Her words speak clearly:

Whereas the institution of women's studies has brought about a radical rethinking of gender relations in society, especially in western societies, this cannot be said of curricular reform on race. Frequently, attempts in this area take an additive approach, adding an article (or two) to existing materials. There has been insufficient re-conceptualization of how race matters in the structuring of social experiences inside and outside the academy. (p. 193)

Building on Ng, I would suggest that the institutionalization of women's studies, gender studies, and more recently, queer studies is another manifestation of what Malinda S. Smith (2016) describes as the "diversification of whiteness." By and large, the organization and implementation of these departments and/or programs extend white racial privilege and power by advancing our understanding of discourses of sex, gender, and sexuality, while simultaneously expunging race and racism from analytical frameworks. Consequently, the focus on gender equity has largely benefitted white able-bodied women, resulting in the development and dissemination of knowledge and experience regarding the heterogeneity of whiteness. What's more, this strategic "escape from knowledge" (Morrison, 1988, p. 136) simultaneously constructs and protects the normative status and importance of the white female self, while maintaining the university as white property (Razack, 2005). In this context, the absence and/or marginalization of Indigenous and racialized minority female scholars reflects a symbolic and material practice that Mary Louise Fellows and Sherene H. Razack (1998) describe as ensuring "the material basis for domination while enabling members of the dominant group to define themselves" (p. 343). In sum, the regulation of Indigenous and racialized and gendered bodies is another example of how the predominantly white professoriate and leadership promote a politics and perspective that reproduces racial inequalities and sustains white supremacy and settler colonial projects (Hong, 2008; Patel, 2015; Smith, 2016).

In addition, the dearth of intellectual breadth and the valuation of a curriculum that is exclusionary allow whites to embrace images that affirm their identity and status as rightful citizens in the settler colonial nation-state. Simply put, the curriculum communicates what Zeus Leonardo (2009) describes as white racial knowledge, a "racial self understanding" based on a "sense of belonging" (p. 235) that is emotional, psychological, and embodied. In this context, whites are taught and understand themselves as not raced – while Indigenous and racialized minorities are repeatedly told that they alone are raced, thereby re-establishing "hierarchies of humanness" (McKittrick, 2006, p. xvii).

Students and faculty are subsequently socialized through the erasure of certain areas of study, voices, and experiences. As a consequence, settler colonial "grammars" (Calderon, 2014, p. 313), or knowledge, is (re)produced, along with inequality (Margolis & Romero, 1998).

In addition to performing the labour that sustains the white property rights of the university, institutions' efforts to own the intellectual property of scholars are a contemporary expression of the settler colonial logic that stole Indigenous land while relying on enslaved and indentured labour to work the land, enforcing a coercive relationship that continues to benefit and maintain their interests and investments (Patel, 2015). Furthermore, in this climate of austerity, departments and programs claim that they can barely teach their core curriculum, that they have no money to teach anything new, or that they have no money to diversify their faculty, leaving the gap between the academy and the community ever wider.

Securing Settler Futurity[7]: The Damage Done

We have seen that colonization materially kills the colonized. It must be added that it kills him [*sic*] spiritually. Colonization distorts relationships, destroys or petrifies institutions, and corrupts [women and] men, both colonizers and colonized.

– Albert Memmi, 1965, p. 151

As we know, knowledge is power. Canadian post-secondary institutions are integral to settler colonialism since education that protects and maintains the needs, interests, and entitlements of the nation-state is a crucial means of securing what Tuck and Yang (2012) describe as "settler futurity" (p. 3). In particular, Canadian universities underwrite settler colonial structures geographically, as well as through curricula, white racial hegemony, and a culture of whiteness.

Located on unceded territory, Canadian universities' geographic domination is tied to settler colonial projects of conquest; the forced removal of Indigenous peoples from the land and the suppression of this violence is one of the ways in which universities are able to create their spaces as white property, since dispossession and exploitation of the land and its resources facilitates the accumulation of capital. The reconfiguration of these spaces is inextricably linked to the predominance of whites as professors, Canada Research Chairs, and administrators.

Returning to Morrison's (1988) metaphor of "unspeakable things unspoken," I am interested in how settler colonialism and systemic racism have damaged interpersonal and social relations and led to the loss of both talent and potential. In his formative text *The Colonizer and the Colonized*, Albert Memmi's (1965) perceptive observations about the psychological, interpersonal, and systemic violence of colonization and its impact on both the colonizer and the colonized remain relevant. I now want to consider how the management of racialized and gendered bodies and the controlling of racialized and gendered bodies of knowledge are needed to sustain the social, moral, and psychological elements of the university as white property. Barbadian writer George Lamming's (1970/1983) autobiographical novel, *In the Castle of My Skin*, takes up the psychology of colonial domination. He describes the violence he endured in the Caribbean as "a different kind of subjugation. It was a terror of the mind; a daily exercise in self-mutilation. Black versus black in a battle for self-improvement" (p. xxxix). Lamming's experiential knowledge resonates with Steve Biko's (1978) assertion that "the most potent weapon in the hands of the oppressor is the mind of the oppressed" (p. 78). Both of their insights offer us a way to think about why some Indigenous and racialized minority scholars engage in behaviours that support the status quo. We are all subject to the discourses of domination; we need not be racialized as white (for example) to reproduce settler colonialism. I would argue that the historical and cultural legacies of violence inform how we see and relate to each other in the present.

Since discussions about equity have rarely moved beyond gender equity, white able-bodied women have been the primary beneficiaries. Racialized minority and Indigenous women have largely been excluded. I maintain that the accomplishment of a primarily white presence represents the consolidation of the university as white property; the rejection of racialized and Indigenous women in particular is synonymous with what Tagore and Herising (2007) refer to as "colonial absenting" (p. 284). Consequently, the "epistemological status of white scholars as the authorized agents of institutional knowledge" (Wiegman, 1999, p. 149) means that students are exposed to a learning environment that is essentially a white racial space. Thus, the university's management of racialized and gendered bodies supports settler colonialism by socializing its inhabitants about the racial order, since the authority and privilege available to whites reinforces their sense of "entitlement, superiority and belonging" (Schick, 2014, p. 92). In an atmosphere where one does not see/hear/imagine diversity, it is difficult for those who are members of underrepresented groups to interact and contribute.

The absence of a critical mass of Indigenous and racialized minority faculty also makes it difficult for the targets of repression to speak up for fear of reprisal. The cultivation of an atmosphere of hostility and terror is not new – it has been fundamental to the colonial rulebook/

reproduction of white racial domination for several centuries (hooks, 1992; Yancy, 2012).

Furthermore, the predominance of white faculty also means that there are few opportunities to provide Indigenous and racialized minority students with mentors, role models, and advisors (Henry et al., 2012; Henry, Dua, Kobayashi et al., 2017; Tremonti, 2016; Zoledziowski, 2017). In addition, when these students do not see themselves reflected – and respected – in the curriculum they study or the professors they encounter, these exclusions reinforce notions of the inherent superiority of whites and the attendant inferiority of Indigenous and racialized minorities in ways that have psychological, embodied, symbolic, and material ramifications. Simply stated, the cultural identities of white students are affirmed at the same time as the cultural identities of Indigenous and racialized minority students are marginalized, distorted, or rendered invisible.

In this context, to what extent are we encouraged and taught to see ourselves as equals? To what extent are we encouraged and taught to see ourselves in each other?

Audre Lorde (1984) speaks to this question in her acclaimed essay "Age, Race, Class, and Sex: Women Redefining Difference." She writes:

> Institutionalized rejection of difference is an absolute necessity in a profit economy which needs outsiders as surplus people. As members of such an economy, we have *all* been programmed to respond to the human difference between us with fear and loathing and to handle that difference in one of three ways: ignore it, and if that is not possible, copy it if we think it is dominant, or destroy it if we think it is subordinate. But we have no patterns for relating across our human differences as equals. As a result, those differences have been misnamed and misused in the service of separation and confusion. (p. 115)

Lorde's linking of the violence of the capitalist economy, difference, domination, and disposability challenges us to examine the university's management of racialized and gendered bodies and the politics of knowledge production, alongside wealth and resource inequities, to consider why certain groups have access to opportunities and privilege while others do not (Bakare-Yusuf, 1999; Hong, 2008; Schick, 2014).

Closing Remarks: Beneath the Cover of White/ness

In this essay, I have sought to identify and analyze some of the settler colonial "grammars," (Calderon, 2014, p. 313), practices, and arrangements, as well as the "strategies of escape from knowledge" (Morrison, 1988, p. 136) that are necessary to sustain white racial hegemony as Canada's population grows more diverse. As a key locus for the affirmation and cultivation of the power and privileges of whites, Canadian post-secondary institutions are a central site of social justice struggles. Located on unceded Indigenous land, Canadian universities are organized to reinforce geographic, economic, and social domination and to demonstrate white supremacy, thereby protecting and bolstering white expectation and authority, as well as the status and property rights of whites (Harris, 1993; McKittrick, 2006; Tuck & Yang, 2012). In addition, whites' majority status reinforces the notion that those who are there secured their job as a result of their singular ability, reinforcing notions of racial superiority. Under the guise of merit and excellence, the systematic underrepresentation of Indigenous and racialized minority scholars and administrators has clearly damaged interpersonal and social relations and led to the loss of both talent and potential, rendering Canadian post-secondary institutions morally corrupt. Moreover, the dearth of intellectual breadth and the valuation of a limited range of perspectives and experiences are not read as a loss but as evidence of the inferiority of those whose absence is not natural, but rather the product of norms and ways of thinking and being that refer largely to those who constitute the norm, namely whites.

Alongside equal measures of cynicism and resignation, combined with a tinge of hope, I am compelled to ask whether those who wield power possess the heart and moral integrity to act. This discussion reveals how the pairing of declarations of racial innocence with the violence of disavowal works in concert to sustain the indifference and the forcefully maintained white naïveté that indicate a particular reckoning with race, which has been, and continues to be, instrumental to the formation and maintenance of white settler colonial structures (Glenn, 2015). Simply put, the safeguards offered by the existence of formal multiculturalism and employment equity facilitate the ongoing resistance to equity within Canadian universities by obscuring the enduring relevance of race as a marker of otherness, as well as hiding the persistence of systemic racism. Thus, while acknowledgment of racial inequality does not ensure the eradication of domination, it is evident that many whites are reluctant to even engage in this form of critique. Given these dynamics, who will disrupt "hegemonic ways of seeing through which [whites] make themselves dominant" (Razack, 1998, p. 10)? Who will acknowledge the interests and experiences of Indigenous and racialized minority scholars?

There remain numerous barriers to equity; however, this fact does not mean that we cannot strive to create more just institutions and work to cultivate relationships that are founded on the principles of equality, integrity, and respect. We cannot eradicate racial inequality and injustice unless we challenge the divisiveness of hierarchies of oppression and recognize the interconnectedness of systems of domination. We are not in a position to challenge injustice on our own; our struggles must be collective (Lorde, 1984; Mohanty, 2003; Razack, 2005).

There is no time like the present to analyze our positions and commit ourselves to broadening our understanding of the intersections of our multiple identities so that we can better respond to the institutional elements of oppression, in conjunction with the individual, embodied, intricacies of our everyday lives both in and outside of the academy (Mohanty, 2003).

Can I get a witness?

Acknowledgments

To the memory of Dr. Lawrence F. Douglas (father, mentor, and sociologist).

NOTES

1 This passage is taken from R. Peck's (2016) documentary *I Am Not Your Negro*, based on the writings of James Baldwin.
2 Every six years, the shifting demographics of the country are captured by Statistics Canada, a federal department responsible for conducting the national census. The Census uses the term "ethnic" (or "ethnocultural") to include both ethnic and racialized groups in its system of classification. Thus, an ethnocultural community/group is identified by the extent to which it shares characteristics that are both specific to, and acknowledged by, that group. These features include cultural traditions, ancestry, language, national identity, country of origin, and/or physical traits.
3 The term "visible minority" is used by all federal institutions and refers to persons, other than Aboriginal peoples, who are "non-white" in race or colour. In Canada, the politics of this term has received much attention, which is beyond the scope of this discussion. Notably, the United Nations Committee on the Elimination of Racial Discrimination suggests that Canada's use of the term "visible minority" is racist: in the words of one committee member, "the term seemed to somehow indicate that 'whiteness' was the standard, all others differing from that being visible" (CBC News, 2007).

4 The term "Aboriginal" refers to all Indigenous people, or those who descend from the original inhabitants of North America. In Canada, the term "Aboriginal peoples" refers to those who identify as First Nations (Indigenous peoples who are neither Inuit nor Métis). In this chapter, the term "Indigenous" will be used; the term "Aboriginal" will only be used in accordance with its original sources (for example, Statistics Canada data).

5 The concept of the "economy of violence" is from Bakare-Yusuf (1999), p. 311.

6 I cite here DuBois (1935/1998), since "the wages of whiteness" is his concept.

7 The concept of "settler futurity" is from Tuck & Yang (2012).

REFERENCES

Agnew, V. (2003). *Where I come from*. Waterloo, ON: Wilfrid Laurier Press.

Backhouse, C. (1999). *Colour coded: A legal history of racism in Canada, 1900–1950.* Toronto, ON: Osgoode Society.

Bakare-Yusuf, B. (1999). The economy of violence: Black bodies and the unspeakable terror. In J. Price & M. Shildrick (Eds.), *Feminist theory and the body: A reader* (pp. 311–23). New York, NY: Routledge.

Biko, S. (1978). *I write what I like*. Chicago, IL: University of Chicago Press.

Block, S. (2017, 29 November). Racialized Canadians continue to face barriers to decent work. *Behind the numbers*. Retrieved from https://behindthenumbers.ca/2017/11/29/racialized-canadians-barriers-to-work/.

Cacho, L.M. (2012). *Social death: Racialized rightlessness and the criminalization of the unprotected*. New York, NY: New York University Press.

Calderon, D. (2014). Uncovering settler grammars in curriculum. *Educational Studies, 50*(4), 313–38. https://doi.org/10.1080/00131946.2014.926904.

Canadian Association of University Teachers (CAUT). (2018a, April). The slow march towards equity. *CAUT Bulletin*. Retrieved from https://www.caut.ca/bulletin/2018/04/slow-march-toward-equity.

Canadian Association of University Teachers (CAUT). (2018b, April). *Underrepresented and underpaid: Diversity & equity among Canada's post-secondary education teachers*. Ottawa, ON: CAUT. Retrieved from https://www.caut.ca/sites/default/files/caut_equity_report_2018-04final.pdf.

CBC News. (2007, 8 March). Term "visible minorities" may be discriminatory, UN body warns Canada. *CBC News*. Retrieved from https://www.cbc.ca/news/canada/term-visible-minorities-may-be-discriminatory-un-body-warns-canada-1.690247.

Dewar, A. (1993). Would all the generic women in sport please stand up? Challenges facing feminist sport sociology. *Quest, 45*(2), 211–29. https://doi.org/10.1080/00336297.1993.10484085.

Du Bois, W.E.B. (1935/1998). *Black reconstruction in America, 1860–1880*. New York, NY: Free Press.

Eisenkraft, H. (2010, 12 October). Racism in the academy. *University Affairs*. Retrieved from https://www.universityaffairs.ca/features/feature-article/racism-in-the-academy/.

Fellows, M.L., & Razack, S.H. (1998). The race to innocence: Confronting hierarchical relations among women. *Journal of Gender, Race and Justice, 1*(2), 335–52. Retrieved from https://scholarship.law.umn.edu/faculty_articles/274/.

Friesen, J. (2011, 25 February). Canadian-born visible minorities earn less. *The Globe and Mail*. Retrieved from https://www.theglobeandmail.com/news/national/canadian-born-visible-minorities-earn-less/article568434/.

Glenn, E.N. (2015). Settler colonialism as structure. *Sociology of Race and Ethnicity, 1*(1), 52–72. https://doi.org/10.1177/2332649214560440.

Gutiérrez y Muhs, G., Niemann, Y.F., González, C.G., & Harris, A.P. (2012). *Presumed incompetent: The intersections of race and class for women in academia.* Logan, UT: Utah State University Press.

Habtemariam, S., & Hudson, S. (2016, 1 March). Canadian campuses have a racism problem. *Toronto Star*. Retrieved from https://www.thestar.com/opinion/commentary/2016/03/01/canadian-campuses-have-a-racism-problem.html.

Harris, C.L. (1993). Whiteness as property. *Harvard Law Review, 106*(8), 1709–95. https://doi.org/10.2307/1341787.

Henry, F., Choi, A., & Kobayashi, A. (2012). The representation of racialized faculty in Canadian universities. *Canadian Ethnic Studies, 44*(2), 1–12. https://doi.org/10.1353/ces.2012.0008.

Henry, F., Dua, E., James, C.E., Kobayashi, A., Li, P., Ramos, H., & Smith, M.S. (2017). *The equity myth: Racialization and Indigeneity at Canadian universities.* Vancouver, BC: UBC Press.

Henry, F., Dua, E., Kobayashi, A., James, C., Li, P., Ramos, H., & Smith, M.S. (2017). Race, racialization and Indigeneity in Canadian universities. *Race, Ethnicity and Education, 20*(3), 300–14. https://doi.org/10.1080/13613324.2016.1260226.

Henry, F., & Tator, C. (2007, 27–30 September). *The rightness of whiteness: Enduring racism in the Canadian academy.* Paper presented at the 19th Biennial Conference of the Canadian Ethnic Studies Association, Winnipeg, MB.

Hong, G.K. (2008). "The future of our worlds": Black feminism and the politics of knowledge in the university under globalization. *Meridians: feminism, race, transnationalism, 8*(2), 95–115. https://doi.org/10.2979/MER.2008.8.2.95.

hooks, b. (1992). Representing whiteness in the black imagination. In L. Grossberg, C. Nelson, & P.A. Treichler (Eds.), *Cultural studies* (pp. 338–46). New York, NY: Routledge.

hooks, b. (1994). *Teaching to transgress: Education as the practice of freedom*. New York, NY: Routledge.

Kobayashi, A. (2007, 26 May–3 June). *Making the visible count: Difference and embodied knowledge in the academy*. Paper presented at the Congress of the Humanities and Social Sciences, Saskatoon, SK.

Lamming, G. (1970/1983). *In the castle of my skin*. Ann Arbor: University of Michigan Press.

Leonardo, Z. (2009). Reading whiteness: Anti-racist pedagogy against white racial knowledge. In B. Ayers, T. Quinn, & D. Stovall (Eds.), *Handbook of social justice in education* (pp. 231–48). New York, NY: Routledge.

Lomax, T. (2015, 18 May). Black women's lives don't matter in academia either, or why I quit academic spaces that don't value black women's lives and labor. *The Feminist Wire*. Retrieved from https://www.thefeministwire. com/2015/05/black-womens-lives-dont-matter-in-academia-either-or -why-i-quit-academic-spaces-that-dont-value-black-womens-life/.

Lorde, A. (1984). *Sister outsider*. Freedom, CA: The Crossing Press.

Margolis, E., & Romero, M. (1998). "The department is very male, very white, very old, and very conservative": The functioning of the hidden curriculum in graduate sociology departments. *Harvard Educational Review*, *68*(1), 1–32. https://doi.org/10.17763/haer.68.1.1q3828348783j851.

McKittrick, K. (2006). *Demonic grounds: Black women and the cartographies of struggle*. Minneapolis: University of Minnesota Press.

Memmi, A. (1965). *The colonizer and the colonized*. H. Greenfeld (Trans.). New York, NY: Orion Press.

Mohanty, C.T. (2003). "Under western eyes" revisited: Feminist solidarity through anti-capitalist struggles. *Signs*, *28*(2), 499–535. https://doi .org/10.1086/342914.

Morrison, T. (1988, 7 October). *Unspeakable things unspoken: The Afro-American presence in literature*. The Tanner Lectures on Human Values, delivered at the University of Michigan. Retrieved from https://tannerlectures .utah.edu/_documents/a-to-z/m/morrison90.pdf.

Ng, R. (1993). "A woman out of control": Deconstructing sexism and racism in the university. *Canadian Journal of Education*, *18*(3), 189–205. https://doi .org/10.2307/1495382.

Patel, L. (2015). Desiring diversity and backlash: White property rights in higher education. *Urban Review*, *47*, 657–75. https://doi.org/10.1007 /s11256-015-0328-7.

Peck, R. (Director). (2016). *I am not your Negro*. Documentary based on the writings of James Baldwin. Los Angeles, CA: Magnolia Home Entertainment.

Ramos, H. (2012). Does how you measure representation matter? Assessing the persistence of Canadian universities' gendered and colour coded

vertical mosaic. *Canadian Ethnic Studies, 44*(2), 13–37. https://doi.org
/10.1353/ces.2012.0010.

Razack, S.H. (1998). *Looking white people in the eye.* Toronto, ON: University of
Toronto Press.

Razack, S.H. (2002). Gendered racial violence and spatialized justice: The
murder of Pamela George. In S. Razack (Ed.), *Race, space and the law:
Unmapping a white settler society* (pp. 121–56). Toronto, ON: Between the Lines.

Razack, S.H. (2005). How is white supremacy embodied? Sexualized racial
violence at Abu Ghraib. *Canadian Journal of Women & the Law, 17*(2), 341–63.

Schick, C. (2014). White resentment in settler society. *Race, Ethnicity and
Education, 17*(1), 88–102. https://doi.org/10.1080/13613324.2012.733688.

Scoffield, H. (2013, 8 May). Canada's immigrant population surges, highest in
the G8. *Global News.* Retrieved from https://globalnews.ca/news/544337
/canadas-immigrant-population-surges-highest-in-the-g8/.

Smith, D.E. (1991). An analysis of ideological structures and how women
are excluded: Considerations for academic women. In J.S. Gaskell, & A.T.
McLaren (Eds.), *Women and education* (2nd ed.; pp. 233–55). Calgary, AB:
Detselig Enterprises.

Smith, M.S. (2007, 26 May–3 June). *Telling tales on white li(v)es, diversity-talk,
and the ivory tower.* Paper presented at the Congress of the Humanities and
Social Sciences, Saskatoon, SK.

Smith, M.S. (2016, 1 March). *Intersectionality blues: Diversity is the new white.*
Race Literacies: A Black Canadian Speaker Series. University of British
Columbia, Vancouver, BC.

Smith, M.S., & Bray, N. (2018). Equity at Canadian universities: National,
disaggregated, and intersectional data. *Academic Women's Association.*
University of Alberta. Retrieved from https://uofaawa.wordpress
.com/2018/06/22/equity-at-canadian-universities-national-disaggregated
-and-intersectional-data/.

Statistics Canada. (2011). Seeking success in Canada and the United States:
The determinants of labour market outcomes among the children of
immigrants. Retrieved from http://www.statcan.gc.ca/pub/11f0019m
/2011331/part-partie1-eng.htm#h2_1.

Statistics Canada. (2017a). Aboriginal people and the labour market.
Retrieved from https://www150.statcan.gc.ca/n1/daily-quotidien/170316
/dq170316d-eng.htm.

Statistics Canada. (2017b). Aboriginal peoples in Canada: Key results from
the 2016 census. Retrieved from https://www150.statcan.gc.ca/n1/daily
-quotidien/171025/dq171025a-eng.htm.

Statistics Canada. (2017c). Immigration and ethnocultural diversity:
Key results from the 2016 census. Retrieved from https://www150
.statcan.gc.ca/n1/daily-quotidien/171025/dq171025b-eng.htm.

Tagore, P., & Herising, F. (2007). Pedagogies of presence. In K. Kumashiro & B. Ngo (Eds.), *Six lenses for anti-oppressive education* (pp. 287–98). New York, NY: Peter Lang.

Tremonti, A. (Host). (2016). The Current, 16 January 2016. In W. Barth (Producer), *The Current* (Radio program). Toronto, ON: Canadian Broadcasting Corporation.

Tuck, E., & Yang, K.W. (2012). Decolonization is not a metaphor. *Decolonization: Indigeneity, Education, and Society, 1*(1), 1–40. https://jps .library.utoronto.ca/index.php/des/article/view/18630/15554

Wiegman, R. (1999). Whiteness studies and the paradox of particularity. *Boundary 2, 26*(3), 115–50. https://muse.jhu.edu/article/3281

Yancy, G. (2012). *Look a white! Philosophic essays on whiteness.* Philadelphia, PA: Temple University Press.

Zoledziowski, A. (2017, 18 October). Lack of faculty diversity can affect studies and career aspirations. *The Globe and Mail.* Retrieved from https:// beta.theglobeandmail.com/news/national/education/canadian-university -report/lack-of-faculty-diversity-can-affect-studies-and-career-aspirations /article36637410/.

6 Invisibility, Marginalization, Injustice, Dehumanization: Precariousness in the Academy

SARIKA BOSE

Since the latter part of the twentieth century, scholarly institutions have been relying more and more on contracting out academic labour in order to make financial room for the administrative labour that has been replacing academics with amenities (Sorbara 2017; Ginsberg 2011; AAUP 2018). The replacement of people with goods arises from the devaluation of expertise in favour of consumer services, and the consumer or marketplace framing of education has resulted in an academic environment that moves ever closer to violating the human rights laid out in the United Nations' Universal Declaration of Human Rights (UDHR). In "By the Numbers: Contract Academic Staff in Canada," the Canadian Association of University Teachers (CAUT) reports that the number of academics employed in Canadian universities as contract labourers has increased by 200 per cent since 1999, with only a 14 per cent increase in tenured faculty, and further notes that roughly one-third of university teachers are not on the tenure track and are paid, on average, up to 67 per cent of a tenured faculty member's salary, however long they may have been teaching (CAUT 2017). In the United States, the number is even higher, with the American Association of University Professors (AAUP) reporting a 73 per cent average of contract academics teaching at universities across the country according to the most recent numbers collected in 2016 (AAUP 2018). This policy of employing academics by contracts that create artificial divisions, marginalization, and shame is leading to the erosion of the institution of higher education itself.

I approach this paper from the position of the contractually hired academic. My lived experience for the last twenty years as an academic in a contractually precarious position has given me first-hand knowledge of the situation faced by many of my similarly positioned colleagues, not only on my own campus but in campuses across the city, the province, and the nation. My role as the representative for contract academic issues in local and national professional associations has exposed me to the broader, common situations of contract academics in Canada and the United States. The personal accounts of the many contract academics I meet at conferences and meetings across North America leave me asking why, using the terminology of Bill Readings (1995), the university is in ruins.

In this chapter, I will examine the condition of the "subaltern" academic, who inhabits a precarious and economically vulnerable space that exists in a system whose primary currency is status – which bases its actions upon the fear of losing privilege and recognizes its own privilege partly through the lack of privilege in others. I will attempt to determine the relationships that connect those marginalized by labour conditions, cultural differences, and racial divisions and imagine some ways in which we can move towards the ideals of education and united community articulated by many universities' mission statements and by the UDHR. Although I will focus on Canada and the United States, I acknowledge that the suffering caused by precarity in academic work has spread globally. Therefore, this chapter's main arguments about subaltern academics and social justice will be framed by the UDHR and draw on the data published by the CAUT and the CCPA (Canadian Centre for Policy Alternatives) as well as the AAUP. My chapter argues that precarity in academic work is not simply an economic but a human rights issue.

In the Preamble to the UDHR, there is a special emphasis on "the dignity and worth of the human person" (United Nations 1948, para. 5). As I consider gendered and ethnic experiences in universities, I am struck by how closely social justice concepts and terminology intersect with the experiences of marginalized faculty in university campuses across North America. Thus, I would like to use an intersectional approach to account for the various overlaps between some of the experiences of racialized contract faculty members in the university and the wider population of contract faculty. In a recent article published in *Academe*, Anne Sisson Runyan (2018) points out that intersectionality is a useful conceptual tool to examine increasingly oppressive hierarchies and divisive attitudes, and seems particularly apt in the context of the proliferation of precarious work (para. 9). However, it is important to note the limits of my chapter's exploration of this issue, which is widespread and complicated. The examples necessarily will be representative, rather than exhaustive: marginalization and invisibility mean data is hard to acquire. Frances Henry and Carol Tater (2009) explain that "the processes of racism intersect with other forms of subjugation," operating "along a series of socially constructed axes" (24). The authors make a case for the necessity of recognizing that "this interlocking framework is important in understanding how power and powerlessness operate in the spaces of the academy" (24). As Richard Moser (2014) says in an article on the adjunct system, the "struggle to reform the new academic labor system is a struggle about freedom. It is fundamentally a political issue and an invitation to citizenship that none of us can afford to refuse" (para. 18).

Article 2 of the UDHR (United Nations 1948) reminds us that "everyone is entitled to all the rights and freedoms set forth in this Declaration, without distinction of any kind, such as race, colour, sex, language, religion, political or other opinion, national or social origin, property, birth or other status."

This chapter will argue that the application of principles of equity needs to extend past the obvious markers of difference such as gender, race, and disability, although there are many intersections between racialized, disabled, gendered, and transgendered faculty and a large part of the modern university's professional academic contract faculty. Readings's (1995) predictions about the dangers of framing academic work within superficial and corporate frameworks of "excellence" have been realized over the last twenty-five years. By clothing discrimination beneath the rhetoric of professionalism and professional ability, the academy often continues to discriminate against and disadvantage contract academics. As Moser (2014) points out, what the next generation learns is "that it is acceptable to discriminate against someone based on the fact that they belong to a certain *class* of employees" (para. 20; emphasis added). In a formerly secure economic sector (Gee 2017, para. 11; Dea 2018), we now have a rapidly growing underclass whose treatment seriously imperils the values outlined by the UDHR as well as the ideals of education declared by universities themselves.

It is worth taking a moment to outline some of the social justice terminology and concepts I will be using. Frances Henry notes in *The Equity Myth: Racialization and Indigeneity at Canadian Universities*: "Today, the term 'racialization' is generally used to identify the process by which ethno-racial groups are among those racialized, created, categorized, inferiorized and marginalized as 'other'" (Henry et al. 2017, 4). Some of the key lenses through which we view race and marginalization of the racialized other, including systems of invisibility and suppression of voices, barring of spaces, violations of hospitality, refusal of citizenship, self-loathing, and participation in Foucault's (1977/1995) contagion model, appear to apply closely to the situation of more and more contract academics in higher education institutions. Like specifically racialized faculty, almost all contract faculty members tend to be reduced to one aspect of their being. In this case, it is disposability. The divisions created by the conditions of employment aren't simply economic but psychological and intellectual, and are ultimately damaging to the scholarly enterprise as a whole.

Henry and Tater (2009) emphasize the importance of recognizing that injustice is not simply a matter of intention but of impact (24). Accounts of experiences by members of the precariat tell a common story of discrimination and exclusion, which result in bitterness, anger, malaise, and despair. Many contract academics find that all their hard-won specialized research and expertise are erased in the consciousness of the rest of the academy due to the practice of the fallacy of false or circular cause and effect: a financial decision to offer fewer tenure-track jobs does not mean that a person who accepts a contract job has little expertise; just because "market forces make it possible to pay people a dehumanizing wage does not make it moral to dehumanize them" (Elliott 2017, para. 16). The dehumanizing treatment of contract academics by current academic culture and by the academic administrative system will be examined in more detail during the course of this chapter. The Preamble to the UDHR makes clear the expectation that "every individual and every organ of society, keeping this Declaration constantly in mind, shall strive by teaching and education to promote respect for ... [the] rights and freedoms" (United Nations 1948, para. 8) that result in "the dignity and worth of the human person" (para. 5). The actual experience of contract academics is that their worth as professionals is constantly under attack, both by the systems that perpetrate practices of humiliation and erasure and by colleagues, staff, and students. Their perception aligns with some of the Copenhagen Psychosocial Questionnaire (COPSOQ)'s categories of psychological stressors (Kristensen et al. 2005): fundamentally, they feel they are the victims of injustice in the academy, the targets of profiling, not just by tenured colleagues and administrators but also by students who learn quickly that, in the corporate academy, money represents value and thus view the poorly paid academic as a less valuable professor than the well-paid, tenured academic. The practice of making the place of so many academics precarious in the academy by refusing "long-term commitment to faculty holding [contingent] positions" (AAUP n.d.) is leading to some of the same types of discrimination experienced by racialized members of society. As Henry reminds us, "the university is a racialized site that still excludes and marginalizes non-White people, in subtle, complex, sophisticated, and ironic ways, from everyday interactions with colleagues to institutional practices that at best are ineffective and at worst perpetuate structural racism" (Henry et al. 2017, 3). For contract academics of colour, marginalization is doubly expanded.

The Importance of Diversity in the Academy

Though not necessarily designed as such, racialization and marginalization are forms of institutional disempowerment. One effective move towards countering marginalization and disempowerment would be to implement hiring policies that pay special attention to the diversity of faculty. In a 2017 study, Bessma Momani and Jillian Stirk report on the advantages of diversity in the workplace:

> An in-depth statistical analysis of the Workplace Employee Survey (WES), a recently released Statistics Canada data set covering more than 7,900 workplaces in 14 industrial sectors with between 15,000 and 20,000 employees from 1999 to 2005, revealed in almost all sectors a significant, positive relationship between ethnocultural diversity and increased productivity and revenue. (Momani and Stirk 2017, 1)

The authors also explain some of the anxieties of employers, who fear that "managing diversity" will result in higher costs. Yet, such data ought to allay this fear in employers, since a diverse population already exists on university campuses in both the student and, to a lesser extent, the faculty population. However, administrative policies and workplace culture are predicated on older models of universities without diversity in either population. The challenge, say Momani and Stirk (2017), "is to change the way we think and the way we work, if we want to truly see the benefits of diversity" (1). They argue that a robust policy of diversity, equity, and inclusiveness will give Canada a global advantage (15). According to CAUT's survey on racialized faculty, as well as Momani and Stirk's report, the 2006 Census reported that just under 21 per cent of Canadian university teachers were members of visible minority groups (CAUT 2018c; Momani and Stirk 2017, 15). Under CAUT's urging, Statistics Canada has now undertaken a more focused census of contract and racialized faculty. The numbers of racialized faculty are now broken down further to show that, although various equity-seeking groups, including women in general and racialized women and men, are disadvantaged in career progress, Indigenous faculty are even further disadvantaged: only 1.4 per cent of Canadian academics report Aboriginal identity, and few Aboriginal, racialized, and other equity-seeking groups are able to secure tenure-track appointments (CAUT

2018c). CAUT has also published its own, extensive nationwide survey on contract academics, which shines a light on current numbers and patterns of employment and types of work (Foster and Birdsell Bauer 2018). The report, *Out of the Shadows: Experiences of Contract Academic Staff*, surveyed 2,606 contract academics from across Canada to find that "women and racialized CAS [contract academic staff] work more hours per course per week than their white male CAS colleagues and are overrepresented in lower income categories" (5).

Enabling Diversity

Although racial and other diversities exist in both the student and faculty populations in universities, diversity is marginalized on every level. Momani and Stirk (2017) consider that, while implementing systems for measuring diversity will help to keep diversity and equity initiatives on track, it is important to remember exactly what is being measured. Though effects of diversity initiatives can be easier to determine through any changes in revenue of a corporation (like today's universities), the authors warn that this measurement is not enough because the goal of diversity initiatives is broader than economics: "Embracing diversity is as much about values as it is about economics" (3). Nevertheless, it is worth stating that their research found the highest positive correlation between economics and ethnocultural diversity out of all Canadian industries within the information and cultural fields. With every 1 per cent increase in ethnocultural diversity, there was an impressive 6.2 per cent increase in revenue (8). Gender diversity also had a positive effect on revenue: for every 1 per cent increase in gender diversity and females in upper management, there was a 3.5 per cent increase in revenue and a 0.7 per cent increase in workplace productivity (14). Despite the positive correlations between revenue and social justice initiatives, however, institutions continue to position revenue and human rights in opposition to each other, suggesting that they are incompatible. Revenue, rather than human rights, becomes the foundation of their approaches to institutional planning (for example, in the areas of curriculum and student recruitment) and hiring.

Despite the growing labour pool of racialized minority Canadians who hold PhDs, in 1991 only 12.73 per cent of faculty positions at Canadian universities were held by people who were racialized minorities; by 2006, the percentage had only risen to 15.54 per cent (Henry et al. 2017, 54). The increase in the racialized minority population, the comparatively high proportion of Canadians who are racialized minorities and hold PhDs, and the persistent scarcity of racialized minority representation at the faculty level in social science and humanities departments suggest that pervasive systemic barriers continue to prevent the hiring of qualified faculty of colour within Canadian universities (Henry et al. 2017, 8). In an earlier study on racism and lack of diversity at Queen's University, Henry reported that some faculty of colour and Aboriginal faculty actively avoided participating in the study due to fear of repercussions (Henry 2004); this mirrors contingent faculty members' lack of trust in the academy and fear of negative consequences when invited to share their own experiences of marginalization and disrespect.

What assumptions are being made by administrators, colleagues, and students if a large proportion of faculty of colour are more likely to be hired only if they are doing research into issues of racialization and marginalization, rather than traditionally "non-racialized" Western subjects? Implicitly denying the validity and value of an academic's scholarly work based on an explicit connection with their ethnicity seems to violate the human right to independent choices and preferences, as well as the right to academic freedom. The lack of connection between principles of social justice and scholarly practice reveals fundamental problems of comprehension and commitment to social justice in the employment of racialized faculty. Even when social justice issues are examined in class, there is a disparity between theory and practice. Andrea Choi (2016) writes a powerful critique from the perspective of students:

> As undergraduate students studying geography, we were encouraged to examine gendered, raced, and classed structures of power through a geographic lens. We would read about geography and feminist methodologies, gender inequality, ethnic segregation, racism, gentrification, and economic marginalization. (370)

Yet, Choi notes, when she came to do her research on equity and employment practices in universities, she realized that the classroom discussions on these topics did not translate into the actual employment practices of those same universities. Although her research focused on Canadian geography departments, Choi suggests that the continuance of "the raced and classed structures of power" (370) is endemic across departments, faculties, and universities. Her surprise and disappointment in realizing that universities do not practice the principles they teach are clear in her article. Moser (2014) expresses deep concern about the "example that the university itself is setting in regard to intellectual activity, citizenship, and democracy" (para. 19). The effect on the future will be serious: "What values are being learned when those who teach and research – who esteem the intellect and hold high the values of citizenship – are apparently held in low regard by society and by the university community itself?" (para. 19).

Working Conditions Are Learning Conditions

The United Nations' definition of "human rights" centres dignity and worth as essential to achieving full human rights (United Nations 1948, 5th statement); as we will see, the working conditions of contract academics leave out many of the basic components that facilitate human dignity and worth through institutions ignoring the work as well as the presence of contract academics in their midst. The slogan "Working Conditions Are Learning Conditions" was used extensively in awareness campaigns by CAUT for several years. The aim was to draw the attention of students, parents, employers, and academic colleagues to the fact that the standard working conditions of contract academics made it difficult for them to offer optimal learning conditions for students. Throughout this section, I will explain how the lack of time and space, which are the working conditions of most contract academics, negatively affect students' essential learning conditions. As Moser's (2014) research demonstrates, the classroom learning experience of students becomes tainted by their experience of the undercutting of the "values of citizenship" within the university (para. 19). That this failure can be directly traced to working conditions is amply borne out by the CAUT's 2018 survey *Out of the Shadows*, which confirmed that more than half of those surveyed (53 per cent) "want a tenure-track university or full-time, permanent college job" (Foster and Birdsell Bauer 2018, 4). The CCPA has also released its report on the state of precarious employment in the academy, *Contract-U: Contract Faculty Appointments at Canadian Universities*, to report on recent numbers: 53.6 per cent of Canadian academics are employed in contract positions (Shaker and Pasma 2018, 5). That figure means that fewer than half of academics in Canada are employed in secure tenure or tenure-track positions that allow them a chance at achieving a life with "dignity and worth" expected by the UDHR (United Nations 1948, 5th statement).

The working conditions of contract faculty have imposed so heavy a burden that they bear a close look. Academics hired on a contract basis face particularly difficult practical and cultural working conditions. The "last minute scholar" encounters the common practice of being offered courses two weeks to three days before they begin, which gives the instructor an almost impossible set of tasks to create and make syllabi available to students within a few days. Since such a time line makes it impossible to order course materials, instructors must either use text materials previously ordered by the department or primarily internet sources, or find some other solution. Lack of preparation time, as well as access to office space and other resources, means instructors have to teach with one hand tied behind their backs. Limited access to and draconian management of library and internet resources leaves the contract academic further disadvantaged because pre-course and post-course access to online library resources and communications is cut off, as is access to physical library materials. Despite their sometimes superhuman effort, demonstrated ability (such as adaptability in teaching university-level courses that aren't their specialization), and dedication to their students, contract academics are subject to anonymous and uncontrolled student evaluations that present results out of context and affect not only their livelihoods but also their overall mental health. They are likely to score low in the COPSOQ's survey within the "effort-reward-imbalance model" (Kristensen et al. 2005, 447). In other words, contract academics feel that none of their efforts are recognized or rewarded.

Contract academics rarely get orientations or negotiate their salaries (and then only within very limited ranges). The culture of "invisibilization" of the contract academic means that neither administrative staff nor their tenured colleagues appear to know of their existence, only of their basic function as stop-gaps in the system. Being perceived as mere cogs in the wheels of the system means contract academics do not have to be treated as human beings; even their physical presence is often ignored by their tenured colleagues. This erasure shuts off avenues for scholarly conversations and collaborations, and for research and funding competitions, unless they can partner with tenured faculty. It is hard to compete with those who have been able to do competitive-level research by taking the sabbaticals and other teaching load reductions to which contract academics have no access. Social exclusion, inability to participate in governance, and discounting of service add to the demoralizing effect of the academic workplace. Inhospitable schedules and transportation costs of time, money, and safety all contribute to the marginalization of contract academics.

Effects of Inequity

The conditions outlined above will allow us to view in greater detail the descriptions and explanations of the effects of inequity in the university. For instance, CAUT's (2018b) study of diversity and equity does not differentiate between contract and tenured academics, but it found that the wage gap between non-Indigenous, non-racialized men and racialized women university instructors is the highest, at 68 cents earned for every dollar earned by non-racialized men (2). The significant economic gap between racialized and non-racialized faculty means that the economically disadvantaged faculty have to take on more work, especially if they are also contract academics. This economic necessity can mean little time to do research that could lead to better opportunities.

Racialized academics can find themselves even more left out of the academic communities at their campuses if their markers of difference are especially noticeable. For example, students might view strong non-standard accents as obstructive to their learning and thus write poor evaluations; native speakers of the dominant language of a university might judge the non-native speakers as less competent or professional, or assign particular characteristics to them based on superficial judgment; and the dominant culture of a university community might create a non-inclusive workplace for a racialized worker. Missed opportunities and discrimination towards racialized workers have a wide range of negative effects on a profession, particularly one that claims to produce citizens and leaders and to serve society. In their 2012 article on managing diversity in the workplace, Brigid Trenerry and Yin Paradies outline the effects of racism in the workplace:

> Racism, which encompass[es] any unfair and unavoidable treatment resulting in unequal power, resources or opportunities across racial, ethnic, cultural and/or religious groups ... has negative outcomes for individuals and society and is commonplace within workplaces ... Workplace racism has been associated with a range of detrimental outcomes, including: poor mental and physical health and wellbeing ... problem drinking ... psychological distress ... reduced productivity and innovation ... reduced organizational commitment and employee perceptions of injustice ... reduced trust and job dissatisfaction ... as well as increased cynicism, absenteeism and staff turnover. (Trenerry and Paradies 2012, 12)

These are hardly conditions that promote employment justice. The UDHR states that everyone "has the right to work, to free choice of employment, to just and favourable conditions of work and to protection against unemployment" (United Nations 1948, art. 23, 1). The lack of employment rights and reasonable working conditions especially affects contract academics, whether they are from equity-seeking groups or not. The damage to them arises not just from the chilly climate of their workplace, but primarily from their built-in financial instability. Unless other income is coming in from outside their precarious jobs, contract academics face straightforward poverty (Harris 2017). However, protections against unemployment are easily dismissed by employers, who can cite financial exigencies for their decisions. In addition, everyone "without any discrimination, has the right to equal pay for equal work" (United Nations 1948, art. 23, 2). The definition of equal work, however, continues to be in dispute, especially when universities calculate that contract academics should be paid only for contact hours with students, ignoring the crucial connections with and existence of research and preparation, for which tenured academics are paid. The UDHR further emphasizes that everyone who works "has the right to just and favourable remuneration ensuring for himself and his family an existence worthy of human dignity" (art. 23, 3). As we see in the many reports on the human cost of precarious jobs, this article of the UDHR is not being followed in the cases of many academic employers. Furthermore, the UDHR's statement on the right "to form and to join trade unions" (art. 23.4) is directly violated by many states in countries such as the United States.

It is not just Canadian academics who are facing the human rights violations that are the effects of precarity in academia. A recent survey by the Service Employees International Union reported that, out of the 773 contract academics surveyed across Florida, "more than 43% experienced three major signs of poverty, such as taking a payday loan, facing eviction or having utilities cut off. A quarter said they've skipped meals, relied on food stamps, or visited a food bank or soup kitchen. Others said they slept in cars or forwent doctors' visits" (McNeill 2017b, para. 5, 6; SEIU/FPSU 2017, 13). In a TIAA study on contract academics (usually termed "adjunct faculty" in the United States), Paul J. Yakoboski (2018) found that, although the average salary per course was $3000, 60 per cent of contract academics were actually earning less (6).

Stories of contract academics living in cars are sadly not unusual. The title of a sensational story published in *The Guardian* in September 2017 says it all: "Facing Poverty, Academics Turn to Sex Work and Sleeping in Cars" (Gee 2017). The article's author, Alastair Gee, was able to interview one middle-aged academic who chose to do sex work as a way to prevent imminent homelessness. The contract academic told her story on condition of her anonymity. There is no evidence to prove she is the only contract academic desperate enough to take the same path. When years of experience and specialized knowledge can earn a fraction of the payment for sex work, which pays $200 an hour (para. 14), it is not surprising that higher education is becoming devalued (Nelson 2010, 90). The poverty of contract academics also leads to homelessness. Gee (2017) writes about Ellen Tara James-Penney and her husband, and about Mary-Faith Cerasoli, who all live in cars because they cannot afford rent on the salaries they are paid. Of the homeless academics, they are the fortunate ones, as they still own cars and can afford to pay for fuel. They are not young enough to start new careers. But more than that, they are trapped in a cycle of hopelessness and cannot imagine any way out. When we look at the UDHR, we see that "freedom from fear and want" features at the top of its Preamble (United Nations 1948, para. 2). The constant fear of layoffs, coupled with the shame of discovery that they are homeless, that they (Ellen Tara James-Penney and her husband) have been reduced to using "cups or plastic bags and baby wipes" instead of a toilet (Gee 2017, para. 28), places some contract academics firmly into the category of "fear and want." Individual university administrators may not be aware of the extent of poverty to which their policies have reduced their contingent employees, but knowing the cost of living in their area must surely lead to some knowledge about a realistic standard of living for such employees. Whether it is deliberate ignorance or careless inaction, universities need to reverse a trend that is leading to such "fear and want." In his book *No University Is an Island*, Nelson (2010) mourns the breaking of the human spirit and the decades of trauma caused by precarious academic employment (91).

The effects on physical health are equally worrying. The COPSOQ recognizes that the consequences of "being exposed to psychological stressors at work" (Kristensen et al. 2005, 438) include "musculoskeletal disorders, cardiovascular diseases, mental disorders, stress, burnout, reduced quality of life, sickness, absence, labor turnover, and decreased motivation and productivity" (438).

One contract academic at Florida's Broward College, Muhammad Rehan, says that he has gone without health care and that "he has to avoid cold foods and drinks because without dental coverage, he can't afford to replace a crown that came off a tooth nine months ago" (McNeill 2017b, para. 15). Maria Lizardi of Valencia College, Florida, reports that she had to pay her medical bills and survive on her savings for three months after prosthetic knee surgery because her employer did not pay for sick leave (SEIU/FPSU 2017, 10). As Rehan notes, "this is no way for anyone to live" (McNeill 2017b, para. 14). The destruction of members of the precariat is literalized in the stories of Robert Ryan, who worked as an "adjunct" at the University of South Florida for twenty years, and Margaret Mary Vojtko, who had worked at Duquesne University in Pittsburgh for twenty-five years, both of whom died of cancer because they could not afford medical insurance: "When she died, [Vojtko] lay in a cardboard casket" (McNeill 2017a, para. 22).

How have universities come to such a low point that, as tuition fees soar, such a large number of its faculty members are paid so little that they lose their dignity, self-worth, health, and even their lives? How is it that their basic human rights simply do not matter anymore? Although the UDHR states that no "state, group or person [has] any right to engage in any activity or to perform any act aimed at the destruction of any of the rights and freedoms" outlined in the declaration (United Nations 1948, art. 30), the academy appears to contravene these principles directly through a corporate model of management that does not take basic human rights into consideration.

Such disheartening trajectories in the career paths of contract academics result in significant mental health challenges, including withdrawal and reclusiveness, as well as depression. There is little understanding of the debilitating psychological effect of the relentless message that one is a fourth-class citizen in the academy. The order of the academic hierarchy is as follows: first come tenured research faculty; second, tenured teaching faculty; third, students; and last, contract academics. Even if opportunities are available to be included in the governance of a department, for example, many contract academics – sometimes the majority – don't attend meetings, which results in charges of apathy and unprofessionalism. It is perhaps not surprising that a workplace that constantly reinforces their outsider and fourth-class status is one that becomes a physical location from which to escape as soon as possible. It is impossible to emphasize sufficiently the despair that comes from that imposed identity. In an article on mental health in the academy, published in the *CAUT Bulletin*, Marianne Jacobsen, chair of the University of Regina Faculty Association's Sessional Advocacy Committee, suggests that precarity itself creates a dangerous mental health challenge: "Working as a sessional instructor is very stressful because you don't know where your next paycheque is coming from" (CAUT 2018a, 19), and this stress and anxiety "cascades through the system" (19).

During an extended strike in 2017 by contract academics within the Ontario Public Services Employees Union, the union distributed a toolkit for measuring stress, which was created jointly by Occupational Health Clinics for Ontario Workers (OHCOW) and the Canadian Centre for Occupational Health and Safety (CCOHS), based on the COP-SOQ. This toolkit for measuring and taking action on mental injury in a workplace acknowledges the reality of the psychological distress that comes from stressful working conditions, whether they come from workload issues, disrespectful or discriminatory environment, or other poor working conditions (OHCOW 2012). It attempts to provide suggestions for remedying the situation. Some of the areas of stress that are acknowledged in this toolkit directly link to the areas identified by Trenerry and Paradies (2012). The Mental Injury Toolkit identifies the following "hazards" to mental health, as defined by COPSOQ: pressure; physical and mental exhaustion due to work overload; anxiety and illness due to harassment and bullying; the uncertainty from "the constant threat of layoff" and from not knowing where or when one will be employed in the immediate future; an emotional toll because there is not enough time to give adequate care and attention to "customers" (here, students); frustration from the lack of control over how work gets done (here, academic freedom); or "because of a lack of support from supervisors or management to do your job" (OHCOW 2012, 3). Even though the conditions of an academic job are extremely stressful for pre-tenure and many tenured academics, they have reached a crisis point for those in contract positions.

In her 2011 study, *Cruel Optimism*, Lauren Berlant explains that people hold on to a dead-end job like a contract academic job in a once proud profession because of "cruel optimism." She asks: "Why do people stay attached to good-life fantasies – say of enduring reciprocity in couples, families, political systems, institutions, markets and at work – when the evidence of their instability, fragility, and dear cost, abounds?" (Berlant 2011, 2). One answer is that people who allow themselves to get stuck in a destructive cycle and be exploited are simply fantasizers, unable to be realistic: "Fantasy is the means by which people hoard idealizing theories and tableaux about how they and the world 'add up to something'" (2). In other words, those who dream have unrealistic and overblown hopes that their lives will be meaningful: to wish to continue to hope against the odds, or to try for a meaningful life, is foolish. Rebecca Snow, who recently left academia to become a full-time writer, agrees that teaching was a fantasy (Gee 2017, para. 39). But perhaps contract academics hold on to their dreams and hopes because, after investing many years in their intellectual lives, their attachment to those intellectual parameters are fundamental to their identities. Instead of sneering that they dare to dream, even if hope is gone, perhaps those responsible for dissolving those hopes could take actions to restore them. Berlant is correct, however, that, in a situation like a precarious position, the very actions that should determine the happiness and well-being of the individual destroy that happiness and well-being. Another factor in the complex relationship between optimism and despair in Berlant's vision is the danger that, "if the cruelty of an attachment is felt by someone/some group, even in a subtle matter, the fear is that the loss of the promising object/scene itself will defeat the capacity to have any hope about anything" (Berlant 2011, 24). Unfortunately, by the time many contract academics come to realize that hope for a stable academic career is gone, it is too late to change to another profession.

The increasingly untenable working conditions of contract academics are leading to a growing movement of leaving academia behind altogether. Lauren Berlant's "cruel optimism" is being rejected in favour of alternate careers. In an article posted on the online platform LinkedIn, Catherine Sorbara (2017) urges fellow academics to "Stop Ignoring the Data and Start Leaving Academia" because "the academic career track is now a dead end career track." Hers is not the only such article, and indeed, there are websites dedicated to instructing academics on how to divorce themselves from the profession for which they trained. These voices speak of a broken academy, which actively aims to make some of its members "poor, mistreated and unhappy," thus "weakening [their] mind[s] and eroding [their] confidence" (Sorbara 2017). The very institution of higher education is under threat due to the "poisoned workplace" practices described by the Ontario Public Services Employees Union (OHCOW 2012).

The Invisible Academic

For several years, the CAUT ran an awareness-raising campaign about the working conditions of contract academics titled "The Invisible Academic" (CAUT n.d.) The generic silhouette of a person in an academic gown and cap drew attention to the disposable nature of the contract academic, who tended to have the same academic credentials as tenured academics but had been hollowed out by the system to become just a black, scholar-shaped smudge on a white background. The seeming lack of interest in the condition of the contract academic by tenured academics contributes to the dehumanization and erasure of identity. As Nathan Elliott (2017) points out, the first step in moving towards fair and equitable treatment for contract academics is to recognize that they exist and that they "eat, sleep, raise children, and seek medical and dental care for all 12 months of the calendar year" (para. 7). The next step is to acknowledge their work, because there is a serious disjunction between the actual and acknowledged existence of that work:

> The eight-month contract creates a bizarre fantasy world every summer. The eight-month faculty member is routinely asked – throughout the summer months – to review textbooks, to prepare syllabi, and to reinvigorate

class lectures in order to deliver thoughtful courses in the fall. (Elliott 2017, para. 9)

Denying that this labour is taking place means that contract faculty, the administration, and sometimes faculty associations and unions are all participating in a "bizarre hallucination" (para. 9).

In a blog essay in which she traces the process of her rejection of the academic life altogether, Ali Colleen Neff summarizes the disenfranchisement and "dehumanization" caused by precarity, using the metaphor of a wound:

> Precarity is hope that sustains past the promise of hope ... Precarity is humiliating ... Precarity quickly becomes a stigma ... Precarity appears as a wound, sometimes temporary, sometimes disabling, that intellectual predators and sexual harassers and snobs and racists can see a mile away ... [T]he microaggressions and racisms ... bubble up within [academic precarity]. (Neff 2017, para. 10)

Data and Invisibility

When one attempts to gather data on contract academics, one comes up against a thought-provoking lack of scholarly data. The absence of a range of rigorous academic research on the topic of contingent faculty itself attests to the success in making contract academics invisible. Contract academics' stories are difficult to gather due to the situation of precarity and a history of discipline for speaking out against their institutions or the general systems of the academy. Many contract faculty are either too afraid or too disillusioned to share their stories or even to fill out anonymous data collection tools such as surveys. The protections and rights listed in the academic freedom policies declared by the CAUT and the AAUP have little clout in the cases of contract academics: precariously employed academics are vulnerable on so many fronts that it can be difficult to protect their jobs on the grounds of an institution's violation of academic freedom. When even Steven Salaita, a former star academic, is forced out of the academy due to public statements he made that raised donor concerns about his political position (AAUP 2015), we can see just how little access the vulnerably employed academic may have to academic freedom rights.

The jobs of contract academics are so precarious that they fall through the cracks within the collective consciousness of the academy. The CCPA report on contract academics, for example, includes a short chapter on "The Challenge of Obtaining Good Data"; their attempt to access data for their report required them to use Canada's Freedom of Information laws to try and get the data directly from the universities themselves (Shaker and Pasma 2018, 12–13). Of the seventy-eight publicly funded universities, only seventy-three participated, but some were so reluctant to share this data that they attempted to charge significant fees to release the information.

Even when academic studies are done using discipline-approved methodologies, Andrea Choi (2016) and other researchers acknowledge the problematic nature of some research on racial diversity in universities. In one study, Audrey Kobayashi (2002) found the only method of finding equity data on racialized geographers in Canadian universities was to check first and last names in the Canadian Association of Geographers Directory of 2000. Henry, Choi, and Kobayashi (2012) reported that the absence of official equity data from universities forced the investigators to scroll through departmental websites, looking at faces and names to determine the numbers of racialized faculty employed. Choi (2016) herself used a similar method in her own research. The superficial nature of the data was reported with frustration by these researchers, but the superficiality of diversity policies is literalized by the methodology used in the study. Momani and Stirk's (2017) report also draws attention to the dearth of data on this issue at workplaces across the spectrum (20). Stirk also suggests that institutional data is of debatable value. Sara Ahmed (2006) points out that many institutions produce publicity images of the "happy, smiling faces" of a diverse university community (124); however, they are more likely to be images of the international students than the university's workforce. A recent Halloween costume on the internet showed a young woman inserting her head into a diversity poster to demonstrate the tokenism of well-meant diversity campaigns on campus. As a woman of colour, I too have been used as the face of diversity in such campaigns. Diversity and equity must be connected to more than the mere physical appearance of an employee, but the danger is that appearance will replace principle. While CAUT and CCPA's attempts to counter the rumour- and assumption-based discussions about race and gender in the contract academic workforce by conducting nationwide surveys have provided some concrete data on contingent employment patterns in higher education in Canada, much more work needs to be done in this area, particularly on racialized and otherwise marginalized equity-seeking groups. Until that hard data are collected, some of the evidence about the lives of contract academics must come from news, social media, and blog posts that do exist.

Denizens, Not Citizens

The lack of belonging in the academy is made clear by the physical and conceptual space inhabited by contract academics and by university mission statements. In *The Precariat Charter: From Denizens to Citizens,* economist Guy Standing (2014) considers that the denial of citizenship in the academy turns precariously employed academics from citizens into "denizens," defined by the *Concise Oxford English Dictionary* (12th ed.) as mere "inhabitants or occupants" of a place. The *OED* expands on this definition to state that a denizen is also considered a "foreigner allowed certain rights in their adopted country." The *OED's* definition of "citizen" is a legal one: a citizen is "a legally recognized subject or national of a state or commonwealth." Other definitions of citizen include such attributes as responsibilities and the underlying assumptions about commitment and belonging. The UDHR asserts that everyone "has the right to a nationality" (United Nations 1948, art. 15). If we see academia as a nation, we see that contract academics exist in limbo – nationless and homeless. The normalization of contingency as the standard model for academic employment has remade the academy from a community to merely a "traveler's hub" (Nelson 2010, 93), where the underemployed become a "stranded resource" (Momani and Stirk 2017, 17). Here is where Nelson's observation meets the concept of the nationless non-citizen. The AAUP stated in its 1970 amendments to the famous "1940 Statement on Academic Freedom": "College and university teachers are citizens, members of a learned profession, and officers of an educational institution" (AAUP 1970, 14).

Yet, contract faculty are treated as intruders, wrongfully inserting and imposing their presence into the academic space. In reality, contract academics are sharply turned away from physical and psychological spaces of belonging. Let us then keep the above perspective on the contract academic's place in the academy in mind as we examine the stated ideals of post-secondary education. In the university setting, the ethical standards are ideally at the highest of levels – these standards are what we aspire to, and they are what give universities the authority to claim they have the right to train the leaders of the next generation. Yale University (n.d.) declares it will "[inspire] leaders worldwide who serve all sectors of society," while Harvard College (n.d.) states it will "educate the citizens and citizen-leaders for our society." In Canada, Queen's University (1996) states that one of its key missions is to encourage "the exemplary service of the University and that of its graduates to the community and the nation and the community of nations." This noble goal is tied to the concept that education is indeed an ideal site for defending human rights. But if the institution itself does not follow the standards it proclaims, how is it possible to train leaders to "serve all sections of society"? How can non-citizens train "citizens" how to be "citizens"?

The AAUP (1970) states that the function of a university, within the academy and beyond, is to promote the "common good" (14). In the academy, the justification for a scholar's existence is the ability to do scholarly work – which includes research and knowledge-making – enabling the next generation to continue to explore ideas, influencing ethical actions for the "common good," and ultimately moving towards the United Nations' ideal of friendship between nations or communities (United Nations 1948, para. 4). In examining the conditions for full participation in the academy, it is clear they are not conducive to contract academics, many of whom are actively barred from participation in departmental life at all levels. Contract academics are not allowed at departmental meetings or are reluctantly included or allowed to serve on departmental committees. The lack of governance rights within their own academic units is almost inevitably amplified in the wider context of a university. As Barnhardt and Phillips (2018) conclude, "the ramifications of silencing and excluding part-time faculty members in decision-making processes are immense and should not be overlooked" (13).

Contract academics are in a liminal space in more ways than one. A huge majority of contract academics across North America report not having professional office space. Here, it is worth considering the implications of being barred from this most basic of resources. Without dedicated office space within their institutions, contract academics cannot meet students to do the component of teaching every instructor necessarily does outside the classroom. For some academics, hallways, student cafeterias, and parking lots have to make do as temporary offices, where it is neither possible to concentrate on intellectual work nor to afford students their right to privacy. When offices are available, they are usually shared, again making it impossible to provide students with privacy. Without offices, it is not possible to offer open office hours or spaces without distractions, which would allow students to drop in to engage in valuable discussions with their professors – discussions that go beyond the superficial administrative tasks of asking for extensions or disputing grades (the commonest content of instructor-student interactions) to conversations about ideas. Not having office space means that the essential work of the academy – to make knowledge and build ideas – becomes almost impossible. Though most contract academics necessarily work at home as well as on campus, it would not be reasonable to expect them to invite students to their homes in order to provide that office space. The inability to be accessible to students and to be without the means of mentoring them not only deprofessionalizes the contract academic; it also "shortchanges the student" (Fredrickson 2015, para. 8). The in-between space the contract academic occupies in the academy is made starkly clear. In a blog post published in 2017, Ali Colleen Neff deeply criticized office spaces. Her account of a real experience with her office, which she framed as a metaphor for the inhospitality of the academy, has now been edited out, and one can only speculate why. She wrote about an academy that dismissed her concerns as hysterical and unimportant simply because she was contingent faculty. The office as a site for anxiety and discrimination is evident in the deep anxiety she felt when she entered her office, the black mould on the walls having been dismissed by an administrator as insignificant, despite its effect on her health. That black mould clearly functions as a metaphor for the rot that she sees infesting the whole institution of higher education, as well as the actual matter of higher education – the mould also spreads to her books – "poison[ing] the whole academy" (Neff 2017). Terra Poirier's book on the spaces occupied by the "non-regular" faculty at Emily Carr University in British Columbia quotes students as saying that the one shared contract academic office is "creepy," because of its concrete and brick wall and its stark lighting, and "hard to find," because it was originally intended as a storage closet (Poirier 2018, 93). As Poirier considers the location and size of the office space shared by eighty contract academics – with cubby holes representing each individual's "office" – she comments that they feel "as though we were banished" (65–6). This characterization of the type of workplace described by many contract academics as poisonous is echoed by the Mental Injury Toolkit document (OHCOW 2012, 3).

The message is that contract academics are merely temporary occupants of whatever minimal academic space is absolutely necessary for the exercise of their contractual duties. In addition to lacking office space, many do not have access to professional development workshops, travel grants, or even departmental resources like photocopying. In addition, there are other institutional barriers, the most disruptive of which is the instant stoppage of internet and library privileges on the last day of a contract. This practice misunderstands the nature of academic work and conflates it with "fast food" work (a metaphor used to indicate unspecialized skills and the disposability and interchangeability of a worker). The contract academic disappears even more effectively from the academy here – students cannot contact them; end-of-term work like deferred exams must be completed by a tenured faculty member (which can have effects on contract instructors' academic freedom and question their professional expertise); and colleagues with whom they might have a chance to do collaborative work also cannot find them. Staff members often collaborate in the corporate marginalizing and "disappearing" of contract academics, not only by interrogating them about their "demands" for necessary academic space beyond their contracts but also by crystalizing the assumptions about contract academics with comments such as "But you knew what you were getting into," thereby presumably absolving the corporate institution from responsibility in perpetuating oppressive systems. This attitude of disdain towards contract academics is learned as part of a corporate culture.

Contract academics, then, are deliberately treated with professional inhospitality, barred not only from professional spaces such as offices but also from opportunities to enter the professional world of ideas. Access to grant applications is often limited, sometimes because these academics do not have the research profile to write strong applications and sometimes because senior administrators will not sign off on applications for those who are considered to be transients in the academy (even if they have been working at an institution for a decade or more). Travel funding for research and conference attendance, for example, is rarely available – the least financially able members of the academy must use their own funds to attend necessarily fewer academic events, where they might exchange knowledge with other academics. The lower salaries – in comparison to tenured ones – earned by contract academics mean they must teach more courses, often as "road scholars" or "freeway fliers" at more than one institution, and usually through the summer in addition to the regular academic year. Some have to take non-academic jobs to supplement their teaching salaries. This scrambling leaves little time for research. They are caught in a vicious cycle: Not being able to produce publications means there is less chance for grants that would enable them to have the research time to produce those publications. Not having a strong publication record means their chances of becoming part of the tenure stream become almost impossible in just a couple of years. "We want researchers, not instructors!" cry senior academics across campuses. But universities also want students. The logical gap between the practical need to have students in seats and the desire by administrators and some tenured academics not to invest their tuition fees in teaching contributes to the in-between identity and unstable space of the contract academic and thus threatens to destabilize academia as a whole. Not only do the lost opportunities in knowledge-making result in the individual marginalization of contract academics, but they also have a significant effect on the world of knowledge itself. The knowledge of at least one generation of academics has been lost, and as fewer and fewer academics are given the time and opportunity to make knowledge, their students will have access to less and less knowledge. Trenerry and Paradies (2012) speak of the loss of innovation when there is workplace inequity (12), but it is not that simple. In fact, many contract academics do create innovative programs and pedagogies, but the academy loses the potential innovative work of many others simply by denying the existence of their work. Lack of institutional support for programs that could truly create "student success" – a commonly declared aim by administrators – on the grounds that innovative programs could not and should not be produced by contract academics results in real harm for future generations. Dismissal of such work by their institutions significantly wastes human resources and impoverishes the academy.

Freedom of Teaching and Impact on Learning

The UDHR asserts that everyone "has the right to freedom of opinion and expression; this right includes freedom to hold opinions without interference and to seek, receive, and impart information and ideas through any media and regardless of frontiers" (United Nations 1948, art. 19). CAUT's Policy Statement on academic freedom is as follows:

> Academic freedom includes the right, without restriction by prescribed doctrine, to freedom to teach and discuss; freedom to carry out research and disseminate and publish the results thereof; freedom to produce and perform creative works; freedom to engage in service to the institution and the community; freedom to express one's opinion about the institution, its administration, and the system in which one works; freedom to acquire, preserve, and provide access to documentary material in all formats; and freedom to participate in professional and representative academic bodies. (CAUT 2018b, para. 2)

The policy provides both ideals and guidelines, but true academic freedom rests on job security. Without assurance of any job continuity, contract academics are apprehensive about exercising academic freedom in the classroom or elsewhere. Richard Moser (2014) notes:

> Adjuncts and graduate students often deliver excellent instruction, but that is in spite of their working conditions. Most contingent faculty members and graduate assistants are so poorly compensated and teach so many

students that they face powerful disincentives to quality instruction ... [C]ontingent faculty members are often forced to rely solely on students to evaluate their work. It is reasonable to expect that such a system of eva- luation makes teachers vulnerable to student pressure for better grades, reluctant to teach controversial subjects, or engage in stressful disputes over plagiarism and cheating. (para. 8)

An article by Eva Swidler (2017) in the *Chronicle of Higher Education* on universities and social justice asks this question about students in higher education:

If what they learn and discuss tiptoes around topics like exploitation, vio- lence, and racism, what are they learning? That these are not important issues to think about? That these are issues to be ignored, or even swept under the rug, lest the boat be rocked? As the American Association of University Professors notes, the conditions of adjunct employment put students at risk of being "deprived of the debate essential to citizenship." To this risk I would add the risk that a primary unintended lesson our students might learn from us is how to neglect justice. (para. 9)

Voices of contingent faculty are suppressed: experience has shown that making waves through complaints about working conditions, or even competing at an uncomfortably professional level with tenured academics, can simply result in contracts not being renewed. Attempt- ing to exercise academic integrity by establishing high standards in classrooms can result in poor evaluations and complaints against instructors. Again, the likely result is non-renewal of contracts. Exercis- ing academic freedom in the classroom by attempting innovative and experimental teaching methods or by teaching unorthodox perspec- tives can also result in contracts that are not renewed, as can exercising academic freedom by criticizing the institution or speaking on public issues. Swidler (2017) notes:

Adjuncts' timidity, or even fear, affects not just students but also the public at large. When contingent faculty members – who account for 70 percent of [American] college instructors – put the renewal of their teaching con- tracts at risk if they dare to advise a group of student activists, or to speak about a controversial issue with a journalist, the role of academics as public intellectuals suffers. (para. 10)

The "common good" is being affected negatively by this culture of fear. It would not be accurate to say that these academics are fired for exercising their academic freedom, because one would need to belong or to have some kind of ownership of one's position in the academy for that to happen. The contract system allows institutions to "disappear" employees for any deviation, perceived or otherwise, from whatever norms are set down for them.

Here we see another aspect of the invisibility spectrum. For some contract academics, the suppressed voice and invisibility have become a choice. Silence and compliance to institutional rules have become the only methods of survival, at the expense of academic freedom and integrity. Many contract academics routinely inflate grades or assign only mid-range grades that are neither too high nor too low so as not to attract the attention of administrators. When they do come to the attention of those in control of their jobs, many package themselves as cooperative team members, attending meetings, taking part in special projects, serving on committees, and so on. Even when hope to some-day advance in their academic careers is gone, their goal becomes to have their contracts renewed, however bad they are, just to survive. Like other equity-seeking workers, contract academics, the shame-ful "others" in the academy, can feel they must do more than ten-ured colleagues, at least on the level of service, so they are not seen as troublemakers.

Swidler (2017) explains: "If your job hangs in the balance, an over-riding concern is to keep the supervisor happy, keep your student evaluations uniformly positive, and keep your head down. For many adjuncts, the ideal is to come to no one's attention" (para. 5). She adds:

> Because your syllabus goes to the department chair at the start of each semester, controversial authors and readings get weeded out. You need to avoid negative comments from students, so you avoid assignments that might challenge anyone's ideas, and you steer classroom conversations away from any topic that might provoke a heated discussion. You don't want to come to the attention of administrators, so you don't participate in speaking events or teach-ins that might draw the ire of powers-that-be. (para. 6)

Swidler is uncompromising in her condemnation of institutions of higher education that hire large numbers of contract faculty, as it not only "changes their relationship to justice" but also "widespread use of adjuncts … affects justice in the larger society" (2017, para. 1). If over 53 per cent of academics in Canada are precariously employed, then, as Dea (2018) points out, the academy is now constituted of only approxi-mately 47 per cent of academics who have real academic freedom, and therefore only 47 per cent are able to be fully engaged in the scholarly mission. Only 47 per cent of academics are now able to speak up against state interference or directives, leading to the conditions for academic work seen in states such as Mexico, Turkey, India, and Hungary.

Ideals of Education

Article 26 of the UDHR sets out the following principles about the purposes of education:

> Education shall be directed to the full development of the human personality and to the strengthening of human rights and fundamental freedoms. It shall promote understanding, tolerance and friendship among all nations, racial or religious groups, and shall further the activities of the United Nations for the maintenance of peace. (United Nations 1948, art. 46)

In their strategic plans and mission statements, several North American institutions of higher education do indeed acknowledge the United Nations' characterization of education as a conduit for unity, tolerance, and friendship among nations. They affirm the primacy of equality and respect for members of the academy, service to the public, and hope for the future. Some sample mission statements of top universities in North America advocate equity and mutual respect as central tenets of their institutions. At the University of British Columbia (2018), for example, the "Mutual Respect and Equity" section of its "Vision and Values" statement says that "the University values and respects all members of its communities"; while Dalhousie University (2014) promises to "foster an environment of teaching and learning excellence, built on innovation, collaboration and respect." The University of Toronto's (n.d.) mission statement says that the university "is dedicated to fostering an academic community in which the learning and scholarship of every member may flourish, with vigilant protection for individual human rights, and a resolute commitment to the principles of equal opportunity, equity and justice." It is essential to recognize the importance of such ideals in a university's foundational policies, and by articulating these ideals, these universities have taken the first step towards putting policies of equity and social justice into practice.

Further, many universities also recognize the importance the AAUP places on the "common good." It translates into the concept of service to the community in the statements of many universities.

For example, McGill University's (n.d.) statement promises to "provide service to society"; Stanford's lofty mission statement, written in 1885 by its founders, is "to promote the public welfare by exercising an influence on behalf of humanity and civilization" (Stanford University 2011). Promoting "public welfare" and inspiring "citizen-leaders" to serve society by "exercising an influence on behalf of humanity and civilization" are large claims, and I would like to suggest that their implementation can only be possible once they are first implemented within the scholarly institutions themselves. A "vigilant protection for individual human rights and a resolute commitment to the principles of equal opportunity, equity and justice" will be only be possible once universities look inward to the practices within their own institutions.

It is true that there are several types of interest groups or communities within a large institution like a university and that each group may have its own aims and functions. However, more effort towards the acknowledgment of silenced groups and towards unity needs to be made. The ideal of friendship among nations is still a distance away in the scholarly world, which insists on the maintenance of the divided communities or "nations"; instead of cooperation, collegiality, and collaboration, the system encourages divisiveness, diminishment, and disrespect. Increasingly, the scholarly world functions on the maintenance of new hierarchies and divisions within communities, rather than on "the development of friendly relations between nations" (United Nations, 1948, para. 4).

Two Nations

The divisions that are created between tenured and untenured faculty are not evident to the wider society, to whose service universities are committing themselves in their mission statements, but they are deeply damaging to "the common good." In 1845, future British prime minister Benjamin Disraeli's novel, *Sybil, or, The Two Nations*, outlined the troubling state of the class divide, classifying it as a conflict between nations:

> Two nations: between whom there is no intercourse and no sympathy; who are as ignorant of each other's habits, thoughts and feelings, as if they were dwellers in different zones, or inhabitants of different planets; or who are formed by a different breeding, are fed by a different food, are ordered by different manners, and are not governed by the same laws. (Disraeli 1845/1998, 66)

Contract and tenured faculty are sometimes so far apart in their experiences in the academy that they even begin to function like Disraeli's two nations. Former AAUP president Cary Nelson (2010) sees the sharp divisions within the community as having created two worlds (94). Even when sharing the same building, Nelson says, "vulnerable and protected faculty" remain "invisible to one another" (94), and "transient 'colleagues' pass unnoticed, like ships blind to each other's passage" (90). Nelson's point about invisibility is perceptive: one group is visible, and one lurks at the margins of academia, invisible, unspeakable, the abominable manifestation of a man-made problem that threatens to devour what is good in the academy. Contract academics often speak of being ignored, looked past, or looked through if they encounter their tenured colleagues, as if they do not exist. As Nelson mentions, many are given schedules in such a way that they do not encounter any colleagues at all: they literally do not enter departmental space, as their work starts after hours for office staff and well after most tenured faculty have left their offices. Racialized contingent faculty, if they do exist, are made doubly invisible by being looked *at* only for their physical presence and, sometimes, appearance and looked *through* because of their professional status. As noted earlier, the silhouette graphic of a past CAUT poster campaign about the "invisible academic" crystalized the situation of the contract academic slowly disappearing into a shadow, with no individual identity, because the individual academic's work itself had become invisible.

It is of deep concern, however, that tenured and contract faculty have not only become two nations instead of one united community of academics; they are also frequently two nations at war. Battle lines are being drawn up in many institutions, with each side full of resentment and suspicion, one bitter and furious that they are consistently shut out of the academy and the other fearful and furious that their own place in the academy may be in jeopardy from the vast hordes looking in. Thomas Docherty's (2014) *Universities at War* characterizes the modern university as a battleground and, like other writers such as Bill Readings (1995), Benjamin Ginsberg (2011) and Cary Nelson (2010), cites his concern about the corporatization of the academy, which creates many of the oppressive practices at the heart of the "war." Richard Moser (2014) concludes that "the new academic labour system has fragmented the faculty, weakening its ability to act as a constituency" (para. 13).

If there is a war, each side characterizes the other as an enemy and as monstrous, a dangerous trend. Cary Nelson (2010) reports that a common practice of assigning only the inconvenient evening courses to contract faculty has resulted in the characterization of contract faculty as "vampires" who are feeding on the curriculum by night (94): the monstrous "other" (Barnhardt and Phillips, 2018, 2). If not a devouring monster, the contract academic is still a manifestation of a scholar's worst fears. In a recent encounter with a graduate student in my own department, I was engaged in a lively conversation about my specialized disciplinary research. The friendly student finally asked why we had not met before. I mentioned that I did not teach graduate courses because I was employed as a sessional faculty member. The melodramatic start by the student and her instant excuse to leave and move to a chair on the opposite side of the room (despite many empty chairs between us) justified my reluctance to tell her about my employment status. This reaction was by no means an unusual one from a graduate student who is determined to stay apart from the contagion of the failed academic, as the corporate academic culture characterizes precariously employed faculty. Contract faculty themselves turn on each other at times, fearing association with other "failures" will cause their own status to plunge. Thus, Foucault's (1977/1995) "contagion model" serves to manage, shame, and discipline from within the ranks of the most vulnerable academics. As Catherine Sorbara (2017) says, "you're told over and over that nothing else but staying in academia is respected" (para.2).

For Nelson (2010), the logic is circular, and culpability lies with tenured and administrative employees, who create working conditions that oppress some workers and then blame those same workers for perpetuating the unworkable working conditions, presumably because they have accepted the jobs. Oppressive and discriminatory behaviour do cause resentment, but, according to Nelson, administrators are now criticizing their targets for making them feel fearful and guilty. In this way, the marginalized faculty members become the oppressors of those they challenge (Henry and Tater, 2009, 34).

Just as the colonial enterprise justified its mission by characterizing the colonized as unworthy of their own privilege by virtue of being less intelligent, lazy, and morally undeveloped, so contract academics seem to be perceived by tenured academics as less intelligent and less hardworking, despite the reality that most contract academics are teaching highly specialized knowledge and skills (including the "service" skills of composition and other entry-level courses) and often teaching at least twice as many courses as tenured faculty. The United Nations' hope that education will promote the maintenance of peace seems to be replaced by the practice of education being used to promote privilege. Artificial barriers, ranging from constantly moving bars for "excellence" to actual barred spaces for contract academics, maintain the divisions between these "nations." As Moser (2014) explains, the "fragmentation of the profession is driven by administrators; yet faculty members are also often complicit in the transformation of tenure from a right into a privilege by allowing or even encouraging the escalation of the requirements for tenure" (para. 15). As such, Nelson (2010) observes that what he calls "contingent culture" (93) has very different behaviours, goals, and attitudes from those of tenured culture towards the academy. Similar criticisms about work ethic and intellectual quality are levelled against tenured academics by contract academics. While tenured academics say contract academics are trying to take what they do not deserve, contract academics say tenured academics do not deserve what they have.

Race and Contract Work

The most obvious example of insulting and discriminatory behaviour comes from staff members and colleagues who say to a scholar's face that s/he/ze was hired because s/he/ze fit into a particular quota for equity-seeking groups, thus erasing merit as a factor in that scholar's ability to get a job. Carl James notes that Frances Henry's 2006 study discovered minority faculty members "are faced with an 'inhospitable' climate and resentment from other faculty members that contribute to feelings of self-doubt as to whether their appointments were based on their qualification or identity, as in 'equity hires' or 'token hires'" (James 2009, 147). The title of Carl James's article "'You Know Why You Were Hired, Don't You?' Expectations and Challenges in University Appointments" reflects a common experience of racialized faculty (James 2017).

In addition, course assignments, especially for contract academics, can be based on gender or ethnic origin; for example, a South Asian female academic might be assigned to teach world literature or postcolonial feminist literature simply because she *looks* like she should be able to do so, even if her specialization is the poetry of John Donne. If she is not engaged in specifically racialized political action or political approaches when she teaches, she is the object of disapproval by others who identify as being in a similar racialized and gendered space. When "visible minority" faculty are hired, they feel they must work extra hard on both scholarship and service. Yet, when their service attempts to bring community issues to light, "they are told that they are of little value in merit and personnel decisions," and such work "costs them dearly when they are being evaluated for promotion or tenure" (Stanley 2006, 721). This scenario was what happened in Patricia Monture's case at the University of Saskatchewan and in Cornell West's case in 2004, when his hip-hop CD for the purpose of making his work more accessible to a wider audience made him the target of criticism by administrators – such work was seen to be undignified and inappropriate to the academy, even though West was attempting to communicate some of his scholarly ideas to the public (James 2009). Those differences in scholarship and research interests that initially brought such scholars into the diversity equation then count against them – as with Indigenous scholars – as their work seems to be unrecognizable when it comes to merit or promotion. When the service is approved by the academy, such as mentoring students who match their minority status, sitting on diversity committees, being the spokesperson or face of their race or other marker of difference, it tends to expand and spiral into impossible workloads, as noted by Henry and Tator (2012) and Minelle Mahtani (2006). Mahtani reports that female faculty members from minority groups had to accept "gargantuan tasks simply because they were seen as being a 'two-fer' – both a woman and a woman of colour" (23).

James (2009) warns that, in universities' eagerness to ensure an authentic voice, a candidate who represents "difference" to the majority culture and equity background of a department might be hired because s/he/ze fits well into the "culture of the faculty," represents "the views of the collegium," and is expected to "become an effective 'Native Informant' – a role (as anthropologists) that minorities are expected to play in representing the academy to, and working with, those considered different" (143). As long as such a scholar seems nonthreatening (143), the academy remains safe and stable. James also points to another problematic area of review: the student evaluation. While more research needs to be done in this area, some preliminary studies suggest that faculty of colour are treated differently by students, who treat the ubiquitous anonymous evaluation forums as ways to express racist and sexist points of view. C.A. Stanley's (2006) research showed that minority groups are often subject to responses that question their credibility and authority from students who equate obvious markers of difference from their norm, as well as precarious employment, with lack of expertise. In recent conversations with students at my institution, I have been told of the general assumption by students that faculty of these equity-seeking groups are considered by them to be second-class scholars who do not know what they are doing, so that students feel cheated in their education. Knowing the power of the anonymous student evaluation in one's employment status, it is no wonder that visible minority and contingent colleagues are so often afraid to make themselves further vulnerable by challenging students on academic or ethical standards, thus having their academic freedom compromised and, in turn, having to compromise their academic integrity.

Non-Performative Speech Acts and Social Justice

Sara Ahmed (2006) points out that mission statements about diversity and inclusion are often just that: statements. To her, they are "speech acts that read as if they are performatives," that is, they appear to commit to certain values or ideals. But "just because an organization is committed to being a diverse organization does not necessarily mean that they are one"; in other words, they are "nonperformatives" (104). This interpretation of the effectiveness of diversity and equity initiatives is echoed by several other scholars, including Audrey Kobayashi (2009) and Patricia Monture (2009). Enakshi Dua's (2009) research finds that diversity training tends to work more effectively with non-academic staff than with faculty. Trenerry and Paradies (2012) reiterate that simply having a diversity or anti-discrimination plan doesn't mean an organization is diverse or anti-discriminatory. Momani and Stirk (2017) recommend *measuring* diversity as a way of managing it: "what gets measured gets done" (2); furthermore, they expect the leader of an organization to ensure meaningful measurement criteria are set in place (18). In practice, there are discriminatory actions, some noticeable perhaps only to the target and others culturally common to particular institutions, in spite of stated policies. The first hurdle is acknowledgment of and recognition by the organization's "managers" or administrators of the existence and true nature of the problem. Ahmed (2006) notes the concerns of many practitioners and academics "that writing documents or having good policies becomes a substitute for action" and that universities are writing the documents simply as a way to manage the university's public image, without any sincere belief in principles of equity (117). It is relatively easy to hire scholars who represent ethnocultural diversity, but it is important to move beyond the numbers (Momani and Stirk 2017, 19). Once they are hired, the diversity-fulfilling candidates' experiences do not necessarily represent that diversity or, indeed, remedy discriminatory attitudes. Patricia Monture (2009) writes of her intense struggle to have her intellectual work recognized because it falls within Indigenous knowledge systems and alternative research methodologies from those familiar to conventional scholarly lenses. She expresses her concern that, when scholars attempt a different path at attaining knowledge, the "result is to make invisible the work that is most important to Indigenous people and communities" (95), thus rendering null the point of diversity initiatives. James (2017) argues:

Even as job advertisements proclaim universities' commitment to equity policies and practices that will bring women, "visible" minorities, Indigenous peoples, and persons with disabilities into faculties, the contexts into which racialized and Indigenous scholars enter remain less than welcoming. [There is the] unspoken expectation that "affirmative action hires" will "deal with diversity issues." (156)

For Momani and Stirk (2017), the responsibility for a remedy lies first with the leadership; their report on diversity quotes Dimitri Girier, then senior advisor on diversity and inclusion at la Banque Nationale and currently chief advisor equity, diversity, and inclusion at the University of Montreal, who says we "need champions at the top who don't just talk about diversity, but demonstrate and recognize the value of inclusion through *daily work*. On ne gère pas la diversité, on la vit [You don't manage diversity, you live it]" (20; emphasis added). Writing a mission statement, creating a strategic plan, or promising to provide leaders for society is a good start, but it is of little value if such a document is called on only occasionally as a response to a crisis or egregious violation of its principles that is evident to the broader public, or if the leader actually maintains or enables structures and systems of marginalization. Instead, actions taken every day are necessary in order to build towards any concrete results in creating a diverse and equitable academy.

Recovering the Academy

It is important to remember that universities have failed to follow the UDHR exhortation that everyone "has the right to a standard of living adequate for the health and well-being of himself and his family, including food, clothing, housing and medical care and necessary social services, and the right to security in the event of unemployment, sickness, disability, widowhood, old age or other lack of livelihood in circumstances beyond his control" (United Nations 1948, art. 25). The representative stories outlined in this paper should serve as a dire warning of what will become the norm in the academic sector if we refuse to act to reverse the trend. Maria Maisto and Seth Kahn (2016) explain that "universities have enacted oppressive employment policies with impunity for so long that they have enculturated faculty into believing there is no need to reject activities or proposals that constitute ethical, if not legal, violations of contingent faculty rights" (para. 10). There is no reason to accept this exploitation passively, or to think that, because one is tenured, one has little or no responsibility to help racialized, contingent colleagues rise well above the current survival-level working conditions. The academy is very much under attack (for example, Vermont Law School's impending loss of tenure), and the current protected jobs may well become as contingent as those that already exist if academics with some power do not act now. The normalization of exploitive practices and the reaction of blame towards those who accept jobs that exploit them further violate principles of social justice. Does the fact that the academy has divisive employment practices mean that the academy and its intellectual enterprise, that of education with its goal of human liberation, must be abandoned? Should academics encountering poor employment practices leave the profession altogether? Are the ideals of education worth fighting for and worth defending from within the academy? When there are fewer jobs than post-graduates, the answer is obvious: if one wants the scholarly life, surrounded by the privileges of the scholarly atmosphere such as intellectual conversations, scholarly colloquia, and scholarly libraries, and one wants to avoid being immersed in a different profession like banking or working in industry, then the only option is to still hold on to the academic job. Instead of leaving academia, perhaps a renewed effort is needed to recover a healthy academy that truly works towards the ideals of inclusivity, public service, and free inquiry declared in so many mission and policy statements. Instead of trying to erase the profession of the academic by dismantling all the conditions that make the above ideals possible, we need to maintain and strengthen the working conditions that make social justice possible. As Elliott (2017) says, "individual heroism will never be sufficient" (para. 33). There must be systematic change, which can be achieved through a refusal to accept artificial divisions between ranks. No dedicated academic wants to be at war with another. The core mission of the academy is to make knowledge; neither knowledge nor its dissemination is possible without academic freedom, something that is only a theoretical right for all the academics who are precariously employed. Ideals of community need to be recovered for all members of the academy. Instead of creating and perpetuating divisions between members of the academy, we need to acknowledge the common purposes of the profession and thus the common aims of all academics. Collegiality, not competition, needs to become a habit, as competition results in only short-term gains. Research projects in teams that do not discriminate on the grounds of rank and insist on equitable pay and working conditions for all will allow knowledge to advance, to be shared between ranks, and to be passed on to future generations. Realistic goals for promotions and permanent positions for the precariat need to be implemented and followed through so scholars who are working as teachers are paid adequately for a life of dignity. Universities must be discouraged from enacting superficial policies that seem to aim for equity and fair employment practices but only achieve a forced picture of fairness by simply firing existing, often long-term contract academics. Workloads need to be examined and brought into line with the UDHR's Article 23.1, which requires "favourable conditions of work," and Article 24, which reminds us that everyone "has the right to rest and leisure, including reasonable limitation of working hours and periodic holidays with pay" (United Nations 1948). The time needed for sleeping, eating, and travelling to different campuses for teaching does not count as "reasonable limitation of working hours." Circular thinking about the contract academic needs to be rejected. An academic who is paid very little, and thus must do two to three times the teaching as a securely employed academic in a research position, simply does not have the time to do the research expected from a scholar who has release time or less teaching to do; there is no justice in then dismissing the precariously employed academic's worth for not doing research. Adequate funding opportunities need to open up so contract academics can afford to do research. National funding bodies, such as the Social Sciences and Humanities Research Council (SSHRC) and the Natural Sciences and Engineering Research Council (NSERC), for example, need to invest in and create a significant number of opportunities for contract academics, just to start catching up and making up for the missed opportunities for which they have been active enablers. Financial accountability within university administrations is also important: financial offices need to be closely audited to see where government funds and tuition fees are actually being spent, and spending needs to be redirected from amenities and administrators to learning in libraries and classrooms. The Canadian government's increasing awareness that precarious employment often intersects with the interests of equity-seeking and other economically disadvantaged groups may lead towards possible legislation to support more secure and equitable jobs in the academic sector. Some provincial governments are also becoming aware that, when a previously stable economic sector becomes unstable, the broader economy also increases in instability, and thus they may also act to support more stable employment. Institutions need to commit to real changes in inclusiveness for all equity-seeking groups, using the readily available measures provided by such reports as that written by Momani and Stirk (2017) and research by such scholars as Ahmed and Dua. The increasing fragmentation of the professoriate in areas of race and employment will shatter the academy if action is not taken to remedy the current state of the profession. As the UDHR asserts, "education shall be directed to the full development of the human personality and to the strengthening of respect for human rights and fundamental freedoms" (United Nations 1948, art. 26).

REFERENCES

AAUP (American Association of University Professors). n.d. "Background Facts on Contingent Faculty Positions." https://www.aaup.org/issues /contingency/background-facts.

– 1970. "1940 Statement of Principles on Academic Freedom and Tenure with 1970 Interpretive Comments." https://www.aaup.org/report /1940-statement-principles-academic-freedom-and-tenure.

– 2015. *Academic Freedom and Tenure: The University of Illinois at Urbana-Champaign*. https://www.aaup.org/report/UIUC.

– 2018. "Data Snapshot: Contingent Faculty in US Higher Ed." https://www .aaup.org/news/data-snapshot-contingent-faculty-us-higher-ed.

Ahmed, Sara. 2006. "The Nonperformativity of Antiracism." *Meridians: Feminism, Race, Transnationalism* 7 (1): 104–26. http://www.jstor.org/stable/40338719.

Barnhardt, Cassie L., and Carson W. Phillips. 2018. "At the Margins of University Work: The Influence of Campus Climate and Part-Time Faculty Status on Academic Values." *JAF: AAUP Journal of Academic Freedom* 9: 1–21. https://www.aaup.org/JAF9/margins-university-work-influence-campus -climate-and-part-time-faculty-status-academic.

Berlant, Lauren. 2011. *Cruel Optimism*. Durham, NC: Duke University Press.

CAUT (Canadian Association of University Teachers). n.d. "Mobilizing Tips for Fair Employment Week." https://bulletin-archives.caut.ca/docs /default-source/fair-employment-week/few-mobilizing-tips.pdf.

– 2017. "By the Numbers: Contract Academic Staff in Canada." *CAUT Bulletin*, October 2017. https://www.caut.ca/bulletin/2017/10 /numbers-contract-academic-staff-canada.

– 2018a. "Academic Anxiety." *CAUT Bulletin*, May June 2018. https://www .caut.ca/bulletin/2018/05/academic-anxiety.

– 2018b."Academic Freedom." CAUT Policy Statement. https://www .caut.ca/about-us/caut-policy/lists/caut-policy-statements/policy -statement-on-academic-freedom.

– 2018c. *Overrepresented and Underpaid: Diversity and Equity among Canada's Post-Secondary Education Teachers*. Ottawa: CAUT. https://www.caut.ca /sites/default/files/caut_equity_report_2018-04final.pdf.

Choi, Andrea. 2016. "Equity, Race, and Whiteness in Canadian Geography." *Canadian Geographer* 60 (3): 369–80. https://doi.org/10.1111/cag.12266.

Dalhousie University. 2014. *Inspiration and Impact: Dalhousie's Strategic Direction, 2014–2018*. https://cdn.dal.ca/content/dam/dalhousie/pdf /about/Strategic-Planning/StrategicDirectionReport-Print.pdf.

Dea, Shannon. 2018. "Academic Freedom in a Non-Ideal World." *University Affairs*, 19 October 2018. https://www.universityaffairs.ca/opinion /dispatches-academic-freedom/academic-freedom-in-a-non-ideal-world/.

Disraeli, Benjamin. 1845/1998. *Sybil, Or, the Two Nations*. Oxford: Oxford University Press.

Docherty, Thomas. 2014. *Universities at War*. Los Angeles, CA: Sage.

Dua, Enakshi. 2009. "On the Effectiveness of Anti-Racist Policies in Canadian Universities: Issues of Implementation of Policies by Senior Administration." In *Racism in the Canadian University: Demanding Social Justice, Inclusion, and Equity*, edited by Frances Henry and Carol Tater, 160–95. Toronto: University of Toronto Press.

Elliott, Nathan. 2017. "The Hidden Costs of Exploiting Contract Faculty." *The Newfoundland and Labrador Independent*, 17 August 2017. https:// theindependent.ca/2017/08/17/the-hidden-costs-of-exploiting -contract-faculty/.

Foster, Karen, and Louise Birdsell Bauer. 2018. *Out of the Shadows: Experiences of Contract Academic Staff*. Ottawa: CAUT. https://www.caut.ca/sites /default/files/cas_report.pdf.

Foucault, Michel. 1977/1995. *Discipline and Punish: The Birth of the Prison*. Translated by Alan Sheridan. New York: Vintage.

Fredrickson, Caroline. 2015. "There Is No Excuse for How Universities Treat Adjuncts." *The Atlantic*, 15 September 2015. https://www.theatlantic .com/business/archive/2015/09/higher-education-college-adjunct -professor-salary/404461/.

Gee, Alastair. 2017. "Facing Poverty, Academics Turn to Sex Work and Sleeping in Cars." *The Guardian*, 28 September 2017. https://www .theguardian.com/us-news/2017/sep/28/adjunct-professors-homeless -sex-work-academia-poverty/.

Ginsberg, Benjamin. 2011. *The Fall of the Faculty: The Rise of the All-Administrative University and Why It Matters*. Oxford: Oxford University Press.

Harris, Alex. 2017. "Part-time Professors Struggle to Put Food on the Table. Some Want a Union to Fix That." *Miami Herald*, 23 November 2017. https:// www.miamiherald.com/news/local/education/article185747328.html.

Harvard College. n.d. "Mission Vision, & History." https://college.harvard .edu/about/mission-vision-history.

Henry, Frances. 2004. "Systematic Racism towards Faculty of Colour and Aboriginal Faculty at Queen's University." Report on the 2003 Study: "Understanding the Experiences of Visible Minority and Aboriginal Faculty Members at Queen's University." Kingston, ON: Queen's Senate Educational Equity Committee.

Henry, Frances, Andrea Choi, and Audrey Kobayashi. 2012. "The Representation of Racialized Faculty at Selected Canadian Universities." *Canadian Ethnic Studies* 44 (1): 1–12. https://doi.org/10.1353/ces.2012.0008.

Henry, Frances, Enakshi Dua, Carl E. James, Audrey Kobayashi, Peter Li,
    Howard Ramos, and Malinda S. Smith. 2017. *The Equity Myth: Racialization
    and Indigeneity at Canadian Universities.* Vancouver, BC: UBC Press.
Henry, Frances, and Carol Tater. 2009. "Theoretical Perspectives and
    Manifestations of Racism in the Academy." In *Racism in the Canadian
    University: Demanding Social Justice, Inclusion, and Equity,* edited by Frances
    Henry and Carol Tater, 22–59. Toronto: University of Toronto Press.
– 2012. "Interviews with Racialized Faculty Members in Canadian
    Universities." *Canadian Ethnic Studies* 44 (2): 75–99. https://doi.org/10.1353
    /ces.2012.0003.
James, Carl E. 2009. "'It Will Happen without Putting in Place Special
    Measures': Racially Diversifying Universities." In *Racism in the Canadian
    University: Demanding Social Justice, Inclusion, and Equity,* edited by Frances
    Henry and Carol Tater, 128–59. Toronto: University of Toronto Press.
– 2017. "'You Know Why You Were Hired, Don't You?' Expectations and
    Challenges in University Appointments." In *The Equity Myth: Racialization
    and Indigeneity at Canadian Universities* by Frances Henry et al., 155–70.
    Vancouver, BC: UBC Press.
Kobayashi, Audrey. 2002. "A Generation Later, and Still Two Percent:
    Changing the Culture of Canadian Geography." *The Canadian Geographer*
    46 (3): 245–48. https://doi.org/10.1111/j.1541-0064.2002.tb00745.x.
– 2009. "Now You See Them, How You See Them: Women of Colour in
    Canadian Academia." In *Racism in the Canadian University: Demanding
    Social Justice, Inclusion, and Equity,* edited by Frances Henry and Carol Tater,
    60–75. Toronto: University of Toronto Press.
Kristensen, Tage S., Harald Hannerz, Annie Høgh, and Vilhelm Borg. 2005.
    "The Copenhagen Psychosocial Questionnaire: A Tool for the Assessment
    and Improvement of the Psychosocial Work Environment." *Scandinavian
    Journal of Work, Environment, & Health* 31 (6): 438–49. https://www.jstor.org
    /stable/40967527.
Mahtani, Minelle. 2006. "Challenging the Ivory Tower: Proposing Anti-Racist
    Geographies within the Academy." *Gender, Place and Culture* 13 (1): 21–5.
    https://doi.org/10.1080/09663690500530909.
Maisto, Maria, and Seth Kahn. 2016. "No Adjunct Left Behind?" *Academe* 102
    (3). https://www.aaup.org/article/no-adjunct-left-behind.
McGill University. n.d. "McGill University Mission Statement and Principles."
    https:/www.mcgill.ca/secretariat/mission.
McNeill, Claire. 2017a. "In Union Push at USF, Adjunct Professors Strive for
    More Respect and a Living Wage." *Tampa Bay Times,* 14 November 2017.
    https://www.tampabay.com/news/education/college/In-union-push
    -at-USF-adjunct-professors-strive-for-more-respect-and-a-living-wage
    _162644741.

– 2017b. "USF Adjuncts to Rally as New Survey Reveals Poverty among Florida Professors." *Tampa Bay Times*, 22 November 2017. https://www .tampabay.com/blogs/gradebook/2017/11/21/usf-adjuncts-to-rally-as -new-survey-reveals-poverty-among-florida-professors/.

Momani, Bessma, and Jillian Stirk. 2017. *Diversity Dividend: Canada's Global Advantage*. Waterloo, ON: Centre for International Governance Innovation. https://www.cigionline.org/publications/diversity-dividend-canadas -global-advantage.

Monture, Patricia. 2009. "'Doing Academia Differently': Confronting 'Whiteness' in the University." In *Racism in the Canadian University: Demanding Social Justice, Inclusion, and Equity*, edited by Frances Henry and Carol Tater, 76–105. Toronto: University of Toronto Press.

Moser, Richard. 2014. "Overuse and Abuse of Adjunct Faculty Members Threaten Core Academic Values." *Chronicle of Higher Education*, 13 January 2014. https://www.chronicle.com/article/overuse-and-abuse-of -adjunct-faculty-members-threaten-core-academic-values/.

Neff, Ali Colleen. 2017. "On Academic Precarity of the Faculty Adjunct." Blog post, 8 November 2017. http://www.alicolleenneff.com/blog/2017/11/8 /on-academic-precarity. [No longer posted. The comment on precarity is quoted in California State University, Dominguez Hills (CSUDH) Task Force. 2018. *Report of the Task Force to Recommend Best Practices for Non-Tenure-Track Instructional Faculty*. Carson, CA: CSUDH, 169–70. https:// www.csudh.edu/Assets/csudh-sites/president/docs/task-force/FINAL -REPORT-Non-Tenure-Track-Faculty-Task-Force.pdf.]

Nelson, Cary. 2010. *No University Is an Island*. New York: NYU Press.

OHCOW (Occupational Health Clinics for Ontario Workers). 2012. "Action on Workplace Stress: Mental Injury Prevention Tools for Ontario Workers." Mental Injury Toolkit. https://www.ohcow.on.ca/mental-injury-toolkit.html.

Poirier, Terra. 2018. *Non-Regular: Precarious Academic Labour at Emily Carr University of Art and Design*. Vancouver, BC: UNIT/PITT Projects.

Queen's University. 1996. "The Mission of Queen's University." https://www .queensu.ca/secretariat/policies/senate/mission-statement-queens-university.

Readings, Bill. 1995. *The University in Ruins*. Cambridge, MA: Harvard University Press.

Runyan, Anne Sisson. 2018. "What Is Intersectionality and Why Is It Important? Building Solidarity in the Fight for Social Justice." *Academe*, November–December 2018. https://www.aaup.org/article/what -intersectionality-and-why-it-important.

SEIU (Service Employees International Union) / FPSU (Florida Public Services Union). 2017. *Life on the Edge of the Blackboard: Florida Adjunct Faculty Survey Report 2017*. http://seiufacultyforward.org/wp-content /uploads/2017/11/Life-on-the-Edge.pdf.

Shaker, Erika, and Chandra Pasma. 2018. *Contract-U: Contract Faculty Appointments at Canadian Universities*. Ottawa: Canadian Centre for Policy Alternatives. https://www.policyalternatives.ca/publications/reports/contract-u.

Sorbara, Catherine. 2017. "Stop Ignoring the Data and Start Leaving Academia." *LinkedIn*, 13 February 2017. https://www.linkedin.com/pulse /stop-ignoring-data-start-leaving-academia-catherine-sorbara-phd.

Standing, Guy. 2014. *A Precariat Charter: From Denizens to Citizens*. London: Bloomsbury.

Stanford University. 2011. "Stanford's Mission." http://web.stanford.edu /dept/registrar/bulletin1112/4792.htm.

Stanley, C.A. 2006. "Coloring the Academic Landscape: Faculty of Color Breaking the Silence in Predominately White Colleges and Universities." *American Educational Research Journal* 43 (4): 701–36. https://doi.org /10.3102/00028312043004701.

Swidler, Eva. 2017. "The Pernicious Silencing of the Adjunct Faculty." *Chronicle of Higher Education*, 30 October 2017. https://www.chronicle.com /article/the-pernicious-silencing-of-the-adjunct-faculty/.

Trenerry, Brigid, and Yin Paradies. 2012. "Organizational Assessment: An Overlooked Approach to Managing Diversity and Addressing Racism in the Workplace." *Journal of Diversity Management* 7 (1): 11–26. https://doi.org /10.19030/jdm.v7i1.6932.

United Nations. 1948. *Universal Declaration of Human Rights*. https://www .un.org/en/universal-declaration-human-rights/.

University of British Columbia. 2018. *Shaping UBC's Next Century: Strategic Plan 2018–2028*. https://strategicplan.ubc.ca.

University of Toronto. n.d. "Mission Statement." https://www.utoronto.ca /about-u-of-t/mission.

Yakoboski, Paul J. 2018. *Adjunct Faculty: Who They Are and What Is Their Experience?* New York: TIAA Institute. https://www.tiaainstitute.org /publication/adjunct-faculty-survey-2018.

Yale University. n.d. "Mission Statement." https://www.yale.edu/about-yale /mission-statement.

7 Refusing Diversity in the Militarized Settler Academy

CAROL W.N. FADDA AND DANA M. OLWAN

Diversity and inclusion have become central mantras of the academy. Across the United States and Canada, universities regularly make public commitments to increase the numbers of minoritized faculty and students by altering academic investments and priorities. Such efforts are meant to engage previously ignored or neglected areas of inquiry and to make diversity a central cornerstone of what the academy does at the pedagogical, curricular, faculty, student, and administrative levels. In the context where diversity and inclusion are floated around and adopted as imperatives of the academy, there is a need to record, measure, and assess their success, as well as the ability of the university to adapt to increased demands for their institutionalization. In response to these calls, the university has adopted diversity measures, ensuring that it fulfils its own mandate. In the *Chronicle of Higher Education*, Ben Myers (2016) speaks of a "diversity index" or a measure of ethnic and racial diversity among faculty and students at universities. In another article, a study claims that, when "minorities account for more than 35 per cent of the student body, a campus climate improves" (Berrett 2015). Through such measurements, diversity becomes a goal that enables the university to present itself as being in a constant process of self-reconfiguration and self-assessment. In other words, the university appears to be committed to confronting evidence of class elitism, racial exclusivity, regionalism, and even gender bias that are articulated in its faculty hiring practices, its student body, and even its curricular offerings. And yet, as scholars have shown, such measures do not in and of themselves alter the university landscape. Without attending to the structural inequalities and impediments on which the university is founded, diversity becomes yet another tool that can be used to assert the university's proclaimed commitment to liberatory education.

In this essay, we map the political and pedagogical implications of institutional adoptions of diversity projects in the militarized, neoliberal, and settler university. We argue that the university is currently engaged in remaking projects that allow it to respond to internal calls and pressure for change and reform. Working at the intersections of anti-imperial, anti-racist, and anti-settler-colonial struggles, our analysis traces the shifts that have taken place at our own academic institution, Syracuse University, which, like other US institutions of higher learning, has and continues to embrace methods of inclusion and diversity that are concomitant with a broader directive in higher education to diversify the academy. We address the implications of being at an institution that has garnered top rankings as a veteran-friendly institution, while simultaneously attending to neoliberal expectations to expand the university through internationalization efforts and the development of institutional discourse and practice around the acknowledgment of Indigenous land and peoples. As Sandy Grande (2018) has argued, "historically, the university functioned as the institutional nexus for the capitalist and religious missions of the settler state, mirroring its histories of dispossession, enslavement, exclusion, forced assimilation and integration" (47). Building on critiques such as Grande's, we ground our analysis in a feminist politics that emerges from the recognition of the importance of embodied knowledge and experiences, and their connection to these ongoing legacies of dispossession. We are invested in exploring how, together, these various but intertwined histories shape one's place and view of institutionalized forms of power, with all the tensions and complexities that such positionalities produce.

Some questions that we contend with on a daily basis and that inform our discussion here include the following: How do we engage students in critical knowledges about Arab and Muslim communities in the United States and the Arab world while resisting institutional co-optation? How do we navigate the labour of challenging the violent erasure of our bodies and our work within and outside our institution? In attending to the call of Indigenous scholars and feminists of colour to "be *in* but not *of* the university" (Grande 2018, 49; emphasis in original), how do we develop strategies that confront the academic violences of disappearance and erasure? In asking these questions, we attend to the ways in which diversity has functioned in our institution to fulfil institutionalized understandings of difference and inclusion that primarily serve institutional versions of development, growth, and profit-making. We are committed to examining how the discourses of diversity, its language, and its attendant practices are wielded and how their particular constructions and manifestations reflect dominant institutional interests and investments.

At the heart of our interrogations of the university structure and our place within it lie the conundrums posed by the politics of visibility and the seductive promises of recognition. Academic institutional "recognition" is neither beneficial nor appealing for racialized minorities because it inevitably carries within it the dissolution of critical speech and action in the service of the institution's lucrative well-being, or what Sara Ahmed (2012) refers to as the "'happy diversity' model, in which 'diversity talk' becomes 'happy talk'" (72). In contrast to such "happy talk," centring academic discourse and praxis that interrogate power differentials and asserting multiple forms of knowledge becomes even more urgent in the regulatory and disciplinary space of the US academy, which ultimately bolsters whiteness and the settler colonial state.

In the work below, we point out how the shifting maps of diversity have been drawn up recently at our current institution in order to reflect on how knowledge production is controlled through the compartmentalization of racialized and minoritized bodies that inhabit the university. We examine three main siloed constructions/definitions of institutional diversity pertaining to Indigeneity, internationalization, and militarization. In doing so, we do not seek to underplay the complex and overlapping ways in which these distinct but intertwined aspects of institutionalized diversity operate. Moreover, this analysis does not provide cures or solutions for the institutional violences on which the settler university is predicated. Rather, we hope to show how the university approaches diversity in a specific way that serves to sever, conceal, or override connections between these strands. We argue that this approach to diversity is part and parcel of the logics of institutional containment and control that characterize the "neoliberal restructuring of the university" that occurs in US institutions of higher learning (Chatterjee and Maira 2014, 12). Such containment and control serve to facilitate and dictate the institution's economic survival, which, as Chatterjee and Maira note, is often predicated on "the profitable business of militarism, incarceration, and war" (12). This chapter thus charts some of these siloed constructions of diversity as enacted at our institution, reflecting on our positioning within and against these practices. We offer this analysis as an act of solidarity with each other and those who dissent within our institution and the broader academic community, and "challenge the dominant codes of belonging and citizenship within the academic nation" (Chatterjee and Maira 2014, 11).

A Note on Positionality

In this chapter, we focus our analysis on Syracuse University because it is where we are currently employed and where we teach and do research. In addition to being shaped by the lived experiences on which we base this analysis, we choose to focus on Syracuse University because we recognize how this institution encapsulates the shifting landscapes of higher education that this chapter, and this edited collection as a whole, engages and seeks to problematize. With the quickly accelerating adjunctification of labour and un/employment in the corporate university (shouldered by and large by faculty from racialized and working-class backgrounds), coupled with an increasing investment in "happy [diversity] talk" (Ahmed 2012, 72), we recognize how our current positions bring with them the responsibility of having to consistently and constantly foreground the complex workings of the nation-state and the racial, capitalist, and colonialist politics constituting the axes of the settler colonial university.

As Indigenous scholars and feminists of colour have pointed out repeatedly, the act of institutionally recognizing racialized and marginalized bodies in the service of so-called diverse and inclusive university environments reasserts the power and colonial hegemony of such institutions. In these spaces, the institutional act of recognizing and naming marginalized bodies becomes a selective form of provisional, arbitrary, and precarious inclusion. Sandy Grande, citing the work of Audra Simpson, Glen Coulthard, and others, shows how "CIS [critical Indigenous studies] scholars argue that 'recognition' – as an equal right, a fiduciary obligation, a form of acknowledgement – functions as a technology of the state by which it maintains its power (as a sole arbiter of recognition) and, thus, settler colonial relations" (Grande 2018, 49–50). With "the academy [serving] as *an arm of the settler state* – a site where the logics of elimination, capital accumulation, and dispossession are reconstituted" (47; emphasis in original), the politics of recognition as enacted by the academy and the acts of racial, ethnic, and national performances that it demands undercut the potentials of institutional critique and dissent. Sara Ahmed (2012) also discusses this integral link between the nation and the academy in *On Being Included*, stating: "Inclusion could be read as a technology of governance: not only as a way of bringing those who have been recognized as strangers into the nation, but also of making strangers into subjects, those who in being included are also willing to consent to the terms of inclusion" (163).

With their goal of legitimizing the university and ensuring its relevancy and perfunctory attendance to multicultural discourses, institutionalized diversity projects necessitate defining and regulating the bodies and roles of racialized and minoritized individuals who inhabit institutional spaces. In other words, the student, faculty, staff, or administrative body of a university is expected to adhere to a shared institutional definition of diversity in order to be recognized as diverse. This definition is not stagnant, however, as it is constantly revisited to ensure institutional saliency in light of shifting national and global political climates, capitalist flows, and, in some cases, student activism. As this chapter will show, the university's definition of diversity changes over time, and those alterations can be read as signposts for evolving or newly emergent institutional interests and alliances. The purported visibility that diversity projects emphasize and the optics of recognition attached to them are not only limited in scope and depth but are premised and contingent on the invisibility and disappearance of othered bodies or "strangers" that do not easily correspond to or fit in the carefully constructed compartments of institutional difference, which are made to align with US binarist racial logics.

As Arab women born and raised in the Arab world, our experiences of US imperial hegemony and its effects on national and transnational politics, global economies, and the day-to-day lives of Arab peoples directly shape our encounters with such hegemony as it is embodied, replicated, and modeled by US academic institutions. Both of us arrived in the United States as adults in pursuit of higher education opportunities in the field of literary studies, having grown up in the Middle East and experienced and understood the effects of US empire and its devastating role in the region we call home across multiple decades and sites. Growing up in Lebanon during the Lebanese War and its aftermath was integral to Carol's understanding of the effect of US empire in material and immediate ways, not only in Lebanon but in the Arab region as a whole. This exposure was shaped by both the hawkish practices of US foreign policy and the seemingly benign global reach of US popular culture, both of which underscored for Carol the complex and powerful role that the United States plays internationally in shaping people's lives – even those who are geographically situated outside of its physical borders. As a Palestinian who was born and raised in the Gulf state of Kuwait, Dana's understanding of the direct effects of US hegemony in the region and their connections to longer histories of Palestinian dispossession was directly impacted by the events that preceded and followed the 1990 Gulf War. Forced to relocate to Jordan from Kuwait, Dana's lived experience of the war planted the seeds for a critical perspective of US military intervention projects that are disguised as liberatory missions abroad. This distrust of US national narratives of benevolence and good will continue to characterize our relationships and positions within the United States, with our new and unfamiliar environments pushing us to reflect on that from a position of consciousness and estrangement.

In other words, while we both understood in our own ways how the United States operated outside of its borders and how the policies it formulated became enacted elsewhere, we would later learn through grounded experiences how this formation is internally organized and how it would seek to interpellate and/or expel us at different historical conjunctures. Having arrived in the United States shortly before 9/11, we both had to immediately negotiate a US landscape in which anti-Arab and anti-Muslim sentiments were rampant and ubiquitous. As international graduate students, we were already negotiating our own status as Arab women within our departments, cohorts, and chosen academic programs. These negotiations became amplified by the recognition that our estrangement within the United States is intimately connected to the experiences of other racial minorities in the US context. The events that occurred on 11 September 2001 and its aftermath indelibly shaped how we understood the connections between the racialization of Arabs and Muslims in the United States and US imperial projects abroad. In saying this, we do not mean to suggest that this event was a start or end point for the difficult negotiations of our dislocations in the US racial landscape. Instead, 9/11, for one, rendered visible continuities and disjunctures between and among people of colour in the United States and Canada that existed long before its occurrence.

These constant negotiations continued into our postgraduate careers, which included bouts of economic uncertainty and precarity endemic to both immigrant and academic life. Both of us have negotiated multiple moves (across the United States and, in Dana's case, Canada) in pursuit of academic employment opportunities, which, for each of us, were often contingent and precarious. During this time, we encountered the US and Canadian immigration systems in an effort to become permanent residents in these nation-states, while fully recognizing how some immigrants are often drawn into multicultural projects of settler colonial states at the expense of Indigenous communities, Black people, racial minorities, and migrants. Our understanding of the workings of power inside and outside the racialized academy is informed, individually and collectively, by these experiences and negotiations, which remain ongoing.

At Syracuse University, Arab women of colour are repeatedly and consistently unrecognized as faculty of colour, as the university systematically adheres to the US Census categorization of Middle Eastern peoples as white. This classification leaves no room for self-identification that can lay bare the limits of constructed racial categories that historically render citizenship contingent on whiteness. Based on US Census categorizations, Arabs are automatically placed in the racial category of white, concealing long histories of discrimination and racialization that well precede 9/11. As Arab American scholars have shown, the classification of Arabs as white emerges from a history of legal exclusion enshrined in US state and citizenship law; in particular, the Naturalization Act of 1790 rendered access to citizenship contingent on whiteness, leading to a slew of what is referred to as prerequisite cases from the early 1900s onwards whereby Arabs went to court to assert their legal whiteness as a way to access US citizenship. Nevertheless, this white categorization has been contested by Arab Americans from around the mid-twentieth century onwards, with various organizations and lobbyists calling for Arab Americans to be recognized as a racial minority in the United States. More recently, the push to create a specific Middle East and North Africa (MENA) ethnic designation on the Census has been overturned by the Trump administration, but Arab Americans continue to fight against the erasures and omissions produced by official US racial categorizations, especially in light of the alarming and increased levels of anti-Arab, anti-immigrant, and Islamophobic sentiments that precede the current political moment.[1]

Our institution's practice of replicating national racial classifications that are based on the Census categorizations problematically inheres Arabs as white. This practice becomes even more troubling given that we are constantly being called on by administrators and colleagues to provide labour and service to fulfil institutional diversity requirements, including serving on search committees, standing committees, and carrying out curricular service. Upon being called to perform this institutional service, our initial impulse was to correct such nonrecognition and erasure, which inevitably requires significant amounts of time and effort, including writing detailed emails to administrators, following up with HR, providing historical and political contexts, and making ourselves available for additional clarification. In other words, the price of potential recognition is additional labour: the work of teaching the institution how to better comprehend diversity and how to further incorporate it into its norms and definitions. We have nevertheless become increasingly attuned to the ways in which this corrective impulse serves to further our own exclusions. By reading the scholarship of other feminists of colour and their critiques of the settler academy, we become cognizant of the fact that this corrective impulse and the recognition it seeks can "function as a technology of the state [and in turn the institution] by which it maintains its power" (Grande 2018, 47).

Corrective approaches problematically move us into the realm of mis-recognition, given the limited and exclusionary axes of racial, national, gender, ethnic, and religious difference that inform institutional diversity. We simply do not fit in or adhere to these axes: therefore, we remain misrecognized. Heeding Robin Kelley's (2016) warning about the pitfalls and dangers of "seek[ing] love from an institution incapable of loving" and following the work of scholars like Sara Ahmed who trouble the politics of institutional belonging, we seek to base our survival within the academy on radical feminist forms of love that hold dissent, non-acquiescent self-representation, and interrogative solidarities and alliances at their centre. We do so, however, with a full critical understanding of the evolving landscapes and maps of inclusion and diversity that the institution constantly draws and redraws to ensure its survival in a corporatized system of higher education contingent on high student enrolment, branding enterprises, and college rankings. Our approach in the institution, and in this chapter, is thus to refuse to engage corrective politics of recognition and invest instead in practices that enable us and others to name ourselves and our experiences on our own terms.

In October 2015, in light of the previous year's THE General Body's student-organized and student-led sit-in demanding that the university administration attend to a host of concerns regarding diversity and transparency on campus,[2] the Chancellor's Workgroup on Diversity and Inclusion was established, made up of faculty, administrators, staff, and student members. The charge given to this workgroup was "to develop solutions on how to further create a more diverse and inclusive climate at the University" (Syracuse University News 2015). In March 2016, the workgroup issued a final report on its discussions and findings, including sections defining diversity and inclusion on campus, and offered thirty-three recommendations for the implementation of short-term and long-term diversity and inclusion measures (Chancellor's Workgroup 2016). The report defines diversity "as the presence and/or representation of the individual and group differences that make us unique. Diversity is not always noticeable and can be invisible ... [In]clusion [is defined] as the deliberate and ongoing act of creating and maintaining systems, practices, and spaces that respect individual and group differences and that systematically address broader issues of discrimination, oppression, and exclusion" (1). Most notably, these differences are outlined as revolving around "experiences regarding race and ethnicity, gender and sexual orientation, internationalization, religious identity, military status, (dis)abilities, and other intersecting identities" (1–2). The language of the report frames diversity as difference in identities/cultures, emphasizing an investment in establishing a welcoming, respectful, and safe environment accessible to all through the removal of structural barriers. The labour that went into compiling the information and crafting the recommendations included in the report should not go unacknowledged, especially given that several of its members belong to minoritized and vulnerable communities. Changing or challenging institutional structures, however, necessitates acknowledging and centring power differentials, not simply expanding institutional grammar to accommodate more inclusionary notions of identity and difference. To their credit, the authors of the report link their recommendations to "systemic issues in higher education, as well as those specific to our campus" (2). However, the report is shaped by a diversity language and politics premised on the logics of inclusion, recognition, and belonging that the institution embraces and celebrates. For us, the question is not about shifting institutional diversity language in order to allow it to include and accommodate more diverse bodies. Rather, we are invested in interrogating how this diversity language – and its institutionalized reviews and revisions – upholds the hierarchical and bureaucratic power structures on which the university remains founded.

Diversity Work and the Politics of Indigenous Recognition

Academic institutions such as Syracuse University have adopted a language of diversity that purports to acknowledge the university's own links to histories of discrimination, marginalization, and violence. One such instance where this link becomes particularly visible is the turn towards Indigenous inclusion, land recognition, and acknowledgment. At Syracuse University, recognition of settler colonial histories takes a variety of material, discursive, and visual forms. For example, in a successful and highly important university initiative called the "Haudenosaunee Promise," the university has developed a unique scholarship program that provides Indigenous students from the Six Nations with funding opportunities that cover the costs of tuition and room and board for the duration of their bachelor's degree. This program was started in 2006 under the leadership of former chancellor Nancy Cantor "to strengthen the relationship between the Haudenosaunee nations and the university," and it has been lauded by Indigenous groups for its role in creating "friendship between the university and the Haudenosaunee, which includes the Mohawk, Oneida, Onondaga, Cayuga, Seneca and Tuscarora nations" (Buckshot 2010). In a campus where the cost of attendance exceeds US$60,000 per year, this initiative is significant and has played an essential role in increasing Indigenous student enrolment at the university at both undergraduate and graduate levels.

Following on the success of this program and its importance for building Indigenous and campus alliances at the material level, the university has renewed its commitment to the program under its new and current leadership. In addition to work on recruiting Indigenous students into the student body and increasing Indigenous student enrolment, the university has extended its practices of inclusion through the adoption of discourse that specifically addresses the university's location on Indigenous lands. In official university discourse and at public and ceremonial events, the university now explicitly pays tribute to the Onondaga Nation on whose ancestral lands the campus exists. Land acknowledgments are visible on most parts of the university's official website and on some departmental sites as well, linking discursive land acknowledgments in the real and virtual worlds. This discursive inclusionary turn has been accompanied with visual signposts of recognition and inclusion such as the flying of the Haudenosaunee flag in major campus locations. Notwithstanding the university's continued support for the "Haudenosaunee Promise" program, Indigenous inclusion on campus has been symbolic and performative, deepening the university's claims to diversity and facilitating its multicultural agendas.

Practices of acknowledgment and recognition of Indigenous lands and peoples such as the ones adopted by Syracuse University highlight how corporatized, privatized, and militarized university campuses in the United States have sought to attend to and reconcile with their settler colonial ongoing and past histories. While land acknowledgment has a long history in Canada and has become a ubiquitous practice on Canadian university campuses and beyond, it is by and large a newly adopted phenomenon in the context of US institutions of higher learning. Due to the limited uptake of this practice, the US Department of Arts and Culture (n.d.) has called on organizations and individuals to adopt the practice of Indigenous land recognition. Its website states: "Acknowledgment is a simple, powerful way of showing respect and a step toward correcting the stories and practices that erase Indigenous people's history and culture and toward inviting and honoring the truth." Importantly, this call is accompanied with the recognition that land acknowledgments are small – but significant – gestures that can become more "meaningful when coupled with authentic relationship and informed action." Framed as a positive step towards greater understanding, recognition is also understood as a tool to better comprehend Indigenous sovereignty and rights, and thus pave the way "toward equitable relationship and reconciliation."

While we do not doubt or underestimate the importance of land acknowledgments and the necessity of institutional programs that support education opportunities for Indigenous communities, we are wary of the widespread, and oftentimes depoliticized, adoption of such practices by university institutions in the settler colonial state. Specifically, we are concerned that these performative recognitions and inclusions are not always accompanied by alliance work that seeks to trouble or undo the logics or material practices on which the settler university remains founded. In his work on the politics of recognition and reconciliation, Glen Coulthard (2014) has shown how recognition is often underpinned by "models of liberal pluralism" that are ill equipped to confront the structural and economic foundations of coloniality (6). Similarly, Penelope Edmonds (2016) has argued that reconciliation, which works in tandem with recognition, "has become part of an international lexicon and a prominent feature of late liberal modernity" (13). Both scholars have placed the turn towards recognition and reconciliation in settler states within a particular historical conjuncture structurally built on the removal and disappearance of the Indigenous. Edmonds goes on to explain how reconciliation, which emanates from utopic impulses and gestures, may in fact "be coercive and repressive" (5).

In an article that explores the pedagogical limits of settler territorial acknowledgments in Canada, Lila Asher, Joe Curnow, and Amil Davis (2018) argue that such practices perform "pedagogical interventions" that intend to simultaneously resist Indigenous erasure and unsettle settlers (319). They are performances intended to evoke the fact of settler colonialism as an ongoing structure and not a past event. And yet, as the authors discussed here make clear, these gestures, when performed regularly, can also become "normalized and rote," thus losing their political significance and power (322). Given this context, it is not surprising that scholars have sought to critically examine the politics of Indigenous recognition and land acknowledgments and the role they can play in shaping Indigenous futurities. Although Indigenous inclusion has not yet been routinized in the US context in the ways which Asher and colleagues see at work in Canada, the problematic politics they and Indigenous scholars such as Coulthard lay bare is already at work in the newly adopted university discourse surrounding Indigenous recognition and inclusion.

Take, for example, the welcome remarks prepared by Chancellor Syverud (2016) in his address to Indigenous students at the Nya wenha Skä•noñh Center. In his speech, Syverud honoured the presence of Indigenous students and their families at the Syracuse campus and provided a long list of university contributions towards recognizing and solidifying the university's "association with Native American students and participation with our Haudenosaunee neighbors." Configured as neighbours who engage in mutual relations, the chancellor also recognized "the deep bond" that exists between the campus and its Indigenous neighbours due to "the fact that the University sits on the ancestral homelands of the Onondaga Nation." In this acknowledgment of fact, the friendly language of bonds and associations serves to conceal the asymmetries of power that structure the relationship of the settler academy to the Indigenous people on whose lands it continues to exist, thrive, and prosper. Posed as a generous and benevolent leader of an institution committed to engaging Indigenous peoples by inviting them to be part of the institution, the chancellor celebrates university-led initiatives for their ability to contribute to programmatic diversity. As Syverud states, "the diversity that these programs bring to the campus makes the entire University a better place. A diversity of perspectives – shaped by different life experiences, cultures, and belief systems – is essential to academic excellence." In turning Indigenous inclusion into a diversity gain, Syverud renders apparent the university's investment in such measures: they are here intended to assist the university in achieving its goal of "academic excellence," a goal that is intimately tied to an extractive logic rooted in profit and profit-making educational models.

Internationalization and the Logics of Profit-Making

Nowhere is the university's profit-making model more fully on display than in its growing internationalization and globalization policies and practices. As scholars have shown, internationalization is now part and parcel of most – if not all – institutions of higher education in the United States and in other settler states such as Canada and Australia. In its 2017 report on internationalization in the US academy, the American Council on Education (ACE) showed how "internationalization continues to gain momentum among U.S. colleges and universities" at a rate that is significantly higher than what was previously reported in 2011 (ACE 2017, 5). The organization releases reports on the status of academic internationalization every five years, basing its findings on surveys submitted to the organization by US institutions of higher education. As the report shows, "a sizeable proportion of U.S. colleges and universities have articulated a commitment to internationalization through their mission statements and/or strategic plans" (7). This commitment has not always been matched with financial support for internationalization efforts, but as the report finds, US universities are becoming more willing to provide administrative support in the fulfilment of this goal. In mapping the state of internationalization in the US academy, the report also investigates the reasons behind this growing trend across university campuses. The report finds that university respondents had a number of reasons for adopting an internationalized agenda. Some universities indicated that improving students' readiness for a globalized world is one of the main reasons for their adoption of internationalizing agendas. Universities placed diversifying their student and faculty bodies as a second reason for their efforts. The third driver for universities' investment in an internationalized campus is the ability to draw international students, and the fourth is "revenue generation." As the report shows, the articulation of revenue as a reason for the widespread embrace of internationalization reflects an "increased (or at least more overt) focus on this as a goal" (5). Although the report notes that revenue generation has become a more explicit goal of internationalization efforts on campuses or one that universities are more willing to acknowledge, it does not establish a direct link between the impulse to attract international students from specific and predominantly resource-rich economies to US campuses and the desire for increased financial revenue.

While universities have successfully represented their interest in internationalization as driven by academic and curricular investments rather than financial concerns, current findings indicate that the US university campus in particular and the US economy at large have benefitted to a great degree from internationalization efforts. In findings published by NAFSA: Association of International Educators, the organization notes "that the more than one million international students studying at U.S. colleges and universities contributed $39 billion to the U.S. economy and supported more than 455,622 jobs during the 2017–2018 academic year" (NAFSA 2018). The numbers are based on a state by state and congressional district analysis of revenue generated by international students and their families to the US economy. NAFSA's information does not reduce international students to their monetary and economic value, but notes the "immeasurable academic, security and cultural value these students bring" to our campuses and local communities. This nod to the "immeasurable" but never clearly stated contributions of international students to diversifying the academic culture of US institutions is reflected in Syracuse University's strategic plan on internationalization. Titled "Internationalization: Enter the Campus, Engage the World," the plan states its goal to "enhance and expand institutional mechanisms to better cultivate, welcome, support, and value the contributions of our international student community, facilitate cross-cultural interaction, and advance cultural understanding" (Syracuse University 2015b). While this feel-good language promotes a welcoming and supportive environment in which international students appear to be valued, nowhere are their contributions to campus life, research, and teaching ever enumerated. Instead, international students are inherently assumed to facilitate cross-cultural interactions and understanding simply by virtue of the international student status on which they are admitted to the US university campus; in other words, it is their physical presence on campus that indexes diversity. Syracuse University (SU) is home to at least 4,000 international students from over 49 countries, with the largest representation of international students being from China, South Korea, and India. These students help the university increase its revenue and fulfil its stated diversity goals. Unsurprisingly, in language about international students, the university often represents internationalization as an essential and always positive goal for the receiving US academic institution. What disappears from view are the material, linguistic, and cultural difficulties and the structural barriers of entry and later integration into the US university campus for international students, barriers that are repeatedly underplayed, concealed, and even ignored in the university's push to diversify and internationalize its student body and academic standing. Here it is also important to note that the lumping of people from racially and nationally diverse backgrounds under the broad and non-specific category of the "international" serves to further distance such communities from minoritized peoples in the United States, including Indigenous, Black, and people of colour communities. In other words, the internationalization of the campus enshrines a binaristic understanding of difference that continually unbinds the global from the local in a way that leaves no room for our overlapping emplacements and serves to undercut potential solidarities between and among people of colour, Black, and Indigenous communities inside and outside of the United States.

In promoting its engagement with the world, university discourse often emphasizes the opportunities opened up to "local" or US students through international and global engagement that takes place outside of the university campus. Steeped in the language of international travel and global discovery, the university's approach to internationalization is often two pronged: On the one hand, under the banner of enhanced cultural diversity, it seeks to increase international student enrolment, bringing the world to the US university campus. On the other hand, it seeks to open and make available study abroad opportunities for students that allow them to explore worlds located outside of the US borders. It thus invites SU students to travel to other countries and immerse themselves in other cultures, which are here posited as different from US culture. In both cases, what disappears from view are the historical conditions that construct the boundaries between what is local and what is global and conceal the uneven ways in which ideas, goods, and peoples traffic and are trafficked between them. As Alissa Trotz (2007) has argued, the push towards campus and curricular diversifications and inclusions under the banner of global engagement "poses considerable challenges in re-narrativizing glo-balization's trajectories to render visible historical encounters that are productive of difference and hierarchy" (1). Trotz's work critiques this embrace, forcefully bringing into view "the amnesia that is required or the particular kinds of histories that must be narrated in order to sus-tain globalization as innocent or recent" (8). Rather than offer a celebra-tory and optimistic view of the global, Trotz's sober analysis reminds us that world engagement has "magnified inequality and displacement to staggering proportions" (14).

With this critical approach in mind, how can we read our own involvement in setting up and running a study abroad program dedi-cated to the study of women and gender in the Arab world, which we first taught in the summer of 2015? How can we understand our own invitation of Syracuse students to our homeland(s) and our curricular efforts to internationalize our curriculum? To address these questions, we begin by providing a brief map of global/international curricular offerings at our campus and the US politics that undergird their exis-tence. At SU, international programs are managed by a study abroad office, Syracuse Abroad, dedicated to helping students "prepare for the world *in the world* with invaluable internships, Signature Seminars, language study at all levels, homestays, field research, and commu-nity engagement projects" (Syracuse Abroad, n.d.; emphasis in origi-nal). The international study abroad program at Syracuse University is highly successful and was ranked "#7 in Study Abroad on US News & World Report." In addition to regularly providing courses in the uni-versity's seven international centres, Syracuse Abroad also offers more than 100 short-term study abroad programs in 60 countries. Among these programs are a few based in the Middle East and North Africa, including destinations such as Morocco, the United Arab Emirates,

Jordan, and Israel. The study abroad program sponsors different types of study abroad opportunities and facilitates students' ability to "direct enrol" in partner institutions in the region such as the University of Tel Aviv. The investment in providing study abroad learning opportunities in Israel is also extended through short-term, faculty-led seminars dedicated to the study of democracy, terrorism, and security – areas of inquiry that neatly converge with the national security agenda and foreign policy goals of the United States.

Militarizing the Academy

The overlap between globalized curricular offerings and the international destinations in which they are based has a longer history, one that is rooted in federal legislation developed in the late 1950s to allow students to pursue educational opportunities abroad that help meet "national security needs" of the United States as a rising global world power and that neatly relegate knowledge to area studies (Lane-Toomey 2014, 121). This process of dividing knowledge between the United States and areas of the world serves to "[locate] the object of its inquiry 'elsewhere'" and thus contributes to the construction of the Middle East as simultaneously marginal and exceptional to the United States (Shohat 2002, 4). As these curricular offerings suggest, study abroad programs are part and parcel of how the settler academy produces global "area studies" knowledge about the Middle East that serves to further the militarized and securitized interests of the US nation-state.

It is important here to note that the US Campaign for the Academic and Cultural Boycott of Israel (USACBI) has specifically called faculty and students to boycott study abroad programs in Israel, linking their reproduction of settler colonial practices that violate Palestinian rights to education and academic freedom with their potential violation of "the rights of US faculty and students and our campus non-discrimination and equal opportunity policies" (USACBI 2018). In an article outlining Syracuse University's role in normalizing Israeli settler colonialism through study abroad programs, the Syracuse-based Palestine Solidarity Collective (2015) notes that "the description of Israel on the study abroad program website fails to acknowledge the ongoing genocide of Palestinian people upon which the state is built and the fact that Palestinians, who already inhabited the land which was being settled, were violently and forcibly removed." Such erasures are, of course, part and parcel of larger US national and transnational discourses that are replicated and embraced on the university level in the service of the settler colonial state.

Our own involvement in the study abroad program at SU (as well as our curricular offerings as a whole) highlights the conundrums, pitfalls, as well as the revisionary possibilities of contending with the globalized and militarized university. It brings us back to Grande's question about how to "be *in* but not *of* the university" (Grande 2018, 49). That is, it compels us to insist on the production of complex knowledges about our communities (and the transnational spaces to which we are intimately connected) from within our US institutional location and in our classes, but in ways that do not cohere with the logics and aims of the settler colonial university. We hoped, in other words, to launch a course that takes up the challenge to "reimagine the study of regions in a way that transcends the ghettoization typical of traditional area studies," especially those that are replicated in gender studies curriculum about women from other and othered places (Shohat 2002, 13). With these concerns and investments in mind, we launched in summer 2015 a study abroad course titled "Global Perspectives, Local Contexts: Women and Gender in the Arab World," which took place in Lebanon and Jordan.

In addition to familiarizing students with some of the major literary, cultural, and sociological texts and trends in the fields of gender studies and feminist Middle East studies, this course was geared towards connecting students with scholars and activists located in the Lebanese and Jordanian contexts working on the ground on issues related to gendered and sexualized identities, human rights discourses, and feminist mobilizations. None of the students (except for one Turkish graduate student) had ever been to the Middle East before, so we had to address from the get-go the kinds of knowledges about Arabs and Muslims that shaped their interest in the course itself and in travelling to the Arab world more generally. Foregrounding our vision for the course was a critical feminist approach that clearly outlines and simultaneously rejects the workings of academic tourism and the fraught implications of US-based students (who have not had much prior exposure to Arab cultures) parachuting into these countries for short-term courses. Rather than seeking to present students with prepackaged sets of knowledges about the course topics and the Arab locations we were in, the main impetus of the course was geared towards having students question and critique hegemonic Western knowledge constructions about the Arab world. With that came an emphasis on the local, in all its complexities, in developing questions about *how* we know rather than merely *what* we know.

That experience was a transformative one for us as teachers as well as for the students who were able to join us on this costly curricular inquiry. Several of them ended up returning to the Arab world to study or work, to hopefully build on the key questions of "how we know" that formed the basis of our study abroad course. While we recognize that the course had reached some of our students in unexpected and important ways, transforming their views of the MENA region and their relationship to it, we also acknowledge that this experience cannot be untied from the larger efforts of the curriculum of globalized diversity that the university promotes or its larger goals of revenue and profit-making. In spite of our best intentions to broaden our students' worlds in ways that acknowledge the hierarchies of power that allow them access to our homelands in the first place, we also recognize that our course is implicated in many of the problematics outlined and critiqued in our work here – a fact that cannot be reconciled, as it is sustained by our being *in* but not entirely *of* the academy or by the various ways in which people and disciplines become paradoxically entangled in policies and practices that enable "profit-making and value-making projects" central to the academy (Agathangelou et al. 2015, 161).

The conundrums of being implicated in, while at the same time resisting, the production of globalized knowledges are not restricted to our study abroad course, but shape in integral ways the courses that we teach on the SU campus and our own presence as Arab women who teach in this highly militarized academic institution. Our courses span topics in Middle Eastern gender studies, critical race and ethnic studies, constructions of genders and sexualities in the "War on Terror," transnational feminisms, as well as Arab and Muslim cultural production in US and transnational contexts. At the core of these courses lies a shared pedagogical commitment to anti-racist, anti-imperial, and anti-Orientalist frameworks, as well as to the critique of hegemonic knowledge productions that serve the university's diversity goals and imperatives. The anti-imperial scholarship that we use in our classes takes up in immediate and direct ways a critique of the long histories of US imperial wars in the Arab world and the seemingly benevolent discourse used to justify violent interventions by placing them in longer and comparative histories of analysis and critique of empire, war, and militarism in the region and beyond it. Such pedagogical investments further accentuate the precarity of our positionalities within the US academy, and Syracuse University specifically, given how the institution has been quickly developing a blatantly militarized agenda that impacts our critical scholarship and pedagogical work, especially work that challenges US settler colonialism at home and abroad.

In 2009, the Veterans Resource Center opened at SU's University College, with the mission to provide "support to student-veterans with a personalized set of services from recruitment to degree completion" (Syracuse University News 2009). The center's mission was significantly expanded with the establishment of the Institute for Veteran and Military Families (IVMF) at SU in 2011, in close collaboration with JPMorgan Chase, a founding member of IVMF. IVMF's (n.d.) mission statement underscores its commitment "to advancing the post-service lives of America's service members, veterans and their families." "Supported by a world class advisory board and public and private partners," the statement continues, "our professional staff delivers unique and innovative programs in career, vocations, and entrepreneurship education and training to post 9/11 veterans and active duty military spouses, as well as tailored programs to veterans of all eras." Such institutionalized support of veterans and the military, however, is by no means restricted to the post-9/11 period, but has a long history at SU, dating back to the Second World War.

In 1944, Chancellor Tolley established the post–Second World War "'uniform admission program,' which ensures all military personnel admission to Syracuse upon return from war" (Office of Veteran and Military Affairs, n.d.). This program was followed over the years by the subsequent implementation of several other veteran- and military-focused programs, many of which are sponsored and supported by the US Department of Defense, including the Defense Comptrollership Program (est. in 1952), the Military Photojournalism Program (est. in 1963), and the National Security Studies (est. in 1996), among others. Most notably, the university's 2015 Academic Strategic Plan explicitly spells out an expanded iteration and a recommitment to the university's military investments (Syracuse University 2015a). One result of such an expanded and expansive iteration (with perhaps the highest price tag) is the construction of the National Veterans Resource Center, a 115,000 square foot complex, centrally located on campus, to house the various military-focused offices and programs, including the Institute for Veterans and Military Families, the Office of Veteran and Military Affairs, and the Army and Air Force ROTC programs. The construction of the National Veterans Resource Center was completed in spring 2020, at the estimated cost of $62.5 million (Burke 2018), with the official opening of the center postponed due to Covid-19 health concerns. It is not a surprise then, given such clear and expansive commitments, that SU was named the number one institution among private schools in the *Military Times'* 2019 Best for Vets rankings, and the fourth among all universities (Syracuse University News 2018).

This brick-and-mortar approach to ensuring that the university's militarization is a visible and strong one is carefully conceived and implemented in close tandem with attendant curricular and research plans, a key factor for the full actualization of institutional militarization. Such curricular and research commitments are clearly indicated in SU's Academic Strategic Plan, which states: "We must leverage cross-University academic expertise to develop and enhance interdisciplinary research in critical areas related to veterans, military affairs, and national security" (Syracuse University 2015a). Linking academic research and interdisciplinary expertise to provide services for veterans is a critical goal, for it lays bare the primary way in which the university is no longer merely a hosting space for veterans post-combat. Rather, with the push to foreground research and expertise in "critical areas related to veterans, military affairs, and national security," the university becomes a main actor in developing, facilitating, and enacting US imperial military projects, whereby, as John Armitage (2005) aptly notes, it becomes "a factory that is engaged in the militarization of knowledge" (221). Of course, the cogs of such a "factory" are contingent on funds that not only ensure its smooth running but determine in elemental ways the kinds of militarized knowledges produced in the military academic industrial complex, as well as their purpose. With the bulk of such funding coming from the Pentagon, Henry Giroux (2008) reminds us of "the kind of pressure that the Department of Defense and the war industries can bring to bear on colleges and universities to orient themselves towards a society in which non-militarized knowledge and values play a minor role" (66). Indeed, with the increased militarization of universities across the United States, it is no wonder that the humanities are considered to be in crisis across university campuses, with specific fields (including women's and gender studies, critical race and ethnic studies, for instance) constantly being devalued and facing the threats of amalgamation, absorption, or disappearance, given that they are deemed by administrators to be insufficient revenue generators with little regard to the kinds of critical knowledges developed and taught in these fields. With that in mind, articulating our role as scholars and teachers who contribute to the development of critical and complex readings of US foreign policies and imperial projects while located in the militarized US academy is a crucial and loaded process.

A Conclusion

In this chapter, we have argued that diversity practices at Syracuse University include three seemingly disparate but interconnected methods: internationalization, Indigenization, and militarization. We have sought to show how the university's approach to each of these areas serves to advance the particular institutional goals of survival, expansion, and financial profit. We have shown how each of these aspects function to enshrine diversity as a university gain and how, in the process, the meaning and practices of diversity are altered in order to legitimize the institution's incorporation of difference. It is nevertheless our understanding that the university's diversity practices go well beyond the three aspects that we outline above, for in recent years institutional engagement with issues of diversity has extended to disability, environmentalism, and LGBTQ rights, showcasing yet again the institution's ability to further expand and/or alter the meaning of diversity in ways that guarantee its ideological and material saliency, continuing relevance, positioning, and perhaps most importantly, its resilience. In choosing to focus on three aspects of diversity, we draw attention to the very specific ways in which diversity projects operate in the historical, geographic, and political conjuncture in which we are located. We have argued that these and other incorporations analyzed in this chapter are never innocent and that, even as critics of these practices, we too are often caught within them.

Against this complicated and thorny historical, political, and racial backdrop, and in light of our recognition of the uneasy space that we and other feminists of colour occupy within these institutions, we find ourselves repeatedly coming back to questions that constantly push us to assess our role in relation to the university's evolving diversity projects: How do we situate ourselves as scholars of colour employed in the militarized US settler academy? How does our often paradoxically precarious presence simultaneously disrupt and resist the academy's ability to incorporate and absorb difference? Can such work, ultimately, confront the settler academy without being digested by it? In her work on mapping belonging and unbelonging in academic institutions, as we note earlier, Sara Ahmed (2012) argues that institutional inclusion/incorporation practices often rely on diversity as "a technology of happiness" (153). This practice depends on the use of people of colour as tools or instruments to achieve the institution's purported anti-racist and equality goals under the banner of diversity (153). Ahmed's work points to the problems with such institutional practices, reminding us that "diversity would be institutionalized when it becomes part of what an institution is already doing, when it ceases to cause trouble" (27). Thus, by the end of her book *On Being Included*, she urges that we – those of us who inhabit the university and its diversity practices – need to become what she calls "the cause of obstruction," or "blockage points" (187). While Ahmed's work helps us understand the necessity of obstructing and blocking the workings of institutionalized diversity, it does not offer a singular praxis. Instead, it opens up multiple possibilities for enacting refusals and continuing "to cause trouble." Such possibilities are always contingent upon questions of power and hierarchy: where we are and who we are shape our enactments of our refusals. At times, these refusals may risk coinciding with institutional diversity practices, and they may even come to be co-opted by the institutions we seek to refuse in ways that we cannot anticipate, control, or prevent. There are times, also, when our refusals will clash with the demand for diversity as institutional happiness and where our presence in academic spaces may become inconvenient, threatening, and even unwelcome.

Our practices for dealing with such challenges are always multiple, shifting, and ongoing; they reflect our commitment to refusals at Syracuse University in particular and the academy in general, refusals that nevertheless involve constant negotiations. They demand that we recognize the paradox of being simultaneously empowered and disempowered as Arab academics employed in the militarized settler academy. Such recognition requires continuous and unrelenting labour that allows for the recognition of the shifting contours of the university and its enduring ability to respond, through absorption, to diversity risks and threats. This labour is only possible through the forming of strong, multigenerational, cross-racial, and transnational coalitional work that rejects the seductions of selective inclusion and allows us to enact and envision academic disruptions. These disruptions are shaped by current, past, and ongoing histories of struggle that exist within and well beyond the academy as a singular site of knowledge production.

NOTES

1 For a discussion of US racial categorization of Arabs as white, see Helen Samhan (1999). See also Sarah Gualtieri (2009).
2 The acronym THE stands for transparency, heterogeneity, equality. For information about THE General Body and its main demands, see its website (https://thegeneralbody.org/). Since the writing of this chapter, #NotAgainSU, a protest movement led by Black students at Syracuse University, has called for a range of institutional changes starting in Fall 2019. Such changes include disarming campus police, freezing tuition, and acknowledging the university's role in upholding and perpetuating white supremacy. The Covid-19 pandemic and the ensuing national and global health crises provided the administration with a rationale to indefinitely

defer further negotiations with #NotAgainSU student protesters. For more information, see "NotAgain SU on Twitter (https://twitter.com /notagain_su).

REFERENCES

ACE (American Council on Education). 2017. "Mapping Internationalization on US Campuses: 2017 Edition." Washington, DC: ACE. https://www .acenet.edu/Documents/Mapping-Internationalization-2017.pdf.

Agathangelou, Anna M., Dana M. Olwan, Tamara L. Spira, and Heather M. Turcotte. 2015. "Sexual Divestments from Empire: Women's Studies, Institutional Feelings, and the 'Odious' Machine." *Feminist Formations* 27 (3): 136–67. https://doi.org/10.1353/ff.2016.0003.

Ahmed, Sara. 2012. *On Being Included: Racism and Diversity in Institutional Life.* Durham, NC: Duke University Press.

Armitage, John. 2005. "Beyond Hypermodern Militarized Knowledge Factories." *Review of Education, Pedagogy, and Cultural Studies* 27 (3): 219–39. https://doi.org/10.1080/10714410500228884.

Asher, Lia, Joe Curnow, and Amil Davis. 2018. "The Limits of Settlers' Territorial Acknowledgements." *Journal of Curriculum Inquiry* 48 (3): 316–34. https://doi.org/10.1080/03626784.2018.1468211.

Berrett, Dan. 2015. "Diversity's Elusive Number: Campuses Strive to Achieve 'Critical Mass.'" *Chronicle of Higher Education*, 9 December 2015. https:// www.chronicle.com/article/Diversity-s-Elusive-Number-/234522.

Buckshot, Sarah Moses. 2010. "Inaugural Class of Haudenosaunee Promise Scholars will Graduate from Syracuse University on Sunday." *syracuse.com*, 15 May 2010. https://www.syracuse.com/news/2010/05/inaugural_class _of_haudenosaun.html.

Burke, Michael. 2018. "Quiet Leader: How a Syracuse University Trustee from Bain Capital Has Influenced Campus-Wide Change." *The Daily Orange*, 26 April 2018. http://dailyorange.com/2018/04/quiet-leader-syracuse -university-trustee-bain-capital-influenced-campus-wide-change/.

Chancellor's Workgroup on Diversity and Inclusion. 2016. "Final Report." Syracuse University, 11 March 2016. https://news.syr.edu/wp-content /uploads/2016/03/Final-Report.pdf.

Chatterjee, Piya, and Sunaina Maira. 2014. "Introduction. The Imperial University: Race, War, and the Nation-State." In *The Imperial University: Academic Repression and Scholarly Dissent*, edited by Sunaina Maira and Piya Chatterjee, 1–50. Minneapolis: University of Minnesota Press.

Coulthard, Glen Sean. 2014. *Red Skin, White Masks: Rejecting the Colonial Politics of Recognition.* Minneapolis: University of Minnesota Press.

Edmonds, Penelope. 2016. *Settler Colonialism and (Re)conciliation: Frontier Violence, Affective Performances, and Imaginative Refoundings*. London: Palgrave MacMillan.

Giroux, Henry. 2008. "The Militarization of US Higher Education after 9/11." *Theory, Culture & Society* 25 (5): 56–82. https://doi.org/10.1177 /0263276408095216.

Grande, Sandy. 2018. "Refusing the University." In *Toward What Justice? Describing Diverse Dreams of Justice in Education*, edited by Eve Tuck and K. Wayne Yang, 47–65. New York: Routledge.

Gualtieri, Sarah. 2009. *Between Arab and White: Race and Ethnicity in the Early Syrian American Diaspora*. Berkeley, CA: University of California Press.

IVMF (Institute for Veterans and Military Families). n.d. "About IVMF: Mission Statement." https://ivmf.syracuse.edu/about-ivmf/.

Kelley, Robin D.G. 2016. "Black Study, Black Struggle." *Boston Review*, 7 March 2016. http://bostonreview.net/forum/robin-d-g-kelley-black-study -black-struggle.

Lane-Toomey, Clara. 2014. "U.S. Government Factors Influencing an Expansion of Study Abroad in the Middle East/North Africa." *Frontiers: The Interdisciplinary Journal of Study Abroad* 24 (1): 121–40. https://doi .org/10.36366/frontiers.v24i1.340.

Myers, Ben. 2016. "The Flagship Diversity Divide." *Chronicle of Higher Education*, 5 January 2016. https://www.chronicle.com/article/the -flagship-diversity-divide/.

NAFSA: Association of International Educators. 2018. "New NAFSA Data: International Students Contribute $39 Billion to the U.S. Economy." Press Release, 13 November 2018. https://www.nafsa.org/about/about-nafsa /new-nafsa-data-international-students-contribute-39-billion-us-economy.

Office of Veteran and Military Affairs. n.d. "Timeline of Veteran Programs at Syracuse University." https://veterans.syr.edu/timeline-of-veteran -programs-at-syracuse-university/.

Palestine Solidarity Collective. 2015. "Normalizing the Israeli Occupation of Palestine in Syracuse University." *Syracuse Peace Council Newsletter*, September 2015. https://www.peacecouncil.net/pnl/september -2015-pnl-845/normalizing-the-israeli-occupation-of-palestine-at -syracuse-university.

Samhan, Helen Hatab. 1999. "Not Quite White: Race Classification and the Arab-American Experience." In *Arabs in America: Building a New Future*, edited by Michael W. Suleiman, 209–26. Philadelphia, PA: Temple University Press.

Shohat, Ella. 2002. "Gendered Cartographies of Knowledge: Area Studies, Ethnic Studies, and Postcolonial Studies." *Social Text* 20, no. 3 (72): 67–78. https://doi.org/10.1215/01642472-20-3_72-67.

Syracuse Abroad. n.d. "Imagine the World Differently." https://suabroad
.syr.edu/.

Syracuse University. 2015a. "Syracuse University Academic Strategic
Plan: Commitment to Veterans." https://asp.syr.edu/the-plan
/commitment-to-veterans-military-connected-communities/.

Syracuse University. 2015b. "Syracuse University Academic Strategic Plan:
Internationalization: Enter the Campus, Engage with the World."
https://asp.syr.edu/the-plan/internationalization/.

Syracuse University News. 2009. "SU Establishes Veterans' Resource Center
to Better Serve Student-Veterans; New Website Launched." *Syracuse
University News: Campus & Community*, 27 August 2009. https://news.syr
.edu/blog/2009/08/27/su-establishes-veterans-resource-center-to-better
-serve-student-veterans-new-website-launched-2/.

Syracuse University News. 2015. "Chancellor's Diversity and Inclusion
Workgroup Members Announced." *Syracuse University News: Campus &
Community*, 16 October 2015. https://news.syr.edu/blog/2015/10/16
/chancellors-diversity-and-inclusion-workgroup-members
-announced-38000/.

Syracuse University News. 2018. "Military Times Names Syracuse No. 1
Private Institution on 2019 Best Colleges for Vets list. *Syracuse University
News: Veterans*, 23 October 2018. https://news.syr.edu/blog/2018/10/23
/military-times-names-syracuse-no-1-private-institution-on-2019-best
-colleges-for-vets-list/.

Syverud, Kent. 2016. "Remarks by Chancellor Syverud at the Nya wenha
Ska:nonh Welcome Luncheon." Syracuse University, 22 August 2016.
https://chancellor.syr.edu/wp-content/uploads/2017/05/Nya-wenha
-Skanonh-Welcome-Luncheon-August-22-2016-1.pdf.

Trotz, Alissa. 2007. "Going Global? Transnationality, Women/Gender Studies
and Lessons from the Caribbean." *Caribbean Review of Gender Studies*
1 (April): 1–18. https://sta.uwi.edu/crgs/april2007/index.asp.

USACBI (US Campaign for the Academic and Cultural Boycott of Israel). 2018.
"We Will Not Study in Israel until Palestinians Can Return: Boycott Study
Abroad in Israel!" https://usacbi.org/2018/03/we-will-not-study-in-israel
-until-palestinians-can-return-boycott-study-abroad-in-israel/.

US Department of Arts and Culture. n.d. "Honor Native Land: A Guide
and Call to Acknowledgment." https://usdac.us/nativeland/.

8 How Canadian Universities Fail Black Non-Binary Students

CICELY BELLE BLAIN

The university is a microcosm for the rest of society, coded by binaries, racism, and inequality. Using the writer's experience at the University of British Columbia (UBC) as a foundation, this chapter will explore the challenges of being Black and non-binary in an institution of higher education.

The university is a site of white privilege in which racialized students need safe spaces to thrive; yet these spaces are challenged, attacked, and underfunded. The university, built on stolen Indigenous land by white colonizers, will always benefit white students and disadvantage racialized communities.

Research suggests that experiences of racism can result in multiple mental health challenges, particularly post-traumatic stress disorder (PTSD)–like symptoms.[1] This finding therefore proves that racialized students are at a profound disadvantage compared to their white counterparts. When the additional intersection of gender is applied to this situation, research shows that female students experience sexism on campus that is a prohibitor to their success, safety, and enjoyment of campus life, a situation particularly well documented through the lens of sexual assault at UBC.[2] However, what is not documented or well researched is the experience of other gender minorities, namely transgender, gender non-conforming, and non-binary students. During the rise of transgender studies in the early twenty-first century, trans identities were yet again folded into a binary narrative (trans women and trans men).[3] But where does this leave those who do not fit into the binary (non-binary, agender, pangender, genderfluid)?

This auto-ethnography will explore the ways in which racial and gender binaries impact the experiences of Black students who identify as non-binary. I attempt to tackle the complexity of accessing Black communities that are perceived as homophobic and transphobic, and then will look at 2SLGBTQIA+ spaces that lack anti-oppressive or decolonial politics.

Terminology

AFAB – assigned female at birth

AMAB – assigned male at birth

cisgender – noting or relating to a person whose gender identity corresponds with that person's biological sex assigned at birth[4]

cisnormativity – the assumption that everyone is cisgender, which normalizes and reinforces the gender binary

femme – commonly associated with a lesbian or queer woman who is feminine in their appearance; however, the term is increasingly used by people of all genders to describe their relationship to femininity. The phrase "women and femmes" is used throughout this chapter to highlight how, regardless of gender, those who present as or are perceived to be more feminine are exposed to greater instances of violence and trauma within patriarchy, whether they exist within the gender binary or not.

FTM – female to male; referring to a transgender man who was assigned female at birth

gender dysphoria – a psychological condition marked by significant emotional distress and impairment in life functioning, caused by a lack of congruence between gender identity and biological sex assigned at birth[5]

gender non-conforming – a state in which a person has physical and behavioural characteristics that do not correspond with those typically associated with the person's assigned or perceived gender

heteronormativity – a system that works to normalize behaviours and societal expectations that are tied to the presumption of heterosexuality and an adherence to a strict gender binary[6] – the presumption that everyone is straight and, furthermore, an enforcement of traditional heterosexual monogamous ideals and gender roles

homonegativity – a term proposed by Hudson and Ricketts in 1980 as a description of a negative attitude towards homosexuality or homosexual people, instead of the term homophobia[7]

microaggressions – everyday verbal, nonverbal, and environmental slights, snubs, or insults, whether intentional or unintentional, which communicate hostile, derogatory, or negative messages to target persons based solely upon their marginalized group membership[8]

MTF – male to female; referring to a transgender woman who was assigned male at birth

non-binary (also written "nonbinary" or "non binary") – for the purposes of this text, a gender identity that signifies not fitting or conforming to the existing societal gender binary (male or female); often used as an umbrella term for other gender non-conforming identities such as genderqueer, agender, genderfluid, genderflux, pangender, demigender, gender non-conforming, or gender variant

transgender – an umbrella word that refers to all the folks who, more or less, do not identify with the genders assigned to them at birth, either wholly or partially[9]

transphobia – discrimination towards people who are trans, transgender, non-binary, or gender non-conforming; may include physical, verbal, psychological, or emotional violence and can appear at an interpersonal or systemic/institutional level

2SLGBTQIA+ – an acronym that stands for two spirit, lesbian, bisexual, transgender, queer, intersex, asexual. The + acknowledges a myriad of gender and sexual identities.

whiteness – "whiteness" as well as "colour" and "Blackness" are essentially social constructs applied to human beings rather than veritable truths that have universal validity. The power of whiteness, however, is manifested by the ways in which racialized whiteness becomes transformed into social, political, economic, and cultural behaviour. White culture, norms, and values in all these areas become normative and natural. They become the standard against which all other cultures, groups, and individuals are measured and usually found to be inferior.[10]

Introduction

The experience of Black non-binary students in the Canadian university is one that, despite being largely undocumented, is generations old. Gender identity and gender expression are concepts that seem "new" in many academic spheres, yet anthropological research indicates that, beyond Eurocentric understandings of gender roles, there are rich histories of gender fluidity. Within the construction of Canadian universities, supremacy of Western ideology, thought, and academia emerged, rendering non-Western language, practice, and tradition as foreign, "other," and inferior. For many Black non-binary individuals, a rejection of Western academia is essential for the reconstruction of our identities. Where, then, does that leave those who are Black and non-binary but exist within the elitist spheres of academia in Canada?

A quick search through academic libraries on research pertaining to non-binary gender identities yields few results and forces the researcher to dodge countless publications about computer science and mathematics. While feminist literature speaks into existence gender non-conformity as it relates to the "female" body, little is documented about gender non-conformity as a means of rejecting or not identifying with being either "man" or "woman." In other words, I perceive that the common understanding of gender non-conformity is an opportunity largely for cisgender women (and occasionally cisgender men) to express themselves in ways that are not typical for their gender. Not conforming to gender has come to mean not conforming to gender roles, particularly at work or in the home. For example, many modern women would describe themselves as gender non-conforming because they work full-time, share chores with their partner, and do handiwork. However, this ideology actually serves to reinforce the gender binary and scripts gender non-conformity into the existing dichotomy. It does not allow for an acknowledgement that there are an infinite number of genders that exist with no relation to "man" or "woman."

In her famous work *Gender Trouble*,[11] Judith Butler unpacks how the feminist movement has historically placed limitations on gender variance by asserting that women are a unified group. This view, she argues, implies that there are things inherent to women that do not exist in other genders and therefore strengthens an already rigid gender binary. Butler is correct in asserting that gender is about expression and performance rather than a reflection of anything core to who we are as humans. Indeed, this ideology is now commonplace in queer theory; gender does not relate to anything innate or biological; rather it is a feeling, it is fluid, and it is expansive.

Although many feminist scholars before Butler fell short of limiting the narrative of feminism to the two traditional genders recognized by mainstream society, many provided cisgender women with the opportunity to dispel traditional stereotypes and roles associated with their gender. Yet, they did not entirely quash the gender binary enough for entirely new non-binary genders to emerge. In many ways, Butler opened this door with her 1990 work.

However, in the past three decades since Butler's visionary work, there has been little improvement in the study of non-binary identities. Why? I surmise it is due to society's angry resistance to undoing their beloved gender binary. From ever-extravagant gender reveal parties to the recent uproar about British retailer John Lewis removing gender markers from children's clothing,[12] it is evident that most of society is not ready to let go of its pink and blue wonderland. In 2016, Susan Cox wrote an article in which she declared that "women coming out as non-binary are throwing other women under the bus."[13] Aside from her wild misunderstanding of what it means to be non-binary, Cox's work seems typical of a white feminist. Feminism has done for her what she needed: she can enjoy privilege in many spheres; the glass ceiling is practically shattered; and being a white, middle-class, heterosexual woman is without much hardship. White feminism has become a contributing factor to the complacency of modern-day feminists towards the plight of women of colour but also towards trans and gender variant communities. Coupled with rampant toxic masculinity upheld by rape culture and heteropatriarchy, cisgender men and women (even those who may perceive themselves as "gender non-conforming") leave no space for non-binary identities to blossom. As Michael Kimmel purports in his work *Guyland,* young white men feel a sense of "thwarted entitlement" as they watch women and minorities claim equal rights and gain freedom from oppression.[14]

Dr. Javid Abdelmoneim recently produced a BBC Two documentary[15] that explored introducing gender neutrality in the lives of young children. While his project did not encompass trans or non-binary identities, he raised many imperative points about the impact of a gender binary on children and their future. When we give children gendered products, particularly clothes with certain slogans on them, we restrict their ability to be gender variant. We encourage them to see themselves within a narrow script that leads to a vulnerable femininity and a toxic masculinity. Young girls in the experiment felt inferior, less intelligent, and obsessed with their appearance, while young boys were aggressive and unable to express their emotions. This experiment proves to me the necessity of undoing the gender binary; for cisgender, transgender, and non-binary communities alike, the gender binary is nothing but restrictive.

When we place a critical race lens on the gender binary, we can clearly see how it has been used as a tool of colonialism, slavery, and oppression in the subjugation of racialized people. In each prominent racial group, there exist tropes and stereotypes based on gender that further criminalize and dehumanize people of colour. For example, as Myra Mendible outlines, "the Latina body" is "hot-blooded, tempestuous, hypersexual, and ... has a big butt."[16] She describes this stereotype as a "convenient fiction," one that is rooted in history, desire, location, politics, and marketing. It reduces Latina women and femmes to a prescribed script within white supremacy. Simultaneously, Latino men are disenfranchised through their perceived relationship to manual labour and criminality. A similar dichotomy takes place in Asian bodies. Asian women and femmes are scripted as docile and subservient, among other tropes, while Asian men are emasculated figures.[17]

I suggest that the gender binary is a sub-tool of white supremacy that creates a schism within racialized communities where whiteness settles itself. Not only does it lead to increased violence towards women of colour, but it also erases and others the experiences of trans and non-binary people of colour. Those who are Black and non-binary exist in a world that not only dehumanizes Blackness but also upholds a restrictive gender binary. In a university setting, this situation forces us to conform, assimilate, and whitewash ourselves while being alienated, harassed, and tokenized.

Blackness within Gendered History

Blackness has been and continues to be scripted through systems of oppression dictated by centuries of white colonial power and enslavement. This situation manifests in present-day rigid gender binaries, particularly those that disproportionately impact how Black communities are perceived and how they interact with one another. Much like the discussed perception of other communities of colour, racial discrimination towards Black people is broken down into subsections based on our relationship to femininity or masculinity. Black women and femmes receive a particular form of violence – as outlined by Moya Bailey in her coining of the term "misogynoir"[18] – that highlights the intersectionality of oppression. Black women and femmes are routinely disenfranchised by a society that is both racist and sexist, while white women are increasingly afforded more privilege and power, regardless of their gender and because of their whiteness. While Black men may experience gender privilege, their Black masculinity renders them dangerous in the white imaginary.

As per Michel Foucault's theory of biopower, society is structured such that some people are folded into life and others into death through government-assisted means of population control.[19] Notably, Achille Mbembe[20] expands on this theory by asking questions about death, and I relate his work to the concept of "body terrorism." Body terrorism, a term coined by the publication *The Body Is Not an Apology*, outlines the war on marginalized populations in its most devastating physical form. From forced sterilization to slavery to sexual harassment to the prison industrial complex, the concept encapsulates the very real and physical impacts of white supremacy.[21] Together, these theories present an understanding of our society that portrays mass incarceration, unemployment, homelessness, sexual violence, discrimination, and injustice as a war on marginalized bodies. These forms of violence are state sanctioned and performed by law enforcement, rendering the most vulnerable and oppressed communities in a state of genocide.

While arguably most predominant and evident in North America, anti-Black violence is a global phenomenon that can be attributed to Eurocentric global dominance and imperialism. What we know as the Atlantic slave trade subsisted on the common agreement of white people that Black people were subhuman and therefore viable as property. Scientific racism served to embolden the disparity between Black and white people. Widely read texts like "Report on Diseases and Physical Peculiarities of the Negro Race"[22] fostered a rampant dehumanization of the Black body.

The gender binary, already well established within a European patriarchal context, became a necessary tool of subjugation within the colonial project of enslavement. Chosen as slaves for their supposed physical strength and lack of civilization, Black Africans were stolen from their homelands and used for three hundred years as a tool for the creation of modern-day capitalism. Within this narrative, male and female slaves were given distinctively different roles, decided upon by white slave owners. These roles and their connotations have led to continued gendered and racialized perceptions of Black people in the present day. As Eric Williams posits in his famous text *Capitalism and Slavery*,[23] while the proletariat were exploited to create wealth for the bourgeoisie, Black bodies were literally the means of production. To cover the land and the domestic sphere, these means required a delineation of gender. As Aliyah I. Abdur-Rahman states, "the vulnerability of all enslaved black persons to nearly every conceivable violation produced a collective 'raped' subjectivity."[24]

The treatment of Black female slaves is well documented; their bodies were used as tools of subjugation and colonialism. Under slavery, Black women were continually assaulted, raped, and violated within a system that gave them no rights or freedom. Against their will, they were used as concubines, reproductive hosts, and objects of pleasure in an overwhelming terrorism of their bodies. Simultaneously, Black women from other parts of Africa were exported to Europe to act as spectacles for a European audience, the most famous given the label "Hottentot Venus."[25] Their curvaceous hips, big bottoms, large breasts, and dark skin were gawked and ogled at by white people. Their bodies were sexualized when they were made to strip naked for onlookers, yet they themselves were devoid of any sexuality within a patriarchal society.

Black men were savage, barbaric, strong, and lascivious. Their carnal desires were a threat to seemingly innocent and pure white women.

Their only purpose was to do physical labour. Thomas A. Foster also brings to light the instances of sexual assault on male slaves. It often took the form of being forced to perform sexual acts on their female counterparts for the pleasure of white onlookers.[26] One slave master is documented as describing this experience as "putting a mare to a horse."[27]

Regarding stereotypes, Elijah G. Ward notes their continuity: "US media stereotypes developed during slavery such as that of the mammy, the jezebel and the wild and hypersexual buck have their latter-day incarnations in the domineering matriarch, the 'welfare queen' and the violent and sexually promiscuous black man."[28]

In 2016, Lena Dunham tweeted her frustration that Black athlete Odell Beckham Jr. paid her no attention at an awards ceremony.[29] Her framing of Beckham as a sexually motivated beast plays into the contemporary narrative of Black men as barbaric and lustful, rooted in centuries of an anti-Black rhetoric. Similarly, the story of Patrice Brown – a fourth grade teacher from Atlanta, Georgia, who was targeted for wearing "inappropriate" and "unprofessional" clothing to teach students[30] – highlights another small piece of the colonial hangover. Brown's body's non-conformity to Western beauty standards renders her oversexualized and objectified, like the "Hottentot Venus."[31] The gender binary continues to be a tool with which white supremacy objectifies, divides, and harms Black bodies.

Blackness and Coming Out

My understanding of Blackness was so tightly scripted through the gender binary that I struggled to find validation for my own gender identity. Much of the exposure I had to non-binary or gender variant communities was white, thin, and androgynous presenting. As a fat, Black, non-binary femme, I struggled with identifying as non-binary. With no access to role models who were non-binary people of colour, I felt pressured to conform to white standards of gender non-conformity. In the same way that white feminism has allowed the misconstruction of gender variance to remain only a form of gender experimentation for cisgender women, white queer communities presented a narrow and exclusive representation of being non-binary.

I grew up believing that queerness (and, although I did not have the language for it, gender variance too) was for white people. I remember a white high school friend coming out as queer in grade ten and me telling her that, if I were gay, I would suppress those feelings in order to live a "normal" heterosexual life. I grew up surrounded by white people, which often caused me to yearn for Black communities and a closer connection to my Black family members. I would learn about queer and trans people through social circles or the media, but every single one was white. The lack of representation of queer and trans people of colour in the media that I consumed was arguably the biggest perpetrator of this misconception. I began to conflate normalcy with heterosexual marriage that, to me, was represented most accurately by Black people who never seemed to stray from that script. From my naïve perspective, Black people seemed to follow a trajectory rooted in simplicity and family. They seemed to live devoid of the complexity of queerness and gender. Whether I wanted that life for myself or not, I accepted very early on that it was my destiny and purpose. In my young imaginary, Black people could not be queer or trans; therefore, I would not even afford myself the curiosity.

While being queer and being transgender are not necessarily the same thing, they are both impacted by the perceived rigidity of the gender binary within society – the idea that there is man and woman and they must copulate. As I discuss my non-binary identity in relationship to my Blackness, I must begin exploring it through the lens of queerness. I was exposed to gay or lesbian identities far before I came to understand gender fluidity or gender variance.

While Black communities are not the most homophobic ethnic group, according to a study by the Public Institute for Religion Research,[32] there are undoubtedly histories of homophobia that took prominence within Black spaces, particularly in the Black church. It can be attributed simply to the fact that "theologically-driven homophobia is reinforced by the anti-homosexual rhetoric of black nationalism."[33] Literal interpretations of the Bible among a minority of Black Christians have led to a criminalization of homosexuality and a rejection of white-dominated biblical revisionism.[34] Some also argue that Black communities may fear or reject sexual experimentation as it is reminiscent of the sexual exploitation and degradation of Black bodies during slavery and thereafter. A final possibility presented by scholar Wesley Crichlow emphasizes the idea of "race survival consciousness" – within the urgency to preserve Black bionationalism, a Black masculinity was upheld against white domination.[35]

My own experiences of Black communities exhibiting homophobia, or at least heteronormativity, seemed to be rooted very strongly in the upholding of the gender binary. As a young queer person, searching for safe spaces on a university campus was challenging yet essential. The University of British Columbia (UBC) is home to over 66,000 students,[36] so being unable to find communities of like-minded or supportive people can leave one feeling isolated and scared. Throughout my first year of university, I was accessing almost exclusively Black spaces through two Afro-Caribbean and African cultural clubs. These are spaces where I sought community, friendship, mentorship, and support.

As an eighteen-year-old, I had considered attending university on the other side of the world to be an opportunity to reinvent myself and be open with all aspects of my identity. I wanted to be free from the restraints of growing up in a small, conservative, predominantly white suburb of London and to gain exposure to more accepting and inclusive communities. I knew that universities had Pride clubs or 2SLGBTQIA+ organizations and was excited to meet other queer people and explore my own sexuality. As a mixed race person, I also wanted to become more connected to my Blackness and felt excited that there was both an African cultural club and a Caribbean association at UBC. I did not realize that these two pieces of my identity would be at odds.

While my experience is not representative of all queer and/or nonbinary Black people, my research and conversations within this community have shown it is a reasonably average experience. The space that I entered was exactly as I had imagined a Black community to be. The community was based largely around Christianity, even though the purpose of the social club was not faith related. Furthermore, many of the conversations, activities, or events revolved around heteroromantic courtship. Many events involved bringing a date or segregating the group by gender (boys versus girls), which emphasized the necessity of heteronormativity within the creation of the space. At first, it was something I attempted to assimilate into. One salient memory was being invited to a "girl's night," where we stayed up late talking about "girl things." I knew immediately that I would have to perform heterosexuality and gender conformity to the best of my ability in order to be accepted into this space. One student asked: "What kind of boys do you like the most? Black, white, Asian, or mixed?" We then went around in a circle offering our attraction ranked by ethnicity. I distinctly remember hoping for a disruption or looking for an escape route so as to avoid answering the heavily heteronormative (and also somewhat problematic) question. As if reading my mind, someone asked: "What would we do if someone in the group was gay?" Through clenched teeth, I joined in the laughter that ensued. "I wouldn't be okay with that ... [I]t's against our religion," she said, subsuming us all into the Christian identity. "We would have to stop being friends with that person." We all brushed it off as an unlikely circumstance – yet I knew it was a foreshadowing.

As Melissa M. Wilcox describes, there is a very prominent perception that 2SLGBTQIA+ identities and Christianity do not mix.[37] Her research shows that many people who are both 2SLGBTQIA+ and Christian must make decisions or sacrifices to find safe communities. For example, some may remain in the closet in order to access religious communities, while others may seek specifically 2SLGBTQIA+ churches, if they are fortunate enough to have one nearby, and some are forced to practise in isolation.[38] While I am not a Christian, the Black community group that I was accessing mirrored many of the predominantly Black and West African churches I had been to.

With Vancouver's Black population being only around 1 per cent,[39] I surmise that the small Afro-Caribbean cultural groups within Vancouver's universities become victim to several social cohesion problems that result in those who are Black and queer and/or gender variant feeling excluded. First, these cultural groups are prone to creating microcosms of Black churches, of which there are several in the Lower Mainland. Through my Black university community, I occasionally attended services in Surrey and New Westminster (just outside of Vancouver), where I witnessed the use of heteronormative propaganda through sermons. Repeatedly, pastors would divide their speeches into addressing men and then addressing women. They made remarks about how women should treat their husbands, made assumptions about the things that men wanted, and of course, supported the superiority of a heterosexual monogamous marriage. While these churches were spaces I could choose to disconnect from, their messages filtered through to the smaller community I was part of at UBC. I needed this space because I wanted to be surrounded by Black people; upon my arrival in Vancouver, I longed for the diversity of London and the evident celebration of Black communities there. Black communities have always congregated in predominantly white or non-Black cities as a refuge from racism and white supremacy; the church has been a pillar of that safety.[40] Yet, remnants of white evangelical thought still reside there and manifest in homophobic and transphobic "family values."

Second, the smallness of these communities allows for little diversity or rebellion. The creation of groups and clubs in campus settings are essential to the success of university students. Within Egolf and Chester's psychological analysis of groups, adolescent and young adult groups are responsible for our identity formation and social competence.[41] The authors highlight that "an adolescent must, first, be accepted into an adolescent group and, thereafter, must conform to its norms in order to receive positive feedback which contributes to identity formation."[42] In our first year of university and therefore in our late adolescence, campus clubs played a crucial role in who we became, whether temporarily or permanently. Entering a group that was already well established and founded upon traditional and Christian values meant that many of us had to conform in order to be accepted. In turn, it meant there was little leniency for diversion or difference. The stringency of the unspoken group rules was reinforced by gossip, shaming, and exile.

The presence of any other queer or transgender group members was not evident to me. Either I was the only one, or they felt equally silenced and invisibilized by the pervasive hetero- and cisnormativity within the space. The space served its purpose as a refuge from the whiteness of the rest of campus; it allowed Black students to bond, connect, seek mentorship and inspiration, and celebrate culture. However, it became so insular that any non-conformity, particularly that perceived to be in proximity to whiteness, was rejected. After I graduated from the university and found different Black communities, I noticed similar group dynamics at play, which again I believe to be a by-product of the extreme marginalization of Black people in Vancouver. The preservation and celebration of Blackness needed to come at the expense of individuality. The rigid gender binary, imposed upon Black communities through slavery and colonialism, continued to present itself within Black spaces. Black women would call one another "sisters," and Black men, "brothers," while events like the "'Sisters' Soiree" or the "'Brothers' BBQ" would reinforce the binary of gender. Of course, this language of kinship is rooted in a combined experience of oppression. As Malcom X said of Black men, "oppression made them brothers; exploitation made them brothers; degradation made them brothers ... humiliation made them brothers."[43] These ideas are not entirely exclusive to Black communities, but as someone who is Black and non-binary, this gendered obsession became oppressive.

Black Masculinity

These environments also paved the way for toxic masculinities to develop. In a group where gender norms are so prominent yet not critiqued, a rigid perception of manhood was present. My earliest memory of this rigidity presenting itself in the group was when an academic discussion somehow devolved into a comparison of women. A respected older student, who was part of the leadership committee, said: "We don't want to date Black women – they are too difficult and strongheaded." He then continued: "I like Asian girls; they are easy and tight." Some audience members gasped or grimaced, but overwhelmingly the crowd laughed and affirmed his statements. This remark was neither the first nor the last such comment, but it was shocking to me how the conversation was so acceptable that it could be had in an academic setting. These conversations are undoubtedly commonplace in all racial groups in North America. Young men are socialized to believe they must perform certain aspects of masculinity to progress into manhood. Unlike many other cultures, Western culture has no specific coming-of-age ritual. Instead, young men must impress one another or those slightly their senior to be accepted into manhood.[44] Often, this performance necessitates the subjugation and oversexualization of women. However, within Black communities, this dichotomy is sometimes exacerbated. Furthermore, this behaviour is often accepted by both cisgender men and women; a preservation of the Black identity and community is more important than the needs of the individual.

As bell hooks discusses in her book on Black men and masculinity, white male slave owners represented the patriarchy as a form of dominance. Female slaves were repeatedly subjugated, often with physical or sexual violence, as male slaves were forced to watch. This dynamic led Black men to yearn for a different version of patriarchy where they could protect their women. However, with no other lived experience, Black men, once freed, in turn dominated their wives and daughters with the same patriarchal violence they had witnessed on the plantation.[45] As time progressed and patriarchy remained steadfast in the shaping of modern America, Black men continued to oppress Black women in order to be accepted by white men. To be a man, it seemed, was to dominate women; and to be seen as racial equals by the dominating whiteness, Black men continued to conform to patriarchy.[46]

During my time at university, several stories of sexual assault became known on campus.[47] Many, of course, remained unknown, but a series of assaults momentarily brought the issues of sexual violence in universities to light. The standard narrative ensued: the university encouraged women on campus to remain safe by dressing appropriately and not walking on campus at night. One evening, the African cultural group was hosting an event on the other side of campus from my residence building. I wrote a message on the wall of the Facebook event page asking if anyone was available to walk with me as it was already dark. No one responded, so I went anyway; but when I arrived at the event, an older male student remarked that he saw my post. "Scared about getting raped?" he asked, laughing.

At this point in my life, I was sadly not immune to the criminalization of the Black male portrayed by North American media. My own experience of violence and oversexualization from Black men, coupled with the pervasive sexism and misogyny I had witnessed with this cultural group at the university (and other Black spaces), led me to fear Black men more than others. As South and Felson outline in "The Racial Patterning of Rape," there is a common misperception that Black men are the biggest threat to all women. Conversely, perpetrators are far more likely to assault those within their communities (read racial group), and the issue is overwhelmingly one of gender rather than race.[48] Black men are not inherently violent. Men are. My skepticism and fear of Black men as a Black woman (as I then identified) was justified in that sexual assault occurs most frequently between known individuals and within racial groups.

Black women are among the least likely to report sexual assault, especially if perpetrated by a Black man. A project by the US National Resource Center on Domestic Violence names several reasons why women of colour are less likely to report sexual and domestic violence. Due to the historical treatment of racialized women within white supremacy, women of colour experience a "strong personal identification based on family structure ... fear of isolation and alienation ... loyalty to both immediate and extended family [and] ... fear of rejection."[49] Many Black women and femmes are acutely aware of the consequences of reporting their community members to the authorities and choose to remain silent rather than tear apart their community. "In the impossible hierarchy of acceptable victimhood, black women who walk willingly into the rooms of men they call 'brother' are considered undeserving of protection from any violence that happens therein," says Hannah Giorgis. "To be a 'good rape victim' is to immediately report your assault to the police (even knowing you will likely never see 'justice'), but to be a good black person is to avoid the police entirely because your life quite literally depends on it. The tightrope walk is impossible."[50]

The dominance of Black masculinity in these spaces created a culture of fear. I believe cisgender women conformed to their roles within patriarchy because the group's leadership was made up of Black men who imbued a traditional gendered dichotomy. Several of the women who I became close with were open-minded about sexuality when we spoke on a one-to-one basis, even if they did play into some heteronormative habits. However, within the group setting, sexist, transphobic, and homophobic tendencies were upheld by the patriarchal environment. Within most social groups, this attitude is a result of peer pressure and groupthink. In Black communities, I think it is exacerbated by the combined experience of intergenerational trauma, systemic racism, and the necessity of kinship faced by Black people for centuries.

Black Queerness in White Spaces

At the end of my first year of university, I began my first relationship with a woman, which led to an unplanned and unscripted "coming out." I immediately began to notice changes in how the African cultural group interacted with me. After a few months, I had been silently ostracized from the group. For a while, I attempted to continue accessing the space but was met with hostility and rejection. This shunning had a severe impact on my mental health. "Experiencing homonegativity has the potential to cause some 2SLGBTQIA+ individuals to be depressed, experience internalized homonegativity, and have other detrimental effects," says Patricia A. Hill,[51] while also alluding to the fact that research on the experiences of Black 2SLGBTQIA+ people within religious communities is sparse.

Instead, I sought the university's 2SLGBTQIA+ community in the hopes of being accepted there. I also became employed in an on-campus position that allowed me to work with 2SLGBTQIA+ youth and meet queer and trans people outside of the university. This experience was my first real escape from the bubble of UBC – which could even be described as a "total institution."[52] UBC is so expansive and home to so many amenities, residences, shops, and people that an entire world exists on the endowment lands, isolated from the rest of Vancouver. As a young international student living, working, studying, accessing support and health care, and socializing on campus, the university became my only reality.

Accessing 2SLGBTQIA+ spaces was transformative in my self-acceptance and affirmation of my identity. 2SLGBTQIA+ teenagers and young people are at the highest risk for violence at home, at schools, and in the community in the United States and Canada, says Elizabeth M. Saewyc.[53] The creation of safer spaces for 2SLGBTQIA+ people within a university environment is therefore essential for their mental health, safety, and well-being. They need to have access to spaces that are free from discrimination and marginalization, and that present specific systems of support for their needs, which may be different from those of their heterosexual and cisgender counterparts.[54] Pride UBC was the first place where I was able to be free and truthful about my identity and my queerness. It was also my first exposure to gender identities that existed beyond the binary. While I knew the term "transgender" before my entry into the 2SLGBTQIA+ community, I did not know that transness could also exist without the gender binary. I did not much desire masculinity or manhood, yet I felt continually removed from womanhood. I had to unlearn and relearn my understanding of gender in order to formulate my own identity. The lack of research, media, and imagery around non-binary people, even within 2SLGBTQIA+ communities, left me still yearning for identity markers that felt apt.

As Luna Ferguson outlines, there exists a metanarrative in which a binary is still pervasive even within gender and transgender studies. Ferguson explains that "the transgender metanarrative in our society is often focused on the lives of binary trans people – trans men and trans women"[55] They argue that "even when we think about the possibility of someone being trans, we assume that they are either a trans man or a trans woman. This elevates the lives of binary trans people while excluding non-binary trans people from social and legal recognition."[56]

I began to realize that so many of the experiences I had had growing up were in relation to being non-binary. My body developed very early on, leaving me exposed to oversexualization from both my peers and elders. Womanhood was projected onto my body well before I even understood what it meant. Like the Hottentot Venus, I was a spectacle in so many of the predominantly white spaces that I grew up in. My body became a site of exotification and fetishization well before I had even developed my own sexual agency. I was receiving all of the tropes and stereotypes placed on Black women without even being aware of my own gender identity. Simultaneously, mentors and teachers tended to place some form of masculinity onto me. For *The Body Is Not an Apology*, I wrote:

> Teachers would tell me to go and play football with the boys, or tell me I was "tough" and "strong." Worse yet, they seemed far less sympathetic towards me if I was struggling or in pain. I was always the perceived aggressor or instigator in playground fights, while in all their feigned innocence, my thin, white counterparts were the victims. I was too big to be a child, too masculine to be a girl, too Black to be innocent and too fat to be pretty. I yearned for a form of femininity that would never be accessible to me while being simultaneously forced into a perceived masculinity.
>
> As girls in my class began to wear make-up and talk about boys, I felt silenced by the conflicting messages I received about my gender. How could I juggle being forced into womanhood by the sexualization of my physical form yet rejected from femininity because of my fatness and my Blackness? I know now, of course, that womanhood and femininity are not related, but within a cisnormative script, pre-pubescent girlhood is a race to mature into the most beautiful woman. I stumbled at the starting line, not knowing that the whole race was rigged … and that womanhood was not really the destination I desired anyway.[57]

I had struggled with this confusion for much of my life, although I never had the language for it. Upon accessing 2SLGBTQIA+ spaces, I became exposed to others who identified as non-binary, genderqueer, gender variant, agender, and so on. I felt drawn to these labels as terms that encompassed my experience. However, something still didn't feel right. It was whiteness.

In contrast to the Afro-Caribbean cultural clubs, the 2SLGBTQIA+ club was a predominantly white space. It was more diverse than a lot of other spaces on campus, yet significantly lacked Black queer and trans people. As Julie Park's research indicates, many student groups on university campuses experience ethnic homogeneity, which limits the amount of interracial contact and friendships that students form, even if the university is diverse overall.[58] The research also points out that students of colour have higher levels of interracial friendship than white students, which I believe impacts the way white students treat students of colour. For students of colour, ethnically homogenous groups are important for feelings of belonging, particularly in institutions where the larger population is predominantly white. By contrast, white-only spaces can become sites of unchecked privilege and racism. White students were shown to be the least likely to have friends of a different race,[59] which I suggest would make them less sympathetic to the instances of microaggressions, discrimination, and systemic oppression experienced by students of colour.

While I did feel a sense of belonging within the 2SLGBTQIA+ groups I accessed both on and off campus, the lack of other Black 2SLGBTQIA+ people played into my preconceived perception that queerness and gender variance were things exclusive to white people. This outlook continued to impact my sense of self and identity. I received the message that in Black spaces you cannot be queer, and in queer spaces you cannot be Black. I grappled with knowing that I was non-binary – I felt neither male nor female, neither man nor woman – and eventually came to settle on the term "agender." To me, agender represents an absence of gender and is not related to the way I present myself, which I would describe as "femme." This is both a personal and a political identity; with my body being hyper visible yet my identity being invisibilized in many spaces, I cannot extricate the politics from my sense of self or my physical form.

While I felt freer and more able to express myself in this community, I was still "othered." Simply, my body as a fat, Black femme did not fit with the prescribed script of a non-binary person. Somehow, non-binary meant androgynous, and androgynous meant masculine. As Kris Nelson explains in their article "4 Harmful Lies the Media Is

Telling You about Androgyny,"[60] "masculinity is recognized as being genderless." Furthermore, whiteness and thinness are also recognized as being gender neutral. The white body is the default body.[61] As Nelson points out, "white non-binary and gender non-conforming folks ... need to acknowledge that the gender binary is a tool of white supremacy and colonial violence."[62] They finish by saying: "All of this leads to a vision of androgyny that denies the experiences and identities of femme non-binary people and focuses almost entirely on cis-women and AFAB trans masculine people."[63] Subsumed by this narrative, I spent a few months attempting to wear button-ups and bowties but felt overwhelmingly disconnected from my sense of self. I also used a chest binder; I wanted to appear more androgynous, which I internalized as appearing more masculine. With size 36K breasts, the garment was painful and ineffective. While some trans and non-binary people experience gender dysphoria, which may impact their relationship with their chest, I do not. Instead, I just felt pressured to appear less feminine in order to distance myself from womanhood. The lack of diverse non-binary imagery and role models both in close proximity and in the media render a feeling of worthlessness and undesirability within young non-binary people of colour.

As I wrote in a *Daily Xtra* article, "I describe my own experience of being non-binary as a political rebellion. For me (but not for everyone), not conforming to the gender binary is a necessary form of survival and personal exploration in a world that strives to oppress Black women. Within Black communities, there is little room for gender non-conformity. Not in the sense that gendered or genderless possibilities are not open to Black bodies, but in the way that blackness is perceived. This is often in rigid gender binaries (man/woman) as opposed to seeing gender as a spectrum or a galaxy of possibilities."[64]

Black and Non-Binary Experiences in the University

I wanted to know if my experiences were similar to others who identified as Black and non-binary and had experience with a Canadian or American university. There is very little existing research on the subject, and while my sample size is small, I believe it is indicative of the gaping hole in academia where Black and non-binary people frantically seek support, community, and validation. Existing research on gender diversity is still heavily entrenched in the gender binary.[65]

I interviewed eight participants. The participants all experienced different types of Blackness (for example, mixed race, dark-skinned, Haitian, African American, white-passing, and South African) and also used different terminology to describe their gender identity and/or expression. Four of the participants identified as "non-binary" and two as "genderqueer"; other identities included "demigender," "androgynous," and "agender flux." The universities they attended include the University of British Columbia, Langara College, Capilano University, Douglas College, and the British Columbia Institute of Technology in Canada; and the University of Texas at Austin and the Savannah College of Art and Design in the United States. Findings showed that 87.5 per cent of the participants experienced racism during their time at university. For 50 per cent of them, it included being called a racial slur or derogatory name; 12 per cent had experienced physical violence.

As I indicated, my own experience of being Black and non-binary was one of feeling silenced and erased in both Black and 2SLGBTQIA+ communities. I asked the participants to outline similar experiences at their universities. The main issues that arose were being ignored or talked over, particularly by cisgender men, and being shut down when bringing up issues pertaining to Blackness and erasure of Black identities, histories, and experiences in class discussions.

One student described a traumatic experience:

> I went to a professor's office after being extremely triggered by a series of African films we watched in class, particularly the discussions that arose from watching these films. Discussions facilitated by a white woman professor ... to a mostly white class (I was one of three Black students in the class). After being triggered by a South African film we watched and having to leave as a result, I tried to express my discomfort during a meeting with my professor ... She spoke over my trauma, instead relaying her own experiences with "doing difficult work" abroad on the African continent. She even expressed disappointment that I didn't stay to discuss my "perspective" with the class because "it could have been a teachable moment." I felt extremely silenced, and worse, told that my pain only mattered so white students could learn from/off of it.

Another expressed the frustration of being silenced:

> Often times white professors, specifically white professors speaking on Black and [people of colour] issues, would quickly shut me down when speaking about Blackness, especially in cases where they compare Black trauma to another group's trauma in a way that ignores that Black folks in Canada experience trauma at the hands of our government/police force, etc. ... I've had one teacher specifically tell me multiple times that "this is not the place for this discussion."

Many participants expressed the pervasiveness of specifically anti-Black racism. One participant summed up their experience of the instances of anti-Black racism: "There's just far too much to name. I encountered anti-Black racism everywhere, almost all the time." A lot of the experiences that the participants brought forth stemmed from stereotypes about Black communities. Some were told by their mentors or peers that they couldn't be trusted because of pervasive perceptions of Black people as criminals. Others reported instances of being presumed uneducated or unintelligent due to their Blackness or African heritage. One person remarked: "[These experiences] aren't incidental. Because whiteness is upheld, valued and engrained into almost every aspect of the university, racism is both pervasive and institutional."

I also asked the participants about their experiences of gender-based discrimination and transphobia: 50 per cent had been called derogatory slurs, and 16.7 per cent had experienced physical violence. These instances of transphobic violence included using birth names as a silencing tactic; students declaring that the use of gender neutral pronouns is "stupid"; or being told that non-binary people are "not really trans." Participants also elaborated how the content of their academic courses reinforces the gender binary and erases the experiences and existence of non-binary people. Some noted that, even within gender studies departments, "binary texts were taught, often without question." One participant mentioned how they were asked to do additional unpaid labour by professors to make sure the class content was not transphobic. Furthermore, textbooks and reading material are rarely vetted for transphobic language; one participant's textbook mentioned transgender identities within the context of pedophilia.

Another salient issue is the lack of gender neutral bathrooms on university campuses for non-binary and gender non-conforming students to access. A 2013 study from the Williams Institute found that 70 per cent of transgender and gender non-conforming people had experienced some kind of negative reaction when using a public bathroom,[66] which can include being told they are in the wrong place, being questioned about their gender, made fun of, verbally abused, physically assaulted, forcibly removed, or sexually assaulted.[67] As Ivan Coyote explains in their TED Talk on the importance of gender-neutral bathrooms, "bathroom bills" that are becoming more prominent across North America only serve to endanger and harm trans people, especially trans youth and children: "They drop out of school, or they opt out of life altogether."[68] UBC does have *A Guide to Gender-Inclusive Single-Stall Washrooms*,[69] but it seems to be in the minority.

Trans and non-binary students also experience misgendering. Misgendering primarily refers to being called by the wrong pronouns or the wrong name. For those who have changed their name, often to one that they feel aligns more with their gender, being called by one's "previous" or "birth" name is considered "deadnaming." It can also include designations of gendered terms such as "dude" or "ladies." "Misgendering can cause psychological harm, moral wrongs, and political disadvantage," states Stephanie Julia Kapusta in "Misgendering and Its Moral Contestability."[70] Kapusta indicates that psychological harm can be caused by microaggressions and can include "chronic health problems, persistent anxiety, fatigue, stress, hypervigilance, anger, fear, depression, shame, and a sense of loneliness." Moral harm refers to "having some significant area of one's social experience obscured from collective understanding."[71] Finally, misgendering can cause political disadvantage by excluding transgender people from necessary elements of social life, for example, the complicated legal process surrounding changing one's gender on a piece of government ID.[72] One study participant noted that professors and peers alike would purposefully misgender or deadname them as a silencing tactic.

Overwhelmingly, for those who are both non-binary and Black, the university does not create space for their identities to be respected, acknowledged, and protected. These students experience a complex and damaging intersectionality of racism, homophobia/queerphobia, and transphobia. "When it comes to social inequality, people's lives and the organization of power in a given society are better understood as being shaped not by a single axis of social division, be it race or gender or class, but by many axes that work together and influence each other,"[73] say Patricia Hill Collins and Sirma Bilge in explaining "intersectionality." In my sample, the intersectionality of the participants' lived experiences places them in a vulnerable position. A viable solution to many of the issues faced by Black and non-binary students in Canadian universities is access to safer spaces. However, the pervasiveness of white supremacy within these spaces, as I described in my own experience, continues to be a barrier for many Black non-binary people.

Two of the participants' experiences mirrored my own very closely. Jerome[74] attended UBC as an international student from the Caribbean. They felt hesitant about accessing the Afro-Caribbean cultural clubs on campus because they perceived these spaces to be homophobic. They explained: "I think I had a lot of internalized racism/anti-Blackness and also associated Caribbean/Black spaces with homophobia because of my experiences growing up ... I saw those spaces as [heterosexual and cisgender] spaces and at the time I really wanted nothing to do with straight/cis[gender] people. So, [I] ended up choosing (whiteness) queerness over culture." They describe this choice as a "big regret" in retrospect. Instead, they spent a lot of time with Pride UBC.

At first, this space was really important to Jerome. "I was coming from a country where I didn't have a lot of access to exploring my queer identity growing up, and wanted a chance to do that here [at] university." However, the group's racism and "cultural incompetency" became too much for Jerome to deal with. They began to realize that few people of colour accessed Pride UBC or felt safe there and that the space was not actively committed to decentring whiteness. This insight caused Jerome to become distant from their racialized queer and trans friends and to realize that their "queerness/gender/trans-liberation was shaped by white queers and did a number on [their] own emotional health and growth around queerness." Ultimately, Jerome became disconnected from their cultural community and found themselves surrounded by white people who were unable to understand their experience, some of these people even overtly racist. Jerome also felt that the few queer and trans people of colour they did meet through these spaces were from Canadian or American backgrounds, leaving them feeling further excluded as someone from the Caribbean.

Omari[75] attended a university in Canada. They also identify as Caribbean and describe themselves as non-binary transmasculine and female-to-male (FTM). Omari became involved in the Pride club at his school but quickly noticed they were the only Black queer person there. Omari says they were described as an "aggressor" by other members of the club when they continually tried to hold the club accountable for things that were racist. They got suspended from the organization and were told "to die since [they are] trans" by the vice president of the club. Being excluded from the organization left them feeling isolated and frustrated. It also led to instances of depression, anxiety, stress, loneliness, suicidal ideation, and self-harm. These impacts were also experienced by the majority of the other participants.[76]

Conclusion

Once Black youth have navigated the treacherous path of uncertainty and defied various odds to be accepted into Canadian universities, they enter a microcosm of society at large. In the same way that all the other institutions we attempt to access are built upon stolen Indigenous land and uphold white supremacy, so too do university campuses. These educational platforms were never built with the intention that students of colour would freely access them; rather, they were planned with the understanding that racialized bodies would be the ones to physically construct them and act as labourers and servants to the privileged elite. Just like other systems meant to measure success or intelligence, universities were built by white people for white people.

The dearth of research and narrative that exists about students at Canadian universities who are Black and non-binary leaves a gaping hole in academia. Black non-binary students experience a challenging dichotomy of racialized transphobia that creates barriers between them and accessing safer spaces. Histories of systemic and institutionalized oppression on Black communities globally have created numerous particularities for the Black community, some of which cause strife within them. The shaping of the Black man within North American history has created a conflicting paradox. In striving for sexual agency and equality with other men, the Black male figure also represents toxic masculinity within closed, religious Black communities. In turn, this contradiction creates unsafe spaces for both cisgender women and queer and trans folks who also wish to access these spaces. Those who exist within the margins of the margins must make choices in accessing communities and are often left completely isolated.

Campus groups are very important to personal development for many university students, yet they can also be sites of exclusivity. Furthermore, with a high likelihood of ethnic homogeneity and a lack of critical inspection or supervision, these spaces can become toxic and violent. Even spaces that are intended to be supportive and inclusive, like Pride clubs and 2SLGBTQIA+ groups, can foster climates of insensitivity if they lack diversity and anti-oppressive education.

The experience of Black non-binary students proves to be overwhelmingly negative. These students experience physical, emotional, and verbal violence and become isolated from a variety of communities. Furthermore, the university lacks infrastructure to offer systems of support or members of staff qualified to deal with instances of racialized transphobia. This situation presents a disproportionate amount of psychological and emotional challenges to Black non-binary students.

In a larger context, 2SLGBTQIA+ communities are often scripted through whiteness, while Black communities are posited as both devoid of sexual exploration and entirely oversexualized. These two damaging stereotypes leave little space for those who are Black and queer, and particularly for those who are Black and gender variant. In the search for our sense of self and our self-determination, we are excluded from communities that are supposed to shape our identities. In both our own minds and in society's imaginary, Black non-binary people cannot exist, because non-binary people are white, and Black people are straight. Yet, we do exist – and we find ourselves caught between violence and invisibility.

NOTES

1 Williams et al., "Cultural Adaptations."
2 Gannage, "Review."
3 Ferguson, "Ferguson: We're Non-Binary Trans – and We Exist."
4 *Dictionary.com*, s.v. "cisgender," accessed 22 November 2017, https://www.dictionary.com/browse/cisgender.
5 *Dictionary.com*, s.v. "gender dysphoria," accessed 22 November 2017, https://www.dictionary.com/browse/gender-dysphoria.
6 Nelson, "What Is Heteronormativity."
7 *Dictionary.com*, s.v. "homonegativity," accessed 22 November 2017, http://www.dictionary.com/browse/homonegativity. See also Hudson and Ricketts, "A Strategy."
8 Rivera, "Microaggressions."
9 TransWhat?, "Glossary of Terms."
10 Henry, Rees, and Tator, *The Colour of Democracy*.
11 Butler, *Gender Trouble*.
12 Hosie, "John Lewis Gets Rid."
13 Cox, "Coming Out as 'Non-Binary."
14 Kimmel, *Guyland*.
15 Abdelmoneim, *No More Boys and Girls*.
16 Mendible, *From Bananas to Buttocks*, 1.
17 Kawahara and Fu, "Psychology and Mental Health of Asian American Women."
18 Bailey, "They Aren't Talking about Me ..."
19 Foucault, *The History of Sexuality*.
20 Mbembe, "Necropolitics."
21 "What Is Body Terrorism?"
22 Cartwright, "Report on Diseases and Physical Peculiarities of the Negro Race."
23 Williams, *Capitalism & Slavery*.
24 Abdur-Rahman, "Black Grotesquerie," 688.
25 Holmes, *African Queen*.
26 Foster, "The Sexual Abuse of Black Men."
27 Ibid., 445.
28 Ward, "Homophobia, Hypermasculinity and the US Black Church," 495.
29 Sherrycj, "Lena Dunham Accused Odell Beckham Jr."
30 D'Oyley, "The News Isn't #TeacherBae's Clothing."

31 Holmes, *African Queen.*
32 Cox, Lienesch, and Jones, "Who Sees Discrimination?"
33 Ward, "Homophobia, Hypermasculinity and the US Black Church." 493.
34 Ibid.
35 Crichlow, *Buller Men and Batty Bwoys.*
36 UBC, "UBC Overview & Facts."
37 Wilcox, *Coming Out in Christianity.*
38 Ibid., 11.
39 World Population Review, "Vancouver Population 2021."
40 Stanford, *Homophobia in the Black Church.*
41 Egolf and Chester, *Forming, Storming, Norming, Performing.*
42 Ibid., 29.
43 Quoted in Lemelle, *Black Masculinity*, 1.
44 Kimmel, *Guyland.*
45 hooks, *We Real Cool.*
46 Ibid., 7.
47 Stewart, "UBC Failed Its Sexual Assault Victims."
48 South and Felson, "The Racial Patterning of Rape."
49 NRCDV, "Domestic Violence in Communities of Colour."
50 Giorgis, "Many Women of Color Don't Go to the Police."
51 Hill, "Spiritual Well-Being of Black LGBT Individuals."
52 Gibbon, Canterbury, and Litten, "Colleges as Total Institutions."
53 Saewyc et al., "Hazards of Stigma."
54 Vaccaro, August, and Kennedy, *Safe Spaces.*
55 Ferguson, "Ferguson: We're Non-Binary Trans – and We Exist."
56 Ibid.
57 Blain, "Mixed-Race, Non-Binary, Queer Fat Femme."
58 Park, "Clubs and the Campus Racial Climate."
59 Ibid.
60 Nelson, "4 Harmful Lies."
61 Ibid.
62 Ibid.
63 Ibid.
64 Blain, "The Political Rebellion."
65 Cayley, "XWHY?"
66 Hermon, "Gendered Restrooms and Minority Stress," 71.
67 Ibid.
68 Coyote, "Why We Need Gender-Neutral Bathrooms."
69 Accessible Washroom Working Group, *Guide to Gender-Inclusive Single Stall Washrooms.*
70 Kapusta, "Misgendering," 504.
71 Fricker, "Silence and Institutional Prejudice," 102.

72 Kapusta, "Misgendering," 505.
73 Collins and Bilge, *Intersectionality*.
74 Name has been changed.
75 Name has been changed.
76 Blain, "Black and Non-Binary."

REFERENCES

Abdelmoneim, Javid, director/host. *No More Boys and Girls: Can Our Kids Go Gender Free?* BBC Two, 2018.
Abdur-Rahman, Aliyyah I. "Black Grotesquerie." *American Literary History* 29, no. 4 (2017): 682–703. https://doi.org/10.1093/alh/ajx028.
Accessible Washrooms Working Group. *A Guide to Gender-Inclusive Single-Stall Washrooms at UBC Point Grey.* Vancouver, BC: Access and Diversity, University of British Columbia, 2006. https://equity3.sites.olt.ubc.ca/files/2010/06 /guide_to_gender_inclusive_single_stall_washrooms_at_ubc_point_grey.pdf.
Bailey, Moya. "They Aren't Talking about Me ..." *Crunk Feminist Collective*, 14 March 2010. http://www.crunkfeministcollective.com/2010/03/14 /they-arent-talking-about-me/.
Blain, Cicely Belle. "Black and Non-Binary in the Ivory Tower." Unpublished interviews and raw research data. Vancouver, BC, November 2017.
– "Mixed-Race, Non-Binary, Queer Fat Femme: How I Fail and Succeed in Finding Liberation." *The Body Is Not an Apology*, 14 August 2019. https:// thebodyisnotanapology.com/magazine/fat-femm-my-f-you-to -traditional-beauty-standards-cicley-blain/.
– "The Political Rebellion of Being Black and Non-Binary." *Daily Xtra*, 9 June 2017. https://www.dailyxtra.com/the-political-rebellion-of-being-black -and-non-binary-73646.
Butler, Judith. *Gender Trouble: Feminism and the Subversion of Identity.* New York: Routledge, 1990.
Cartwright, Samuel. "Report on the Diseases and Physical Peculiarities of the Negro Race." *New Orleans Medical and Surgical Journal*, 1851.
Cayley, Mair. "XWHY? Stories of Non-Binary Gender Identities." PhD diss., University of British Columbia, 2016.
Collins, Patricia Hill, and Sirma Bilge. *Intersectionality.* Cambridge, UK: Polity Press, 2016.
Cox, Daniel, Rachel Lienesch, and Robert P. Jones. "Who Sees Discrimination? Attitudes about Sexual Orientation, Gender Identity, Race, and Immigration Status: Findings from PRRI's American Values Atlas." *Public Religion Research Institute (PRRI)*, 21 June 2017. https://www.prri.org /research/americans-views-discrimination-immigrants-blacks-lgbt-sex -marriage-immigration-reform/.

Cox, Susan. "Coming Out as 'Non-Binary' Throws Other Women under the Bus." *Feminist Current*, 10 November 2016. https://www.feministcurrent.com/2016/08/10/coming-non-binary-throws-women-bus/.

Coyote, Ivan. "Ivan Coyote: Why We Need Gender-Neutral Bathrooms." TED Talk, November 2015. https://www.ted.com/talks/ivan_coyote_why_we_need_gender_neutral_bathrooms.

Crichlow, Wesley E.A. *Buller Men and Batty Bwoys: Hidden Men in Toronto and Halifax Black Communities*. Toronto: University of Toronto Press, 2004.

D'Oyley, Demtria Lucas. "The News Isn't #TeacherBae's Clothing – It's the Exploitation of Her Body." *Essence.com*, 16 September 2016. https://www.essence.com/2016/09/16/teacher-bae-patrice-brown-exploitation.

Egolf, Donald B., and Sondra L. Chester. *Forming, Storming, Norming, Performing: Successful Communication in Groups and Teams*. 2nd ed. New York: IUniverse, 2007.

Ferguson, Luna. "Ferguson: We're Non-Binary Trans – and We Exist." *Western News*, 9 November 2016. https://news.westernu.ca/2016/11/non-binary-trans-people-yes-exist/.

Fricker, Miranda. "Silence and Institutional Prejudice." In *Out from the Shadows: Analytical Feminist Contributions to Traditional Philosophy*, edited by Sharon L. Crasnow and Anita M. Superson, 287–304. Oxford: Oxford University Press, 2006.

Foster, Thomas A. "The Sexual Abuse of Black Men under American Slavery." *Journal of the History of Sexuality* 20, no. 3 (2011): 445–64. https://doi.org/10.1353/sex.2011.0059.

Foucault, Michel. *The History of Sexuality*. London: Penguin Books, 1992.

Gannage, Charlene M. "Review of *Racism, Sexism, and the University: The Political Science Affair at the University of British Columbia*, by M. Patricia Marchak." *Canadian Public Policy/Analyse de Politiques* 24, no. 1 (1998): 122–3. https://doi.org/10.2307/3551735.

Gibbon, Heather M., Richard M. Canterbury, and Larry Litten. "Colleges as Total Institutions: Implications for Admission, Orientation, and Student Life." *College and University* 74, no. 2 (1999): 21–7.

Giorgis, Hannah. "Many Women of Color Don't Go to the Police after Sexual Assault for a Reason." *The Guardian*, 25 March 2015. https://www.theguardian.com/commentisfree/2015/mar/25/women-of-color-police-sexual-assault-racist-criminal-justice.

Henry, Frances, Tim Rees, and Carol Tator. *The Colour of Democracy: Racism in Canadian Society*. Toronto: Nelson Education, 2010.

Hermon, Jody L. "Gendered Restrooms and Minority Stress: Public Regulation of Gender and Its Impact on Transgender People's Lives," *Journal of Public Management & Social Policy* 19, no. 1 (2013): 65–80. http://www.jpmsp.com/volume-19/vol19-iss1.

Hill, Patricia A. "Spiritual Well-being of Black LGBT Individuals When Faced with Religious Homonegativity." PhD diss., Walden University, 2015. ProQuest.

Holmes, Rachel. *African Queen: The Real Life of the Hottentot Venus.* New York: Random House, 2007.

hooks, bell. *We Real Cool: Black Men and Masculinity.* New York: Routledge, 2004.

Hosie, Rachel. "John Lewis Gets Rid of 'Boys' and 'Girls' Labels in Children's Clothing." *The Independent,* 2 September 2017. https://www.independent.co.uk/life-style/john-lewis-boys-girls-clothing-labels-gender-neutral-unisex-children-a7925336.html.

Hudson, Walter W., and Wendell A. Ricketts. "A Strategy for the Measurement of Homophobia." *Journal of Homosexuality* 5, no. 4 (1980): 357–72. https://doi.org/10.1300/J082v05n04_02.

Kapusta, Stephanie Julia. "Misgendering and Its Moral Contestability." *Hypatia* 31, no. 3 (2016): 502–19. https://doi.org/10.1111/hypa.12259.

Kawahara, Debra, and Michi Fu. "The Psychology and Mental Health of Asian American Women." In *Handbook of Asian American Psychology,* 2nd ed., edited by Frederick T.L. Leong et al., 181–96. Thousand Oaks, CA: Sage, 2007. https://psycnet.apa.org/record/2006-11867-011.

Kimmel, Michael S. *Guyland: The Perilous World Where Boys Become Men.* New York: Harper, 2010.

Lemelle, Anthony J. *Black Masculinity and Sexual Politics.* New York: Routledge, 2010.

Mbembe, Achille. "Necropolitics." Translated by Libby Meintjes. *Public Culture* 15, no. 1 (2003): 11–40.

Mendible, Myra, ed. *From Bananas to Buttocks.* Austin: University of Texas Press, 2007.

Nelson, Kris. "4 Harmful Lies the Media Is Telling You about Androgyny." *Everyday Feminism,* 1 January 2016. https://everydayfeminism.com/2016/01/lies-media-tells-androgyny/.

– "What Is Heteronormativity – And How Does It Apply to Your Feminism? Here Are 4 Examples." *Everyday Feminism,* 24 July 2015. https://everydayfeminism.com/2015/07/what-is-heteronormativity/.

NRCDV (National Resource Center on Domestic Violence). "Domestic Violence and Communities of Color." Women of Color Network (WOCN) Facts & Stats Collection. Harrisburg, PA: NRCDV, 2006. http://www.doj.state.or.us/wp-content/uploads/2017/08/women_of_color_network_facts_domestic_violence_2006.pdf.

Park, Julie J. "Clubs and the Campus Racial Climate: Student Organizations and Interracial Friendship in College." *Journal of College Student Development* 55, no. 7 (2014): 641–60. https://doi.org/10.1353/csd.2014.0076.

Rivera, David P. "Microaggressions: More than Just Race." *Psychology Today*, 17 November 2010. https://www.psychologytoday.com/blog /microaggressions-in-everyday-life/201011/microaggressions -more-just-race.

Saewyc, Elizabeth M., et al. "Hazards of Stigma: The Sexual and Physical Abuse of Gay, Lesbian, and Bisexual Adolescents in the United States and Canada." *Child Welfare: Journal of Policy, Practice, and Program* 85, no. 2 (2006): 195–213.

Sherrycj. "Lena Dunham Accused Odell Beckham Jr. of Not Paying Attention to Her and Things Got Messy." *BuzzFeed Community*, 3 September 2016. https://www.buzzfeed.com/sherrycj/lena-dunham-accused-odell -beckham-jr-of-not-payin-22v22.

South, Scott J., and Richard B. Felson. "The Racial Patterning of Rape." *Social Forces* 69, no. 1 (1990): 71–93. https://doi.org/10.2307/2579608.

Stanford, Anthony. *Homophobia in the Black Church: How Faith, Politics, and Fear Divide the Black Community*. Santa Barbara, CA: Praeger, 2013.

Stewart, Michael. "UBC Failed Its Sexual Assault Victims on Every Level." *HuffPost Canada*, 27 November 2016. https://www.huffingtonpost.ca /michael-stewart1/ubc-sexual-assault-allegations_b_8657208.html.

TransWhat? "Glossary of Terms." https://transwhat.org/glossary/.

UBC (University of British Columbia). "UBC Overview & Facts." https:// www.ubc.ca/about/facts.html.

Vaccaro, Annemarie, Gerri August, and Megan S. Kennedy. *Safe Spaces: Making Schools and Communities Welcoming to LGBT Youth*. Santa Barbara, CA: Praeger, 2012.

Ward, Elijah G. "Homophobia, Hypermasculinity and the US Black Church." *Culture, Health & Sexuality* 7, no. 5 (2005): 493–504. https://doi.org/10.1080 /13691050500151248.

"What Is Body Terrorism?" *The Body Is Not an Apology*. https://thebody isnotanapology.com/about-tbinaa/what-is-body-terrorism/.

Wilcox, Melissa M. *Coming Out in Christianity: Religion, Identity, and Community*. Bloomington: Indiana University Press, 2003.

Williams, Eric Eustace. *Capitalism and Slavery*. Chapel Hill, NC: University of North Carolina Press, 1944.

Williams, Monnica, et al. "Cultural Adaptations of Prolonged Exposure Therapy for Treatment and Prevention of Posttraumatic Stress Disorder in African Americans." *Behavioral Sciences* 4, no. 2 (2014): 102–24. https://doi .org/10.3390/bs4020102.

World Population Review. "Vancouver Population 2021." https://world populationreview.com/world-cities/vancouver-population/.

9 Interrogating White Supremacy in Academia: Creating Alternative Spaces for Racialized Students' Scholarship and Well-Being

BENITA BUNJUN

Academic institutions within Canada, a white settler society, remain troubling sites of racial exclusion and racial disentitlement with a lack of critical Indigenous and race scholarship and scholars. Undergraduate and graduate Indigenous, Black, and students of colour across multiple intersections of Indigeneity, gender, sexuality, citizenship, language, international/exchange, place of origin, accents, migration, displacement, and disciplines experience a diversity of both embodied and material isolation, silencing, erasure, and exclusion. Additionally, Indigenous, Black, and faculty of colour engaging in critical scholarship and pedagogy experience defensiveness from students for unsettling whiteness and happiness in the classroom.

Drawing on the work of Sara Ahmed (2000, 2009), this chapter examines how and why racialized, and particularly politicized, students and faculty[1] are produced as "bodies out of place" in Western Eurocentric academia while being constructed as unsettling the "happiness" that constitutes white supremacy within it. By interrogating the intersectional deployments and effects of "bodies out of place," I demonstrate that such academic sites of colonial encounters (Mawani, 2009) simultaneously reproduce and contest nationalist discourses of (un)belonging, racialization, and (dis)entitlement (Bunjun, 2011; Thobani, 2007). Such nationalist discourses are embedded both in and outside the classroom within larger imperial and global positionings and racial taxonomies. I further analyze a variety of racialized students' networks and argue that it is imperative for alternative and subversive educational models to emerge within and outside academia to nurture racialized students' scholarship and well-being.

By engaging with critical race and critical whiteness theories, academia in Canada can be understood as a site of colonial encounters of differently positioned subjects within simultaneous contact zones (classrooms, instructors' offices, libraries, student/campus services, departments) within a white settler society. Mawani (2009) refers to a colonial contact zone as "a space of racial intermixture – a place where Europeans, aboriginal peoples, and racial migrants came into frequent contact, a conceptual and material geography where racial categories and racisms were both produced and productive of locally configured and globally inflected modalities of colonial power" (p. 5). University spaces, such as classrooms, are powerful sites of sociopolitical/geopolitical local and global intermixing of a diversity of international students, domestic students, and instructors across racialization, class, gender, trans/non-binary, and ability.

Critical race theory emerges from the scholarship and lived experience of African American, Latinx, and Asian American legal scholars, practitioners, and activists in the 1990s (Bell, 1992; Crenshaw, Gotanda, Peller, & Thomas, 1995; Matsuda, Lawrence, Delgado, & Crenshaw, 1993). Collins (2019) explains that, "as an interdisciplinary endeavor that drew from and reached beyond legal scholarship, critical race theory advanced antiracist analyses of late twenty-first-century racial practices" (p. 90). The field of critical whiteness studies surfaces from the scholarship of critical race and challenges notions of colour blindness while reconfiguring whiteness as an unmarked racial category. The hegemonic naturalization and institutionalization of colour blindness is a new form of racial rule across all relations. Critical race theory includes "ever-evolving, heterogeneous explanations of resistance to global racism" (Collins, 2019, p. 90). Feminist critical race and anti-racist scholars have consistently demonstrated the pervasiveness of coloniality within the academy, resulting in the erasure and marginality of critical race and Indigenous scholarship (Ahmed, 2012; Bunjun, 2014; Carty, 1991; Collins, 2019; Henry et al., 2017; Henry, 2015; Monture-Angus, 2010; Smith, 2010). Hence, the importance of understanding the making and reproduction of Canada as a white settler society becomes imperative to understanding academic spaces of intermixing.

Canada as a White Settler Society

My community and scholarly pedagogical entry point begins with Canada as a white settler society. Sherene Razack (2002) states:

A white settler society is one established by Europeans on non-European soil. Its origins lie in the dispossession and the extermination of Indigenous population by the conquering European. As it evolves, a white settler society continues to be structured by a racial hierarchy. In the national mythologies of such societies, it is believed that white people came first and that it is they who principally developed the land; Aboriginal peoples are presumed to be mostly dead or assimilated. European settlers thus become the original inhabitants and the group most entitled to the fruits of citizenship. (p. 1)

Attached to these white settler mythologies, there exists white amnesia and the ongoing denial of conquest, genocide, chattel slavery, and the exploitation of racialized bodies for labour. The "white fantasy" as described by Hage (2000) is enveloped in reproducing the myth that Canada was peacefully settled and not colonized through the process of *terra nullius* (empty uninhabited lands). Even though such lands were already inhabited nations, they "were simply legally *deemed to be uninhabited* if the people were not Christian, not agricultural, not commercial, not 'sufficiently evolved' or simply in the way" (Culhane, 1998, p. 48; emphasis in original).

As a nation, Canada is contradictory and contested. Its colonial construction can only exist with the continuing dispossession of Indigenous peoples. The nation is able to imagine its community of those who truly belong by the constant dispossession of those who do not belong to the nation. Himani Bannerji (2000) explains that discourses of national belonging involve "certain ideas regarding skin colour, history, language (English/French), and other cultural signifiers – all of which may be subsumed under the ideological category 'white'" (p. 64). Europeanness is represented as whiteness, which translates into Canadianness. Furthermore, embedded in this construction of Canada is a particular notion of nation and state formation. Bannerji criticizes Anderson's[2] concept of "imagined communities" because he does not examine the contradictions and tensions that may exist in the imagined community, nor does he question the type of imagination at work. Ahmed (2000) also refines this concept:

The production of the nation involves not only image and myth-making – the telling of "official" stories of origin – but also the everyday negotiations of what it means "to be" that nation(ality). The production of the nation involves processes of self-identification in which the nation comes to be realised as belonging to the individual (the construction of the "we" as utterable by the individual). (p. 98)

Linda Carty's (1999) scholarship on the construction of empire and the creation of the "Other" also offers an understanding of such discourses of nation-building. Carty explains that the Other emerged as a "stratification based on skin colour and exemplified through England's positioning of its inhabitants in relation to those of the colonies, particularly in relation to the Africans" (pp. 36–7). She asserts that "by the late 18th century England, one of the smallest countries in Europe, would 'own' and 'rule' most of the world" (p. 36). England's mission to civilize the Indigenous and Third World peoples of its colonies through colonial encounters contributed to the social construction of the Other (Carty, 1999; Devereux, 1999; Valverde, 1992). "Constructing the Other would give legitimacy to the belief in white superiority and its 'civilizing' mission" (Carty, 1999, p. 36). Discourses of the uncivilized heathens, savages, and pagans run parallel to those discourses of racialization and Christianity. The merging of discourses of inferiority was reproduced within the colonial empire. Hence, the nation and nationalist is formed, imagined, and sustained through colonial anxieties and encounters with the stranger as the Other.

Ahmed's (2000) ontology of strangers, as articulated in *Strange Encounters*, provides the theoretical framework for analyzing the presence and encountering of strangers in constructing the dominant "I" or "we" within national and institutional discourses. The making of the stranger is ultimately about the making of the self and how one embodies the self in relation to encounters and contact with strangers. It is through this theoretical understanding that Ahmed argues: "There are techniques that allow us to differentiate between those who are strangers and those who belong in a given space" (p. 22). Ahmed analyzes how the stranger is recognized as stranger prior to their appearance as a body identified as not belonging and out of place. She examines how the dominant subject of the nation ensures that the boundaries are maintained and enforced in order to keep the stranger out. If the stranger appears to cross the line or come too close, fear accumulates, demanding that the stranger be expelled in order to secure imagined purity and spatial formation.

> We can consider how nations are invented as familiar spaces, as spaces of belonging, through being defined against others who are recognised, or known again, as strange and hence strangers. In some sense, the stranger appears as a figure, as a way of containing that which the nation is not, and hence as a way of allowing the nation to be. (Ahmed, 2000, p. 97)

By already recognizing the stranger as not belonging and out of place, the demarcation and enforcement of boundaries crystallize the place *we* inhabit as home (Ahmed, 2000). Such boundaries are to be maintained and enforced in order to ensure that those we recognize as strangers and who have been determined as not belonging do not contaminate or threaten property, space, and person. Ultimately Ahmed affirms that "recognizing strangers is here embedded in a discourse of survival: it is a question of how to survive the proximity of strangers who are already figurable, *who have already taken shape*, in the everyday encounters we have with others" (p. 22; emphasis in original). Therefore, the intermixing of individuals across power relations within academic sites becomes embedded in how the stranger will be constructed, accommodated, managed, and/or excluded as a form of gatekeeping for the survival of the institution and nation.

Displacing White Entitlement

In this section, I draw on my experience as a faculty of colour, teaching from a critical intersectional race and feminist perspective in sociology at various universities, by analyzing some students' evaluations to exemplify the unsettling of white students. This critical race feminist pedagogy interacts with curricula focusing on histories, policies, law, resistance, and discourses of colonialism, patriarchy, and capitalism that have predominately been omitted, misrepresented, and silenced. This unsettling that I invoke in the classroom produces deep resentment, defensiveness, and unproductive guilt that constructs me and many racialized politically aware students as the "feminist killjoys" theorized by Sara Ahmed.

Here, I draw on the course "Canadian Society," a third-year full-year course taught at a university in Canada by two different instructors; each instructor independently taught one term. The instructor teaching part one was a white female tenured faculty, who was often described in the student evaluations as providing a much safer environment where information was presented as "less biased," "more objective," and "more neutral." For example, the following students articulate how my invocation troubled and unsettled their white selves:

> I did not feel like this class was in any way a "Canadian Society" class. The entire focus was on racial and ethnic inequality, white supremacy, and colonization and often without even a focus on Canada ... I felt insecure and attacked for being a white middle-class student in this class. I understand the value in what she was trying to teach but the manner in which it was done made me defensive and far less receptive to learning. (Student G)

There are other issues that are important in Canadian Society than just the White Settler Society. I signed up for the course to learn about culture, diversity, ethnicity, gender, government, race, religion ... She could have made an effort to stay more neutral and academic. (Student F)

I felt very uncomfortable in this class, as a White, middle-class person. I understand the long-lasting effects that colonization and Europeans have had on Canada, as I am a 3rd-year Sociology major. However, I have never felt so attacked in a classroom situation because of my background. I felt very defensive, which was not conducive to a beneficial learning environment for me. (Student E)

The above comments demonstrate that, to bring comfort and joy, the course "Canadian Society" should be absolved of its teaching of the history of colonialism and white supremacy, and should only reproduce and naturalize the happy image of Canada. It is I who "should be" reinforcing such benevolent imaginations and perform as the grateful, joyful woman of colour who MUST (re)produce happy national subjects by infusing the learning experience in the classroom of white academia with positivity, objectivity, and neutrality.

Ahmed (2009, 2010) offers the important theoretical framework of the "feminist killjoys." She explains that feminist killjoys did not present themselves as the happy and smiling Other but rather as the feminists who kill the joy of the nation and its national subjects.[3] I refer to *killjoy moments* as pivotal events in the classroom where the faculty of colour not only contextualize hegemonic relations but further "unsettle" the happiness that has been fabricated in the making of a white supremacist nation. Ahmed (2009) specifically recognizes politicized women of colour and Indigenous women who point out forms of racism and exclusion within as "feminist killjoys."[4] hooks (2000) and Ahmed (2000) describe how the proximity of the racialized body causes tension and anxieties for white subjects by unsettling happiness. Ahmed (2009) explains:

Happiness becomes a condition of membership: you have to be happy for them ... You cannot speak about racism; that's too unhappy as it causes them to lose their right to happiness, resting as it is on an ego ideal of being good and tolerant. You certainly should not speak of whiteness, which would implicate them in the force of your critique. You have to stay in the right place to keep your place. (p. 48)

In the classroom, white students and racialized students who invoke whiteness learn to recognize and reject curricula that contest the reproduction of a white settler society and homonationalism.[5] The response during the first month from many students reflects comments such as "Benita is racist towards white people"; "This is uncomfortable"; "There is too much content on First Nations"; and she/the content "is so negative."[6] Racialized and white students invoke the field of whiteness by defending imperialism and nationalist discourse of white entitlement, which revolves around the "hard-working pioneers" who developed and civilized the lands and its Natives. The killjoy challenges institutional hegemonic academia and the hierarchies of power within knowledge creation and distribution. This disruption has taken place because the killjoy has accidentally been welcomed as the stranger through multicultural benevolent discourses of a white settler society. The stranger now disrupts white heterosexual middle-class entitlement and happiness through the emergence and practice of anticolonial pedagogy, which produces her as biased, partial, and lacking objectivity.

The Field of Whiteness and National Power

The presence of Indigenous, Black, and racialized faculty, staff, and students in the Canadian academy produce national anxieties that contest the *field of whiteness*. Ghassan Hage (2000) theorizes belonging to the nation and national accumulated capital. He explains that citizenship is the primary formal marker of national belonging: "The act of taking on citizenship has also been termed 'naturalization,' implying a process of acculturation, of belonging to a national cultural community" (p. 49). Some academics equate citizenship with national belonging, but Hage disagrees. He argues that all categories describing dominant groups "[refer] to cultural possessions which allow their holders to stake certain claims of governmental belonging relative to the weight of the capital in his or her possession" (p. 56). Hage recognizes that the value of each capital is "constantly fluctuating, depending on various historical conjunctures as well as the internal struggle within the field of national power" (p. 57).

Hage (2000) defines the useful concept of "the field of national power," which he asserts is the "field of Whiteness" (p. 57). He explains that whiteness is not a fixed category but rather "an ever-changing, composite cultural historical construct" (p. 58). This construct originated in opposition to Blackness and Brownness, fabrications of colonial relations, where "White has become the ideal of being the bearer of 'Western' civilization ... Whiteness is itself a fantasy position and a field of accumulating Whiteness" (p. 58). Accordingly, Hage argues that "Third World-looking people" are then classified "with very low national capital and ... are invariably constructed as a 'problem' of some sort within all White-dominated societies" (p. 59).

The students' comments above explain the process of unsettlement that they experienced and hence vocalized in multiple ways, claiming that they were the ones who were made to feel bad for being who they were and the ones who experienced discrimination, and ultimately, that they experienced "reverse racism" upon their national bodies which rightfully belong. I displaced their traditional comfortable selves in white academia. One critically engaged student discusses why and how some of their classmates experienced such discomforts:

> I heard some students in the class complaining that there was a sort of "feminist agenda" operating and that even though they were white they aren't settlers; however, I think that is nonsense. It seems to me that the issue for these people is that they had to confront their privilege and were made to feel uncomfortable.
>
> In a sense, [the white tenured faculty's] class was *safer* in that students were not forced to confront their privilege and their complicity in perpetuating systems of domination and inequality. However, I think that this semester [with Benita Bunjun] was much more useful for the very reason that people were made to feel uncomfortable. If people look at these issues without examining how they are complicit in the production of them, then they cannot become aware that they are part of the problem. This class had the effect of making people understand their social location and how their unique positionality plays into the different issues we examined. Therefore students were (hopefully) able to see how they sometimes benefited from and contributed to systems of oppression. I think that this kind of awakening really forces people to at least examine their own social situation and is much more likely to contribute to larger social change. (Student A)

Hence, throughout the term, I was consistently compared to another white faculty who taught the first part of the course – an inevitable comparison between a white heterosexual faculty with tenure and me, a racialized queer faculty without tenure. Such comparisons included the guaranteed *safety, comfortability, and happiness* that the white faculty offered, which brought reassurance and reproduction of a hegemonic classroom environment and further created a hierarchy of scholarly legitimacy. How dare I teach from a critical race feminist perspective while centring historically omitted material! Further, how dare *I* project my full subjectivity as other white faculty have done for decades! How dare I speak about the Other and at times as the Other! It appears that I have committed a great crime, not only by exposing Canada's colonial white supremacist history but, even more devastatingly, by invoking guilt and defensiveness. This comparison between myself and the other faculty produced the construction of me as the "unhappy ungrateful queer instructor of colour" who shed her unhappiness onto those who are either happy white settlers or happy grateful settlers of colour; both invest in the invocation and deployment of the field of whiteness.

Many students of colour within our classrooms, including racialized international students, have often found comfort in reproducing the white nation-state with the hope of belonging and acceptance, and become what has been referred to as the "model minority." According to Kalman-Lamb (2013), the model minority "represent the ideal immigrant citizen: English-speaking, middle class/bourgeois, disciplined, and hard-working. As such, they serve a disciplinary function for other immigrants by demonstrating how it is they should act and producing a standard against which they are evaluated" (p. 238). Douglas (2012) also explains the refusal or denial of white supremacy and white privilege by white subjects and also by racialized minorities.

For Canada and its academic post-secondary institutions, the field of whiteness produces and facilitates the claim of legitimate white Canadianness and white academics. This field of national power is further complicated when "this dynamic of accumulation reaches its limitations ... when it comes face to face with those whose richness in national capital does not come from a struggle to accumulate and 'be like' White Australians [Canadians], but who appear 'naturally' White Australians [Canadians]" (Hage, 2000, p. 61). How one accumulates such capital is an important determinant of its national recognition and legitimacy. Therefore, "no matter how much national capital a 'Third World-looking' migrant accumulates, the fact that he or she has acquired it, rather than being born with it, devalues what he or she possesses" (p. 62) in comparison to the "naturally" white Canadian national subject.

Bodies Out of Place: The Ejection of White Entitlement and Happiness

The mere presence of a racialized politicized body within white academia is itself a form of resistance that deeply disrupts spatial, symbolic, political, and affective white entitlements. In particular, as a racialized South Asian queer feminist, my presence and pedagogy has been defined by white liberal academia as an encroachment that threatens its heteronormative middle-/upper-class field of whiteness. By attempting to not reproduce such a landscape of the grateful racialized feminist, the feminist killjoy emerges and is constructed as the most threatening due to not catering to white institutional and national entitlements as natural and inevitable. It is our colonial encounters with administrations, students, and each other within such bourgeois intellectual institutions that produce differently positioned strangers. Our influence as racialized strangers who were never meant to teach within white academia is deeply troubling. If we were meant to walk the halls of white academia, it was only through processes of servitude such as cleaners, cooks, and clerical staff. Through the processes of colonization and immigration, the imperial multicultural project has brought forth racialized subjects into spaces that were solely for white subjects (Hage, 2000), for example, the presence of Indigenous bodies and bodies of colour who intellectually entered and carved academic spaces within a white settler society. Ahmed (2009, 2010) emphasizes that *some bodies* are constructed as negative and are encountered as being negative. Frye (1983) explains that "it is often a requirement of oppressed people that we smile and be cheerful. If we comply, we signify our docility and our acquiescence in our situation" (p. 2). Therefore, those who are oppressed must show and demonstrate signs of happiness and gratefulness, and hence those who do not may be perceived as negative, angry, hostile, undeserving, and unhappy.

Ahmed (2010) introduces the concept of "happiness duty" (p. 59). Happiness, she explains, can be constructed as a duty that functions as a debt owed that must be returned in the form of happiness. As politicized faculty of colour who experience processes of exclusion while being policed, disciplined, and regulated, we are taught that we must be thankful for the opportunity, paid work, and space, and perform the happiness duty to predominately white academics, administrators, staff, and students. Ahmed (2010) emphasizes that bodies pass as happy in order "to keep things in the right place" (p. 59). Those who are willing to speak out about their unhappiness or refuse to make others happy become objects and symbols of the troublemaker or killjoy. "The feminist killjoy 'spoils' the happiness of others; she is a spoilsport because she refuses to convene, to assemble, or to meet up over happiness" (p. 65). Student Z below articulates her understanding and transformation as a student engaging with critical thinking:

I know Benita will most likely get plenty of negative comments, but I enjoyed her class. I think there was initial negative reaction because compared to [the white tenured faculty] Benita is more "intense" and presents more

critical and "controversial" views on society. Also Benita's course was hea-
vier on theory compared to [the white tenured faculty's], that is, since [the
white tenured faculty's] barely had any, which contributed to the general
dislike. I feel that students who took this course without a general interest in Canadian society (because it is a required course) generally ended
up feeling negative about Benita's class because it is more rigorous and
demanding. I liked it, however, and I found it worth my time since I learned a lot from this course, and it inspired me to become more active in
social issues. (Student Z)

Hence, I not only destroy happiness and joy but also become attributed
as the origin of bad feeling and unhappiness. Some students thus construct feminist killjoys as unhappy people who ruin *their* space, *their*
symbols, *their* politics, and *their* emotions. But other students, who dare
to open their minds and hearts, experience the benefits from such scholarship and pedagogy. By introducing different pedagogical styles, theoretical frameworks, and critical praxis, many students like Student Z
have benefitted from how such transformative learning has impacted
every aspect of their lives and relations. What has been the most threatening, especially to white students, has been the process of unsettling
the grand narrative of Canada as good and benevolent, and the myth
that it was peacefully settled. Often any critiques of the nation-state,
including the military, governments, and laws, as well as symbolic
forms of entitlement such as hockey, the maple leaf, and the Canadian
anthem, have provoked moments of anger and the need to protect the
nation from such critical engagement.

    When the feminist killjoy within academic spaces is seen to be dis-
turbing the fragility of the space, spatial entitlements are then threatened, because spatial happiness is undermined as it interacts with other
forms of entitlement. Often what does not get noticed is what makes
the feminist killjoy courageously perform and speak in the way that
she does. What are the invocations and deployments of power relations that produce the effects of excluding her, denying her scholarship,
and omitting her subjectivity? Ahmed (2010) also explains that feminist
killjoys, such as queer working-class women of colour feminists, are
seen to get into trouble because they are already read as being trouble before anything happens. Hence, power relations of exclusion and
representation are already invoked prior to the possible deployment
of these power relations across difference. For example, a feminist killjoy teaching "Canadian Society" as someone not born in Canada, or a
racialized person teaching English composition, will be seen as not sufficiently competent, legitimate, or scholarly.[7] Such explicit and implicit

bias is purposefully embedded in organizations in order to create legitimacy for white subjects of the nation and alleviate their fears of Indigenous, Black, and racialized encroachment. Douglas (2012) argues that,
because the majority of professors are white, it is easy to float the idea
that white people are best suited to become authority figures. Not only
does this idea have an influence on creating the "legitimate" scholar as
well as determining the "best" candidate to be teaching, but Douglas
further argues that, by only having white professors, the language and
what is being taught by white professors influence students' perspectives on the topic.

Many evaluations from the sociology course showed that a number
of students were well aware of the attacks that I would experience from
their own friends and classmates, not only for teaching critical content
within an intersectional analysis but for daring to teach, articulate, and
speak about the field of whiteness. Student T provides an example of
critical awareness, exhibiting both a scholarly manner as well as an
awareness of power within the classroom while also demonstrating
compassion:

> I am aware Benita will probably get many scathing reviews. From the time
> I have spent with my classmates, I believe that this is because they were not
> ready to have their ways of thinking changed by someone who comes off
> so strongly. This is very unfortunate in a sociology class. A major frustration
> for me and a small selection of my classmates was the fact that they often
> discounted ideas brought up by Benita, probably *just because it was Benita
> that was saying them*. Benita's analysis of Canadian society went very deep,
> and I strongly appreciate this although many of my classmates might not.
> I truly believe that everyone at [this university] should be taking this class
> with her and learning what she teaches. (Student T; emphasis in original)

Therefore the killjoys are seen as disrupting unity and fracturing the
climate of the classroom because they speak out against the intersecting racist, classist, transphobic, nationalist, and ableist talk and culture
within white academia's everyday discourses. Unfortunately, in this
case, the feminist killjoy faculty of colour is attributed as the cause of
unhappiness, and her critical engagement is read as targeting the happiness of her students rather than aimed at what nonwhite subjects
are unhappy about. Ahmed (2010) articulates how certain bodies are
encountered as being negative:

> Does bad feeling enter the room when somebody expresses anger about
> things, or could anger be the moment when the bad feelings that circulate

through objects get brought to the surface in a certain way? Feminist subjects might bring others down not only by talking about unhappy topics ... but by exposing how happiness is sustained by erasing the very signs of not getting along. Feminists do kill joy in a certain sense: they disturb the very fantasy that happiness can be found in certain places. To kill a fantasy can still kill a feeling. It is not just that feminists might not be happily affected by the objects that are supposed to cause happiness but that their failure to be happy is read as sabotaging the happiness of others. (p. 66)

The killjoy becomes what Ahmed (2010) describes as "affectively alien," because she affects others in the wrong way. Her "proximity gets in the way of other people's enjoyment of the right things, functioning as an unwanted reminder of histories that are disturbing, that disturb an atmosphere" (p. 56). Many Indigenous, Black, and racialized scholars have written about their experiences of inequities, exclusion, discrimination, backlash, and discipline within predominately white academics spaces as instructors (tenured, untenured, sessionals), staff, and administrators (Douglas, 2012; Dua, 2009; Edwards, 2014; Henry, 2015; Monture-Angus, 1995, 2010; Verjee, 2013). Not only different degrees and intensities of white entitlement and its relationship to space, land, and territory are questioned but the emotions, symbols, and politics attached to the making and sustaining of such white entitlement within the field of whiteness are also interrogated.

Critical Reflections and Lessons from Racialized Students in Academia

Drawing on several racialized student initiatives over the last fifteen years at several universities on Coast Salish territories, this section demonstrates the pivotal importance of such sites of racialized students' academic well-being. I draw on the following networks, where I was either a student member or later a resource sessional/tenure-track faculty, to support such significant spaces of survival for Indigenous, Black, and students of colour. The main theme that is dominant in all the networks is the acknowledgment that universities were exclusive colonial projects for the white elites who taught and continue to teach the naturalization of the field of whiteness. Racialized students and faculty come to understand that their presence troubles and unsettles white students and faculty. It is ultimately a site of political, affective, and social regulation and control where racialized Others must be reproduced and regulated within Canada. Therefore, academia becomes a powerful sociopolitical geographical space of the accumulation of national entitlement embedded in colonial discourses and encounters of racialization, whiteness, and Othering. Whiteness, again, becomes a marker of national belonging and global mobility/ entitlement.

Racialized students have repeatedly explained[8] that they are expected to bring comfort and joy to white students in the classroom, group work, and student services. Here again, they must know their place by reproducing and naturalizing the happy image of Canada by performing happiness for their white national classmates, professors, and student service providers. They must do so by showing thankfulness, appreciation, and gratefulness. Anything to the contrary demonstrates disruption, chaos, and ungratefulness requiring management and disciplining of the racialized subject. This performance that is expected of the Other produces the effect of academic violence upon the intellectual, physical, and emotional well-being of racialized graduate and undergraduate students. The students' narratives of academic violence provide evidence of bodily injury and trauma within classrooms; from professors, officers, student services, and supervisors; and as precarious employees of the university. The most discussed aspect of academic violence is invoked in the classroom, either through the curriculum and/or the instructor's pedagogical standpoint.

Based on my consulting and coordination work with the Academic Well-Being of Racialized Students (AWRS) project and with a group of social work students, several areas of academic violence experienced by these students can be determined. First, students articulated how the erasure, omission, appropriation, and silences about non-Eurocentric knowledges and histories, which often represented themselves, brought forth experiences of invisibility and erasure of their self, family, and community. The majority of those who perpetuated this erasure were white professors whose pedagogical style often resulted in violence and displacement of racialized students' knowledges, histories, and lived experiences. White national bodies were seen as the legitimate keepers, transferers, and experts of knowledge. For example, students found it very difficult to bring forth their experiences of displacement, war, and migration, as they felt the instructor or classroom environment was unwelcoming. The irony of the capitalist marketing and recruitment of international students is that such students pay significantly higher tuition for the very same Eurocentric knowledge that their ancestors fought against during times of struggle for independence in the colonies.

Monture-Angus (1995) recalls her time as an Indigenous law student who experienced academic violence as her courses engaged in an erasure of the colonial relationship between Canada and Indigenous nations. She states:

> I was so shocked I could not say and did not say a word about the total disappearance of First Nations, First Nations history and belief, or the colonial relations Canada was building upon. The entire system of property law in this country is built on a lie – that colonial myth ... None of my colleagues knew the impact that Canada's colonial past was having on me as an Aboriginal person in my class at law school and this compounded the experience of alienation and isolation. Nobody in that law school was conscious of the fact that they were lying and I was overwhelmed at being expected to quietly participate in the disappearance of my people. (p. 81)

Monture-Angus's experience described above is one that is common for many Indigenous students in academic institutions across settler societies. Cote-Meek's (2014) research focuses on the specific challenges and barriers experienced by Indigenous students in the academic colonial space of the classroom, a site where Indigenous students must consistently negotiate culture and racism. Indigenous students and students of colour are repeatedly marked as different and outsiders, both racially and culturally. The classroom is a powerful space of colonial encountering between the instructor (possibly a teaching assistant) and differently positioned students: "what is transmitted in that space and the relationships that occur in that space are all affected by longstanding and ongoing colonial and imperial practices" (Cote-Meek, 2014, p. 91).

Second, the lack of praxis in many disciplines that preached the importance of connecting to community and to those being studied brought forth deep contradictions and hypocrisy within such disciplines. Students found it difficult to reconcile with this tension and disagreement. White faculty presented themselves as exalted subjects who are seen as the most objective and legitimate, and are rewarded with the mandate to teach about the Other, not only to the Other but also to other white subjects about one's place in the world. This form of exaltation is discussed by Thobani (2007), who argues that the process of legitimization and belonging produces national subjects as exalted. This exaltation reinforces the subject to experience the self as preferred and differently valued above all Others. Thobani illustrates that the act of exaltation began at contact through colonization and the construction of Canada and Canadian identity as legitimate by law and by policies such as the Indian Act, immigration, and citizenship. This belief that one is above all Others produces discourses of what is right and good, and becomes the basis for the foundation of the nation through white supremacy. Hence, the creation of white Canada is based on processes of exclusions and exaltation, which are profoundly embedded in our institutions and organizations.

The third identified area of academic violence is the assumption that international and exchange students are "incompetent" because of the intersecting identities of being racialized, having an accent, and coming from the "Third World." Students' narratives discuss the pressure to identify a preferred name to use as members of the academic community, a name that is not a name they prefer but rather one preferred by those of dominant white settler society. International students' learning experiences in Canada have largely erased their intersectional identities and experiences regarding language, citizenship, and geography, which has resulted in weak pedagogical variations and accommodations. Exchange students shared that they are constructed as invisible, needy, dependent, or "the annoying exchange students."[9] They are also pressured to construct themselves first and foremost by invoking Anglo names to bring comfort and happiness to their administrators, teachers, and classmates. Adopting Anglo names results in the abandonment of their traditional ancestral and spiritual names given at birth from extended family and community. This practice can be understood as the production of ancestral and epistemic violence, while prioritizing the English worldview. I recall the many times when white students, who feel a sense of solidarity with me due to my being a dominant accent English speaker, complained that they should not have to hear or work with instructors or students with "non-Canadian accents." One of these students stated: "I pay good tuition and should not have to hear or be taught by someone with an accent."[10] This view, along with racist and inaccessible pedagogical styles and exclusive curriculum, results in a complex series of tensions and contradictions that impede international racialized students' academic well-being.

Fourth, racialized students in their multiplicity, specificity, and diversity are often homogenized, erasing difference across ethnic, racialized, and geographical groups. This form of essentializing results in the lack of space for intellectual integrity and knowledge production. Through the AWRS project, participants were able to articulate pieces of themselves that have never or rarely been able to emerge or be recognized in the classroom. These include the complexities of ancestral and family histories of war, displacement, migration, racial profiling, and other forms of exclusion. The lack of space, pedagogy, and curriculum interact to create a system of Eurocentric, white supremacy paradigm default. Thobani (2007) provides an explanation for understanding this Eurocentric paradigm default when she discusses the naturalization of exaltation:

> Rather than simply denoting "natural" human qualities, exaltation as a technique of power politicizes these characteristics, defining the national community as a whole as possessive of these, regardless of the actual attributes of individual members. It elevates the human status of this political – and politicized – subject as a civilized and worthy subject, hence deserving of certain rights and entitlements, and as capable of exercising these rights with the appropriate measure of responsibility. Yet, even as exaltation elevates, it simultaneously "naturalizes" these qualities as essential aspects of the human nature of national subjects, as intrinsic to the superior order of their humanity. (p. 87)

Cote-Meek's (2014) research on Indigenous students in colonized classrooms highlights the denial of racism as the most frustrating act of racism experienced by the students. Often, students are asked to perform their culture or history or "be the Native expert," which results in racist voyeurism, and at other times, they are constructed as not sufficiently intelligent or "not university material." Additionally, Indigenous or Native studies courses are not acknowledged as academic courses – a form of institutional racism. As Cote-Meek points out, "Aboriginal professors [and] Aboriginal students find themselves having to contend with racialized constructions of inferiority that attach [to] Native-based programs and Native studies courses" (p. 105).

Hence, Indigenous, Black, and students of colour across multiple identities and lived experiences – such as working multiple jobs; being a single parent; living in poverty; having a family history of residential school and child apprehension; being of mixed race identity or a refugee; having experienced displacement, war, or migration; being a descendant of slaves/indentured labourers; as well as histories of birthplace – have no place in the classroom. Monture-Angus (1995) demonstrates her anger in response to her colonial academic experience as an Indigenous law student and later as a law professor: "What I am naming as anger feels more like thunder, thunder in my soul. Sometimes, it is quiet distant rumbling. Other times it rolls over me with such force that I am immobilized" (p. 68). The student's entire self and full subjectivity cannot exist other than as the exotic, the stranger, and the Other for the exalted national subject. To facilitate for their full subjectivity to emerge is a threat to the national story, as it displaces the national narrative of white settler multicultural Canada. Hage (2000) has defined this situation as the discourse of Anglo decline and displacement, which draws on the *worrying nationalist* who is deeply invested in discourses of white nation fantasy exhibiting white supremacy. Similarly, worrying nationalists fear the racialized Other's presence and leadership within white academia. This fear of displacement and Other-stranger-danger anxieties produced nationalist hegemonic responses of essentialism, exclusion, and racialization.[11] Racialized politicized bodies trouble academic spaces, as it is a body out of place that speaks, contests, and unsettles hierarchies of power creating *discomfort* and *unhappiness*.

Alternative Spaces for Racialized Students' Scholarship, Resistance, and (Cou)Rage

In this section of the chapter, I would like to discuss two recent projects and student initiatives focused on creating spaces of anti-colonial feminist student organizing that I have been part of in some capacity. In the above section, I described the different manifestations of academic violence, and it is precisely this academic violence experienced by Indigenous, Black, and students of colour that has motivated the visioning and creation of spaces of anti-colonial feminist student organizing. Such transformative and transgressive spaces are pivotal tools not only for intellectual rigour and scholarship but also for resistance, survival, mentorship, love, organizing, friendship, and guidance, while holding each other accountable based on individual and collective capacities.

The first initiative that I will discuss is the Centre for Race, Autobiography, Gender, and Age (RAGA) Graduate and Undergraduate Student Networks on Coast Salish territories in British Columbia. Below is the mandate:

> The RAGA Undergraduate and Graduate Student Networks are informal, independent, and volunteer groups that strive to build a supportive network of under/graduate students from UBC [University of British Columbia] who are engaging in critical race feminisms and Indigenous frameworks to facilitate our journey through under/graduate school. The Networks aim to specifically decrease isolation by networking and sharing information/resources while also supporting each other to remain focused on our courses, research and completing our degrees. We hope the space will promote the building of a peer community and encourage group support, as well as one-on-one support. We recognize that racialized students (Indigenous and students of colour) experience additional barriers in the academic institution and therefore a priority goal of the

Networks is to strive to centre and support Indigenous students and students of colour. The Networks value reciprocity, responsibility, confidentiality, trust, and understanding as we aim to share lessons learned during our academic trajectories.[12]

The Graduate Network was initiated in March 2010 with a group of Indigenous students and students of colour, including myself. Over the years it has grown to include over sixty-two MA and PhD students from various disciplines, such as the Institute of Gender, Race, Sexuality and Social Justice; Social Work; Interdisciplinary Studies Graduate Program; Sociology; Educational Studies; Law; Education; Rehabilitation Science (Medicine); Political Science; and Geography.

The summer of 2013 saw the creation of the Undergraduate Network, which grew to include over sixty-one undergraduate students from Sociology; Biology; Psychology; Institute of Gender, Race, Sexuality and Social Justice; First Nations Studies; Geography; Political Science; Anthropology; and Health Sciences. The RAGA Undergraduate and Graduate Students' Networks are unique to UBC, as no other space on campus exists to provide the specific and distinct support particular to racialized (Indigenous students and students of colour) under/graduate students. The networks' commitment to ensuring that racialized students remain focused on accomplishing their degrees is pivotal to building community both on and off campus. Over the next few years since their inception, the networks grew to include not only students from UBC but also from Simon Fraser University, Langara College, Douglas College, Kwantlen Polytechnic University, and other institutions.

Through the evaluation process conducted by the networks, members expressed the importance of such networks. Students shared that they have benefitted from such a network because of the decrease in isolation due to networking and the sharing of resources, especially scholarly and self-care resources, which are not provided by the university. In particular, graduate students appreciated the workshops that provided knowledge on how to navigate graduate school, especially the complexities of supervisory committees, relationships with the supervisor, and research ethics applications. Undergraduate students very much appreciated workshops that focused on how to submit an abstract for, or how to present at, conferences. Another important feedback from students was that the RAGA Student Networks were a pivotal space of creating community care, which would ensure the completion of undergraduate and graduate degrees, as the students experienced academic violence. Many expressed that the space provided a level of love and care rarely found in academic spaces. For many Indigenous students, it was another space that provided valuable and imperative relations between Indigenous peoples of Turtle Island with immigrants, settlers of colour, and descendants of African slaves.

The networks were predominately housed in the RAGA Centre of the Jack Bell Building at UBC. This space provided by the university president in 2010 was very much consistently under threat for a variety of reasons. RAGA was often constructed as a space for Others, a space to be appropriated by white feminists, a space that the administration wanted to package and at times store in a closet. The storing of RAGA, out of sight, out of space was most evident in the summer of 2015 when a number of administrative forces came together to ensure RAGA would lose its current location through a process of erasure and loss of autonomy. Students organized in the best way that they could and over time were able to reclaim the space. This victory was a significant one for the RAGA Student Networks, not only because the space was not lost but also because the students consistently interrogated the administration, which resulted in exposing multiple levels of white supremacy within the institution but also within academic feminist spaces.

The second initiative that I will discuss is the Academic Well-Being of Racialized Students (AWRS) project, which was an alternative school centring six racialized student interns from UBC and Simon Fraser University (SFU). This initiative was funded through my postdoctoral research with the Centre for Gender, Social Inequities, and Mental Health at Simon Fraser University – Harbour Centre. The project promoted the academic well-being of racialized students by centring interdisciplinary critical Indigenous, race, and feminist scholarship, community knowledge, and social justice work. This project derived from my earlier work with students through the Women of Colour Mentoring Program/Network, the Indigenous Women and Women of Colour Leadership Program, and more recently, the RAGA Graduate and Undergraduate Students' Networks.

The project focused explicitly on providing relevant skills, networks, resources, and mentorship to racialized students while promoting their academic and overall well-being. The internship positions were open to undergraduate and graduate students committed to promoting anti-colonial social justice work and building relevant partnerships with community groups in the Vancouver Lower Mainland. The Internship Program focused on a multiple-level mentorship/peer framework, which provided skills building, peer support, and mentorship through a reciprocal process between undergraduate students, graduate students, and myself as a postdoctoral researcher.

The project interns represented racialized students across their multiple intersecting positionalities of queerness, ability, class, citizenship, gender, parenthood, mixed-race identity, birthplace, language, health, (non)international student, and area of study. The interns selected were two SFU undergraduate students from health sciences and social and behavioural sciences; two UBC undergraduate students from psychology and the Institute of Gender, Race, Sexuality and Social Justice; one SFU MA student from gender, sexuality and women's studies; and one UBC MA student from social work.

The interns received hands-on experience assisting with the administration of the Internship Program and the RAGA Graduate and Undergraduate Students' Networks. They strengthened their networking with community groups engaged in critical social justice work while outreaching, building, and strengthening relations across Indigenous and Black/African communities, and communities of colour. The interns engaged in developing and delivering workshops on the academic well-being of racialized students in white academia. Additionally, they engaged in research on racialization and mental health in British Columbia and Canada as a whole, including conducting literature reviews. They built and developed strong critical Indigenous, race, and feminist scholarship. Lastly, they coordinated the Racialized Students Conference in the spring of 2014, and hence developed important skills of conference coordination and the building of responsible communities. Most importantly, interns built long-term sustainable relations among emerging racialized scholars/activists while strengthening inter/intra-generational relations.

Exit Reflections of AWRS Interns

The following narratives are drawn from the interns' exit interview surveys, which centre the profound, explicit implications of such an initiative. In order to maintain some level of confidentiality, the interns' names have been removed and replaced with a pseudonym number.

> The AWRS project permitted I explore very personal issues that had impacted my journey through academia. It was incredibly intellectually stimulating to invest time in discussing with other people of colour on issues related to race relations, whiteness, coloniality and imperialism. Looking back at the experience, I realize that the environment was an invaluable space to learn and share.

We corroborated and affirmed one another's experiences with tokenization in the classroom, which has, for me, translated into the very same tokenization in professional settings. In this way, AWRS was a space of capacity-building. Though our meetings did not eliminate our life-long experiences with racial marginalization, it served to affirm that we possess immense capacity to organize, engage and agitate systems and institutions. It made me trust that my racialization did not hinder me from academic excellence. (Student 20)

AWRS met my academic needs as it was an alternative academia. I read my entry evaluation prior to completing this exit survey. Back then, as a fourth year international university student at UBC, there was in me a defiance, fear of failure and a desperate need to create, to do something tangible that was relevant ...
Being emotionally fragile and very obstinate by nature, I could not reconcile these teachings in the very mainstream classes. AWRS helped me in various ways to incorporate these teachings within an alternative academia.
The strengths of the AWRS Project were that it included a mentor who was not only patient, kind, gentle, considerate and thoughtful but as well as grasped a strong critical analysis and facilitation skills to navigate through such emotional and vulnerable spaces. (Student 30)

It created a safe space where one could be vulnerable and open up to the group. I felt safe, supported and comfortable in the spaces AWRS provided. I could cry and not feel ashamed or embarrassed and in the end, know I am not being judged for it.
All of the workshops were so meaningful to me as they were steps closer to grounding myself, where I come from and who I am. The workshops where we presented our ancestral roots and history and the art workshop were the most meaningful to me as they made me realize the self-hatred I held for myself and the bitterness I felt towards my parents for my upbringing. The workshops made me love myself, my parents and my people. (Student 10)

This became a space for an international POC [people of colour] to explore and create my own materials while sharing thoughts about race, migration background, a changing understanding of sex and gender, as well as Indigenous sovereignty, without getting low grades for it. In most classes, these discussions never qualified as knowledge by the standards/ criteria of marking.

This project taught me to face and explore the fears which I held even from myself. **I feared knowing my ancestors**. It was a self-protective measure which backfired. (Student 30)

The AWRS project provided the skills, resources, and space for a diversity of racialized students including international, exchange, and domestic students. The six interns were able to explore and engage with their own experiences and histories of family, migration, survival, war, displacement, resistance, grief, and communities. Multiple media such as art, poetry, activism, protest, and community building were drawn upon to bring forth such complex experiences and histories individually and collectively within the group. This process often resulted in very painful and vulnerable moments of remembering ancestors' struggles for survival due to different forms of conflict, persecution, wars, apartheid, and violence while recognizing and appreciating the courage, resilience, and love across generations. One of the interns discusses the process below:

Even though I recognized my mental fragility, I did nothing to prepare myself to engage in this process. The presentation forced me to face this fear. However, prior to presenting on that day, I burned a pot, left a shared space unlocked with all windows open, and almost got hit by a car. This process unhinged me, but it also pieced me [together] in the long run. I no longer fear losing my grandmother, the last surviving link to my people. AWRS taught me to study my people's lineage without breaking apart. I also understood how significant mother tongues can be when it comes to connecting and developing relationships with people of similar backgrounds. (Student 40)

Conclusion

In this chapter, drawing on my own experiences as a faculty and on students' voices, I have exposed the various visceral ways in which colonial academia has disfigured racialized Others' lives, bodies, intellect, and relations. I have also demonstrated the vision, resilience, and community that survive coloniality in the academy every day. I end this chapter by arguing that racialized feminist killjoys are pivotal to the institutional academic sites as they *provide the motivating force for institutional change and the necessary source of energy to engage and transform knowledge and scholarship*. For Audre Lorde (1997), it is the feminist killjoy who engages in cou(rage) and anger as she states that "anger is loaded with information and energy" (p. 280). She further asserts:

> I cannot hide my anger to spare you guilt, nor hurt feelings, nor answering anger; for to do so insults and trivializes all our efforts. Guilt is not a response to anger; it is a response to one's own actions or lack of action. If it leads to change then it can be useful, since it is then no longer guilt but the beginning of knowledge. Yet all too often, guilt is just another name for impotence, for defensiveness destructive of communication; it becomes a device to protect ignorance and the continuation of things the way they are, the ultimate protection for changelessness. (p. 282)

This conception of killjoy and anger, or thunder for Monture-Angus, as not merely inhibiting or impeding but rather as the energy that moves, transgresses, and transforms individuals and academic spaces has benefitted many students. Hence, the dissatisfaction and disappointments with white academia contribute to the politicized racialized feminist engagement in envisioning a different site of critical learning, knowledge creation, and the necessary integrity to nurture all students differently based on their intersecting positionalities and specificities. What emerges from this chapter is an intersectional analysis of the feminist killjoy who interrupts national happiness within white academic institutions of a white settler society by threatening the naturalized field of whiteness.

Ahmed (2000) analyzes how the stranger is recognized as a stranger prior to their appearance as a body identified as not belonging and out of place. She examines how the dominant subject of the nation ensures that the boundaries are maintained and enforced in order to keep the stranger out. If the stranger appears to cross the line or come too close, fear accumulates, demanding that the stranger be expelled in order to secure imagined purity and spatial formation. By already recognizing the stranger as not belonging and out of place, the demarcation and enforcement of boundaries crystallize the place we inhabit as home. I demonstrate how racialized students across their intersectional complexities as "bodies out of place" are constructed as strangers who must learn to know their place in order to keep their place, yet, they also interrupt such national makings through community/collective resistance and care. They must strive to maintain autonomy, relevance, and creativity in order to pursue the creation of non-hegemonic spaces, spaces of collective care and determination.

NOTES

1 Those who engage in challenging and transforming institutional inequities, oppressions, and injustices within multiple academic spaces experience backlash and persecution differently than those who do not.
2 See Benedict Anderson's (1991) *Imagined Communities.* Anderson discusses the making of the nation through processes of nationalism resulting in constructing the imagined communities – those who see themselves as belonging as national subjects.
3 Ahmed (2009) suggests that "there is a relationship between the negativity of certain figures and how certain bodies are encountered as being negative" (p. 48).
4 Ahmed (2009, 2010) draws on feminists who have been constructed as killjoy feminists, such as Audre Lorde (1984), bell hooks (2000), and Aileen Moreton-Robinson (2003).
5 See Puar's (2007) work on homonationalism.
6 Comments shared with me by students as they were told by other students.
7 For further discussion of this point, see Gutiérrez y Muhs, Niemann, González, & Harris (2012).
8 Over a period of fifteen years, I have worked extensively with racialized students in women's and gender studies, sociology, social work, and social justice departments and programs – as a coordinator, instructor, consultant, and mentor. Here, I refer to a collection of their experiences as shared with me during office hours, workshops, classrooms, and conferences. My scholarly and community engagement work with the academic well-being of racialized students informs my analysis, pedagogy, and scholarly work.
9 This experience was expressed during several meetings where exchange students were present and supported the coordination of the student conference – Racialized Students Resistance.
10 This comment was expressed openly during class discussions in a Canadian university while I was teaching a women's studies class.
11 This concept is discussed by Ahmed (2012, 2000), Douglas (2012), Gutiérrez y Muhs et al. (2012), Hage (2000), and Monture-Angus (2010, 1995).
12 The RAGA mandate is taken from RAGA Graduate and Undergraduate Student Networks reports from my personal archives.

REFERENCES

Ahmed, S. (2000). *Strange encounters: Embodied others in post-coloniality.* New York: Routledge.

Ahmed, S. (2009). Embodying diversity: Problems and paradoxes for black feminists. *Race, Ethnicity and Education, 12*(1), 41–52. https://doi.org /10.1080/13613320802650931.

Ahmed, S. (2010). *The promise of happiness*. Durham, NC: Duke University Press.

Ahmed, S. (2012). *On being included: Racism and diversity in institutional life*. Durham, NC: Duke University Press.

Anderson, B. (1991). *Imagined communities*. New York: Verso.

Bannerji, H. (2000). *The dark side of the nation: Essays on multiculturalism, nationalism and gender*. Toronto: Canadian Scholars' Press Inc.

Bell, D. (1992). *Faces at the bottom of the well: The permanence of racism*. New York: Basic Books.

Bunjun, B. (2011). *The (un)making of home, entitlement, and nation: An intersectional organizational study of power relations in Vancouver Status of Women, 1971–2018*. (Unpublished doctoral dissertation). University of British Columbia, Vancouver, BC.

Bunjun, B. (2014). The racialized feminist killjoy in white academia: Contesting white entitlement. In G. Yancy & M.G. Davidson (Eds.), *Exploring race in predominantly white classrooms: Scholars of color reflect* (pp. 147–61). New York: Routledge.

Carty, L. (1991). Black women in academia: A statement from the periphery. In H. Bannerji, L. Carty, K. Dehli, S. Heald, & K. McKenna (Eds.), *Unsettling relations: The university as a site of feminist struggles* (pp. 13–43). Toronto: Women's Press.

Carty, L. (1999). The discourse of empire and the social construction of gender. In E. Dua & A. Robertson (Eds.), *Scratching the surface: Canadian antiracist feminist thought* (pp. 35–47). Toronto: Women's Press.

Collins, P.H. (2019). *Intersectionality: As critical social theory*. Durham, NC: Duke University Press.

Cote-Meek, S. (2014). *Colonized classrooms: Racism, trauma, and resistance in post-secondary education*. Halifax, NS: Fernwood Press.

Crenshaw, K., Gotanda, N., Peller, G., & Thomas, K. (Eds.). (1995). *Critical race theory: The key writings that formed the movement*. New York: New Press.

Culhane, D. (1998). *The pleasure of the Crown: Anthropology, law and First Nations*. Burnaby, BC: Talonbooks.

Devereux, C. (1999). New woman, new world: Maternal feminism and the new imperialism in the white settler colonies. *Women's Studies International Forum, 22*(2), 175–84. https://doi.org/10.1016/S0277-5395(99)00005-9.

Douglas, D. (2012). Black/Out. In G. Gutiérrez y Muhs, Y.F. Niemann, C.G. González, & A.P. Harris (Eds.), *Presumed incompetent: The intersections of race and class for women in academia* (pp. 50–64). Salt Lake City: Utah State University Press.

Dua, E. (2009). On the effectiveness of anti-racist policies in Canadian universities: Issues of implementation of policies by senior administration. In C. Tator & F. Henry (Eds.), *Racism in the Canadian university: Demanding social justice, inclusion, and equity* (pp. 160–95). Toronto: University of Toronto Press.

Edwards, K.T. (2014). "The whiteness is thick": Predominantly white classrooms, student of color voice, and Freirian hopes. In G. Yancy & M. del Guadaloupe Davidson (Eds.), *Exploring race in predominantly white classrooms*. New York: Routledge.

Frye, M. (1983). *The politics of reality: Essays in feminist theory.* Trumansburg, NY: Crossing Press.

Gutiérrez y Muhs, G., Niemann, Y.F., González, C.G., & Harris, A.P. (Eds.). (2012). *Presumed incompetent: The intersections of race and class for women in academia.* Salt Lake City: Utah State University Press.

Hage, G. (2000). *White nation: Fantasies of white supremacy in a multicultural society.* New York: Routledge.

Henry, A. (2015). "We especially welcome applications from members of visible minority groups": Reflections on race, gender and life at three universities. *Race, Ethnicity and Education, 18*(5), 589–610. https://doi.org /10.1080/13613324.2015.1023787.

Henry, F., Dua, E., James, C.E., Kobayashi, A., Li, P., Ramos, H., & Smith, M. (2017). *The equity myth: Racialization and Indigeneity at Canadian universities.* Vancouver, BC: UBC Press.

hooks, b. (2000). *Feminist theory: From margin to centre.* London: Pluto Press.

Kalman-Lamb, N. (2013). The athlete as model minority subject: Jose Bautista and Canadian multiculturalism. *Journal for the Study of Race, Nation and Culture, 19*(2), 238–53. https://doi.org/10.1080/13504630.2013.789219.

Lorde, A. (1984). *Sister outsider: Essays and speeches.* Freedom, CA: Crossing Press.

Lorde, A. (1997). The uses of anger. *Women's Studies Quarterly, 25*(1/2), 278–85. https://www.jstor.org/stable/40005441.

Matsuda, M.J., Lawrence III, C., Delgado, R., & Crenshaw, K. (1993). *Words that wound: Critical race theory, assaultive speech and the first amendment.* Boulder, CO: Westview Press.

Mawani, R. (2009). *Colonial proximities: Crossracial encounters and juridical truths in British Columbia, 1871–1921.* Vancouver, BC: UBC Press.

Monture-Angus, P. (1995). *Thunder in my soul.* Toronto: Fernwood Publishing.

Monture-Angus, P. (2010). Race, gender, and the university: Strategies for survival. In S. Razack, M. Smith, & S. Thobani (Eds.), *States of race: Critical race feminism for the 21st Century* (pp. 23–35). Toronto: Between the Lines.

Moreton-Robinson, A. (2003). I still call Australia home: Indigenous belonging and place in a white postcolonizing society. In S. Ahmed, C.

Castameda, A.M. Fortier, & M. Sheller (Eds.), *Uprootings/regroundings: Questions of home and migration* (pp. 23–40). New York: Berg.

Puar, J.K. (2007). *Terrorist assemblages: Homonationalism in queer times.* Durham, NC: Duke University Press.

Razack, S. (2002). When place becomes race. In S. Razack (Ed.), *Race, space and the law: Unmapping a white settler society* (pp. 121–56). Toronto: Between the Lines.

Smith, M. (2010). Gender, whiteness, and other: Others in the Academy. In S. Razack, M. Smith, & S. Thobani (Eds.), *States of race: Critical race feminism for the 21st Century* (pp. 37–58). Toronto: Between the Lines.

Thobani, S. (2007). *Exalted subjects: Studies in the making of race and nation in Canada.* Toronto: University of Toronto Press.

Valverde, M. (1992). When the mother of the race is free: Race, reproduction, and sexuality in first-wave feminism. In F. Iacovetta & M. Valverde (Eds.), *Gender conflicts: New essays in women's history* (pp. 3–26). Toronto: University of Toronto Press.

Verjee, B. (2013). Counter-storytelling: The experiences of women of colour in higher education. *Atlantis, 36*(1), 22–32. Retrieved from https://journals .msvu.ca/index.php/atlantis/article/view/3183.

10 Dreaming Big in Small Spaces: Prefiguring Change in the Racial University

JIN HARITAWORN

As I make final touches to this chapter in 2019 Toronto, a queer-phobic "Positive Christian Space" demonstration is marching through Toronto's gay village at Church and Wellesley Streets. The alt-right has become a regular presence in our streets, universities, and social media feeds. It's been over a year since Doug Ford became premier of Ontario and three years since Donald Trump became US president. Justin Trudeau is about to get re-elected as Canadian prime minister, barely, with massive losses on the left. In Europe, where I'm from, the far right is also gaining hegemonic status, both in and outside the parliaments. All over the world, it seems, racism is coming out unabashedly, from Brazil to Kashmir to Palestine.

We live in a context not unlike the one described by Octavia Butler, the science fiction writer whose heroines, often Black and queer, fend for themselves and their chosen kin in landscapes of unfettered violence and chaos (see, for example, Butler, 1993). Butler's visionary dystopias are recapturing the imaginations of many contemporary artists and activists who are dreaming up better futures (Brown, 2019). They are fertile grounds for what many have called prefigurative politics: a politics whose means reflect the ends – a politics where we live as if these futures are already here.

Given the atrophied horizons of the bigger social movements, which nostalgically orient themselves towards the lowest common denominator, where is this politics currently possible? This chapter begins with the small spaces and scales that I, a trans of colour academic teaching multiracial and multigender classrooms in a working-class suburb in Canada, have felt some power to reshape in ways that sometimes ripple on to larger spaces. While written from a location that does not readily entail a critical mass or large-scale change, my work both performs from and echoes imagined community. One point of inspiration is my queer of colour lineage that is indebted to Black feminism and expansive of earlier intersectional moments (Brown, 2019; Lorde, 1984; Davis, 2013). I also write alongside a growing number of critical race, Black, and Indigenous theorists who have turned their critical attention to their own workplaces (for example, Ahmed, 2012; Austin, 2013; Ferguson, 2012; Gutierrez y Muhs, Niemann, González, & Harris, 2012; Henry et al., 2017; Hale, 2008; Moten & Harney, 2004; Ng, 1993; Shum, 2015; Shiekh, 1999; Sudbury & Okazawa-Rey, 2009; Rodriguez, 2012; Smith, 1999). Writers have focused on the changing relationship between the university and its racialized and colonized "others" from one that was explicitly antagonistic – as memorialized through the heavily punished strikes and occupations by Black, Indigenous, and racialized students since the late 1960s, from the Bay Area to Montreal – to one that appears to be accommodating and even desiring of difference, repackaged and depoliticized as "diversity" (Ahmed, 2012; Austin, 2013; Ferguson, 2012; Hong, 2008). As a result, a chosen few are now able to perform themselves as privileged symbols of this liberal multicultural diversity regime, often through single-issue performances of gender, sexuality, or disability (Smith, 2010). However, women and queers of colour have highlighted the personal and collective cost of becoming docile subjects, as characterized in the title of the groundbreaking collection *Presumed Incompetent* (Gutierrez y Muhs et al., 2012). As Rod Ferguson (2012) and Grace Hong (2008) both argue, we are faced with a contradictory situation where Black feminism and other subjugated knowledges are included in programs and curricula, while the subjects who produced them are shut out or cycled through revolving doors to the "point of exhaustion, breakdown, and death" (Hong, 2008, p. 105; see also Douglas, 2012).

Beyond this sobering reality, writers have insisted on the agentive possibilities of an activist scholarship that is in service of communities (Sudbury & Okazawa-Rey, 2009; Hale, 2008). Written from several snapshots of my own evolving life, between 2016 and 2019, this chapter walks a similar tightrope. On the one hand, reality checks are still needed, especially for trans people of colour and others whom the university (including in its diverse faces) treats as unintelligible, "new," and falling outside of existing infrastructures of recognition and redress. At the same time, the following pages insist that there remains room for agency, both resistant and allied. They acknowledge the damage, but do not make it their permanent dwelling. They take inspiration from fellow activist scholars to ground our work in our desire (Tuck, 2009; Turtle Tank, n.d.), pleasure (Brown, 2019), intense dreams (Million, 2013), and sense of self or purpose (Pulido, 2008). This chapter, therefore, is also a methodological invitation to manifest knowledge in ways – and genres – that move us closer to our desire and beyond the realist strategies and horizons of most social movement scholarship (Kuumba, 2001). Following this path has meant getting creative, grappling with ghosts (Gordon, 2011), meditating with ancestors – both blood and chosen – and blurring the lines of fantasy and non-fiction, manifesto and autobiography, and ritual and analysis.

The pages ahead touch upon various sites and settings of intellectualism: the debates following the North American elections, the trans of colour–taught classroom, and the realpolitik of the neoliberal institution.[1] Drawing on the ever-growing chorus of intellectuals of colour questioning our role in the racial university, I argue that we need to both become fierce allies, who affirm for each other violences and complicities – some of which we have extensively researched, others we have yet to fully name – and step into our power to manifest other futures and rehearse the relationships that might get us there.

Refusing to Do Our Jobs

There are certain moments that indicate neoliberal multiculturalism (Melamed, 2011) may be on its way out. Terrifyingly and thankfully. It is 2016, and I'm checking Facebook after the US election. Progressive academics in particular are busy performing outrage against the incoming Trump regime and rehearsing their belief in a path to progress from which we will now unfortunately err for a few years. Some maintain that this departure from the onward and upward line was due to some mistake, be it voting lethargy among progressives and people of colour or the Democrats' failure to bet on Bernie Sanders, Hillary Clinton's more left-leaning competitor in the campaign for the 2016 Democratic Party nomination for president. At times, this thinking goes along with a reification of the university as the birthplace of justice, whose mission is to school an apolitical public in the dangers of fascism, along such lines as "Things are terrible right now. Luckily we teach critical thinking."

In the years since, the performativity of liberal outrage has not translated into expanding spaces that begin with the experiences of those who are most vulnerable. On the contrary, the progress fatigue that has ushered in Donald Trump, Doug Ford, and other ultra-right figures and parties is also observable in the bigger social movements themselves and in the intellectuals whom they have produced. There is a discernable lack of fight-back to the ever more brazen stripping away of (tiny) gains and (remaining) entitlements, from trans rights to social assistance, among the more privileged, who in more optimistic times might have been hailed as allies. Instead, there appears to be a nostalgia for earlier times, when things were simpler – when reproductive justice, for example, mainly meant cis-women's abortion rights – and a growing defensiveness around subjects that are considered "new" or "the p.c. that goes too far," often personified by Black, Indigenous, and people of colour on intersections that are considered excessive.

Two years later, in 2018, our social media feeds are again filled with outrage as the Ontario PC Party, a month after the Trump administration's call to redefine sex as "a biological immutable condition determined by genitalia at birth," passes a resolution to debate whether the party should recognize what they describe as "gender identity theory" (Hanssmann, 2018; Rocca, 2018). The resolution is dismissed two days later by the PC Party's own premier Ford, after already doing its discursive work. The debate works to actively reduce trans lives to figments of academic theory, albeit a theory that only claims to be scientific for it is, the resolution claims, a "highly controversial, unscientific 'liberal ideology'" (Rocca, 2018). It recalls earlier moves by conservative governments to take control over education to fix meanings of race, gender, and sexuality – from the recent repeal of the sex ed curriculum by the Ontario PC Party (which also centred around teaching about trans identity as well as consent), to the outlawing of ethnic studies in schools in Arizona and other US states, to section 28 of the Local Government Act in Britain (1988–2000), which attempted to prevent teachers from "promoting" "homosexuality" or its "acceptability" as "a pretended family relationship."[2] Similarly, the resolution to debate recognition of gender identity calls for the removal of this ideology's "teaching and promotion … from Ontario schools and its curriculum" (Rocca, 2018). Education thus, once again, becomes a battleground over racialized and gendered lives – though one in which the left, and in particular the winners of earlier rounds of single-issue struggles, have yet to fully engage.[3] Missing from these debates over pronouns and trigger warnings are the by now well-rehearsed anti-violence frameworks by Black, Indigenous, and racialized feminist, trans, and queer intellectuals, who have highlighted the constitutive role of sexual violence and the colonial gender binary in bringing racial capitalism and settler colonialism to Turtle Island – an unfinished project that these moral panics serve to escalate (Donahue, 2011; Incite!, 2006; NYSHN, FSIS, & NMS, 2014).

However dissident the above social media sound bites appear, they communicate an exaltation, as Sunera Thobani (2007) might say, of the critical scholar and the settler institutions and ideologies that produce and reproduce them: from the liberal state that progressively grants us rights and protections to the neoliberal university, which I more properly refer to as the racial and colonial university,[4] that teaches its logics of meritocracy, equal opportunity, and free speech to elite and non-elite populations alike. The critical scholarship performed in this moment of a state-sanctioned hyper-racism that has gone too far, even for older liberal elites, then, remains dedicated to the very institutions that have brought and upheld white supremacy to and in these lands. It resuscitates them as compelling objects, as antidotes to a slippery slope that they themselves form part of. Indeed, the liberal outrage that was performed on social media did not translate into a mass movement or a large-scale redistribution of activist or academic resources.

At the same time, there are certain aspects to "this moment" that are worth attending to. The outrage against Trump and Ford, rehearsed through a constant repetition of the question "How did we get here?," is clinging to an older model of white supremacy as freedom and equality, however brief its life span was in retrospect, that now appears to have reached its expiry date. Indeed, as the return of the word "fascism" to our shared political vocabulary suggests, white supremacy is increasingly presenting itself in its birthday suit. The question of how we got here, and what the hell we are doing – phrased more politely as "What is the role of the professional intellectual in this moment?" – can thus be posed in a different way that brings to the fore a different moment: one that does not birth but escalates the wars, misleadingly periodized as "on" terror, crime, drugs, and poverty. Many have shown that these wars are really reincarnations of a much older war – on Black and Indigenous peoples, on Muslims, on poor people, trans and queer people, sick, disabled, and mad people of colour – that rarely appears as "fascist" and worth revolting against (Conway, 2017; Saleh-Hanna, 2015). The spatial coordinate and temporal precedent of this war is not the Holocaust, but the arrival of Europeans in the Americas, Africa, Asia, and the Pacific. It is the vibrant afterlife of the settlement/plantation, in Tiffany King's (2013) insightful words, and, I would add, its allied institutions: the prison, the border, *and the university*. To re-pose these questions in the timeline of the settlement/plantation renders us sensitive to how our training prepares us for positions that, while often glorified as critical thinking, might more appropriately be described, following Moten (2016), as jobs in the enclosure (see also Moten & Harney, 2004). As other activist scholars, such as Joy James and Edmund Gordon (2008) and Chinyere Oparah (Sudbury, 2009), have also argued, the racial and colonial university trains its teachers to become overseers, handmaidens of capitalism, and reproducers of the next generation of prison wardens.

The question, in this refracted historical horizon, is not how we can play Clinton to Trump. Nor is it reducible to the slogans of equity, diversity, and inclusion that have traditionally governed discussions of racism in the university. Rather, we must ask what we have to contribute to the self-defense of Black, Indigenous, and people of colour communities in this war, which, while far from new, has indeed just escalated. The next section suggests ways of divesting the classroom – that glorified but dramatically underused space for rehearsing relationships, building people power, and marvelling otherwise – from the logics of the racial and neoliberal university. In contrast to any glorified notion of critical thinking or free speech, I argue that our job there is far from a renewal of our professional identities. It is, rather, a refusal to do our jobs.

Beyond the Glorified Teacher

Many of us have stayed for the students: for our POC [people of colour] students who feel they have no place in the university or in the world; for our QTPOC [queer and trans people of colour] students who need to be in the company of somebody who will let them come out and come into themselves on their own terms and in their own language and who won't mind them hiding beyond middle-class aspirations like "getting into graduate school." At the same time, we are well aware of the neoliberal traps of "staying for the students." Thus, students, too – especially, but not only, those white, cis, and/or male students for whom our classroom is often the only place where they have to confront the facts of racial/colonial capitalism and cis-heteropatriarchy – have a hard time respecting us and regularly reinscribe us as affectable subjects (da Silva 2007). When we help these students understand how their history was mutually created with and deeply imbricated with structures of oppression that entrapped and strangled people from other communities, our teaching is deemed too "political," even as the neoliberal university decorates itself with us. We regularly receive worse evaluations, and more complaints, than our white colleagues. We perform an enormous amount of free labour to compensate for the university's own inability to deal with race, coloniality, class, gender, and sexuality. Yet our service record, just like our skin, is always "too thin."

– Bacchetta et al. (2018)

In our co-authored article in the *Critical Ethnic Studies* special issue on "The Academy and What Can Be Done," Paola Bacchetta, Fatima El-Tayeb, Jillian Hernandez, S.A. Smythe, Vanessa Thompson, Tiffany Willoughby-Herard, and I wrestled with a question we often pose to ourselves: Why do you stay? One of the answers we came up with, but immediately problematized, is "It's for the students." Grace Hong, in her exploration of the violent terms of inclusion for Black feminist scholarship, rightly describes the academy as a hostile environment where "racialized and gendered bodies" are managed to the "point of exhaustion, breakdown, and death" (Hong, 2008, p. 105). It does not matter how hard we try to pass as worthy of its merits.

We might take this point as a warning of the dangers in glorifying the teacher. The reality is that the work we are doing is not always the work that needs to be done, and it is becoming harder to do the latter. We write books that may or may not be read, let alone change lives. We make our students write papers when they could be organizing. We are radicals rather than revolutionaries in James and Gordon's (2008) sense: We "show up" to work when we could do more important things. We spend long hours sitting through departmental meetings, equity committee meetings, and union meetings. We write references, tenure files, and grant applications for American Sign Language interpretation for events that will make programs that work hard to uphold white, masculine, cis, able-bodied norms of scholarship look deceptively inclusive. We battle with bureaucrats in order to get people paid. We lose sleep over that hire that will never materialize, or if it does, then only to diversify the status quo. We work to keep each other in our units. We work for rent and to redistribute resources to our students, colleagues, and community members. This work is dispiriting and often sickening, so we make sure it is divided fairly in a way that collectivizes the costs. We share the dirty work and appreciate the shifts that each person takes so that we can all do our share of the real work, and stay fed and well. This is one of the tasks of equity politics in the racial/colonial university.

I am not going to tell you what the real work is because it will take a lot of us to figure it out together. If there is something hopeful about this moment, it is that many are now ready to build. However, I will suggest that we can do much more to pry spaces and resources away from the enclosed university. The spaces that we have are limited, and they are steeped in violence and complicity. My generation of un/professional[5] intellectuals, of queers of colour who have jumped the gate, know this. Gender studies, schmender studies: we are unaffiliated, and we do not waste too much of our breath on performing diversity in the sideshow (James & Gordon, 2008). All that we touch still changes (Butler, 1993). At times we work magic. We transform classrooms for which no pedagogy of the oppressed was written. We humanize these rooms where we experience lateral violence and sexual assault at the hands of colleagues and students, not by giving up an authority we never had, nor by accepting that we are powerless. We transform these hostile spaces into communities where we build and share power and responsibility. In these rooms, students become comrades to each other and to us. They use institutional evaluation forms against the institution rather than against us. They resolve conflicts and give and receive critiques in ways that divest from the institution's punitive and individualizing culture of competition and complaint. We transfigure our classrooms and hallways into spaces where we can name the necropolitical status quo, then get to the business of inverting its violent logics. We divest these resources away from the university and reinvent them as sites to be liberated so that we may dream up and live marvellous futures, here and now (Haritaworn, Moussa, & Ware, 2018). We reclaim literacy from its elite use as a tool of distinction to its insurgent uses. We use it to fertilize our imagination, to write ourselves into community that doesn't (yet) exist, and to give each other reality checks. We retool reading and writing from methods of domination to methods of communication that source promiscuous memories and visions of the future. These visions provide collective road maps that help us value and nurture each other, not only to stay alive but to thrive. We re/member ourselves and our communities inside and outside these walls as human, as more than human, as interdependent. We teach and learn contents and methods that are in the service of radical movements (Sudbury & Okazawa-Rey, 2009). Our peoples' perseverance in these hostile halls is not a tribute to benevolent reason but to successive generations of students, faculty, and staff who have refused to do their job, blocking roads and occupying campuses in order to make unreasonable and excessive demands: like free tuition, like real education, like an end to exploitation, racial profiling, and the neoliberal carceral university itself.

Beyond the Critical Scholar

This work entails continuous reality checks to remind us that the university is far from innocent; that it arrived here on the same ships as the electoral regimes that ushered in Trump. As Linda Tuhiwai Smith (1999) and others have pointed out, the university has played a privileged role in reproducing colonialism and imperialism: educating the next generation of colonizers and those who strive to become (like) them. We must not expect recognition from this university, even if it wears the face of a brown president, a female dean, or a woman of colour or queer person of colour heading the union's race/equity/

LGBT/feminist/diversity caucus. We cannot afford the cruel optimism (Berlant, 2006) of directing dreams towards the next promotion
or the next invitation to write this article, give that keynote, or serve
on that committee. We cannot invest all our hope in the cis-gender
elder to whom we have long looked up, to then find her struggling
to recognize our contribution and return our identificatory gaze. We
cannot afford to disintegrate every time we get disinvited again, once
the price of engaging us becomes greater than our waxing and waning
exploit as the latest token of diversity. We must not accept all invitations, and we must refuse to bear their costs alone.

Sometimes we do fall apart. And sometimes we become models of
integrity, mirrors that reflect dignity in the face of repeated attempted
disposal, mirrors that reflect each other whole. Sometimes we are the
lone party pooper, the most juniorized presenter, and the only one paying our own airfare, the one whose pronouns are messed up (again),
the one who misses half the conference because we got lost looking for
the accessible bathroom. On a button sold in the mid-2000s, disabled
intersex transgender and intersex activist Emi Koyama[6] told us to just
pee everywhere when organizers disregard our basic access needs and
don't seem to notice or care if we're able to stay in the room or not. We
cannot internalize these messages, and we must not allow the university – including in its diverse face – to suck our lifeblood, our capacity
to vision, and be part of a future that is not more of the same, not more
terrible than the present.

I do not mean these words trivially. We must support the survival
struggles of labour and refuse to reduce these to the arrested careers of
the white middle-class cis-men and cis-women for whom the tenure track
was built. Instead, we must uphold those targeted by chronic exhaustion, attrition, and premature death, those who are presumed incompetent long after gaining their PhDs (Douglas, 2012). We must do better to
keep each other alive, to mirror each other's worth. We must fight for our
capacity to continue living, both in but especially beyond these walls.

This work requires that we become disloyal to the university. We
"abuse its hospitality [and] spite its mission," as Moten and Harney
(2004, p. 101) write. We refuse its mythologies of respectability and
professionalism, of equal opportunity, of merit and promotion. We join
the undercommons and move to the kitchen table when the beer bars
and the picket lines become themselves sites of violence. We learn from
Black students, Palestinian students, Indigenous students, trans and
queer of colour students, who are already creating alternative safety
nets and communities of care. We join struggles to resist racial profiling
on campus, not because we do not want to be mistaken for criminals,

nor because we feel entitled to campus resources over those who are always already in the wrong institution.

We refuse anti-intellectualism, and we do not romanticize those non-academic structures that are equally shot through with racial capital and liberal multicultural cis-heteropatriarchal hierarchies, such as the non-profit sector or the arts industrial complex. We learn to be community members rather than walking credit machines or punch bags onto whom centuries of internalized oppression can be safely projected. The relationships we build are reciprocal and sustainable. They anticipate the world we want to live in.

We are human, we learn from mistakes, and we are not respectable. We do not aspire to be recognized by white reason and white law. We do not buy into their lies of meritocracy and equal opportunity. We do not distance ourselves from the labels criminal, madman, pervert, and prostitute that stick to our eternally youthful, affectable bodies (Ahmed, 2014; da Silva, 2007). We appreciate each other's worth and merits, but we refuse to be exalted. We were let in accidentally, mistaken as docile and diverse. And so we work harder to betray the privileges that got us here – from class and gender conformity, to shade and ability, to non-Black or non-Indigenous descent, to rescuable genealogies that are not from here.

We critique, and we explore models of accountability that divest from the punitive, isolating, and competitive logics of the neoliberal university; that see the harm we have experienced in this and other institutions, and the harm we sometimes inflict as a result. We strive to compassionately hold each other accountable and to create bigger, safer, and healthier communities in the process. The incitement to be "with her/him/them" also applies to female, racialized, and transgender academics who spend too much of their brilliant energy on fending off perceived intruders, often those who work on intersections deemed "too far out": "X is not into homonationalism"; "Y has fought in the university all her life." Or, more honestly maybe: "I need a job. X or Y might have a job." We feel compassion for the damage. We do not glorify in order to then demonize. But we do not throw each other under the bus. Respecting elders and humanizing the traumatized behaviours of oppressed colleagues, mentors, and students cannot mean getting stuck in cycles of abuse. We move beyond exploitative family models and explore our own models of mentorship and comradeship that build rather than destroy people power. We become the ancestors that we have always wanted. It may well take several generations to heal from the violence of the racial/colonial university.

We thus end on a horizon that is larger than any numerologies of celebrity. Our citational practices work to remember, to unarchive, to heal erasure (Haritaworn, Moussa, & Ware, 2018). They reanimate worlds. They join unfinished revolutions. They step into our responsibility to make sure that we, that the peoples we are allied to, will not only survive but thrive.

Conclusion

Written at several moments between 2016 and 2019, this chapter has laboured towards closing a gap in existing activist and critical race scholarships by drawing traces in the mud that mark and acknowledge what makes the university a hard place to survive, especially for those run over on intersections deemed excessive. I have argued that existing equity infrastructures are constrained, not only by their tendency to remain single issue but also by their conjuncture with a neoliberal multiculturalism whose institutional logics we remain magnetized towards, even as it reaches its expiry date. As white supremacy is starting to rid itself of its tokens and transitional objects,[7] and progressive movements shrink towards the lowest common denominator, which roads to transformation close in front of us and which open up?

This chapter has made a two-fold attempt to both acknowledge the harm done and the demand to go further. I have argued that each of us can do much more to expand the ground we have left for dreaming up alternatives, for tapping the spaces we have access to, for liberatory potential. We may not have a lot. But what we do have could stretch boundlessly towards energizing our collective imaginations. On these marvellous grounds (Haritaworn, Moussa, & Ware, 2018), we become emboldened to assert impossible dreams. We prefigure a future beyond these wars.

NOTES

1 Other sites that I was tempted to write about include the gender, sexuality, or ethnic studies classroom/conference/hiring committee, the local "mommies" group, the women of colour or intersectionality panel at the radical conference, and the neighbourhood film festival. Like the classroom, these sites are dramatically underexplored spaces for teaching, learning, and organizing for a different world that could be re-sourced for building the energy and people power to dig ourselves out of the mess we are

in, but they often stay overly loyal to neoliberal multiculturalism, cis-heteropatriarchy, and institutionalized hierarchies.

2 See Local Government Act 1988, UK Public General Acts, 1988, c. 9, Part IV, Miscellaneous, Section 28. Retrieved from https://www.legislation.gov.uk /ukpga/1988/9/section/28.

3 I am not dismissing the strong push back to save public education led by teachers' unions and parents' groups, which has mobilized inspiring numbers to take to the streets and prevent worse things from happening. Still, I think we could go much further in proactively reshaping education at all its intersections and learning from prefigurative spaces grounded in anti-racism, as illustrated and modelled by Freedom School, the queer and trans–led Toronto-based summer camp and Saturday school for Black children (http://freedomschool.ca/).

4 The longer-standing debate about the neoliberal university, while interesting and relevant, frequently ignores or sidelines the ongoing role of the university in racial capitalism (Robinson, 1983) and colonialism (Smith, 1999). In this longer *durée*, precarity is nothing new for Black, Indigenous, and people of colour, who have only just begun to be hired and admitted on a larger scale. Rather, as I argue, it is necessary to interrogate the university as a racial and colonial project that has always sought to fulfil certain functions in the reproduction of white supremacy and the economic and social regimes that have accompanied its arrival and maintenance on these lands.

5 My notion of the un/professional intellectual builds on Gutierrez Rodríguez's (2013) engagement with Gramsci's (1996) distinction between the professional intellectual, who is paid to serve the institution, and the organic intellectual, who works for the movement and theorizes from their own and their communities' lived experiences.

6 Emi Koyama has an online store, where she sells her buttons (http://store .eminism.org/).

7 In my work on the racialization of homophobia in Western nationalisms, I have borrowed the term "transitional objects" from developmental psychology in order to describe how the figure of the queer lover who deserves rights and protections on account of their resemblance to white cis-heteropatriarchal family norms eases our transition between a diversity-oriented regime of neoliberal multiculturalism into one of outright punishment and neglect (Haritaworn, 2015).

REFERENCES

Ahmed, S. (2012). *On being included: Racism and diversity in institutional life.* Durham, NC: Duke University Press.

Ahmed, S. (2014). *The cultural politics of emotion*. Edinburgh: Edinburgh University Press.

Austin, D. (2013). *Fear of a Black nation: Race, sex, and security in sixties Montreal*. Toronto: Between the Lines.

Bacchetta, P., El-Tayeb, F., Haritaworn, J., Hernandez, J., Smythe, S.A., Thompson, V., & Willoughby-Herard, T. (2018). Queer of color space-making in and beyond the academic industrial complex. *Critical Ethnic Studies Journal, 4*(1), 44–63. https://doi.org/10.5749/jcritethnstud.4.1.0044.

Berlant, L. (2006). Cruel optimism. *differences, 17*(3), 20–36. https://doi.org/10.1215/10407391-2006-009.

Brown, A.M. (2019). *Pleasure activism: The politics of feeling good*. Chico, CA: AK Press.

Butler, O. (1993). *Parable of the sowers*. New York: Warner.

Conway, E. (2017). Another moment in the long history of white reconstruction. Interview with Dylan Rodriguez. *The Real News Network*, 28 August 2017. Retrieved from https://therealnews.com/drodriguez0824white.

da Silva, D.F. (2007). *Toward a global idea of race*. Minneapolis: University of Minnesota Press.

Davis, A. (2013). *Feminism and abolition: Theories and practices for the 21st century*. Talk at the University of Chicago. *Beyond Capitalism Now*, May 2013. Retrieved from https://beyondcapitalismnow.wordpress.com/2013/08/08/angela-y-davis-feminism-and-abolition-theories-and-practices-for-the-21st-century/.

Donahue, J. (2011). Making it happen, Mama: A conversation with Miss Major. In E. Stanley & N. Smith (Eds.), *Captive genders: Trans embodiment and the prison industrial complex* (pp. 267–80). Oakland, CA: AK Press.

Douglas, D. (2012). *Black/Out*: The white face of multiculturalism and the violence of the Canadian academic imperial project. In G. Gutiérrez y Muhs, Y.F. Niemann, C.G. González, & A.P. Harris (Eds.), *Presumed incompetent: The intersections of race and class for women in academia* (pp. 50–64). Logan: Utah State University Press.

Ferguson, R. (2012). *The reorder of things: The university and its pedagogies of minority difference*. Minneapolis: University of Minnesota Press.

Gordon, A.F. (2011). Some thoughts on haunting and futurity. *Borderlands, 10*(2). Retrieved from http://averygordon.net/files/GordonHaunting Futurity.pdf.

Gramsci, A. (1996). Aufzeichnungen und verstreute Notizen für eine Gruppe von Aufsätzen über die Geschichte der Intellektuellen, §§ 1–3. *Gefängnisbriefe, 7*(12–15). Hamburg, DE: Argument.

Gutierrez y Muhs, G., Niemann, Y.F., González, C.G., & Harris, A.P. (Eds.). (2012). *Presumed incompetent: The intersections of race and class for women in academia*. Logan: Utah State University.

Hale, C.R. (Ed.). (2008). *Engaging contradictions: Theory, politics, and methods of activist scholarship*. Berkeley, CA: GAIA Books.

Hanssmann, C. (2018). Trump's anti-trans memo opens door to escalating state surveillance. *Truth Out*, 27 October 2018. Retrieved from https://truthout.org/articles/trumps-anti-trans-memo-opens-door-to-escalating-state-surveillance/.

Haritaworn, J. (2015). *Queer lovers and hateful others: Regenerating violent times and places*. London: Pluto.

Haritaworn, J., Moussa, G., & Ware, S.M. (2018). Marvelous grounds: An introduction. In J. Haritaworn, G. Moussa, & S.M. Ware (Eds.), *Marvelous grounds: Queer of colour histories of Toronto* (pp. 1–20). Toronto: Between the Lines.

Henry, F., Dua, E., James, C.E., Kobayashi, A., Li, P., Ramos, H., & Smith, M.S. (2017). *The equity myth: Racialization and indigeneity at Canadian universities*. Vancouver, BC: UBC Press.

Hong, G.K. (2008). "The future of our worlds": Black feminism and the politics of knowledge in the university under globalization. *Meridians: feminism, race, transnationalism, 8*(2), 95–115. https://www.jstor.org/stable/40338753.

Incite! Women of Color Against Violence (Eds.). (2006). Introduction. In *The color of violence: The INCITE! anthology* (pp. 1–10). Cambridge, MA: South End Press.

James, J., & Gordon, E.T. (2008). Activist scholars or radical subjects. In C.R. Hale (Ed.), *Engaging contradictions: Theory, politics, and methods of activist scholarship* (pp. 367–73). Berkeley, CA: GAIA Books.

King, T.L. (2013). *In the clearing: Black female bodies, space and settler colonial landscapes*. (Doctoral dissertation, University of Maryland, College Park).

Kuumba, M.B. (2001). Introduction. In *Gender and social movements* (pp. 1–2). Lanham, MD: Rowman & Littlefield.

Lorde, A. (1984). Uses of the erotic: The erotic as power. In *Sister outsider* (pp. 53–9). Berkeley, CA: Crossing Press.

Melamed, J. (2011). Reading Tehran in Lolita: Making racialized and gendered difference work for neoliberal multiculturalism. In G. Hong & R. Ferguson (Eds.), *Strange affinities: The gender and sexual politics of comparative racialization* (pp. 76–110). Durham, NC: Duke University Press.

Million, D. (2013). *Therapeutic nations: Healing in an age of Indigenous human rights*. Tucson: University of Arizona Press.

Moten, F. (2016). Collective head. *Women & Performance 26*(2–3), 162–71. https://doi.org/10.1080/0740770X.2016.1232876.

Moten, F., & Harney, S. (2004). The university and the undercommons: Seven theses. *Social Text, 22*(2), 101–15. https://doi.org/10.1215/01642472-22-2_79-101.

Ng, R. (1993). "A Woman out of control": Deconstructing sexism and racism in the university. *Canadian Journal of Education / Revue canadienne de l'éducation, 18*(3), 189–205. https://doi.org/10.2307/1495382.

NYSHN (Native Youth Sexual Health Network), FSIS (Families of Sisters in Spirit), & NMS (No More Silence). (2014). *Supporting the resurgence of community-based responses to violence.* Retrieved from http://www.nativeyouthsexualhealth.com/march142014.pdf.

Pulido, L. (2008). FAQs: Frequently (un)asked questions about being a scholar activist. In C. Hale (Ed.), *Engaging contradictions: Theory, politics, and methods of activist scholarship* (pp. 341–66). Berkeley: University of California Press.

Robinson, C.J. (1983). *Black Marxism: The making of the black radical tradition.* Chapel Hill: University of North Carolina Press.

Rocca, R. (2018). Ontario PC Party passes resolution to debate recognition of gender identity. *Global News,* 17 November 2018. Retrieved from https://globalnews.ca/news/4673240/ontario-pc-recognize-gender-identity/.

Rodriguez, D. (2012). Racial/colonial genocide and the "neoliberal academy": In excess of a problematic. *American Quarterly, 64*(4), 809–13. https://doi.org/10.1353/aq.2012.0054.

Rodríguez, Encarnación Gutiérrez. (2013). *Intellektuelle Migrantinnen – Subjektivitäten im Zeitalter von Globalisierung: Eine postkoloniale dekonstruktive Analyse von Biographien im Spannungsverhältnis von Ethnisierung und Vergeschlechtlichung.* Vol. 21. Springer-Verlag.

Saleh-Hanna, V. (2015). Black feminist hauntology: Rememory the ghosts of abolition? *Champ penal / Penal field,* XII. https://doi.org/10.4000/champpenal.9168.

Shiekh, I. (Director). (1999). *On STRIKE: Ethnic studies 1969–1999* [Documentary film]. Center for Asian American Media. Retrieved from https://www.youtube.com/watch?v=0xovOLk9qE8.

Shum, M. (Writer/Director). (2015). *Ninth floor* [Documentary film]. National Film Board of Canada. Retrieved from https://www.nfb.ca/film/ninth_floor/.

Smith, L.T. (1999). *Decolonising methodologies: Research and Indigenous peoples.* London: Zed Books.

Smith, M. (2010). Gender, whiteness and the "other others" in the academy. In S. Razack, M. Smith, & S. Thobani (Eds.), *States of race: Critical race feminism for the 21st century* (pp. 37–58). Toronto: Between the Lines.

Sudbury, J. (2009). Challenging penal dependency: Activist scholars and the anti-prison movement. In J. Sudbury & Margo Okazawa-Rey (Eds.), *Activist scholarship: Antiracism, feminism, and social change* (pp. 17–35). London: Routledge.

Sudbury, J., & Okazawa-Rey, M. (2009). Introduction: Activist scholarship and the neoliberal university. In J. Sudbury & Margo Okazawa-Rey (Eds.), *Activist scholarship: Antiracism, feminism, and social change* (pp. 1–16). London: Routledge.

Thobani, S. (2007). *Exalted subjects: Studies in the making of race and nation in Canada*. Toronto: University of Toronto Press.

Tuck, E. (2009). Suspending damage: A letter to communities. *Harvard Educational Review, 79*(3), 409–28. https://doi.org/10.17763/haer.79.3.n0016675661t3n15.

Turtle Tank. (n.d.). *Radical purpose: Our compass home through a crucial evolutionary stage*. Retrieved from https://turtletank.co/our-approach-1.

Contributors

Beverly Bain is a Black queer radical feminist anti-capitalist scholar, organizer, and public intellectual. She has over forty years of experience working in the areas of feminism, anti-violence, and anti-racism in Canada. Bain teaches on the Black queer diaspora, feminism, anti-racism and decolonialism, diasporic sexualities, and gender and police violence in women and gender studies in the Department of Historical Studies at the University of Toronto, Mississauga Campus. Bain frequently delivers lectures on gender, anti-Blackness, sexuality, abolition, and liberation. She is interviewed regularly in the media on Black queer organizing, and on policing and abolition. Bain is published in numerous books and journals, including *Queerly Canadian*, 2nd edition; *We Still Demand: Redefining Resistance in Sex and Gender Struggles*; *Canadian Women's Studies*; *Fireweed*; and *The Conversation*.

Cicely Belle Blain is a queer Black poet, artist, and community organizer who has been a settler on Coast Salish lands for four years. Originally from London, England, they have been working on bringing social justice, accessibility, and inclusivity to spaces, mainly at UBC, where they studied European studies and Russian. Cicely Belle's previous and ongoing projects include co-founding a chapter of the Black Lives Matter movement in Vancouver, archiving the history of racialized student activism across North America with the UBC Centre for Race, Autobiography, Gender and Age, and being the program assistant for BC's queer and trans summer camp, CampOUT. They have also worked with the Positive Space Campaign and the Global Lounge, both at UBC, which have been instrumental in fuelling their passion for community building, intercultural understanding, and safer space creation. They spend their spare time writing teen fiction, painting, and winning at pub trivia.

Sarika Bose teaches Victorian literature, drama, children's literature, and composition at UBC. A recent publication is the Broadview Press edition of Dion Boucicault's 1859 anti-slavery melodrama *The Octoroon*, and recent research interests include the state of academic freedom in universities. She has been serving as the UBC Faculty Association's Contract Faculty Committee chair since 2014, and has established research and pedagogy initiatives for contract faculty in partnership with the Faculty Association, the Centre for Teaching and Learning Technologies, and UBC Library.

Benita Bunjun is an associate professor at Saint Mary's University in the Department of Sociology and Criminology. She is currently the acting chair of the Department of Social Justice and Community Studies. She received her PhD in interdisciplinary studies at the University of British Columbia and completed a postdoctoral fellowship at Simon Fraser University with the Centre for Gender, Social Inequities and Mental Health. Dr. Bunjun is the past president of the Canadian Research Institute for the Advancement of Women. She was also the coordinator of the Centre for Race, Autobiography, Gender and Age (RAGA) at UBC. She has taught sociology at both the University of British Columbia and Simon Fraser University, as well as at the UBC Institute for Gender, Race, Sexuality and Social Justice. Her research examines organizational and institutional power relations with an emphasis on discourses of nation-building. Other research areas include colonial gendered encounters, academic well-being of racialized students, mental health and labour, and (im)migrant/indentured labour.

Delia D. Douglas holds a PhD in sociology from the University of California, Santa Cruz. Her scholarship is interdisciplinary and is attentive to the continuing significance of the legacies of enslavement, imperialism, and settler colonialism. Her research and teaching interests consider struggles for social justice with a focus on critical race and gender studies, Black diaspora studies, equity and higher education, and sports studies. She is the anti-racism practice lead for the Rady Faculty of Health Sciences at the University of Manitoba.

Enakshi Dua is a professor in the School of Gender, Sexuality and Women's Studies at York University. She is graduate director of the Graduate Program in Gender, Feminist and Women's Studies at York University. She teaches critical race theory, anti-racist feminist theory, post-colonial studies, and feminist theory. She has published extensively on theorizing racism and anti-racism, the racialized and gendered histories of immigration processes, racism in Canadian universities, equity and anti-racism policies, and the racialization of masculinity and femininity. She has also published on women and health, and globalization and biodiversity. Dr. Dua's notable publications include *Scratching the Surface: Canadian Anti-Racist Feminist Thought*; "The Hindu Woman's Question"; "From Subjects To Aliens: Indian Migrants and the Racialisation of Canadian Citizenship"; *Decolonising Anti-Racism*; *Theorizing Anti-Racism: Linkages in Marxism and Critical Race Theories* (with Abigail Bakan); and *The Equity Myth: Race, Racialization and Indigeneity in Canadian Universities* (with Frances Henry, Audrey Kobayashi, Carl James, Howard Ramos, and Malinda Smith). She has more than thirty years of experience in anti-racist work in the community as well as within the academy. Within the academy, she has held a number of administrative positions that address gender, anti-racist, and equity issues. She has served as director of the Centre for Feminist Research, chair of the CAUT Equity Committee, co-chair of the Subcommittee to the Joint Committee of the Collective Agreement on Equity at Queen's University, and as the York University Faculty Association's equity officer.

Carol W.N. Fadda is an associate professor of English at Syracuse University, where she teaches critical race and ethnic studies, transnational and diasporic studies, and Arab American literatures and cultures. A recipient of an NEH summer grant and a Future of Minority Studies Fellowship, her essays on gender, race, ethnicity, war trauma, and transnational citizenship in Arab and Arab American literary texts have appeared in a variety of journals and edited collections. She is the author of *Contemporary Arab American Literature: Transnational Reconfigurations of Home and Belonging* (NYU Press, 2014), which analyzes the ways in which depictions of Arab homelands in Arab American literary and cultural texts from the 1990s onward play a crucial role in reshaping cultural articulations of US citizenship and belonging. Her current book project is titled *Carceral States and Dissident Citizenships: Narratives of Resistance in an Age of "Terror."* She serves as the editor of the Critical Arab American Studies book series at Syracuse University Press.

Jin Haritaworn is an associate professor of gender, race and environment at York University. They have authored various publications, including two books, numerous articles (in journals such as *GLQ*, *Society & Space*, and *Sexualities*), and four co/edited collections (including *Queer Necropolitics*), which are widely read and taught on both sides of the Atlantic. Their latest book, *Queer Lovers and Hateful Others: Regenerating Violent Times and Places*, is on queer gentrification and criminalization, anti-Muslim racism, and queer of colour kitchen tables in Berlin. Jin have made foundational contributions to several debates, including homonationalism, intersectionality, transnational sexuality studies, and queer of colour space and politics.

Min Sook Lee has directed numerous critically acclaimed feature documentaries, including Donald Brittain Gemini winner *Tiger Spirit*; Hot Docs Best Canadian Feature winner *Hogtown*; Gemini nominated *El Contrato*; and Canadian Screen Award winner *The Real Inglorious Bastards*. Lee is a recipient of numerous awards, including the Cesar E. Chavez Black Eagle Award and the Alanis Obomsawin Award for Commitment to Community and Resistance. Canada's oldest labour arts festival, Mayworks, has named the Min Sook Lee Labour Arts Award in her honour. Lee's most recent feature, *Migrant Dreams*, tells the undertold story of migrant workers struggling against Canada's Temporary Foreign Worker Program (TFWP) that treats foreign workers as modern-day indentured labourers. In 2017, *Migrant Dreams* was awarded Best Labour Documentary by the Canadian Journalists Association and garnered the prestigious Canadian Hillman Prize, which honours journalists whose work identifies important social and economic issues in Canada. Lee is an associate professor at OCAD University; her area of research and art making focuses on counter hegemonic narratives of resistance, migrant justice, borderless worlds, and feminist working-class cultural praxis.

Dana M. Olwan is an assistant professor of women's and gender studies at Syracuse University. Her research is located at the nexus of feminist theorizations of gendered and sexual violence and solidarities across settler borders and states. In support of her work, she has received a Future Minority Studies Fellowship, a Social Sciences and Humanities Research Council art/research grant, and a Palestinian American Research Council grant. Her work has appeared or is forthcoming in *Signs: Journal of Women in Culture and Society*, the *Journal of Settler Colonial Studies*, *American Quarterly*, and *Feminist Formations*. She is completing her first book manuscript, *Traveling Discourses: Gendered Violence and the Transnational Politics of the "Honor Crime."*

annie ross is an Indigenous teacher and artist working within community inside the Canadian west. Dr. ross teaches at Simon Fraser University.

Audra Simpson is a political anthropologist whose work focuses on contextualizing the force and consequences of governance through time, space, and bodies. Her research and writing is rooted within Indigenous politics in the United States and Canada, and crosses the fields of anthropology, Indigenous studies, American and Canadian studies, gender and sexuality studies, as well as politics. Her recent research is a genealogy of affective governance and extraction across the United States and Canada. Her book *Mohawk Interruptus: Political Life across the Borders of Settler States* (2014, DUP) won the Sharon Stephens Prize (AES), the "Best First Book Award" (NAISA), as well as the Lora Romero Award (ASA), in addition to honorable mentions. It was a Choice Academic Title for 2014. In 2010, she won the School of General Studies "Excellence in Teaching Award."

Sunera Thobani is a professor in the Department of Asian Studies at the University of British Columbia. Her scholarship focuses on critical race, post-colonial, and feminist theory; globalization, media, citizenship, and migration; South Asian women's, gender and sexuality studies; and violence, Muslim women, and the War on Terror. The author of *Exalted Subjects: Studies in the Making of Race and Nation in Canada* (University of Toronto Press, 2007) and *Contesting Islam, Constructing Race and Sexuality* (Bloomsbury Academic Press, 2020), Dr. Thobani has also co-edited *Asian Women: Interconnections* (Canadian Scholars' Press, 2005) and *States of Race: Critical Race Feminist Theory for the 21st Century* (Between the Lines, 2010). Her research is published in numerous peer-reviewed journals, including *Borderlands*, *Feminist Theory*, *The Supreme Court Review*, *International Journal of Communication*, and *Race & Class*, among others. Dr. Thobani has served as director of the Race, Autobiography, Gender and Age (RAGA) Centre at UBC; the Ruth Wynn Woodward Endowed Chair in Women's Studies at Simon Fraser University; and the president of the National Action Committee on the Status of Women. She is a founding member of Researchers and Academics of Colour for Equity (RACE), the cross-Canada network promoting the scholarship of academics of colour and of Indigenous ancestry, and the recipient of the Sarah Shorten Award from the Canadian Association of University Teachers (2017).

Printed and bound by CPI Group (UK) Ltd, Croydon, CR0 4YY

16/04/2025

14658333-0005